Tools for Financial Management

Tools for Financial Management

Emphasis on Inflation

Leon Shashua
Israel Bank of Agriculture

Yaaqov Goldschmidt
Tel-Aviv University and
Heshev—the Inter Kibbutz Unit
for Management Services

LexingtonBooks
D.C. Heath and Company
Lexington, Massachusetts
Toronto

Library of Congress Cataloging in Publication Data

Shashua, Leon.
Tools for financial management.

Includes bibliographical references and index.
1. Business enterprises—Finance. 2. Corporations—finance. 3. Industrial management—Effect of inflation on. 4. Inflation (Finance)
I. Goldschmidt, Yaaqov. II. Title.
HG4026.S45 1982 658.1′5 82-47951
ISBN 0-669-05720-7

Published simultaneously in Canada

Printed in the United States of America

International Standard Book Number: 0-669-05720-7

Library of Congress Catalog Card Number: 82-47951

Contents

	Figures	xi
	Tables	xiii
	Foreword Jimmye S. Hillman	xvii
	Preface and Acknowledgments	xix
Part I	*Basic Managerial Tools*	1
Chapter 1	**Interest, Growth, and Indexation**	3
	Compounding and Discounting	3
	Growth and Decay Measurements	8
	Various Interest Rates	14
	Interest during Inflation	18
	Indexation	21
Chapter 2	**Periodic Charges and Annuities**	25
	Periodic Capital Charges	25
	Ordinary Annuities	29
	Annuities during Inflation	32
	Varying Annuities	34
	Annuities Due (Advanced Payments)	40
Chapter 3	**Statistical Tools**	43
	Measures of Dispersion	43
	Distribution Curve	49
	Measures of Association	54
	Statistics of Extremes	61
	Relations between Means	66
	Statistical Significance	69
Part II	*Capital Budgeting*	77
Chapter 4	**Loans and Bonds Analysis**	79
	Some Simple Calculations	79
	Methods of Loan Repayment	84
	Gains on Loans	88

	Outstanding Principal	93
	Present Value of Interest Payments	95
	Inflation Adjustment of Interest Rates	98
	Loan Indexation	100
	Price and Yield of Bonds	103
Chapter 5	**Investment Evaluation**	109
	Payback Period	109
	Discounted Cash Flow	113
	Internal Rate of Return	117
	Periodic Capital Expense Method	120
	Income Tax and Financial Leverage Considerations	125
	Investment Evaluation during Inflation	131
Chapter 6	**Investment Evaluation under Uncertainty**	135
	Analysis Using Risk-Adjusted Cash Flow	135
	Analysis Using Risk-Adjusted Discounting Rate	138
	Sensitivity Analysis	141
	Cost of Failure	146
Chapter 7	**Rate of Return and Cost of Capital**	151
	Accounting-Derived Rates of Return	151
	Required Rate of Return for Capital Budgeting	155
	Actual versus Required Rates of Return	157
	Cost of Capital and Financial Leverage	159
	Lenders' Cost of Capital during Inflation	161
Part III	*Assets Accounting and Analysis*	167
Chapter 8	**Single Assets Valuation and Accounting**	169
	Valuation of Fixed Assets	169
	Depreciation Methods	172
	Implications of Depreciation Methods	178
	Present Value (PV) of Depreciation Schedules	182
	Inventory Valuation	187
	Effect of Inflation on Inventory Accounting	192
	Income Tax Considerations	193

Chapter 9 **Stock of Assets Analysis** 197

Depreciation of a Stock of Assets 197
Life Span of a Stock of Depreciable Assets 200
Turnover of Stock of Inventory 202
Ratio of Book Value to Acquisition Cost 204
Ratio of Accumulated to Current Depreciation 209
Analysis of Outstanding Debt 210

Chapter 10 **Inflation Adjustment of Stock of Assets** 213

Revaluing Depreciation Expenses 213
Revaluing Fixed-Assets Acquisition Cost 217
Revaluing Book (Depreciated) Value 218
Timeseries Revaluation 220
Revaluing Cost of Materials Used 228
Revaluing Stock of Inventory 230

Chapter 11 **Profit Measurement during Inflation** 233

Asset Revaluation in Financial Statements 233
Financial Statement Adjustments 235
Inflation Effects on Profit 239

Part IV *Costing and Pricing* 245

Chapter 12 **Framework of Costing** 247

Managerial Cost Statement 247
Analyzing the Cost Items 250
Mechanism of Costing 252
Cost-Volume-Profit Relationships 257
Relationship between Productivity and Size 263
Types of Costs 265

Chapter 13 **Costing Procedures** 267

Cost-Accounting Methods 267
Costing Intermediate Goods 270
Costing Internal Services 273
Overhead and Joint Cost Allocation 276
Costing Capital and Assets Services 279
Variance Analysis 283
Costing during Inflation 284

Chapter 14	**Pricing Products and Services**	291
	Tools for Pricing	292
	Market Pricing Methods	294
	Cost-Plus Pricing Methods	297
	Pricing for Seasonal and Peak-Load Demand	303
	Pricing during Inflation	305
	Strategies in Pricing a New Product	307
Part V	*Financial Management*	309
Chapter 15	**Financial Statement Analysis**	311
	The Financial Report	311
	Analyzing Financial Statements	315
	Performance Ratios	318
	Rating the Company's Financial Standing	322
	Application and Implication of Ratio Analysis	326
	Inflation Distortions in Financial Ratios	332
Chapter 16	**Financing Management and Control**	335
	Tools of Financing Management and Control	335
	Approving the Cash Budget	336
	Revision of the Cash Budget	339
	Current Financing Management and Control	342
Chapter 17	**Valuing Acquisitions**	343
	Analysis of the Candidate	343
	Accounting and Appraisal Methods of Valuation	344
	Economic Method of Valuation	347
	The Hybrid Method of Valuation	350
	Valuing Acquisitions for Merger	352
Chapter 18	**Uncertainty Analysis**	357
	Source and Measures of Uncertainty	358
	Screening of Risky Projects	359
	Risk Aversion and Risk Premium	362
	Certainty Equivalent in Practice	366
	Diversification to Reduce Risk	371
Chapter 19	**Effects of Inflation on Financial Activities**	375
	Overtaxation of Equity	376

Capital Erosion 378
Effect of Inflation on Liquidity 383
Rules for Producing, Investing, Borrowing, and Saving 388
Rules for Combatting the Effects of Inflation 389

Appendix A Capital-Recovery Factors 393

Appendix B Add-On Factors for Finding the Average Interest Rate 401

Index 405

About the Authors 411

Figures

3–1	Distribution Curve	50
3–2	Frequency Distribution	51
3–3	Frequency Distributions	53
3–4	Scatter Diagram	56
3–5	Scatter Diagram and Regression Line	57
3–6	Confidence Region	70
4–1	Installment versus Equal Principal Payment	89
12–1	Breakeven Analysis	258
12–2	Contribution-Volume Curve	261
13–1	Variance Analysis	285
18–1	Distribution of Returns	361
18–2	Risk Curve	363
18–3	Kinked Utility Function	367

Tables

1–1	Future-Value Factors of Single Payment	5
1–2	Present-Value Factors of Single Payment	7
1–3	Annual Effective Rates from Periodic Rates	15
1–4	Annual Rates from Daily Rates	17
1–5	Inflation-Free Rates of Interest	20
1–6	Inflation-Compensated Rates of Interest	21
2–1	Capital-Recovery Factors	26
2–2	Add-On Factors for Finding the Average Interest Rate	28
2–3	Future-Value Factors of Annuity	30
2–4	Present-Value Factors of Annuity	32
2–5	Present-Value Factors of a 10 Percent Growth Annuity	36
2–6	Equivalent Periodic Charge Factors of $1 Increments of a Gradient Annuity	39
3–1	Standard Normal Distribution	52
3–2	Data for Scatter Diagram and Regression Line	55
3–3	Student's *t* Table	71
4–1	Repayment Schedule and Outstanding Principal under Various Loan Repayment Methods	85
5–1	Internal Rate of Return, Constant Cash Flow	111
5–2	Internal Rate of Return, Declining Cash Flow	112
5–3	Investment Evaluation Financed by Equity	127
5–4	Loan Evaluation	129
5–5	Investment Evaluation Financed by Loan	130
5–6	Investment Evaluation during Inflation Financed by Equity	133
5–7	Loan Evaluation during Inflation	134
6–1	Risk Premium of an Investment	137

6–2	Probabilities and Loss Integral: Normal Distribution	144
7–1	Nominal Pretax Required Rates of Return on Loaned Equity	163
7–2	Nominal Pretax Required Rates of Return on Loaned Capital	165
8–1	Depreciated and Book Value under Various Depreciation Methods	172
8–2	Book Value as a Percentage of Acquisition Cost	180
8–3	Present-Value Factors of Depreciation Schedule (SYD)	185
8–4	Present-Value Factors of Depreciation Schedule (DDB with Switch)	186
8–5	Ratio of Present Value of SYD to Straight-Line Schedules	186
8–6	Value of Inventory and Units Used under Various Valuation Methods	188
9–1	Factors for the Sum-of-the-Years' Digits (SYD)	199
9–2	Factors for the Double-Declining Balance (DDB) with Switch	200
9–3	Ratio of Book Value to Acquisition Cost (SL)	207
9–4	Ratio of Book Value to Acquisition Cost (SYD)	208
9–5	Ratio of Book Value to Acquisition Cost (DDB)	209
10–1	Revaluation Factors for Depreciation and Acquisition Cost (SL)	215
10–2	Revaluation Factors for Book Value (SL)	219
10–3	Factors for the SYD Method	220
10–4	Factors for the DDB Method	221
10–5	Revaluation Factors for Inventories under FIFO	230
10–6	Revaluation Factors for Inventories under the Average Method	231
11–1	Company X Balance Sheets, Flow-of-Funds Figures, and Adjusted Balance Sheet	237

11–2	Company X Timeseries Balance Sheets—1979 and 1980	243
12–1	Cost Statement for Product A	248
12–2	Performance Evaluation for Product A	250
12–3	Cost Flow among Cost Centers	253
12–4	Cost Accounting Sheet, Company X	255
12–5	Section of Company X Cost-Accounting Sheet	256
13–1	Income Statements, Department B	270
13–2	Interdepartmental Service Cost Allocation	275
13–3	Internal Transportation Cost Allocation	277
13–4	Overhead Allocation	278
13–5	Joint Cost Allocation	280
15–1	Framework of a Balance Sheet	312
15–2	Company X Balance Sheets of December 31, 1979, and December 31, 1980	313
15–3	Company X Income Statements for December 31, 1979, and December 31, 1980	314
15–4	Company X Flow-of-Funds Statement for 1980	314
15–5	Company X Common-Size Financial Statements for 1979 and 1980	315
15–6	Rating Corresponding to Relative Ratios	323
15–7	Company X Ratios and Ratings for 1980	324
15–8	Company X Ratios and Timeseries Ratings for 1975 and 1980	326
15–9	Financial Ratio Averages for Selected Industries	328
15–10	Effect of Scale on Financial Ratios	329
15–11	Effect of Inflation on Financial Ratios	330
16–1	Projected Income Statement	337
16–2	Projected Flow-of-Funds Statement	338
16–3	Consolidated Cash Budget	339
16–4	Cash Budget—Production	340

16–5	Cash Budget—Capital Account	341
16–6	Monthly Cash Budget and Report	342
18–1	Unit-Risk Premium Coefficients	370

Foreword

Inflation is an economic illness and appears to be a modern fact of life. It respects no person or institution. It affects private and public fortune alike and ultimately blurs financial and economic judgment. Though elusive as to definition, effect, and solution, inflation, nevertheless, can be treated as a physician treats a disease.

We are fortunate to have two skilled practitioners who, in similar fashion to previous works, have dissected the "patient"—financial management—and have come up with a packet of holistic remedies to make him well. Professors Goldschmidt and Shashua have vast experience with inflation surgery and approach each problem from both its practical and its theoretical side.

This book covers a wide range of topics in the field of managerial accounting, statistics, economics, and finance and their interaction with inflation. Normally, such diverse subject matter could be found only in a variety of books such as those in fields of engineering economics, mathematics of finance and investment, cost accounting, capital budgeting, and inflation accounting. The authors have succeeded in presenting the material in an easy and simple fashion, which is a distinct advantage, especially for managers.

Rules of thumb and examples are given simply, without impairing the correctness and the thoroughness of particular subject matter. Novel techniques are introduced in almost every chapter. The treatment of the effects of inflation, uncertainty, and the stock of assets in chapters 6, 9, 10, 18, and 19 is, to a large extent, new.

We at the University of Arizona benefited greatly by the presence of Professors Goldschmidt and Shashua during the 1979–1980 academic year. They were invited to further study and develop the effects of inflation in the agricultural sector on irrigation development and financial management in general. Their research and writings are in some instances no less than pathbreaking.

Jimmye S. Hillman
Department of Agricultural Economics,
University of Arizona

Preface and Acknowledgments

This book is a comprehensive treatment of the subject of financial management, under both stable and inflationary conditions. It covers a wide range of topics, from elementary computations of interest to quite sophisticated techniques for project evaluation under uncertainty. The presentation of the material is in the form of rules and examples to make it easy and simple to study, to comprehend, and to apply. In collecting and developing these rules, we have borne in mind the rationale of simplicity and compactness, while adhering to correctness and reliability.

The text is meant for managers and professionals, as well as students, in various fields of business and economics. The tools expounded in this book provide the practioner with estimates regarding the magnitude, direction of change, and sensitivity of estimates of a problem at hand. It opens the door to the manager to follow, understand, and direct the activities of his professional staff and advisors. In addition, the book can be used as an auxiliary text in university and vocational courses for both teachers and students.

Having hundreds of rules and tools in many fields of business presented in one handy reference will certainly benefit many users. Because of the encyclopedic nature of the book, it is liberally cross-referenced.

The book contains nineteen chapters grouped into five parts. Each subject is first developed for stable price level conditions and is then followed by an analysis of the effects of inflation. Three chapters (10, 11, and 19) are devoted to specific subjects related to inflation. This volume contains more than 500 rules and tools, as well as about 400 numerical examples and illustrating tables. About a fifth of the rules have been developed specifically for this book; chapter 2: rules 2, 10, and 17; chapter 3: rules 16, 24, and 27; chapter 4: rules 13, and 38–40; chapter 5: rules 13, 14, and 21; chapter 6: rules 1, 2, 8, 9, and 14; chapter 7: rules 9, 10, 13–15, and 19; chapter 8: rules 26, 27, 30, 31, 33, 34, 44, and 45; chapter 9: rules 2, 4, 5, 11, 12, 15, 17, and 21–23; chapter 10: rules 4, 5, 9–16, and 23; chapter 11: rules 14 and 15; chapter 12: rules 17 and 21–27; chapter 14: rules 8, 12, 13, 18, 19, and 28; chapter 15: rules 10, 11, and the section "Rating the Company's Financial Standing"; chapter 16; chapter 17: rules 2, 3, and 4; chapter 18: the section "Certainty Equivalent in Practice"; and chapter 19: rules 2–10 and the section "Rules for Combatting the Effects of Inflation."

Acknowledgments

Thanks and appreciations are extended to Professors Jimmye S. Hillman and Sol D. Resnick of the University of Arizona for inviting us to develop the subject of the effects of inflation on economics and management, and also for their considerable assistance in the project. Special thanks are due to Professor Hillman for mutually stimulating discussions on the subject of inflation; his ideas and attitude inspired our study. We appreciate Mrs. Norma Stevens' devotion and patience in typing the manuscript.

Acknowledgment is made to the office of Water Research and Technology, U.S. Department of the Interior, for partial financial support for Yaaqov Goldschmidt.

Finally, we would like to express our appreciation to the many authors of books and articles from which we drew important material used in this book. Acknowledgments are given in footnotes only to sources from which specific rules were drawn.

Part I
Basic Managerial Tools

1 Interest, Growth, and Indexation

The arithmetic of interest calculations is the cornerstone to our monetary system. Any transaction, whether in cash or in credit, implies some interest calculation. Money has a time value; a dollar received now is worth more than a dollar received some time later on. The linking chain among units of money to be received, or to be paid, at different points in time, is the concept of the interest rate.

The subject of interest calculations is often studied as early as in elementary school. However, because of its importance, and because of the various interest schemes used in commercial circles, a review of the subject would benefit students in almost any field.

This chapter covers various schemes of interest calculations and approximations used in real life. It also covers phenomena of nonmonetary growth and decay that behave similarly to the compounding of interest. Interest calculations during inflation and the use of price indexes are outlined in the final sections.

The brief tables and the rules not only illustrate the text but also indicate the order of magnitude of the effects of the interest rate and the length of the period involved. Detailed tables for the main factors can usually be found in various texts and financial tables.

Compounding and Discounting

Interest is the cost of using money; it is quoted as a rate (percentage). The interest rate is calculated by dividing the interest payment by the principal.

Rule 1: Simple interest. Simple interest rate is the amount of interest paid at the end of each period on $1 of principal. The amount of interest on a $1 principal taken for n periods is

$$n \times i$$

where i is the interest rate per period and n is the number of periods.

Example. A $100 loan is taken for 90 days; the annual interest rate (for 360 days) is 20 percent.

Solution: The interest rate for 90 days is

$$i = \frac{0.20}{360} \times 90 = 0.05 = 5\%$$

The amount of interest is

$$100 \times 0.05 = \$5$$

Compounding

When the accumulated interest is paid at the end of several periods, it is called compound interest. Compounding means that the interest on a principal is automatically reinvested (added to the principal at the end of each interest period) to earn additional interest.

Rule 2: Compound interest. The amount of compound interest accrued at the end of n periods on a \$1 principal is

$$(1 + i)^n - 1$$

Example. A \$100 loan is taken for 5 years; the annual interest rate is 18 percent.
Solution: The amount of accumulated interest is

$$100[(1 + 0.18)^5 - 1] = \$128.77$$

Rule for approximation. The total amount of compound interest on \$1 is approximately equal to the simple interest amount plus half its square; that is

$$ni + \frac{(ni)^2}{2}$$

Example. Consider the previous example.
Solution: The simple interest amount on \$1 is

$$5 \times 0.18 = \$0.90$$

The compound amount of \$1 is

$$5 \times 0.18 + \frac{(5 \times 0.18)^2}{2} = \$1.30$$

The total accumulated amount is

$$100 \times 1.30 = \$130$$

Rule 3: Future value of a principal. The future value of a principal is the total of the principal A plus the amount of interest. In the compound-interest case, the future value is

$$A(1 + i)^n$$

where A is the principal.
The future value of a \$1 principal is given by the factor

$$(1 + i)^n$$

Example. \$100 is invested at 10 percent annually for 5 years.
Solution: The future value is

$$100(1 + 0.10)^5 = \$161.05$$

Table 1–1 illustrates some future values of \$1.

Rule 4: Future value of cash flow. The future value of a given cash flow is the sum of the future values of each separate periodic amount. Consider the following cash flow which is received at the beginning of each period:

Period:	1	2	3
Payment:	A	B	C

Table 1–1
Future-Value Factors of Single Payment

Periods	*6%*	*12%*	*18%*	*24%*	*30%*
5	1.34	1.76	2.29	2.93	3.71
10	1.79	3.11	5.23	8.59	13.79
15	2.40	5.47	11.97	25.20	51.19

The future value at the end of the third period is

$$A(1+i)^3 + B(1+i)^2 + C(1+i)^1$$

When the periodic amounts are constant (that is, $A = B = C$), use the future value factor of annuity to save computations (rule 5, chapter 2).

Example. Consider the cash flow pattern in rule 4, where $A = 100$, $B = 200$, and $C = 100$; the interest rate is 20 percent a year.
Solution: The future value at the end of the third year is

$$100(1+0.20)^3 + 200(1+0.20)^2 + 100(1+0.20)^1 = \$580.80$$

Discounting (Present Value)

Discounting is the reverse of compounding. Just as $1 that is invested will "grow" over time, $1 that is due in the future is worth less at present. Discounting enables you to determine how much to invest initially to accumulate $1 in the future. The discounted value is also called the present value.

Rule 5: Discount interest payment. The total amount of discount interest on $1 principal is equal to

$$1 - (1+i)^{-n}$$

Example. A bill of $100 is to be paid at the end of 5 years from today. How much is the total discount amount if the bill is paid today? The interest rate is 18 percent.
Solution: The amount is

$$100[1 - (1+0.18)^{-5}] = \$56.29$$

Rule 6: Present value of a principal. The present value of a given payment in the future is

$$\frac{B}{(1+i)^n}$$

where B is the payment in the future.
The present value of a $1 payment in the future is given by the factor (defined as the reciprocal of the future value)

$$\frac{1}{(1 + i)^n}$$

Example. A borrower promises to pay \$100 at the end of 5 years. The interest rate is 10 percent annually.
Solution: The present value of this amount is

$$\frac{100}{(1 + 0.10)^5} = \$62.09$$

Table 1–2 illustrates some present values of \$1.

Rule 7: Present value of cash flow. The present value of a given cash flow is the sum of the present value of each separate periodic amount. Consider the cash flow in rule 4. The present value at the beginning of the first period is

$$\frac{A}{(1 + i)^0} + \frac{B}{(1 + i)^1} + \frac{C}{(1 + i)^2}$$

where $(1 + i)^0 = 1$.
When the periodic amounts are constant (that is, $A = B = C$), use the present value factor of annuity to save computations (rule 7, chapter 2).

Example. Consider the present value of cash flow where $A = 100$, $B = 200$, and $C = 100$; the interest rate is 20 percent a year.
Solution: The present value at the beginning of the first period is

$$\frac{100}{(1 + 0.20)^0} + \frac{200}{(1 + 0.20)^1} + \frac{100}{(1 + 0.20)^2} = \$336.11$$

Rule 8: Transforming present value to future value. The present value multiplied by the compounding factor provides the future value; that is

Table 1–2
Present-Value Factors of Single Payment

Periods	*6%*	*12%*	*18%*	*24%*	*30%*
5	0.747	0.567	0.437	0.341	0.269
10	0.558	0.322	0.191	0.116	0.073
15	0.417	0.183	0.084	0.040	0.020

$$\text{Present value } (1 + i)^n = \text{Future value}$$

Example. Consider the previous example. The future value of the cash flow at the end of the third year is

$$336.11\ (1 + 0.20)^3 = \$580.80$$

Growth and Decay Measurements

Given the value of a variable on two distant dates, the ratio of the two values provides the total growth or decay (negative growth) over the period. From this value the average growth or decay per period can be derived.

Growth

Rule 9: Total growth. The growth between two dates is

$$G = \frac{\text{Value at end of period}}{\text{Value at beginning of period}} > 1$$

Rule 10: Deriving the total growth. Given the periodic (annual) growth rate, the total growth for the whole period is computed by the future value (Rule 3), that is,

$$G = (1 + i)^n$$

where i is the periodic annual rate of growth and n is the number of periods (years).

Example. A company produces 1,000 units per year. The number of units will increase by 8 percent per year for 10 years.
Solution: The volume of production in the tenth year will be

$$1{,}000(1 + 0.08)^{10} = 2{,}159 \text{ units}$$

Rule 11. Deriving the Growth rate. Given the total growth, the periodic growth rate is approximated by

$$i \cong \frac{0.38\ G}{n}$$

This rule is applicable for $G < 3$.
The exact formula is

$$i = \sqrt[n]{G} - 1$$

Example. The production volume increased from 1,000 units in 1970 to 2,159 units in 1980.
Solution: The total growth, G, is

$$\frac{\text{Volume in 1980}}{\text{Volume in 1970}} = \frac{2{,}159}{1{,}000} = 2.159$$

The annual growth rate is approximately,

$$\frac{0.38 \times 2.159}{10} = 0.082 = 8.2\%$$

The exact solution is

$$\sqrt[10]{2.159} - 1 = 0.08 = 8\%$$

Rule 12: Deriving the Growth Period. Given the periodic growth rate and the total growth, the corresponding period is approximated by

$$n \cong \frac{0.38G}{i}$$

This rule is applicable for $G < 3$. The exact formula is

$$n = (\log G)/\log(1 + i)$$

Example. The annual growth rate is 8 percent and the total growth is 2.2
Solution: This growth process takes approximately

$$\frac{0.38 \times 2.2}{0.08} = 10.45 \text{ years}$$

The exact figure is 10.2 years.

Rule 13: Time needed to double the principal (rule of seventy). You want to know how long it would take to double a given amount of money, given that the money earns compound interest. Alternatively, you want to find the required interest rate needed to double the principal after a given number of years.

To find the required period, divide 0.7 by the given interest rate. Alternatively, to find the interest rate, divide 0.7 by the given number of periods. The rule holds for moderate interest levels (up to 15 percent). The formula is

$$i \times n \cong 0.7$$

where i is the interest rate (compounded daily) and n is the number of periods.

Example. An investor puts \$100 in an account that carries 10 percent interest per annum.
Solution: This sum will be doubled after

$$n \cong \frac{0.7}{i} = \frac{0.7}{0.1} = 7 \text{ years}$$

Note: When the annual inflation rate is 10 percent, the price level will be doubled after 7 years.

Example. It is expected that a \$100 standing loan will be redeemed after 10 years at a value of \$200.
Solution: This loan bears an annual interest rate of

$$i \cong \frac{0.7}{n} = \frac{0.7}{10} = 0.07 = 7\%$$

Decay (Negative Growth)

Rule 14: Total decay. The decay (negative growth) between two dates is

$$D = \frac{\text{Value at end of period}}{\text{Value at beginning of period}} < 1$$

Rule 15: Deriving the total decay. Given the periodic annual negative growth rate d, the total decay for the whole period is computed by

$$D = (1 - d)^n$$

where d is the periodic decay rate.

Example. A company produces 2,159 units per year. The amount produced will decrease by 8 percent per year for 10 years.
Solution: The volume of production in the tenth year will be

$$2{,}159\ (1 - 0.08)^{10} = 938 \text{ units}$$

Note: An annual decay rate of 8 percent, as shown here, differs from the annual growth rate of 8 percent shown in the example for rule 10.

Rule 16: Relation between growth and decay rates. A growth rate of i corresponds to a decay rate of

$$d = i/(1 + i)$$

Example. Given a growth rate of 0.08, the corresponding decay rate is

$$0.08/(1 + 0.08) = 0.0741$$

Suppose the decay rate in the previous example is 7.41 percent; then the volume of production in the tenth year will be

$$2{,}159\ (1 - 0.0741)^{10} = 1{,}000 \text{ units}$$

Rule 17: Deriving the decay rate. Given the total decay D, the periodic decay rate d is approximated by

$$d \cong \frac{0.35}{nD}$$

This rule is applicable for $D > 0.3$. The exact formula is

$$d = 1 - \sqrt[n]{D}$$

Example. The production volume decreased from 2,159 units in 1970 to 1,000 units in 1980.
Solution: The total decay is

$$\frac{\text{Volume in 1980}}{\text{Volume in 1970}} = \frac{1{,}000}{2{,}159} = 0.4632$$

The annual decay rate is approximately

$$\frac{0.35}{10 \times 0.4632} = 0.0756 = 7.56\%$$

The exact solution is

$$1 - \sqrt[10]{0.4632} = 0.0741 = 7.41\%$$

Rule 18. Deriving the decay period. Given the periodic decay d and the total decay D, the corresponding period is approximated by

$$n = \frac{0.35}{dD}$$

This rule is applicable for $D > 0.3$. The exact formula is

$$n = (\log D)/\log(1 - d)$$

Example. The annual decay rate is 7.4 percent and the total decay is 0.5. Solution: This decay process takes approximately

$$\frac{0.35}{0.074 \times 0.5} = 9.46 \text{ years}$$

The exact figure is 9.02 years.

Growth and Decay during Inflation

The total and periodic growth or decay, as computed in the previous section, are in nominal terms and may include the effect of inflation.

Rule 19: Total growth in real terms. The real, inflation-free growth between two dates is

$$\frac{G}{P_T/P_0}$$

where P_T is the price index at the end of the period and P_0 is the price index at the beginning of the period.

Example. The value of sales increased from \$1,000 in 1973 to \$1,828 in 1980. The respective price indexes are 153 and 230.
Solution: The nominal growth is

$$1{,}828/1{,}000 = 1.828$$

The real, inflation-free growth is

$$\frac{1.828}{230/153} = 1.216$$

The annual real rate is

$$\sqrt[7]{1.216} - 1 = 0.0283 = 2.83\%$$

Rule 20: Growth rate in real terms. The periodic growth rate in real, inflation-free terms is

$$\frac{1 + i}{1 + p} - 1$$

where i is the nominal growth rate and p is the inflation rate.

Example. The nominal rate of growth in the sales value during the 1973–1980 period was 9 percent per year. Suppose the average annual inflation rate during this period was 6 percent.
Solution: The annual rate of growth, in real terms, is

$$\frac{1 + 0.09}{1 + 0.06} - 1 = 0.0283 = 2.83\%$$

Rule 21: Decay rate in real terms. The periodic decay rate in real, inflation-free terms is

$$1 - \frac{1 - d}{1 + p}$$

where d is the nominal decay rate.

Example. The nominal rate of decay in the sales volume during the 1973–1980 period was 8.4 percent per annum. Suppose the average annual inflation rate during this period was 6 percent.
Solution: The annual rate of decay, in real terms, is

$$1 - \frac{1 - 0.084}{1 + 0.06} = 0.1358 = 13.58\%$$

Various Interest Rates

Sometimes the interest is not stated in annual terms, nor is it paid at the end of the period. The relations between the various rates and the regular effective rate are required for comparison and analysis.

Monthly versus Annual Interest Rate

Because interest is compounded periodically, the annual rate of interest does not equal the sum of the monthly or quarterly rates. For example, if the monthly rate is 1 percent, then the annual effective rate is more than 12 percent (1 percent times 12 months). If the periodic (monthly, quarterly, or semiannual) rate is stated, what is the effective annual rate, and vice versa?

Rule 22: Deriving the annual effective rate. Given the periodic nominal interest rate the effective annual rate is computed by

$$i = (1 + j)^n - 1$$

where i is the annual effective interest rate, j is the interest rate per period, and n is the number of periods in a year.

Example A. The stated interest rate on a loan is 12 percent per annum. The loan is repaid by monthly installments; thus the monthly rate is 1 percent, paid at the end of each month.
Solution: The effective annual interest rate is

$$i = (1 + 0.01)^{12} - 1 = 0.1268 = 12.68\%$$

Given the annual nominal rate of interest, which is equal to $j \times n$, and using the previous formula, the figures in table 1–3 are computed.

Table 1–3
Annual Effective Rates from Periodic Rates
(percentages)

Annual Nominal $(j \times n)$	Semiannual $(n = 2)$	Quarterly $(n = 3)$	Monthly $(n = 12)$
6	6.09	6.14	6.17
12	12.36	12.55	12.68
18	18.81	19.25	19.56
24	25.44	26.25	26.82
30	32.25	33.55	34.49

Example B. Given a 6 percent semiannual rate, or a 3 percent quarterly rate, or a 1 percent monthly rate, the annual nominal rate is 12 percent. The effective annual rates can be derived from table 1–3: 12.36 percent, 12.55 percent, and 12.68 percent, respectively.

Rule 23: Deriving the periodic rate. Given the annual interest rate, the equivalent periodic rate is

$$j = \sqrt[n]{1 + i} - 1$$

Example. A company wants to charge its subsidiaries 16 percent per annum for the use of the capital that it provides. The company requires a quarterly repayment schedule of interest.
Solution: The equivalent quarterly interest rate is

$$j = \sqrt[4]{1 + 0.16} - 1 = 0.0378 = 3.78\%$$

Daily versus Annually Compounded Interest

You want to compare the returns of two alternative compounding procedures: daily and annually. The daily compounding approximates a continuous growth process.

Rule 24: Deriving the annual compounded rate. Given an annual interest rate that is compounded daily, the equivalent interest rate for compounding that is carried out once in a year is approximated by

$$i \cong j + \frac{j^2}{2}$$

where i is the annual interest compounded annually and j is the annual interest rate compounded daily. The exact formula is

$$i = e^j - 1$$

where e is 2.71828.

Example. A bank applies 12 percent interest per annum on a savings account, compounded daily.
Solution: This rate is equivalent to an annual compounded rate of approximately

$$i \cong 0.12 + \frac{0.12^2}{2} = 0.1272 = 12.72\%$$

The exact result is 12.75 percent.
Given the annual rate of interest, and using Rule 24, the rates in table 1–4 are calculated.

Rule 25: Daily versus monthly compounding. When the interest rate is low, the effective rate resulting from daily compounding is very near to that of monthly compounding.

Rule 26: Deriving the daily compounding rate. Given an annual interest rate i that is compounded annually, the equivalent annual interest j, when compounded daily, is approximated by

$$j \cong i - \frac{i^2}{2}$$

The exact formula is

$$j = \ln(1 + i)$$

where *ln* is logarithm to base e.

Example. Your money carries 10 percent interest, which is compounded annually.

Table 1–4
Annual Rates from Daily Rates
(percentages)

Nominal rate	6.00	12.00	18.00	24.00	30.00
Effective rate	6.18	12.75	19.72	27.12	34.99

Solution: This rate is equivalent to an annual rate compounded daily of approximately

$$j \cong 0.10 - \frac{0.10^2}{2} = 0.095 = 9.5\%$$

The exact solution is 9.53 percent.

The Discount Rate versus Regular Interest

Sometimes the interest is paid in advance by deducting it from the principal. The interest rate in this case is called the discount rate. This procedure is practiced for short-term loans (for example, 3 months). You want to know the interest rate in regular terms—that is, in terms of the end of the period.

Rule 27: Deriving the regular rate. Given the discount rate, the regular rate is

$$i = \frac{d}{1 - d}$$

where i is the regular interest rate (simple interest) and d is the discount interest rate.

Rule 28: Deriving the discount rate. Given the regular rate, the discount rate is

$$d = \frac{i}{1 + i}$$

Example A. From a \$200 loan, \$10.80 is discounted; that is, you receive only \$189.20, while you repay \$200 after 6 months.
Solution: The regular end-of-the-period (6 months) interest rate is

$$\frac{200}{189.20} - 1 = 0.0571 = 5.71\%$$

Alternatively, given a discounting rate of

$$1 - \frac{189.20}{200} = 0.054 = 5.4\%$$

The regular interest rate for this period can be calculated from this rule as follows:

$$\frac{0.054}{1 - 0.054} = 0.0571 = 5.71\%$$

Example B. A merchant requires an annual return of 12 percent on his capital. He practices discount interest in loaning money to his clients. Solution: The discount rate to be used is

$$d = \frac{0.12}{1 + 0.12} = 0.1071 = 10.71\%$$

Interest during Inflation

Inflation causes a decline in the purchasing power of money, which in turn causes prices to increase. Inflation also causes the interest rate to rise. As a result, during inflation the stated nominal rate includes compensation for the reduction in the real value (purchasing power) of the money.

The investor confronts two problems: Given the nominal rate, what is the cost of capital at constant (real) prices—that is, the interest rate free of the effect of inflation? This rate is called here inflation-free rate (real rate). Given the preinflation cost of capital, what is the nominal rate that fully compensates for the effect of inflation? This rate is called here inflation-compensated rate.

Inflation-Free Interest

The inflation-free rate of interest is the stated nominal rate corrected for the effect of inflation to yield the real rate of interest.

Rule 29: Deriving inflation-free rate. The real, inflation-free rate of interest is approximated by

$$i - p$$

where i is the stated, nominal rate of interest and p is the inflation rate. This formula is inaccurate for high rates of inflation. The exact formula is

$$\frac{i - p}{1 + p} = \frac{1 + i}{1 + p} - 1$$

Example. The stated, nominal rate of interest is 17 percent and the inflation rate is 8 percent.
Solution: The inflation-free rate of interest is approximately

$$0.17 - 0.08 = 0.09 = 9\%$$

The exact figure is

$$\frac{0.17 - 0.08}{1 + 0.08} = \frac{1 + 0.17}{1 + 0.08} - 1 = 0.833 = 8.33\%$$

Rule 30: Negative inflation-free rate. When the inflation is higher than the stated, nominal interest rate (that is, when $p > i$), the inflation-free rate of interest will be negative.

Example. Consider the previous example, but using an inflation rate of 20 percent.
Solution: The inflation-free rate of interest is

$$\frac{0.17 - 0.20}{1 + 0.20} = \frac{1 + 0.17}{1 + 0.20} - 1 = -0.025 = -2.5\%$$

The minus sign implies that the principal loses 2.5 percent a year because the inflation rate is higher than the interest rate. This is a gain to the borrower and a loss to the lender.

Table 1–5 illustrates some inflation-free rates of interest.

Rule 31: Conditions for using inflation-free rate. Use the inflation-free rate for discounting or compounding values that are stated in real prices.

Table 1–5
Inflation-Free Rates of Interest
(percentages)

	Nominal Interest Rate				
Inflation Rate	*6*	*12*	*18*	*24*	*30*
6	0	5.7	11.3	17.0	22.6
12	−5.4	0	5.4	10.7	16.1
18		−5.1	0	5.1	10.2
24			−4.8	0	4.8

Rule 32: After-tax interest rate. When the interest payments are tax-deductible, the tax effect must be taken into account. When the interest is tax-deductible, the real, after-tax, inflation-free rate of interest is

$$\frac{i(1 - t) - p}{1 + p}$$

where i is the stated, nominal rate of interest; p is the inflation rate; $i(1 - t)$ is the after-tax rate of interest; and t is the income tax rate.

Example. Consider the example for rule 29, where $i = 0.17$ and $p = 0.08$, but the income tax is 46 percent rather than zero.
Solution: The after-tax, inflation-free rate of interest is

$$\frac{0.17\ (1 - 0.46) - 0.08}{1 + 0.08} = 0.0109 = 1.09\%$$

To illustrate the after-tax inflation-free rates, consider the nominal rates in table 1–5 as after-tax rates.

Inflation-Compensated Interest

During inflation the interest should provide compensation for the decline in the real value of the principal.

Rule 33: Deriving inflation-compensated rate. The inflation-compensated rate of interest is approximated by

$$i^* + p$$

where i^* is the real, preinflation interest rate and p is the inflation rate. This formula is inaccurate for high rates of inflation. The exact formula is

$$i^*(1+p)+p=(1+i^*)(1+p)-1$$

Example. The preinflation rate of interest was 5 percent. The inflation rate is 15%.
Solution: The inflation compensated interest rate is approximately

$$0.05+0.15=0.20=20\%$$

The exact figure is

$$(1+0.05)(1+0.15)-1=0.2075=20.75\%$$

Table 1–6 illustrates some inflation-compensated rates of interest. For deriving the after-tax inflation-compensated rate of interest, see Chapter 7.

Indexation

The rise in the general price level (prices and costs) caused by inflation is measured by a general price index,usually the Consumer Price Index or the GNP Implicit Price Deflator. The changes in the price level of various types or groups of commodities are measured by specific price indexes, such as the construction index or the motor vehicles and equipment index. A price index states the price level at some period in time relative to the price level at some base date or year. The index at the base is 100.

Indexation is a procedure of using some price index to state monetary values at different points in time in terms of constant prices, or vice-versa. The procedure is similar to that of compounding or discounting.

Table 1–6
Inflation-Compensated Rates of Interest
(*percentages*)

	Preinflation Interest Rate				
Inflation Rate	*6*	*12*	*18*	*24*	*30*
6	12.4	18.7	25.1	31.1	37.8
12		25.4	32.2	38.9	45.6
18			39.2	46.6	53.4
24				53.8	61.3

Changing the Base Period

Every price index is stated in terms of a base period whose level is equal to 100.

Rule 34: Setting a new base. A given index number in period T can be changed to a new base of period t by

$$\frac{P_T}{P_t} \times 100$$

where P_T is the price index at date T, the base of which should be changed; P_t is the price index at date t, the date for the new base; and date T is later than date t.

Example. Consider the following index numbers:

	19 x 1	*19 x 5*	*19 x 9*
Old index	100	120	200
New index		100	?

Solution: The index number for 19 *x* 9, related to the 19 *x* 5 base, is

$$\frac{200}{120} \times 100 = 166.7$$

Rule 35: Linking to old base. A given index number in period T, whose base period is t, can be linked to an old base period, by

$$\frac{P_T \times P_t}{100}$$

where P_T is the price index at period T with respect to the new index and P_t is the price index at period t with respect to the old index.

Example: Consider the following index numbers:

	19 x 1	*19 x 5*	*19 x 9*
Old index	100	350	?
New index		100	130

Solution: The index number for 19 *x* 9, related to the 19 *x* 1 base, is

$$\frac{130 \times 350}{100} = 455$$

Inflating and Deflating by Price Index

Inflating or deflating is a procedure of restating monetary values at different points in time in terms of constant prices—that is, in terms of the money units of some base period.

Rule 36: Inflating. Inflating is a procedure of restating a given value in terms of the price level in a later date. A given value in date t is inflated, to be stated in terms of the price level of a later date T, by

$$M_T = M_t \frac{P_T}{P_t}$$

where M_T is the current value at date T; M_t is the value at date t, in terms of the price level at date t; P_T, P_t is the price index at date T or t; and date T is later than date t.

Example. The acquisition cost of an asset was $1,000 in 1970. You want to know the cost of this asset in terms of the price level of 1980. The respective price levels are 115 and 235.
Solution: The cost of the asset in 1980 dollars is

$$1{,}000 \times \frac{235}{115} = \$2{,}043$$

Rule 37: Relation between inflation and compounding. The procedure of inflating is similar to compounding, where the compounding factor is the average inflation rate between the two dates—that is

$$\frac{P_T}{P_t} = (1 + p)^{T-t}$$

where p is the average inflation rate.

Deflating, on the other hand, is similar to discounting.

Rule 38: Deflating. Deflating is a procedure of restating a given value in terms of the price level on an earlier date. A given value of date T is deflated, to be stated in terms of the price level of an earlier date t, by

$$M_t = M_T \frac{P_t}{P_T}$$

Example. It is estimated that an asset will cost $1,000 in 1985. You want to know the cost of this asset in terms of the price level of 1980. The price index in 1980 is 235 and the anticipated price index in 1985 is 378.
Solution: The cost of the asset in 1980 dollars is

$$1{,}000 \times \frac{235}{378} = \$622$$

2 Periodic Charges and Annuities

The present and future values of a cash flow series can be calculated using the compounding and discounting techniques. However, when the series of payments received is uniform (constant, increasing, or decreasing) it is called an annuity. Special formulas for annuities can reduce the calculation work considerably.

An annuity (also called a uniform series) is a series of equal periodic payments. Periodic capital charges are also a series of payments that repay a given principal (for example, a loan or investment).

The formulas and rules for annuities assume uniform periodic payments. However, even when the actual amounts are not equal, the rules may provide workable approximations. An annuity may vary; that is, the periodic payments will decrease or increase over time by a constant rate or amount. The assumed periodic charge may be a good way to approximate a cash flow that varies over time.

The formulas and rules in this chapter provide analytical factors that are determined by the rate of interest and the number of periods involved. Brief tables are provided for purposes of illustration and to show the order of magnitude of the resulting factors. Detailed tables for the main factors can usually be found in various texts and financial tables. Detailed tables for two types of factors (capital recovery and interest add-on factors) are provided in appendixes A and B.

Periodic Capital Charges

Periodic capital charges are computed to arrange repayment of a given principal (such as a loan or investment) over a given number of periods by means of equal end-of-period payments, including both principal repayment and interest payment.

Rule 1: Capital recovery. You want to set up a uniform series of end-of-period payments to amortize (repay) a given amount of money taken today. The periodic payment is called capital recovery.

The periodic capital recovery on a principal is approximated by

$$A\left(\frac{1}{n} + 0.67i\right)$$

where A is the principal, i is the cost of capital (interest or rate of return) per period (year), n is the number of periods (years) for repayment, and 0.67 is the approximated interest add-on factor (rule 2). The periodic capital recovery factor on a \$1 principal is approximated by

$$\frac{1}{n} + 0.67i$$

The exact formula is

$$CR_{n,i} = a_{\overline{n},\, i}^{-1} = \frac{i}{1-(1+i)^{-n}}$$

where $a_{\overline{n},\, i}^{-1}$ is the capital recovery factor.

Rule for memorizing. The exact formula is the interest rate divided by the total discount amount on \$1 (rule 5, chapter 1).

Example A. You intend to invest \$100 in a machine that will be disposed of after 5 years without a salvage value. The cost of capital is 12 percent. Solution: The annual capital charge is approximately

$$100\left(\frac{1}{5} + 0.67 \times 0.12\right) = \$28.04$$

The exact figure is \$27.74

Table 2–1 illustrates some capital recovery factors for \$1. More detailed tables are presented in appendix A.

Example B. A \$1,000 loan should be repaid by five equal end-of-year payments. The interest rate is 10 percent per annum.
Solution: The annual payment (capital recovery) is approximately

Table 2–1
Capital-Recovery Factors

Periods	*6%*	*12%*	*18%*	*24%*	*30%*
5	0.238	0.277	0.320	0.364	0.411
10	0.136	0.177	0.223	0.272	0.323
15	0.103	0.147	0.196	0.250	0.306

$$1{,}000\left(\frac{1}{5} + 0.67 \times 0.10\right) = \$267$$

The corresponding capital recovery factor in appendix A (for 5 periods and 10 percent) is 0.2638; hence, the exact annual payment is

$$1{,}000 \times 0.2638 = \$263.80$$

Rule 2: The interest add-on factor. The interest add-on factor is a number between 0.5 and 1.0. The use of this number simplifies interest calculations. It is denoted throughout this book by the letter k. For most practical situations

$$k = 0.67$$

The value of k depends on the life span in question

$$k \geq \frac{n+1}{2n}$$

For example, when $n = 2$, then k is greater than 0.75; when $n = 1$, then $k = 1$. The exact formula is

$$k = \frac{a_{\overline{n|}, i}^{-1} - \dfrac{1}{n}}{i}$$

where $a_{\overline{n|}, i}^{-1}$ is the capital recovery factor for n and i (rule 1); i is the cost of capital (interest or rate of return) per period (year); n is the number of periods (years) for repayment; k is the interest add-on factor.

$k \cong 0.60$ for $ni < 1$
$k \cong 0.67$ for $ni = 1$ to 2
$k \cong 0.70$ for $ni = 2$ to 3
$k \cong 0.75$ for $ni = 3$ to 4.

Table 2–2 illustrates some interest add-on factors. A more detailed table is presented in appendix B.

Table 2–2
Add-On Factors for Finding the Average Interest Rate

Periods	*6%*	*12%*	*18%*	*24%*	*30%*
5	0.623	0.645	0.665	0.684	0.702
10	0.598	0.642	0.681	0.715	0.745
15	0.605	0.668	0.721	0.764	0.798

Example. Suppose a $100 loan is to be repaid by 12 monthly payments. The interest rate is 2 percent per month.
Solution: The monthly payment is approximately

$$100\left(\frac{1}{12} + 0.60 \times 0.02\right) = \$9.53$$

The corresponding k value in Appendix B (for 12 periods and 2 percent) is 0.561; hence, the exact monthly payment is

$$100\left(\frac{1}{12} + 0.561 \times 0.02\right) = \$9.46$$

Rule 3: The average interest component in capital charges. The average interest rate to be charged to the user of assets, in addition to the depreciation charges, can be computed by using the interest add-on factor (rule 2). The average interest component is

$$ki$$

Example 4. A machine that cost $1,000 is expected to serve 10 years and produce 100 units annually. The company's cost of capital is 12 percent per annum. You want to know how much interest to be charged to each unit produced.
Solution: The average annual interest charges on the machine are

$$1{,}000 \times 0.67 \times 0.12 = \$80$$

The interest charge per unit is 80/100 = $0.80

Rule 4: Effect of a change in interest rate. A one percentage point change in the interest rate or in the rate of return changes the periodic capital charges by less than one percentage point. To arrive at the approximate incremental change in the periodic charge, multiply the change in the interest rate by 0.67 (rule 2).

The exact result of a change in the interest rate is found by comparing the capital recovery factors that correspond to the former and the new interest rates.

Example. The interest rate on a loan has been raised from 10 percent to 15 percent—that is, an increase of five percentage points.
Solution: The annual repayments on a $1 loan would increase by approximately

$$0.05 \times 0.67 = 0.0335$$

For the exact figure, suppose the loan is taken for 10 years. Then the annual repayments (on a $1 loan) are 0.199 for a 15 percent loan and 0.163 for a 10 percent loan. The difference is 0.036.

Ordinary Annuities

An ordinary annuity is a series of equal payments, each made at the end of the respective period, as follows:

Period:	1	2	3	...	n
Payment:	A	A	A	...	A

Rule 5: Future value (Compound Amount) of Annuity. The future value of a constant cash flow (annuity) is the sum of the future values of each payment, including the interest charges (rule 3, chapter 1). The factor for the future value (compound amount) of an ordinary annuity of $1 per period (where $A = 1$) is approximated by

$$n(1 + 0.67ni)$$

This rule holds for the range $ni < 1.5$. The exact formula is

$$FVA_{n,i} = s_{n,i} = \frac{(1 + i)^n - 1}{i}$$

where $s_{n,i}$ is the future value factor for annuity.

Rule for memorizing. The exact formula is the compound interest amount of \$1 (rule 2, chapter 1) divided by the rate of interest.

Example. A sum of \$100 is deposited at the end of each year for 10 years in a savings account that bears 10 percent interest per annum.
Solution: The accumulated sum, at the end of year 10, is approximately

$$100 \times 10\ (1 + 0.67 \times 0.10 \times 10) = \$1{,}670$$

The exact figure is \$1,593.74.
Table 2–3 illustrates some future value factors for annuities of \$1 per period.

Rule 6: Sinking fund. A sinking fund is a desired amount to be accumulated at the end of a given time by means of equal end-of-period payments. The reciprocal of the future value factor of an annuity is the sinking fund factor.

The sinking fund factor for accumulating \$1 in the future is approximated by

$$\frac{1}{n} - 0.33i$$

This rule holds for the range $ni < 1.5$.

The factor for a sinking fund is the capital recovery factor minus the interest rate; that is,

$$a_{n,\,i}^{-1} - i$$

where $a_{n,\,i}^{-1}$ is the capital recovery factor (rule 1).

Example. You want to accumulate a fund of \$1,000 at the end of 5 years by means of equal end-of-year payments that will bear 12 percent interest annually.

Table 2–3
Future-Value Factors of Annuity

Periods	*6%*	*12%*	*18%*	*24%*	*30%*
5	5.64	6.35	7.15	8.05	9.04
10	13.18	17.55	23.52	31.64	42.62
15	23.28	37.28	60.97	100.82	167.29

Solution: The end-of-year payment is approximately

$$1{,}000\left(\frac{1}{5} - 0.33 \times 0.12\right) = \$160$$

The corresponding capital recovery factor in table 2–1 is 0.277; hence, the exact payment is

$$1{,}000\ (0.277 - 0.12) = \$157$$

Rule 7: Present Value of Annuity. The present value of an ordinary annuity, as presented in the scheme at the beginning of the discussion of ordinary annuities, is the sum of the present (discounted) values of each payment (rule 6, chapter 1).

The factor for the present value of an ordinary annuity of \$1 per period (when $A = 1$) is approximated by

$$\frac{n}{1 + 0.67ni}$$

This rule holds for the range $ni < 2$.
The present-value factor of annuity is the reciprocal of the capital recovery factor (rule 1). The exact formula is

$$PVA_{n,i} = a_{n,i} = \frac{1 - (1 + i)^{-n}}{i}$$

where $a_{n,i}$ is the present-value factor of annuity.

Rule for memorizing. The exact formula is the total discount amount on \$1 (rule 5, chapter 1) divided by the rate of interest.

Example. An investor deposits \$100 at the end of each year for 5 years in an account that bears 10 percent per annum.
Solution: The present value of this annuity is approximately

$$100 \times \frac{5}{1 + (0.67 \times 5 \times 0.10)} = \$375$$

The exact figure is \$379.08.
Table 2–4 illustrates some present-value factors for annuities of \$1 per period.

Table 2–4
Present-Value Factors of Annuity

Periods	*6%*	*12%*	*18%*	*24%*	*30%*
5	4.21	3.60	3.13	2.75	2.44
10	7.36	5.65	4.49	3.68	3.09
15	9.71	6.81	5.09	4.00	3.27

Rule 8: Present value of an infinite series. In some cases the stream of payments (ordinary annuity) is infinite—for example, the returns from land. In this case the present value is

$$\frac{E}{i}$$

where E is the annual uniform payment.

Example. The anticipated annual return from an acre of land is $100. The interest rate is 5 percent per annum.
Solution: The present value of this cash stream is

$$\frac{100}{0.05} = \$2{,}000$$

Note: This value is the maximum you would be ready to pay for this acre of land.

Annuities during Inflation

Payments may increase over time because of inflation or because of real growth. The periodic payments will increase every period by a constant percentage. The series of the end-of-period payments is

Period, end:	1	2	...	n
Payment:	$A(1+g)$	$A(1+g)^2$	...	$A(1+g)^n$

The periodic payments A are stated in terms of the price level at the beginning of the first period. The actual first payment at the end of period 1 will already be higher by $(1+g)$. In other words, the level of A is that which is intended to be paid as a series, stated in constant prices. The series of payments will grow by the rate g per annum.

Consider a series of payments A stated in constant prices. Because of inflation, the periodic payments will increase over time by the rate of inflation. The rate of interest (cost of capital), on the other hand, is in nominal terms, a rate that is constant over time.

Rule 9: Present value of inflated annuity. The present value of an ordinary annuity that grows nominally by inflation is computed in two steps.

1. Compute the inflation-free rate of interest (rule 29, chapter 1).

2. Compute the present value by using the resultant inflation-free rate of interest—that is

$$A(a_{n,i^*})$$

where A is the periodic payment at constant prices; a_{n,i^*} is the present-value factor of annuity (rule 7), discounted by i^*; and i^* is the inflation-free rate of interest $= (i - p)/(1 + p)$.

Example. An investor undertakes to pay \$100 at the end of each year for 5 years. The payments are indexed by the inflation rate. The annual interest rate is 20 percent. The expected annual inflation rate is 18 percent. Solution: The inflation-free interest rate is

$$\frac{0.20 - 0.18}{1 + 0.18} = 0.0169$$

The present value of the series is

$$100(a_{5.0.0169}) = 100 \times 4.756 = \$475.60$$

Rule 10: Inflation higher than interest. When the inflation-free rate of interest i^* turns out to be negative (that is, the inflation rate is higher than the nominal rate), the present value is approximately

$$A(s_{n,i^*})\ (1 + i^*)$$

where s_{n,i^*} is the future value factor of annuity (rule 5), compounded by i^*; and i^* is the inflation-free rate of interest disregarding the negative sign.

Example. consider the previous example, but the interest rate is 16 percent rather than 20 percent.

Solution: The inflation-free interest rate is

$$\frac{0.16 - 0.18}{1 + 0.18} = -0.0169$$

The present value of this series is

$$100(s_{5,0.0169})\,(1 + 0.0169) = 100 \times 5.172 \times 1.0169 = \$525.94$$

Varying Annuities

Annuity varies when the periodic payment increases or decreases at each period by a given rate or by a given amount. Even when the actual periodic amounts increase somewhat irregularly, the varying series may provide a convenient way to estimate the actual conditions.

Rule 11: Equivalence to ordinary annuity. A varying annuity can be transformed to the equivalent of an ordinary annuity by taking the present value of the varying annuity and multiplying the result by the capital recovery factor; that is,

$$\left(\sum_{t=1}^{n} \frac{E_t}{(1 + i)^t}\right) a_{n,\,i}^{-1}$$

where E_t is the payment in period t.

Example. Consider the following cashflow

Year, end:	1	2	3
Payment:	100	110	120

The annual interest rate is 10 percent.
Solution: The equivalent ordinary annuity of this series, given that $a_{3,0.10}^{-1} =$ 0.4021, is

$$\left(\frac{100}{(1 + 0.10)} + \frac{110}{(1 + 0.10)^2} + \frac{120}{(1 + 0.10)^3}\right) 0.4021 = \$109.36$$

The varying annuity in this example is equivalent to a 3-year ordinary annuity, each payment equals \$109.36.

Growth Annuity

A growing annuity is an ordinary annuity where each periodic payment A increases in real terms by a given percentage g, as follows:

Period, end:	1	2	3	...	n
Payment:	A	$A(1+g)$	$A(1+g)^2$	...	$A(1+g)^{n-1}$

The periodic payments are exposed to a nominal growth by a given percentage each period, denoted by g; and the interest rate (or cost of capital) denoted by i.

Rule 12: Present value of a growing annuity. The present value of a growing annuity whose first payment is $\$A$, is

$$A \times \frac{1 - \left[\frac{1+i}{1+g}\right]^{-n}}{i-g}$$

where A is the first payment, g is the growth rate, and i is the interest rate.

Example. A machine that will serve for 5 years incurs \$100 annual maintenance costs at the beginning of the first period. It is anticipated that these costs will increase by 10 percent at the end of each period; that is, the cost at the beginning of the second year will be \$110. The annual interest rate is 15 percent and is constant over time.
Solution: The present value of this growing annuity is

$$100 \times \frac{1 - \left[\frac{1+0.15}{1+0.10}\right]^{-5}}{0.15-0.10} = \$398.55$$

Suppose the annual growth is anticipated to be 20 percent, rather than 10 percent; this growth rate is larger than the interest rate ($i = 0.15$). Then the present value is \$474.26.
Table 2–5 illustrates some present values of growing annuities of \$1, growing at 10 percent per period.

Table 2–5
Present-Value Factors of a 10 Percent Growth Annuity (First Payment $1)

Periods	*6%*	*12%*	*18%*	*24%*	*30%*
5	5.09	4.31	3.70	3.22	2.83
10	11.21	8.24	6.31	4.99	4.06
15	18.58	11.84	8.14	5.96	4.59

Decay (Negative Growth) Annuity

A decaying annuity is an ordinary annuity where each periodic payment, A, declines by a given percentage, g, as follows:

Period, end:	1	2	3	...	n
Payment:	A	$\frac{A}{(1+g)}$	$\frac{A}{(1+g)^2}$	...	$\frac{A}{(1+g)^{n-1}}$

Rule 13: Present value of a decay annuity. The present value of a decaying annuity whose first payment is $\$A$, is computed in two steps.

1. Compute the discounting rate that results from the decay rate and the interest rate; that is,

$$h = (1 + g)(1 + i) - 1$$

2. Compute the present value by using the resultant discounting rate, and multiply the result by $(1 + g)$; that is,

$$A(1 + g)a_{n,h}$$

where A is the first payment; g is the annual rate of decay; i is the interest rate; h is the discounting rate; and $a_{n,h}$ is the present-value factor of annuity (rule 7), discounted by h.

Example. The current income from an orchard that will live for 5 years is $100 per acre. This income is expected to decrease by 7 percent each year. The annual interest rate is 10 percent.
Solution: The discounting rate is

$$h = (1 + 0.07)(1 + 0.10) - 1 = 0.177$$

The present value is

$$100(1 + 0.07)a_{5,0.177} = 107 \times 3.149 = \$336.94$$

Rule 14: Determining the withdrawal rate from a fund. In certain cases the rate of decay is determined by the decisionmaker—for example, in the case of withdrawal from funds. The withdrawal rate (the decay rate) is determined by

$$g = (1 + i)\left(\frac{A}{B}\right)^{\frac{1}{n}} - 1$$

where A is the fund at the beginning of the period, and B is the fund at the end of the period.

Example. Suppose a retired person realizes his income needs are decreasing. He has a fund of \$20,000. He wants to get an annual income of g percent of his outstanding balance, and still have \$10,000 at the end of 10 years. The interest rate is 10 percent.
Solution: The withdrawal rate is

$$(1 + 0.10)\left[\frac{20{,}000}{10{,}000}\right]^{\frac{1}{10}} - 1 = 0.179 = 17.9\%$$

Thus, he can withdraw in the first year

$$0.179 \times 20{,}000 = \$3{,}580$$

Gradient Annuity

Gradient annuity is an ordinary annuity where each payment increases by a constant amount B, as follows:

Period, end:	1	2	3	...	n
Payment:	0	B	$2B$	...	$(n-1)B$

Rule 15: Present value of increasing gradient series. The present value of a gradient annuity, which grows periodically by a constant amount, B, is

$$B\left[\frac{a_{n,i}}{i} - \frac{n}{i(1 + i)^n}\right] = B[n(1 - k)a_{n,i}]$$

where B is the first payment, the constant periodic increment; and $k \cong 0.67$ is the interest add-on factor (rule 2).

Example. A machine that will serve for 5 years incurs \$100 maintenance the first year. This cost will increase each year after the first year by \$10; that is, the respective costs will be \$100, \$110, \$120, \$130, \$140. The annual interest rate is 15 percent.
Solution: The present value of the \$100 series is

$$100a_{5,0.15} = \$335.22$$

The present value of the \$10 gradient series is

$$10 \times \left[\frac{3.352}{0.15} - \frac{5}{0.15(1+0.15)^5}\right] = \$57.75$$

The total present value is \$392.97.

Rule 16: Gradient versus growth. In the case of a growth annuity (rule 12), the basic payment is \$$A$ and the growth is g percent. In the case of a gradient annuity, consider B as a percentage of A, which is the basic payment of the growth annuity; that is, calculate B/A. Then the two cases can be compared.

The growth annuity yields a higher present value than the gradient annuity for an equal increase or decrease on \$1, that is, when

$$\frac{B}{A} = g$$

The reason is that the growth and gradient annuities work similarly to compound and simple interest, respectively. For example, the present value of the growth annuity (see the example for rule 12) is \$398.55, whereas the present value of the gradient annuity (the example for rule 15) is \$392.97.

Rule 17: Equivalent periodic charges of a gradient. The equivalent periodic charge of the gradient annuity is computed by multiplying the present value of the gradient by the capital recovery factor. The formula for a direct computation is

$$B[n(1-k)]$$

Example. consider the previous example where $B = \$10$, $n = 5$ and $i = 0.15$.
Solution: The relevant k factor (appendix B) is 0.655. The equivalent periodic charge of the gradient annuity is

$$10[5(1 - 0.655)] = \$17.25$$

Alternatively, the equivalent periodic charge can be calculated by multiplying the present value figure, as calculated in the previous example (\$57.75), by the capital recovery factor (rule 1); that is

$$57.75(a^{-1}_{5,0.15}) = 57.75 \times 0.2983 = \$17.23$$

Note: The regular, incorrect, average charge of the gradient is

$$(10 + 20 + 30 + 40)/5 = \$20$$

Table 2–6 illustrates some equivalent periodic charges for \$1 increments of a gradient annuity.

Rule 18: Present value of decreasing gradient series. When the periodic payments are decreasing by a constant amount, B (that is, B is negative), the factor for the value of the series is the same as above (for an increasing series) with a minus sign.

Example. The current annual income from an orchard that will live for 5 years is \$100. This income will decrease each year from the second year on by \$10. The annual interest rate is 15 percent.
Solution: The present value of the \$100 series is

$$100(a_{5,0.15}) = 100 \times 3.3522 = \$335.22$$

Table 2–6
Equivalent Periodic Charge Factors for \$1 Increments of a Gradient Annuity

Periods	*6%*	*12%*	*18%*	*24%*	*30%*
5	1.88	1.77	1.67	1.58	1.49
10	4.02	3.58	3.19	2.85	2.55
15	5.93	4.98	4.19	3.55	3.03

The present value of the gradient series, as computed in the example for rule 15, is \$57.75. The total present value is

$$335.22 - 57.75 = \$277.47$$

Annuities Due (Advanced Payments)

Annuity due (also called advanced payments) is a series of equal payments, each made at the beginning of the respective period, as in the case of rent or insurance payments. In contrast, in ordinary annuities the payments are made at the end of the period.

Rule 19: Relations between due and ordinary. The relation between the two annuities is given by $(1 + i)$. That is, the future value and present value due equal the ordinary annuity multiplied by $(1 + i)$. The capital recovery and sinking fund factors due equal the ordinary annuity factors divided by $(1 + i)$.

Rule 20: Future value (compound amount) of annuity due. The factor for future value (compound amount) of an annuity due is

$$s_{n,i}(1 + i)$$

Alternatively, use the factor for ordinary annuity for $n + 1$ periods, and deduct one, that is

$$(s_{n+1,i}) - 1$$

Example: A sum of \$100 is deposited at the beginning of every month for 12 months at 1 percent per month. (Thus, $n + 1 = 13$).
Solution: The accumulated future value is

$$100(s_{13,0.01} - 1) = 100\ (13.809 - 1) = \$1{,}280.09$$

Example. Consider the example for rule 5, where the solution is \$1,593.74 (the exact solution). Suppose the payments are deposited at the beginning rather than at the end of the year; then the future value is

$$1{,}593.74\ (1 + 0.10) = \$1{,}753.11$$

Rule 21: Present value of annuity due. The factor for present value of an annuity due is

$$a_{n,i}(1 + i)$$

Alternatively, for calculating purposes, use the factor for ordinary annuity for $(n - 1)$ periods, and add one—that is

$$a_{n-1,i} + 1$$

Example. A sum of \$100 is deposited at the beginning of every month for 12 months at 1 percent per month. (Thus, $n - 1 = 11$).
Solution: The present value is

$$100(a_{11,0.01} + 1) = 100\ (10.368 + 1) = \$1{,}136.80$$

Example. Consider the example for rule 7, where the solution is \$379.08 (the exact solution). Suppose the payments are deposited at the beginning rather than at the end of the year.
Solution: The present value is

$$379.08\ (1 + 0.10) = \$416.99$$

Rule 22: Capital recovery of annuity due. The capital recovery factor for an annuity due is the factor for ordinary annuity divided by $(1 + i)$; that is

$$a_{n,i}^{-1}\ /(1 + i)$$

The periodic payment is carried out at the beginning of the period rather than at the end of the period.

Example. A sum of \$1,000 should be repaid by five equal beginning-of-year payments. The annual interest rate is 10 percent.
Solution: The annual beginning-of-year payment (capital recovery) is

$$\frac{1000\ (a_{5,0.10}^{-1})}{1 + 0.10} = \frac{1000 \times 0.2638}{1.10} = \$239.82$$

For comparison, the end-of-year payment is \$263.80 (example B for rule 1).

3 Statistical Tools

The business manager requires a basic understanding of the main statistical tools used in data analysis. The objective is two-fold: a knowledge of statistics enables the manager to understand the jargon used by his analyst, and more important, it gives him some independence in drawing his own conclusions based on the submitted analysis.

This chapter presents simple and useful rules and tools for statistical data analysis. The emphasis is on arriving at quick answers and orders of magnitude concerning the properties of a data series, basic relationships among variables and their degree of association, detection of changes in a process, evaluation of sample results, and other techniques. Statistical analysis is also important in risk and uncertainty analysis, both of which are necessary in most business decisions.

The approximating rules are based on the assumption that the samples are drawn from a more or less normal or symmetrical distribution.

Measures of Dispersion

Measures of dispersion or variation indicate the scattering of observations about some given point of location. The point of location may be the mean, median, extreme point, or any other point. The measures of dispersion are needed to describe the behavior of individual items within the population. They are needed especially for significance tests between estimates from different samples (see the section on statistical significance later in this chapter).

Range

The range is the difference between the largest and the smallest observation in a sample. Range can be used by itself to represent the variation within the sample or used to find other measures of dispersion, such as standard deviation. It is also used to find the required sample size that will adequately represent the population.

The range is the simplest measure of dispersion. However, it has a serious limitation because it is not constant but depends on the sample size. The larger the sample size, the larger is the range.

Rule 1: Indication of variation. For any given sample of size n (that is, number of observations), the larger the range, the larger the variation.

Rule 2: Spread of ranges. The expected spread of ranges in samples of size n is from about 0.6 to about 1.4 of the average range.

Example A. Suppose the range in a given sample is 10; in a second sample the range may fall between 6 and 14.

Example B. The range of the current ratio figures for a group of companies (the first sample) is 2.1. Then, the expected range of another group (a second sample) is expected to fall between 1.26 and 2.94. If the range of the second group of companies lies outside this range, this may mean that the conditions changed (the sample represents different types of companies or a different period) and you cannot compare the results.

Rule 3: Representative sample size. The required sample size, so that at most p percent of the population is not represented by the observed range, is approximated by

$$\frac{1.5}{p}$$

where p is the expected proportion of the population not represented by the sample.

Example. You want to ensure that your sample represents at least 95 percent of the population data range; that is, at most, only 5 percent are not represented.
Solution: The required sample size should be larger than

$$\frac{1.5}{0.05} = 30 \text{ observations}$$

Rule 4: Relative range. The range is expressed in terms of units of the variable under analysis. Comparisons between various populations or different variables necessitate a measure independent of the units by which the variable is measured. Thus, for comparative purposes, a relative measure is required.

To calculate the relative range, divide the range by the sample mean. The larger the relative range, the larger is the relative variation.

Example. You want to compare the variations of two financial ratios for which the following data is available:

	Current ratio	*Returns on assets*
Range:	3.90 − 1.03	0.11 − 0.01
Mean:	2.10	0.06

Solution: The relative ranges are

$$\frac{3.90 - 1.03}{2.10} = 1.37 \qquad \frac{0.11 - 0.01}{0.06} = 1.67$$

The relative range (dispersion) of the ratio of returns on assets is larger than that of the current ratio.

Standard Deviation (SD)

The standard deviation is a measure of variation that describes the average scattering of observations about the mean. Its square is called variance.

Rule 5: Estimating SD from a range. Given a random sample of size n, an estimate of the standard deviation (SD) can be approximated from the range, as follows:

$$\frac{\text{Range}}{\text{Number of SD}}$$

The number of standard deviations (SD) in the range can be approximated from the following table:

Size of sample (n):	2	5	10	20	30	100
Number of SD in the range:	1	2.33	3	3.75	4	5

Example. The range of the current ratio figures for a sample of twenty companies is 2.9.
Solution: Since the sample size is 20, the number of SD is 3.75. The standard deviation is about

$$\frac{2.90}{3.75} = 0.77$$

Rule 6: Estimating SD from quartiles. The quartile deviation is a measure of dispersion usually used when the observations are ordered according to their value; that is, the data are ordered from the smallest to the largest value. The quartile deviation is the difference between the 25 percentile and the 75 percentile.

For symmetrical and nearly symmetrical distributions, the standard deviation is approximated by dividing the quartile deviation by 1.5; that is

$$\frac{Q_{0.75} - Q_{0.25}}{1.5}$$

where Q is the quartile.

Example. Checking Dun and Bradstreet's Key Business Ratios, you find the following ratios of net profits to net sales for two manufacturing industries in 1978:

	Drugs	*Bakeries*
Upper quartile	10.54	4.13
Lower quartile	2.84	0.92

Solution: The respective standard deviations are approximately

$$\frac{10.54 - 2.84}{1.5} = 5.13 \qquad \frac{4.13 - 0.92}{1.5} = 2.14$$

Rule 7: Subjective estimation of SD. When data are unavailable, the range is estimated by subjectively specifying the optimistic high value $x_{(n)}$ and the pessimistic low value $x_{(1)}$. The standard deviation will be about one-fourth of this subjectively estimated range; that is,

$$\frac{x_{(n)} - x_{(1)}}{4}$$

Example. The returns from a new process are estimated to be between 10 percent and 20 percent.
Solution: The standard deviation is approximated to be

$$\frac{20 - 10}{4} = 2.5\%$$

Rule 8: Exact estimation of SD. The formula for calculating the standard deviation is

$$S = \sqrt{\frac{\Sigma(x_i - \overline{x})^2}{n - 1}}$$

where S is the standard deviation, x_i is the value of observation i, $\overline{x}$ is the average value for the sample, and n is the number of observations. The formula in rule 8 is an estimate of the standard deviation of the population, given that the population is very large.

Example. Consider the data in the first two columns in table 3–2 later in this chapter, regarding monthly production during 10 months.
Solution: The standard deviation is

$$\sqrt{\frac{27.6}{10 - 1}} = 1.75$$

Applying rule 5, the standard deviation is approximated from the range. The range of the amount produced (table 3–2) is $6 - 1 = 5$ and the number of standard deviations in the range of ten observations is three (see table in rule 5). Hence, the expected standard deviation is approximately

$$\frac{5}{3} = 1.67$$

Rule 9: Size correction factor. For a small population, the standard deviation of the population is smaller than the standard deviation of the sample by the following correcting factor:

$$\sqrt{1 - \frac{n}{N}}$$

where n is the number of units in the sample and N is the number of units in the population.

Example. The standard deviation of the current ratio figures for a sample of 20 companies is 0.77. There are 150 companies in the industry.
Solution: The standard deviation for the industry is approximately

$$0.77\sqrt{1-\frac{20}{150}}=0.72$$

Coefficient of Variation

The standard deviation is expressed in terms of units of the variable under analysis. Comparisons between various populations or different variables necessitates a measure independent of the units by which the variable is measured. Thus, for comparative purposes, a relative measure is required—the coefficient of variation. This measure plays an important role in risk and uncertainty analysis.

Rule 10: Calculating the coefficient of variation. To calculate the coefficient of variation, divide the standard deviation by the sample mean; that is

$$C=\frac{S}{\bar{x}}$$

where S is the standard deviation and $\bar{x}$ is the average. The larger the coefficient, the larger the relative variation.

The coefficient of variation is meaningful only when the mean is substantially different from zero. For comparison purposes, the distributions should be transformed so that they will have the same point of origin.

Rule 11: Standardization for calculating the coefficient. One way to standardize the data is to subtract the lowest value observation from every one of the observations in the given sample. In this way, all the data will start from zero.

Example. You confront the following figures pertaining to a large sample of companies:

	Sales to receivables	Current ratio
Mean	7.7	2.3
Standard deviation	3.5	0.9
Lowest value	4.0	1.0

Solution: The respective adjusted coefficients of variation are approximately

$$\frac{3.5}{7.7 - 4.0} = 0.95 \qquad \frac{0.9}{2.3 - 1.0} = 0.69$$

Without adjustment, the respective figures would be 0.45 and 0.39, which should not be compared because they are based on different points of origin.

Distribution Curve

A distribution curve shows the probability that an observation will take on a value less than or equal to a specified number. The range of the curve is from zero probability to a maximum of one. The shape of the curve differs for different events. Variables with random errors are usually described by the normal distribution. When the distribution is unknown, it can be constructed from sample data. This value is known as the empirical distribution.

Empirical Distribution Curve

The probability that an observation in your sample data takes on a value less than or equal to a specified number can be estimated from the cumulative frequency of the sample, as follows.

Rule 12: Constructing the distribution curve. To construct the empirical distribution curve, rank your data in order of magnitude starting with the lowest value as follows:

$$x_{(1)} < x_{(2)} < \ldots x_{(i)}$$

Then compute the fraction of the total number of observations, $F_{(x_i)}$, *with values less than or equal to a given level,* x_i, by means of

$$F_{(x_i)} = \frac{i}{n + 1}$$

where $x_{(i)}$ is the value of the ith ranked observation (for example, $x_{(2)}$ = the value of the second ranked observation), and $F_{(x_i)}$ is the fraction of total observations below observation i having value $x_{(i)}$. Most distribution curves are S-shaped. The fraction $F_{(x_i)}$ as computed above is a point on the curve.

Example. You want to estimate the percentage of companies that have a current ratio lower than 1.8. The sample includes 20 companies. The value of the fifth lowest observation takes the value of 1.8.
Solution: The percentage of companies having a value of at most 1.8 is about

$$\frac{5}{20+1} = 0.24 = 24\%$$

Rule 13: Graphing the distribution curve. To construct a distribution curve, graph the fractions, $F_{(x_i)}$, as ordinates against the respective level of observation, x_i, as abscissa, and smooth the curve. The resulting curve is depicted in figure 3–1. From this curve you can read the fiftieth percentile (the median), the twenty-fifth and seventy-fifth percentiles (the quartiles), or the tenth, twentieth, . . . , ninetieth percentiles (the deciles).

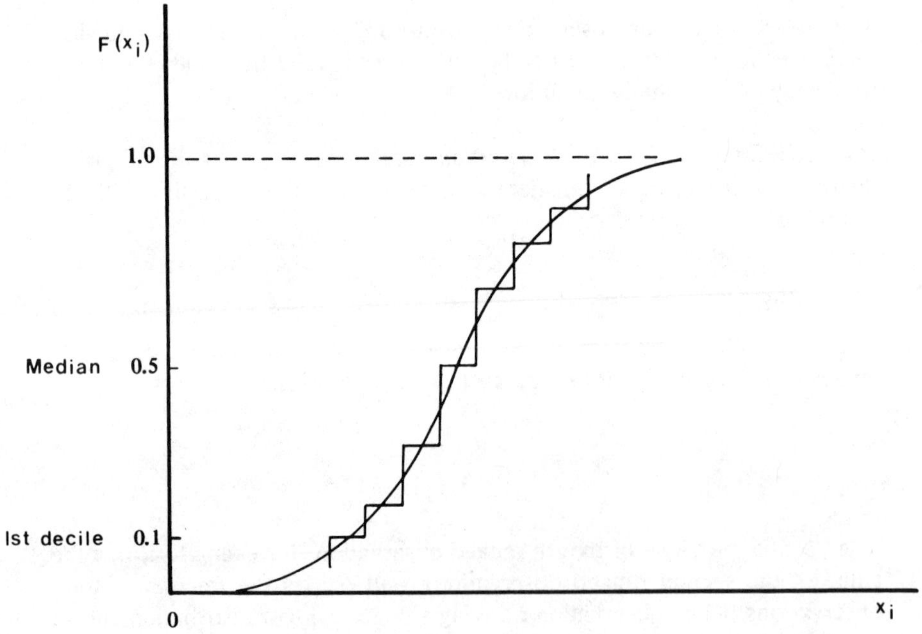

Figure 3–1. Distribution Curve

The Normal Distribution

The normal distribution is a very common distribution in statistics, mainly because averages and sums of samples are normally distributed, no matter what the parent distribution. This distribution is symmetric about the mean; half the data in the population are below the mean and half are above. Because of its symmetric property, the mean (average), median (the middle measure), and mode (the most probable) are equal.

Rule 14: Number of standard deviations in the range. The normal distribution is characterized by an infinite range, although, for practical purposes, the range is about five standard deviations. To put it differently, 99 percent of the population are included in the range of the mean ±2.5 standard deviations, as depicted in figure 3–2. Hence symmetric distributions, with finite ranges, can be approximated by the normal distribution.

Rule 15: Properties of the normal distribution. Some of the properties of the normal distribution can be inferred from the curve in figure 3–2; these properties are summarized in table 3–1. For example, the figures in table 3–1 show that the percentage of all data below one standard deviation from the mean is 15.9 percent.

Example. The data on a group of companies show that the average of the current ratio is 2.1 and the standard deviation is 0.77. You want to know the percentage of companies with a current ratio smaller than one.

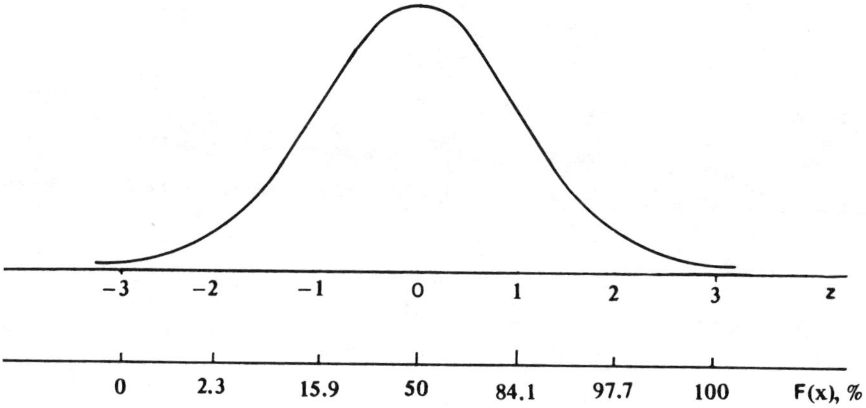

Figure 3–2. Frequency Distribution

Solution: The number of standard deviations included between the average current ratio and the level below one is

$$\frac{2.1 - 1.0}{0.77} = 1.43 \text{ standard deviations}$$

Table 3–1 shows that the number of companies with a current ratio less than one is about 8 percent.

Skewness

The distribution curve may or may not be symmetric about the mean. A curve is symmetric when the mean equals the median. An asymmetric curve may be positively skewed (mean larger than median), or negatively skewed (mean smaller than median), as depicted in figure 3–3.

Most economic and business phenomena are positively skewed. For example, income is limited at zero at the left tail of the distribution and may reach very high levels at the right tail.

Table 3–1
Standard Normal Distribution

Standard Deviation from the Mean z	*Frequency (Ordinate)* $f(z)$, %	*Probability (Area under the Curve)* $F(z)$, %
−2.5	1.75	0.6
−2.0	5.40	2.3
−1.5	12.95	6.7
−1.2	19.42	11.5
−1.0	24.20	15.9
−0.8	28.97	21.2
−0.6	33.32	27.4
−0.4	36.83	34.5
−0.2	39.10	42.1
0	39.89	50.0
0.2	39.10	57.9
0.4	36.83	65.5
0.6	33.32	72.6
0.8	28.97	78.8
1.0	24.20	84.1
1.2	19.42	88.5
1.5	12.95	93.3
2.0	5.40	97.7
2.5	1.75	99.4

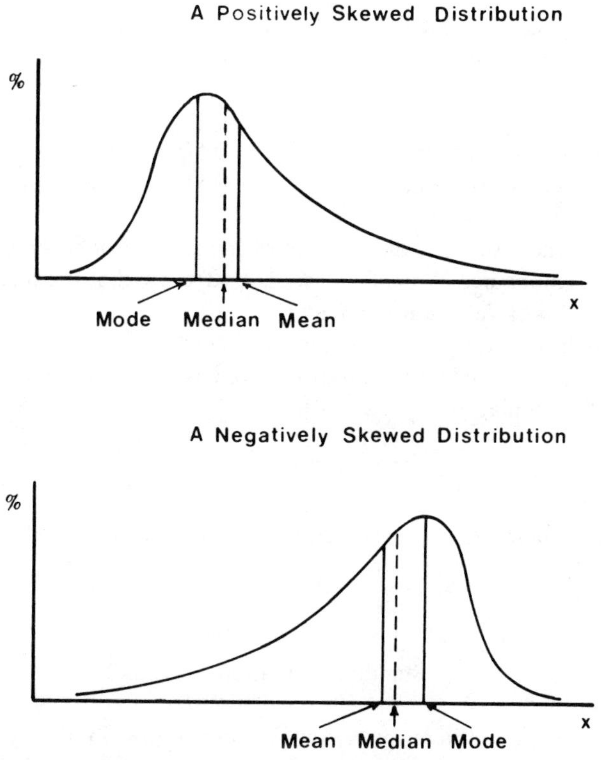

Figure 3–3. Frequency Distributions

Rule 16: Indication of skewness. The curve is skewed when

$$[x_{(n)} - \bar{x}] \substack{\gg \\ \ll} [\bar{x} - x_{(1)}]$$

where $x_{(n)}$ is the largest observation; $x_{(1)}$ is the smallest observation; $\bar{x}$ is the average; » is much larger, indicating positive skewness; and « is much smaller, indicating negative skewness.

Example. You know that the richest people's income is much farther from the average than the poorest people's income. Hence you can infer that the income distribution is positively skewed.

Rule 17: Ratio of median to mean. When a distribution is highly skewed (the coefficient of variation is over 0.5), the use of the average is misleading. It is better to use the median as a benchmark.

For positively skewed distributions, the larger the coefficient of variation, the higher is the skewness as measured by the ratio of the median to the mean; that is

Coefficient of variation:	0.20	0.50	0.70	1.00
Ratio of median to mean:	0.98	0.89	0.81	0.70

Example. You know that the distribution of the ratio of debt to equity in a given group of companies is highly skewed. You know that the mean is 2.5 and the coefficient of variation is about 1.

Solution: Using the ratios of median to mean, in rule 17, the ratio corresponding to a coefficient of variation of one is 0.7. Thus, given that the mean is 2.5, the median is approximately

$$2.5 \times 0.7 = 1.75 .$$

Rule 18: The coefficient of skewness. The coefficient of skewness is approximated by

$$\frac{3\ (\text{mean} - \text{median})}{\text{Standard deviation}}$$

with a range of -3 to $+3$ in terms of standard deviations. In other words, the maximum deviation of the median from the mean is one standard deviation.

In general, for positively skewed distributions, the coefficient of skewness is twice to three times the coefficient of variation (for standardized data with zero origin see rule 11). In comparison, for symmetrical distribution, the skewness is zero and there is no relationship between the coefficient of variation and the skewness. For symmetrical distributions (with a zero point of origin) the coefficient of variation is usually smaller than 0.33.

Rule 19: Transforming to symmetric distribution. A positively skewed distribution can be transformed to a nearly symmetric distribution by taking the logarithm of the variables. Once the distribution is approximately symmetric it is legitimate to use the tables of the normal distribution (table 3–1).

Measures of Association

The relationship between any two variables can be examined through the use of an association measure. Such a measure should indicate the degree of the association, its direction, and its predictive power.

Measures of association are used to examine the relationship between two sets of observations on two variables. The form of this relationship is estimated using a regression model. The degree of the association is measured using the correlation coefficient.

The tools discussed in this section are usable in almost all scientific fields and especially in business and in economics. In these fields, relationships are, generally, not exact; therefore, an average relationship is sought. The question is whether the estimated relationship is reliable and can be applied for forecasting purposes. The extent of errors in using the estimated relationship can also be determined by using association measures.

Rule 20: Preparing a scatter diagram. The simplest way to examine the relationship between two variables, given that the number of observations is not large, is to prepare a scatter diagram. This is done be plotting the observations in a two-dimension diagram.

Example. Consider the data in the first three columns in table 3–2.
Solution: These data are depicted in a scatter diagram in figure 3–4. There is a positive relationship between the amount produced and cost; that is, the larger the amount produced, the higher the cost.

Regression Line

The regression line is a straight line that gives the best estimate of a linear relationship between two variables in a sample. That is, given values on one

Table 3–2
Data for Scatter Diagram and Regression Line

Observation (Month)	*Amount Produced* x	*Cost* y	$x_i - \bar{x}$ x'	$y_i - \bar{y}$ y'
1	2	5	−1.8	0.2
2	1	3	−2.8	−1.8
3	2	4	−1.8	−0.8
4	3	4	−0.8	−0.8
5	6	6	2.2	1.2
6	5	5	1.2	0.2
7	4	6	0.2	1.2
8	6	5	2.2	0.2
9	5	6	1.2	1.2
10	4	4	0.2	−0.8
Total	38	48		
Average	3.8	4.8		

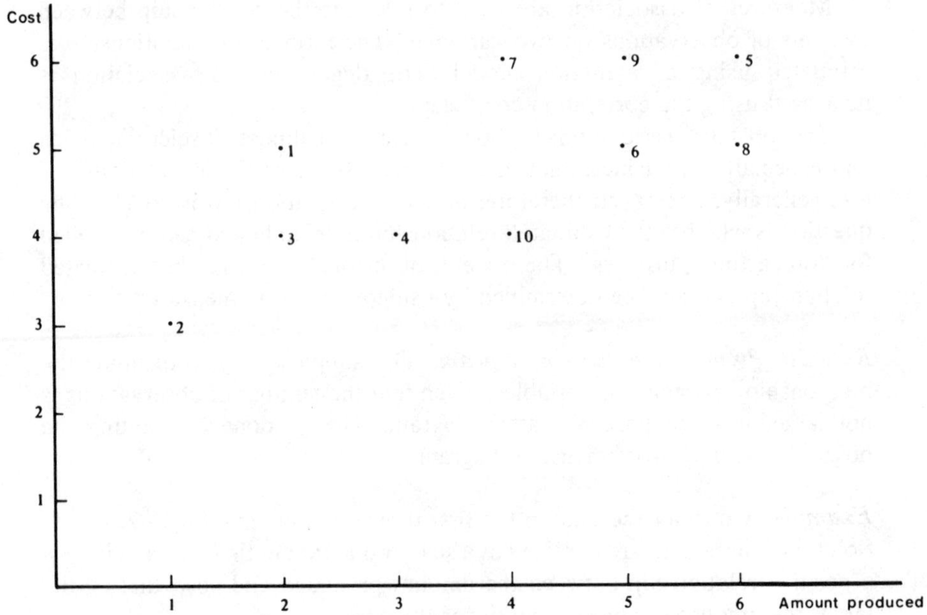

Note: Data from table 3–2.
Figure 3–4. Scatter Diagram

variable, you can estimate the corresponding value of the second variable, with a minimum error.

The regression line is formulated as

$$y = a + bx + e$$

where y is the variable that depends on the variable x and e is the error term indicating deviation from the regression line.

Given the level of x, we seek the best estimate of the coefficients a and b, and consequently, the best estimate of y. The coefficient b is the slope of the regression line, while a is the intercept.

The regression line passes through the point of the means of y (denoted as $\bar{y}$) and x (denoted as $\bar{x}$); hence, the regression line can also be written as

$$y = \bar{y} + b(x - \bar{x}) + e$$

Rule 21: Regression for a small sample. When the sample size is small, it is easy to graph a scatter diagram. Pass a line through the point of the means of

y and x so that the sample data lie around this line; about half the observations lie above the line and half below.

Example. Consider the data in the first three columns in table 3–2.
Solution: The averages are

$$\bar{y} = 48/10 = 4.8; \quad \bar{x} = 38/10 = 3.8$$

The respective points are depicted in figure 3–5, which is a scatter diagram. The line passes through the intersection of $\bar{x}$ and $\bar{y}$, so that five points are below the line and five points are above.

Rule 22: Approximating the regression coefficients from a scatter diagram. To estimate the coefficients of a regression line, determine the intercept a from the scatter diagram, and compute b as follows:

$$\frac{\bar{y} - a}{\bar{x}}$$

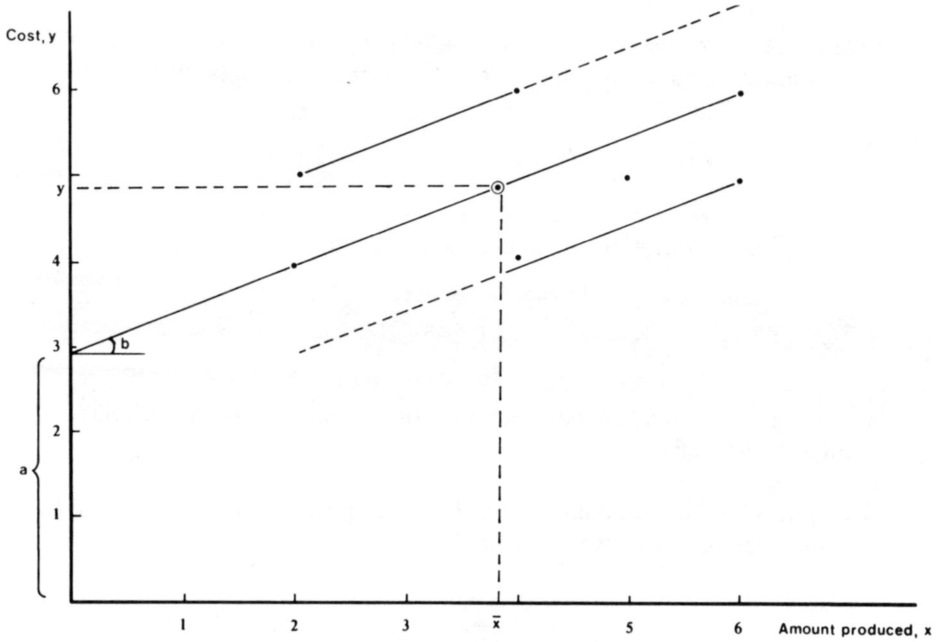

Figure 3–5. Scatter Diagram and Regression Line

Example. Checking figure 3–5 we see that a is approximately 3; using the averages from table 3–2, b is approximately

$$\frac{4.8 - 3.0}{3.8} = 0.47$$

That is, the fixed cost is about \$3, and the variable cost is about \$0.47 per unit.

Rule 23: Regression for a large sample. When the sample is fairly large, delineate two groups: the smallest 5 to 10 x observations and the largest 5 to 10 x observations (denoted by group 1 and 2, respectively), and the corresponding y values. Then, take the sum of each group. The coefficient b is approximated by

$$\frac{y_2 - y_1}{x_2 - x_1}$$

where $y_{2,1}$ is the sum of y for group 2 or 1 and $x_{2,1}$ is the sum of x for group 2 or 1.

Rule 24: Approximating regression coefficient from ranges. The b coefficient is always smaller than the ratio between the two ranges; that is

$$b \leq \frac{R_y}{R_x}$$

where $R_{y,x}$ is the range of y or x.The exact formula is

$$b = r\frac{S_y}{S_x}$$

where $S_{y,x}$ is the standard deviation of y or x, and $r \leq 1$ is the correlation coefficient (rule 26).

Example. Checking the data in table 3–2, the range of y is between 3 and 6 and the range of x is between 1 and 6. Thus,

$$\frac{R_y}{R_x} = \frac{6 - 3}{6 - 1} = 0.6$$

The b coefficient is below 0.6; that is, the variable cost is below \$0.60 per unit.

Rule 25: Exact estimation of the regression coefficients. The exact formulas for the regression line are

$$b = \frac{\Sigma\, y'x'}{\Sigma x'^2}$$

where $y' = y_i - \bar{y}$ and $x' = x_i - \bar{x}$; both are deviations of observation i from the average.

$$a = \bar{y} - b\bar{x}$$

Example. The regression line for the data in the three left-hand columns in table 3–2 is partially calculated in the two right-hand columns in table 3–2. The resultant coefficients are

$$b = \frac{11.6}{27.6} = 0.42 \quad a = 4.8 - 0.42\,(3.8) = 3.2$$

That is, the fixed cost is \$3.20 and the variable cost is \$0.42 per unit.

Correlation Coefficient

The direction and degree of the association between two variables ranges from -1 to $+1$. A zero measure indicates no relationship. A level of 1 indicates a perfect positive relationship; that is, all the points lie on a straight line and the line is sloping upward. The level of -1 indicates a perfect negative relationship. Any degree smaller than 1 indicates that some error is expected in using the relationship for prediction purposes. The higher the degree of association, the smaller the error or uncertainty of the forecasts or estimates.

Rule 26: Calculating the correlation coefficient. If the linear regression coefficient b is known, the correlation coefficient r is approximated by

$$r \cong b\frac{R_x}{R_y}$$

where $R_{x,y}$ is the range of x or y. The exact formula is

$$r = b\frac{S_x}{S_y}$$

where $S_{x,y}$ = standard deviation of x or y. The formula for calculating r directly from the sample data is

$$r = \frac{\sum y'x'}{\sqrt{\sum y'^2 \sum x'^2}} = \frac{\sum y'x'}{nS_xS_y}$$

Example. Consider the data in table 3–2 and the previous example (where $b = 0.42$).
Solution: The range of x is 5 units and of y is \$3. The correlation coefficient is, approximately,

$$0.42 \times \frac{5}{3} = 0.7$$

The exact result is

$$\frac{11.6}{\sqrt{9.6 \times 27.6}} = 0.71$$

Rule 27: Deriving the correlation coefficient from a scatter diagram. When the regression line is missing from a scatter diagram, or when the relationship is not linear you can still find the correlation coefficient.

Draw two parallel lines that enclose most of the points in the scatter diagram (say 90 to 95 percent of the points, to exclude possible outliers). This represents the range of the errors around the imaginary regression line. Determine the vertical distance between the two parallel lines.

The correlation coefficient is approximated by

$$\sqrt{1 - (R_e^2/R_y^2)}$$

where R_e is the range of error, the vertical distance between the parallel lines; and R_y is the range of the y observations, excluding the outliers.

Example. Consider the scatter diagram in figure 3–4.
Solution: Two parallel lines are drawn through the extreme high points and through the extreme low points. The vertical distance between these lines is

approximately two units (dollars). The coefficient of correlation is approximately

$$\sqrt{1-(2^2/3^2)} = 0.75$$

Rule 28: The coefficient of determination. The square of the correlation coefficient (r^2) is called the coefficient of determination. It indicates the proportional reduction in the error variance, as illustrated in the following example.

Example. Consider the example for rule 26 where $r = 0.71$. The coefficient of determination is $0.71^2 = 0.5$. This means that the regression line explains 50 percent of the variance (error) of y about its mean. However, 50 percent of the variance is still unexplained by the regression line.

Statistics of Extremes

Statistical analysis often reports the behavior of the average characteristics of the population, such as the behavior of means and dispersions in different samples. Statistics of extremes, on the other hand, describes the behavior of an individual item in the population, such as the behavior of the largest or smallest value in different samples. This technique is important in analyzing cases of rare events.

The Return Period.

The return period of a given value, X_m, is the average time needed to obtain an observation with a larger or smaller value than the given one. The observations should be made at regular intervals of time.

Rule 29: Calculating the return period. For X_m larger than the median, the period needed to obtain a value larger than X_m, is on the average

$$\frac{1}{1 - F_{(m)}}$$

where $F_{(m)}$ is the fraction of observations having values equal to or less than the given value.
For X_m smaller than the median, the period needed to obtain a value less than X_m is, on the average

$$\frac{1}{F_{(m)}}$$

Example. The rainfall records of a given region indicate that the probability of an annual rainfall of up to 15 inches is 80 percent (eight times in 10 years), and the probability of an annual rainfall up to 5 inches is 10 percent (once in 10 years).
Solution: The average return period of a rainy year (above 15 inches) is

$$1/(1 - 0.80) = 5 \text{ years}$$

Once in 5 years the expected rainfall would be at least 15 inches. The average return period of a drought is

$$1/0.10 = 10 \text{ years}$$

The distribution of the results of the application of this rule for the return period is highly skewed to the right (positively skewed), the median being about 70 percent of the mean, and the coefficient of variation is very high ($C = 1$).

Rule 30: The range of a return period. For practical purposes the actual return period may fall in the range of from one-third to three times the average value (arrived at by rule 29).

Example. The average return period of a drought was 10 years. Then, the actual event may happen any time between 3 and 30 years, with a median value of 7 years.

Distribution of Rare Events

In many cases of rare events, it is sufficient to deal only with the probability that the event will exceed a certain value. The forecast of the size value itself may be either unreliable or redundant. If a drought destroys your crop, the quantity of rainfall in that year does not matter. If you are speculating in the stock market, you may be able to forecast the probability of a price fall or a price rise in the market, but you will not be able to obtain a reliable forecast about the level of prices.

Rule 31: Probability of exceedance. The probability of exceeding a given level in the next n observations is approximated by

$$n(1 - F_{(x)})$$

where $F_{(x)}$ is the population percentile for level x and $n =$ number of observations considered. The exact formula is

$$1 - F^n_{(x)}$$

Similarly, the probability of receiving less than a given level in the next n observations is approximated by

$$nF_{(x)}$$

The exact formula is

$$1 - (1 - F_{(x)})^n$$

Example A. The rainfall records of a given region indicate that the probability of receiving up to 20 inches of rain is 1 percent—that is, once in 100 years.
Solution: The probability of receiving more than 20 inches in the next 10 years is approximately

$$10(1 - 0.99) = 0.10 = 10\%$$

The exact figure is 9.56 percent.

Example B. Suppose the probability of receiving zero returns on a new project in a given year is 5 percent—that is, once in 20 years.
Solution: The probability of receiving zero returns or less in the next 5 years is approximately

$$5 \times 0.05 = 25\%$$

The exact figure is 22.6 percent.

Rule 31 shows that while the event is rare (1 percent and 5 percent in examples A and B), the probability that such an event will occur in the next n years may be quite high. The larger the n, the larger the probability.

Outlying Observations in a Sample

Often a question is raised whether a given observation in a sample may be rejected as an outlier. An outlier is an observation not pertaining to the assumed distribution; that is, an outlier is an observation that is drawn under different conditions than the others in the sample. An extremely large (or small) observation will distort your estimates (such as the mean, standard deviation, or range).

Rule 32: Detecting an outlier. An observation is considered as an outlier when

$$\frac{X_{(n)} - X_{(n-2)}}{X_{(n-1)} - X_{(n-2)}} > 3$$

where $X_{(n),\ (n-),\ (n-2)}$ is the largest, or the second, or the third largest observed value.[1]

When the computed result is considerably higher than 3 (for example, 4) discard the observation. If the sample contains more than one outlying observation, repeat the application of rule 32.

Example. You have the following ordered data:

100, 98, 50, 40, 35, 30, 22, 10, −10

Solution: The second largest observation implies

$$\frac{98 - 40}{50 - 40} = 5.8$$

Because 5.8 is much larger than 3, both the first (100) and second (98) largest observations should be discarded. The smallest observation implies

$$\frac{-10 - 22}{10 - 22} = 2.67$$

Because 2.67 is smaller than 3, the smallest observation is not an outlier.

Rule 33: Determining an outlier. A more accurate rule for determining an outlier is by the following set of steps[2]:

1. Compute the variable A:

$$A = \frac{X_{(n)} - X_{(n-1)}}{S}$$

where $X_{(n),(n-1)}$ is the largest or the second largest value and S is the standard deviation, which should be given a priori or calculated by ignoring $X_{(n)}$.

2. Compare the results with the relevant E's in the second line:

Sample size:	10	20	30	100
Value for E	1.5	1.3	1.2	1.0

3. If the result in step 1 is larger than the corresponding E, then $X_{(n)}$ is an outlier and should be rejected, with a 5 percent risk of being wrong.

Example. You have the following data:

25, 50, 40, 75, 30, 22, 10, 5

Solution: The approximated standard deviation, using rule 5 and ignoring the largest observation, is

$$S = \frac{50 - 5}{3} = 15$$

$$A = \frac{75 - 50}{15} = 1.67$$

The table in step 2 in rule 33 shows that for 10 observations the required E is 1.5. Because 1.67 is higher, the largest observation should be discarded. Note: With rule 32, the largest observation cannot be discarded with certainty (the ratio is 3.5).

Rule 34: Estimating the next extreme. The value of an observation that would follow the largest observation in the sample is approximated by

$$3X_{(n)} - 2X_{(n-1)}$$

where $X_{(n)}$ is the largest value in the sample. Similarly, for the smallest observation

$$3X_{(1)} - 2X_{(2)}$$

where $X_{(1)}$ is the smallest value in the sample.

Example. Consider the following data: 220, 230, 250, 300
Solution: The expected largest value following the value 300 is approximately

$$3(300) - 2(250) = 400$$

The expected value preceeding the value 220 is approximately

$$3(220) - 2(230) = 200$$

Relations between Means

The arithmetic mean is the simplest measure of location of a series of values. However, for skewed distributions and grouped data, this simple measure is not adequate. Other measures such as the geometric and the weighted mean are superior to the arithmetic mean. The relation between the arithmetic and the other two means generally sheds light on the nature of the distribution.

Geometric Mean

Rule 35: Calculating the geometric mean. The geometric mean in a series of n positive numbers is the nth root of their product; that is

$$\bar{x}_g = \sqrt[n]{x_1 x_2 x_3 \ldots x_n}$$

where $\bar{x}_g$ is the geometric mean, x_i is the value of observation i, and n is the number of observations.

Example. The geometric mean between 4 and 9 is

$$\sqrt[2]{4 \times 9} = 6$$

The arithmetic mean is

$$\frac{4 + 9}{2} = 6.5$$

The geometric mean can also be derived by taking the antilogarithm of the arithmetic average of logarithms of the n numbers. This fact indicates that for positively skewed distributions, such as returns on a portfolio, the geometric mean is more representative of the central location than the arithmetic. The reason is that the log transformation of positively skewed data generally yields a more symmetrical distribution (rule 19).

Rule 36: Relation between geometric and arithmetic means. The geometric mean is always smaller than the arithmetic mean. The larger the dispersion among the observations, the smaller the geometric mean.

The geometric mean of a large set of data is approximated by

$$\bar{x}\left(1 - \frac{C^2}{2}\right)$$

where $\bar{x}$ is the arithmetic mean and C is the coefficient of variation (rule 10), when $C \leq 1$.

Example. Two portfolios have the same expected return (mean) but different standard deviations, as follows:

Portfolio	*Mean*	*Standard Deviation*
1	10%	5%
2	10%	2%

Solution: The respective coefficients of variation are

$$5 / 10 = 0.5 \quad 2 / 10 = 0.2$$

The geometric means are

Portfolio 1 $$10\left(1 - \frac{0.5^2}{2}\right) = 8.75$$

Portfolio 2 $$10\left(1 - \frac{0.2^2}{2}\right) = 9.80$$

Rule 37: Effect of dispersion on geometric mean. The smaller the standard deviation (or the variance or the coefficient of variation), the larger the geometric mean.

Rule 38: Estimating the median. For business variables (generally positively skewed) the geometric mean is much closer to the median than the arithmetic average.

Weighted Average

Rule 39: Calculating the weighted average. The weighted average among a series of numbers is computed by weighting each number by a specific weight; that is

$$\bar{x}_w = \frac{\sum x_i w_i}{\sum w_i}$$

where $\bar{x}_w$ is the weighted average, x_i is the value of (observation) i, and w_i is the weight for observation i. The arithmetic average is a special case of the weighted average, where all the weights are equal.

Example. Consider the following data:

Security:	*a*	*b*	*c*	*d*
Values ($)	100	500	50	350
Returns (%)	10	15	20	5

Solution: The weighted average return is

$$\frac{(100 \times 10) + (500 \times 15) + (50 \times 20) + (350 \times 5)}{100 + 500 + 50 + 350} = 11.25\%$$

The arithmetic average is 12.5 percent.

Rule 40: Relation between weighted and arithmetic means. The weighted average is larger than the arithmetic average when the correlation between the variable and the weights is positive, and smaller than the arithmetic average when the correlation is negative; that is

$$\bar{x}_w = \bar{x}(1 + rC_x C_w)$$

where r is the correlation coefficient between x and the weights (w), and C is the coefficient of variation.

Example A. When the portfolio includes a relative large quantity of high-yield shares and a small quantity of low-yield shares, the weighted average will be larger than the arithmetic (simple) average, and vice versa.

In the example for rule 39 the opposite case is illustrated. Security *c* with a relatively small quantity has a high yield, while security *d* with a relatively high quantity has a small yield. That is, the correlation between the yield and the weights is negative; therefore, the weighted mean is smaller than the arithmetic mean.

Example B. The arithmetic average of the current ratio (current assets to current liabilities) in a sample of firms was found to be higher than the weighted average. The latter is computed by summing the numerator of all firms, summing the denominator for all firms and then dividing the aggregate numerator by the aggregate denominator. The variable here is the current ratio, while the weights are the current liabilities.

The fact that the arithmetic (simple) average is higher than the weighted average indicates that the correlation between the ratio and the denominator in the ratio is negative. In other words, small firms have higher ratios than large firms, which means that small firms hold a relatively higher level of working capital than larger firms.

Statistical Significance

Unless you are dealing with the whole population, estimates from samples (such as mean or standard deviation) include errors due to sampling. In the statistical jargon, we state that a sample estimate is distributed about some given value, thus differing from the true population value. Of course, it is not always possible to know the true value; hence, the statements based on the sample are probabilistic in nature.

Rule 41: Standard errors of some estimates. The standard deviation of a sample estimate is called the standard error. The standard errors are used for calculating confidence regions. The approximated standard errors of various sample estimates are listed in the following table, in relation to the standard deviation of the population as a whole.

Sample estimate	*Standard error*
Mean, $\bar{x}$	$S / \sqrt{n}$
Proportion, P	$\sqrt{P(1-P)/n}$
Standard deviation, S	$S / \sqrt{2n}$
Coefficient of variation, C	$C / \sqrt{2n}$
Correlation coefficient, r	$1 / \sqrt{n}$
Regression coefficient, b	$\sqrt{(b_{max}^2 - b^2)/(n-2)}$

where b_{max} is equal to $S_y/S_x = b/r$.

Example A. In a sample of 25 observations the mean value is found to be 10 with a standard deviation of 7.5.
Solution: The standard error of the mean is approximately

$$\frac{S}{\sqrt{n}} = \frac{7.5}{\sqrt{25}} = 1.5$$

Example B. In a sample of 100 items drawn at random, the proportion of defectives was found to be 10 percent.

Solution: The standard error of this proportion is approximately

$$\sqrt{\frac{0.10\,(1-0.10)}{100}} = 0.03 = 3\%$$

Confidence Region

The confidence region is the interval in which the true estimate falls *P* percent of the time (for example, 95 percent). The complement of the confidence percentage (5 percent), which is called the confidence coefficient, indicates the maximum risk level that the true estimate lies outside the confidence region.

The confidence region is depicted in figure 3–6, given that the total area under the curve is 100 percent.

Rule 42: Calculating the confidence region. The confidence region for a true value, given the sample estimate (such as mean or standard deviation) and its standard error, is approximated by

$$X_e \pm 2S_e$$

where X_e is the sample estimate and S_e is the standard error of the sample estimate (rule 41). For exact results, the number 2 in the formula should be substituted by Student's *t* value, which can be found in tables in statistic texts. Some figures of *t* are shown in table 3–3 for two levels of risk and different sample sizes.

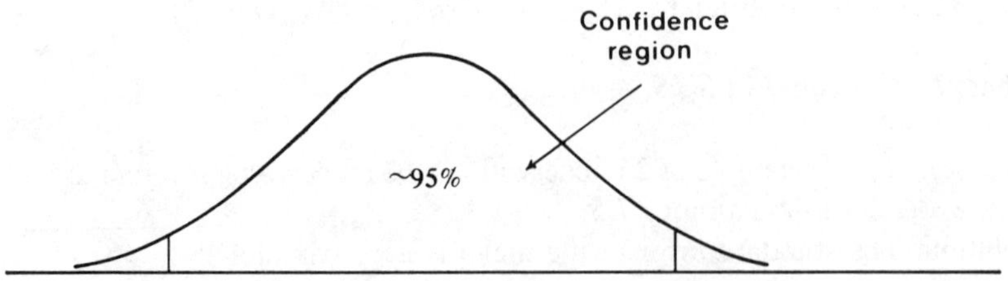

Figure 3–6. Confidence Region

Example. Consider example B for rule 41, where 10 percent of the items were found to be defective, with a standard error of 3 percent.
Solution: The confidence region is

$$0.10 \pm 2(0.03) = 10\% \pm 6\%$$

The true proportion of defectives is in the range of 4 to 16 percent, with 95 percent confidence. There is at most a 5 percent risk that the true proportion is outside this range.

Example. In a sample of 20 observations, the average amount of labor input was 10 hours per unit with a standard deviation of 7.5 hours per unit.
Solution: The standard error (rule 41) is

$$\frac{7.5}{\sqrt{20}} = 1.677$$

The confidence region is

$$10 \pm 2(1.677) = 10 \pm 3.35$$

The true average lies between 6.65 and 13.35 hours per unit, with 95 percent confidence. There is at most a 5 percent risk that the true average lies outside this range.

For a 10 percent risk, the t value to be used is 1.725 (table 3–3). The confidence region is

$$10 \pm 1.725\ (1.677) = 10 \pm 2.89$$

The range is between 7.11 and 12.89.

Table 3–3
Student's *t* Table

	Sample Size				
Risk Allowed (%)	*5*	*10*	*15*	*20*	*30*
5	2.571	2.228	2.131	2.086	2.042
10	2.015	1.812	1.753	1.725	1.697

Rule 43: The allowed risk for confidence region. The allowed risk level that is used in determining the confidence region depends on the cost of a wrong decision. The more serious is the error of a wrong decision based on the sample, the lower should be the allowed risk.

Example. In business, the maximum allowed risk is usually 5 to 10 percent, in agriculture and biology 1 to 5 percent, and in medicine very low.

The Rejection Criterion

Given the true population estimate, you want to know whether the sample estimate is significantly different from the true estimate at some maximum risk level of error. If it is different, it should be rejected.

Rule 44: Calculating the rejection criterion. The rejection criterion that a sample estimate differs from the population estimate is when

$$\frac{X_p - X_e}{S_e} > 2$$

where X_p is the estimate of the population, X_e is the estimate of the sample, and S_e is the standard error of the sample estimate (rule 41). For exact results, the number 2 in the formula should be substituted by Student's t from table 3–3.

Example. The average current ratio in the industry is 2.2. The average current ratio that is calculated from a sample of 16 companies is 1.5 with a standard deviation of 1.8.
Solution: The standard error of the mean is

$$1.8 / \sqrt{16} = 0.45$$

The rejection criterion is

$$\frac{2.2 - 1.5}{0.45} = 1.56$$

Because the result is smaller than 2 (or the t value of 2.131 in table 3–3), we infer that the sample satisfactorily represents the population. Alternatively, we state that the sample average does not differ significantly from that of the population.

Rule 45: Calculating the acceptance criterion. When the true estimate, X_p, is assumed to be zero, as in correlation and regression coefficients, then the acceptance criterion that the sample estimate differs significantly from zero is when

$$\frac{X_e}{S_e} > 2$$

For exact results, the number 2 in the formula should be substituted by the Student's t value from table 3–3.

Example. A sample of 12 observations for the past 12 months shows that the correlation between the sales and variable unit cost is 0.3. Is the relationship reliable?
Solution: The standard error of the correlation coefficient (rule 41) is approximately

$$\frac{1}{\sqrt{n}} = \frac{1}{\sqrt{12}} = 0.29$$

The acceptance criterion is

$$\frac{0.30}{0.29} = 1$$

This value is considerably less than 2; hence we conclude that in this brief period of 1 year, no relationship exists between sales and variable unit cost; that is, the estimate is not significantly different from zero.

Revising the Sample Estimate

Various estimates regarding an estimated value from different sources (such as samples or outside information) can be combined to yield a revised estimate with a higher reliability. The following procedure assumes normality of the distributions and independence among the samples.

Rule 46: Calculating the revised estimate. The revised estimate is a weighted average of the various sample estimates. The weights are the reciprocal of the variances (the square of the standard deviation); that is

$$\frac{\sum X_i I_i}{\sum I_i}$$

where X_i is the sample ith estimate and I_i is the reciprocal of its variance. The revised estimate will have a standard error of

$$\sqrt{1 / \sum I_i}$$

Example. The overhead cost per unit of input has been measured by a regression analysis (rules 21–25) in three departments. The samples yielded the following data:

Sample (department)	1	2	3
Regression coefficients, b	5	4	6
Standard error of b	2	3	4

Solution: Looking at each sample, only in the first department was the regression coefficient significantly different from zero (the estimate is larger than 2 standard errors).

To find the revised estimates, first calculate the respective values of I_i:

$$\frac{1}{2^2} = \frac{1}{4}; \quad \frac{1}{3^2} = \frac{1}{9}; \quad \frac{1}{4^2} = \frac{1}{16}$$

The revised regression coefficient is

$$\frac{\left(5 \times \frac{1}{4}\right) + \left(4 \times \frac{1}{9}\right) + \left(6 \times \frac{1}{16}\right)}{\frac{1}{4} + \frac{1}{9} + \frac{1}{16}} = 4.89$$

The standard error of the revised estimate is

$$\sqrt{\frac{1}{\frac{1}{4} + \frac{1}{9} + \frac{1}{16}}} = 1.54$$

Using the acceptance criterion (rule 45), the ratio of the sample estimate to the standard error is

$$\frac{4.89}{1.54} = 3.2$$

Because this acceptance ratio is larger than 2, the result is reliable. Although the data from each individual department was not reliable, the combined data is reliable with 95 percent confidence. Thus, the overhead cost is about $5 per unit ($4.89).

Notes

1. This ratio is known as the Galton ratio; see E.J. Gumbell, *Statistics of Extremes* (New York: Columbia University Press, 1958) p. 56.

2. This rule is known as the Irwin's criterion; see A. Hald, *Statistical Theory with Engineering Applications* (New York: Wiley, 1952), p. 335.

Part II
Capital Budgeting

4 Loans and Bonds Analysis

Lending and borrowing are an integral part of business activities. In the course of conducting a business, money transactions are continuously made in the form of cash and credit. Credit is, of course, related to loans. Correct financial decisions necessitate a thorough understanding of the loan's mechanism on the one hand and an analysis procedure for quick answers on the other. You will find the use of rules of thumb and simple tools especially useful in day-to-day decisions regarding loans.

Loans analysis covers the economic costs and benefits aspects resulting from the loan's action: the terms and type of the loan, the stipulated sums to be reimbursed, the tax aspects, the effect of the borrower's discounting rate, and the effects of the anticipated inflation. Accounting aspects of the interest expenses and the payments on principal, as well as the outstanding balance of the loan at any time, are considered.

Bonds are types of long-term loans that are sold to the public. This chapter includes an analysis of the variables required for decisions to buy or sell a bond from the investor's point of view.

Some Simple Calculations

Some useful calculations and rules regarding various aspects of commercial loans are presented in the following section of this chapter.

Rule 1: Interest on installment contracts. An installment contract, such as a purchase of merchandise to be paid in equal installments, is often offered for cash payment at a discount. The discount sum implies a certain rate of interest.

The interest rate implied in equal installment payments, rather than cash payment at a discount, is approximated by

$$\frac{B - A}{0.6An}$$

where A is the cash payment, B is the sum of installment payments; 0.6 is the interest add-on factor for $ni < 1$ (rule 2, chapter 2); and n is the number of installment payments. When the rate of discount on cash purchase is stated, then the interest rate on the installment payments is approximated by

$$\frac{d}{0.6n(1-d)}$$

where d is the discount percentage equal to $(B-A)/B$ and $(1-d)$ is the cash equivalent of the loan.

Example. Merchandise can be bought for $1,000 cash, or paid by 12 monthly equal payments of $100 each.
Solution: The interest rate is approximately

$$\frac{100 \times 12 - 1{,}000}{0.6 \times 1{,}000 \times 12} = 0.0278 = 2.78\% \text{ per month}$$

The exact figure is 2.92 percent. Suppose the discount percentage is given—that is, $d = 0.167$. Then the interest rate is approximately

$$\frac{0.167}{0.6 \times 12(1-0.167)} = 0.0278 = 2.78\%$$

Rule 2: Interest on a fund. Consider a fund in which money is added and withdrawn continuously. You want to estimate the periodic rate of interest earned on the money in the fund.

The annual interest rate earned by a fund is approximated by

$$\frac{2I}{A+B-I}$$

where I is the total amount of interest earned during the year, A is the amount of fund at the beginning of the year, and B is the amount of fund at the end of the year, including I.

Example. Your balances in a retirement fund are $10,000 on January 1, 1979, and $12,000 on January 1, 1980. The monthly payments to the fund were $100.
Solution: The amount of interest received is

$$12{,}000 - 10{,}000 - 12 \times 100 = \$800$$

The interest rate is approximately

$$\frac{2 \times 800}{10{,}000 + 12{,}000 - 800} = 0.0755 = 7.55\%$$

Partial Payments on a Contract

In short-term transactions, you are expected to pay both principal and interest as one payment on the maturity date. If you make a partial repayment before maturity date, the interest should be duly reduced. The computations may be carried out in two alternative ways, which provide different results (rules 3 and 4).

Rule 3: Partial payment to repay principal. Each partial payment is considered as principal repayment. Hence, all the payments, original and partial, are assumed to earn simple interest (rule 1, chapter 1) from the original date to the repayment date.

Example. A $1,000 loan, at 10 percent simple interest, should be repaid after 6 months. A sum of $200 was repaid after 2 months and $300 after 5 months.
Solution: The original sum to be repaid is

$$1{,}000\left(1 + 0.10 \times \frac{6}{12}\right) = \$1{,}050$$

The accumulated amount of the $200, paid 4 months before maturity, is

$$200\left(1 + 0.10 \times \frac{4}{12}\right) = \$206.67$$

The accumulated amount of the $300 is

$$300\left(1 + 0.10 \times \frac{1}{12}\right] = \$302.50$$

The total value of the partial payments is $509.17. The balance due is

$$1{,}050 - 509.17 = \$540.83$$

Rule 4: Partial payment to repay interest. Each partial payment is used to pay the interest accrued and the residual is used to reduce the principal.

Example. Consider the example for rule 3.
Solution: The accrued interest for the first 2 months (up to the first partial payment) is

$$1{,}000 \times 0.10 \times \frac{2}{12} = \$16.67$$

The principal is reduced to

$$1{,}000 - (200 - 16.67) = \$816.67$$

The accrued interest on this sum for 3 months is

$$816.67 \times 0.10 \times \frac{3}{12} = \$20.42$$

The principal at the end of the fifth month is reduced to

$$816.67 - (300 - 20.42) = \$537.09$$

The balance due at the end of the sixth month is

$$537.09\left(1 + 0.10 \times \frac{1}{12}\right) = \$541.57$$

Mix of Two Loans

Often the mix of the loans should be determined under stress. Rules 5 and 6 enable you to calculate easily the weighted interest rate of a given mix of two loans and the required proportion of the loan package when the weighted average interest rate is predetermined.

Rule 5: Determining the weighted interest rate. Given the values and weights of two variables, the resultant weighted average value is

$$P_1 + w_2(P_2 - P_1)$$

where $P_1 < P_2$; P_1, P_2 are the value of variables 1 or 2; and w_2 is the weight of variable 2.

Example. A company takes out a mix of two loans, 70 percent of which carry 12 percent annual interest and 30 percent of which carry 20 percent annual interest.
Solution: The average rate of interest of this mix is

$$12 + 0.30\,(20 - 12) = 14.4\%$$

Rule 6: Determining the mix of loans. Given the value of two variables and the weighted average value, the required mix is

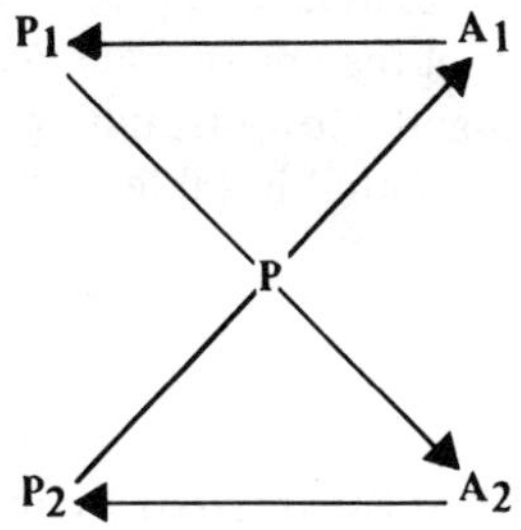

$$A_1 = P - P_2$$
$$A_2 = P_1 - P$$

where P is the value of the mix (weighted average) and A_1, A_2 are the required proportions in the mix of variables 1 or 2.

Example. A company takes out two types of loans: one at 20 percent (P_1) and the other at 12 percent (P_2) annual interest. The weighted average is set to be 17 percent (P).
Solution: The amount of each loan is

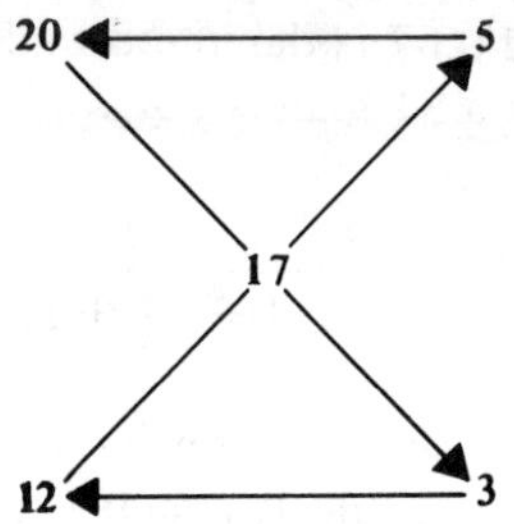

$$A_1 = 17 - 12 = 5$$
$$A_2 = 20 - 17 = 3$$

That is, the loan package should include five units of the 20 percent loan and three units of the 12 percent loan. This implies that the mix is made up of $5/8 = 62.5$ percent of the first loan and 37.5 percent of the second loan.

Methods of Loan Repayment

The major methods for loan repayment are summarized in this section.

Example. Consider a \$100 loan at 10 percent annual interest, to be repaid over 5 years, with payment at the end of each year. The repayment schedule of principal and interest, and the outstanding balance under the various repayment methods, are presented in table 4–1.

Installment Loan

An installment loan is repaid (amortized) by means of equal end-of-period amounts. Each periodic payment is composed of interest expense (on the principal) and repayment of the principal. The relative amounts of these components change in each payment. The interest component declines over time (because the outstanding principal declines), while the principal repayment increases.

Rule 7: Periodic repayment of installment loans. The end-of-period payment on an installment loan is approximated by

$$A\left(\frac{1}{n} + 0.67i\right)$$

where A is the loan principal, n is the periods for loan repayment, i is the rate of interest per period, and 0.67 is the interest add-on factor (rule 2, chapter 2). The exact formula for a \$1 loan is

$$(CR_{n,i}) = \frac{i}{1 - (1 + i)^{-n}}$$

where $CR_{n,i}$ is the capital recovery factor for n and i (also called installment loan amortization factor; (see rule 1, chapter 2; appendix A).

Example. Consider the \$100, 10 percent loan in the previous example, to be repaid (principal and interest) by five equal payments.

Table 4–1
Repayment Schedule and Outstanding Principal under Various Loan Repayment Methods

Year End	*Outstanding Balance*	*Interest on Balance*	*Principal Repayment*	*Total Annual Payment*
Installment loan				
0	$100.00			
1	83.62	$10.00	$16.38	$26.38
2	65.60	8.36	18.02	26.38
3	45.78	6.56	19.82	26.38
4	23.98	4.58	21.80	26.38
5	—	2.40	23.98	26.38
			100.00	
Equal-principal-payment loan				
0	$100.00			
1	80.00	$10.00	$20.00	$30.00
2	60.00	8.00	20.00	28.00
3	40.00	6.00	20.00	26.00
4	20.00	4.00	20.00	24.00
5	—	2.00	20.00	22.00
			100.00	
Standing loan				
0	$100.00			
1	100.00	$10.00	$—	$10.00
2	100.00	10.00	—	10.00
3	100.00	10.00	—	10.00
4	100.00	10.00	—	10.00
5		10.00	100.00	110.00

Solution: The annual end-of-year repayment is approximately

$$100\left(\frac{1}{5} + 0.67 \times 0.10\right) = \$26.70$$

The exact figure is 100 $(CR_{5.0.10}) = 100 \times 0.2638 = \$26.38$. The factor $(CR_{5.0.10})$ is taken from appendix A; the entry for five periods and 10 percent.

Rule 8: Monthly or quarterly payments. Usually, installment loans are repaid by monthly or quarterly installments, but the interest rate is stated in annual terms. In this case, the number of periods in the exact formula in the previous example is stated in months or quarters, and the annual interest rate is stated per period; that is

$$i = j/m$$

where i is the stated periodic interest rate, j is the stated annual interest rate, and m is the number of repayment periods in a year (12 or 4). The conventional amortization tables are constructed on this basis. In these cases, the effective rate differs from the stated rate (see rule 22, chapter 1).

Example. Consider a $100 loan at 10 percent annual interest, to be repaid by sixty equal monthly payments rather than by five equal yearly payments.
Solution: The monthly stated interest rate is

$$0.10 / 12 = 0.00833$$

The exact monthly payment is

$$100 \times \frac{0.00833}{1 - (1 + 0.00833)^{-60}} = \$2.1245$$

Note: The sum of the 12 monthly payments ($12 \times 2.1245 = \$25.49$) is lower than the yearly payment ($26.38) for two reasons: 1. The monthly payments should be compounded rather than added together to be comparable. 2. The effective rate of interest in each computation differs (rule 22, chapter 2).

Rule 9: Average interest component in a repayment. The average interest component in the repayment charges (the so-called add-on rate) over the whole repayment schedule is approximated by

$$0.67i$$

The exact formula is ki, where k is the interest add-on factor (rule 2, chapter 2; and appendix B).

Example. Consider the example under rule 7.
Solution: The average interest rate is approximately

$$0.67 \times 0.10 = 0.067 = 6.7\%$$

For the exact figure, we find in appendix B that k for 5 years and 10 percent interest is 0.638. Hence, the exact average interest rate is

$$0.638 \times 0.10 = 0.0638 = 6.38\%$$

Equal-Principal-Payment Loan

An equal-principal-payment loan is repaid by means of periodic equal amounts of principal and declining interest payments. The interest is paid in each period on the outstanding balance at the beginning of the period. As the interest payment declines, the total periodic payment declines over time.

Rule 10: Periodic repayment of equal-principal-payment loan. The end-of-period payment on an equal-principal-payment loan is

$$E_t = A\left[\frac{1}{n} + i\left(\frac{n-t+1}{n}\right)\right]$$

where E_t is the payment in period t ($t = 1, 2, \ldots, n$); A is the loan principal; t is a given period; and n is the number of periods of loan repayment.

Example. Consider the $100 loan at 10 percent interest in the first example in this section, but the principal is to be repaid by five equal payments plus interest on the outstanding balance.
Solution: The repayment at the end of the first year is

$$100\left(\frac{1}{5} + 0.10 \times \frac{5-1+1}{5}\right) = 20 + 10 = \$30$$

Rule 11: Average interest component in a repayment. The average interest component in the repayment charges (the so-called add-on rate) of an equal-principal-payment loan, over the whole repayment schedule, is

$$\frac{i(n+1)}{2n}$$

Note: This sum is always smaller than that of an equal installment loan as $k \geq (n+1)/2n$ (rule 2, chapter 2).

Example. Consider the previous example.
Solution: The average interest rate is

$$\frac{0.10(5+1)}{2 \times 5} = 0.06 = 6\%$$

Comparison between Loan Repayments

The periodic payments on an installment loan and on an equal-principal-payment loan differ. The respective repayment schedules (principal and interest) are depicted in figure 4–1.
Note that the payments in figure 4–1 for the installment loan are lower than the equal-principal payments during the early years, and vice versa in the later years.

Rule 12: Superiority between loans. Because the borrower usually benefits from the loan (because the rate of return on the investment is higher than the interest rate on the loan), an installment loan is superior to an equal-principal-payment loan. There are also liquidity advantages from an installment loan.

Rule 13: Determining the date of breakeven repayment. The intersection of the two repayment schedules in figure 4–1 is approximately after

$$1 + 0.33n \text{ periods}$$

where n is the number of periods of loan repayment and 0.33 is one minus the interest add-on factor (rule 2, chapter 2).

Example. Consider two types of loans (installment and equal-principal payment) to be repaid in 5 years.
Solution: The level of the periodic repayment on both loans will be equal after approximately

$$1 + (0.33 \times 5) = 2.65 \text{ years}$$

This result can be seen by comparing the periodic repayments in table 4–1.

Gains on Loans

The borrower's rate of return on an investment is usually higher than the rate of interest on the loan that finances the investment. This difference provides a gain on the loan that is required as a premium for the risk involved in taking out the loan. During inflation the gain may be especially high because the interest on loans usually lags behind the fully adjusted inflation-compensated rates (see the section later in this chapter on present value of interest payments).

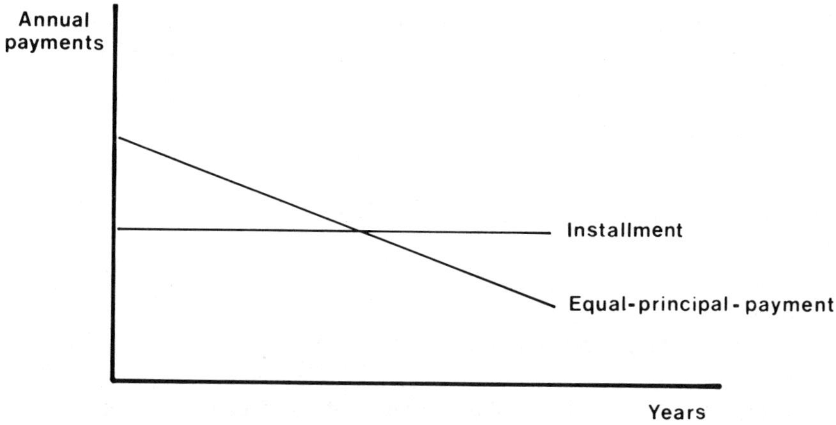

Figure 4–1. Installment versus Equal Principal Payment

The gain on a loan may be computed in present-value terms and in periodic terms.

Gain on an Installment Loan

The gain on a loan is the difference between the loan's principal and the after-tax economic cost of the loan.

Rule 14: Determining the economic cost of a loan. The economic cost of a loan to a borrower is the present value of the loan's repayment schedule; it is derived by using the borrower's required rate of return (cost of capital) for discounting. Because the interest payments are tax-deductible, the tax savings on these payments should be taken into account in computing the present value.

Rule 15: Total gain on a loan. The total after-tax gain on an installment loan (in present-value terms) is

$$A[1 - (CR_{n,i}/CR_{n,r})]$$

where A is the loan principal; $CR_{n,i}$, $CR_{n,r}$ are capital-recovery factors for i or r (rule 1, chapter 2); i is the interest rate on the loan, after-tax (rule 32, chapter 1); r is the required rate of return, after-tax, and equals the discounting rate; and n is the number of periods of loan repayment.

Rule 16: Periodic gain on a loan. The equivalent average gain per period is computed by multiplying the total gain by the capital-recovery factor, using the borrower's cost of capital; that is

$$A(CR_{n,r} - CR_{n,i})$$

The average gain per period is approximated by

$$A0.67\ (r - i)$$

where 0.67 is the interest add-on factor (rule 2, chapter 2).

Example. You want to take out a $100 loan at 10 percent annual interest, to be repaid over 5 years by equal payments. The after-tax cost of capital is 9 percent, and the tax rate is 40 percent.
Solution: The after-tax interest rate is

$$0.10\ (1 - 0.40) = 0.06 = 6\%$$

The total after-tax gain on the loan (in present-value terms) is

$$100\ [1 - (0.237/0.257)] = \$7.78$$

The average annual after-tax gain is

$$100(0.257 - 0.237) = \$2.00$$

The approximated figure is

$$100 \times 0.67\ (0.09 - 0.06) = \$2.00$$

If the risk from taking the loan is evaluated to be higher than $7.78 in present-value terms, or higher than $2.00 per year, do not take the loan.

Factors Affecting the Gain on a Loan

Two factors affect the gain on a loan: the difference between the rate of return on investment and the interest rate on the loan, and the term of the loan—that is, the repayment period.

Rule 17: Effect of loan repayment period. When the rate of return on an investment is higher than the rate of interest on the loan, then the longer the repayment period, the higher the gains on the loan. There are also liquidity advantages from longer-term loans.

Example. Consider the previous example, with the loan to be repaid over 15 years rather than 5 years.
Solution: The total after-tax gain on the loan (in present-value terms) is

$$100[1 - (0.103/0.124)] = \$16.94$$

The average annual gain is

$$100(0.124 - 0.103) = \$2.10$$

The total gain on the 15-year loan in this example is higher than that on the 5-year loan in the previous example because the borrower, who benefits from the loan, holds the loan for a longer time. The periodic gains, however, are almost the same, because they, too, will exist for 15 years rather than for 5 years.

Rule 18: Effect of rate of return. The gains on a loan depend mainly on the difference between the rate of return on investment and the interest rate on the loan. The larger this difference the larger the gain on the loan.

A borrower may lose by taking out a loan when the rate of return on the investment is lower than the rate of interest on the loan. In this case the economic cost of a loan (rule 15) is higher than the principal of the loan.

Example: A sensitivity analysis. A \$100 loan at 15 percent interest is to be repaid by five equal end-of-year payments. The loan will be invested in a project yielding 20 percent to 12 percent. There is no income tax.
Solution: The gain, in present-value terms, assuming $r = 0.20$, is

$$100[1 - (0.2983/0.3344)] = \$10.80$$

Assuming $r = 0.12$, the gain is

$$100[1 - (0.2983/0.2774)] = -\$7.53$$

The profitability of the loan ranges from a \$10.80 gain to a \$7.53 loss, depending on the yield from the project for which the loan is used.

Gains on Other Types of Loans

The economic cost of and the total gains on any type of loan are computed by the same procedure as that used for installment loans. The formulas, however, differ.

Rule 19: Gain on equal-principal-payment loan. The total gain on an equal-principal-payment loan (in present-value terms) is

$$A[k(r - i)\mathrm{PVA}_{n,r}]$$

where A is the loan principal; k is the interest add-on factor for r (rule 2, chapter 2; and appendix B); r is the required rate of return, after tax; i is the interest rate on the loan; and $PVA_{n,r}$ is the present value of annuity for n and r (rule 7, chapter 2).

The equivalent average gain per period is

$$A[k(r - i)]$$

Example. You want to take out a $100 loan at 10 percent interest per year. The principal will be repaid over 5 years by equal payments. The after-tax cost of capital is 9 percent, and the tax rate is 40 percent.

Solution: The after-tax interest rate is

$$0.10\ (1 - 0.40) = 0.06 = 6\%$$

The after-tax total gain on the loan, in present-value terms, given that k for 0.09 is 0.634 (appendix B) and $PVA_{5,0.09} = 3.89$, is

$$100[0.634(0.09 - 0.06)3.89]\ \$7.40$$

The average annual after-tax gain is

$$100[0.634\ (0.09 - 0.06)] = \$1.90$$

The gain in this example is slightly lower than that for the installment loan (see the example for rule 16).

Rule 20: Gain on a standing loan. The principal of a standing loan is repaid at the end of the contract, whereas the interest is paid at the end of each period.

The present value of the total gains on a standing loan is

$$A(r - i)\ (PVA_{n,r})$$

The periodic gain on a standing loan is

$$A(r - i)$$

Example. Consider the previous example with the principal to be repaid at the end of the fifth year.
Solution: The total gain (in present-value terms) is

$$100(0.09 - 0.06)\ (\text{PVA}_{5,0.09}) = 3.00 \times 3.89 = \$11.67$$

The annual gain on the loan is

$$100(0.09 - 0.06) = \$3.00$$

The gains in this example are larger than those for the other loans because the outstanding balance is higher in every year than the balance in the other loans.

Outstanding Principal

The outstanding balance of a loan changes for each period.

Rule 21: Outstanding balance of an installment loan. The outstanding balance of an installment loan, at a given date, is approximated by

$$\frac{\text{Periodic payment}}{1\,/\,v + 0.67i}$$

where v is the number of remaining periods of loan repayment, 0.67 = interest add-on factor (rule 2, chapter 2), and i = interest rate. The exact formula is

$$\frac{\text{Periodic payment}}{CR_{v,i}} = A(CR_{n,i}/CR_{v,i})$$

where A is the original principal, $CR_{n,\,i}$, CR_{vi} are capital-recovery factors for n or v and i (rule 1, chapter 2), i is the interest rate, and n is the number of periods of loan repayment.

Example A. Consider a \$100 5-year installment loan at 10 percent annual interest. The annual repayment is \$26.38. You want to know the outstanding balance at the end of year 2.
Solution: The outstanding balance after 2 years is approximately

$$\frac{26.38}{1/3 + 0.67 \times 0.10} = \$65.88$$

The exact figure is \$65.60.

Example B. A \$100 loan at 1 percent per month is repaid by 120 equal payments. You want to know the outstanding balance at the end of 40 payments.
Solution: The outstanding balance of the loan is

$$100(CR_{120,0.01}/CR_{80,0.01}) = 100(0.01435/0.01822) = \$78.76$$

Rule 22: Periodic repayments of an outstanding loan. Given the level of an outstanding balance of an installment loan, the periodic repayment is determined by

$$B(CR_{vi})$$

where B is the outstanding balance and v is the number of remaining periods of loan repayment.

Example. Consider the exact outstanding balance in example A for rule 21.
Solution: The annual repayment is

$$65.60\ (CR_{3,0.10}) = 65.60 \times 0.4021 = \$26.38$$

Rule 23: Value of an outstanding loan. The value of an outstanding balance of an installment loan is derived by applying the rule for the gain on a loan (rules 14–20) to the outstanding balance of the principal. The economic cost of an outstanding loan is

$$\frac{B_t(CR_{v,i})}{CR_{v,r}}$$

where B_t is the outstanding balance at the end of period t and $CR_{v,i}$, $CR_{v,r}$ are capital-recovery factors for i or r, when both are after-tax.
The gain on the loan is the outstanding balance less its economic cost.

Example. The outstanding balance of your mortgage is $11,500. The $165 monthly payments, which are based on 12 percent annual interest (that is, 1 percent per month) are spread over 10 years. Your desired pretax rate of return is 1.5 percent per month. You pay income tax at the rate of 30 percent.
Solution: The after-tax monthly rates are

$$0.01\ (1 - 0.30) = 0.007$$
$$0.015\ (1 - 0.30) = 0.0105$$

The economic cost of the outstanding loan is

$$\frac{11.500\ (CR_{120,0.007})}{CR_{120,0.0105}} = \frac{11{,}500 \times 0.012345}{0.014697} = \$9{,}660$$

The gain on the loan is

$$11{,}500 - 9{,}660 = \$1{,}840$$

Rule 24: Outstanding balance of an equal-principal-payment loan. The outstanding balance of an equal-principal-payment loan in any given period is

$$B_t = A[1 - (t/n)]$$

where B_t is the outstanding balance at the end of period t, A is the original principal, t is the number of periods elapsed, and n is the number of periods of loan repayment.

Example. Consider a $100 loan at 10 percent annual interest to be repaid by 5 equal principal payments.
Solution: The outstanding balance after 2 years ($t = 2$) is

$$100[1 - (2/5)] = \$60$$

Present Value of Interest Payments

The periodic payments on a loan usually include both interest and principal repayments. Because the interest payments are tax-deductible (deductible from income before income tax is levied), the figure of the present value of the future interest payments can be useful for investment analysis.

Rule 25: Present value of interest payments. The present value of the future interest payments on a loan is approximated by

$$A\left[\frac{i}{r}\left(1-\frac{1}{n(CR_{n,r})}\right)\right]$$

where i and r are after-tax rates. This formula is derived for the equal-principal-payment loan, but it provides satisfactory results for an installment loan. However, when the rate of interest (i) and return on investment (r) are relatively high (say, above 10 percent) this formula overstates the results.

Example: You want to take out a $100 loan at 20 percent annual interest, to be repaid by five equal yearly payments. The after-tax rate of return on investment is 15 percent and the tax rate is 40 percent.
Solution: The after-tax interest rate on the loan is

$$0.20(1-0.40)=0.12$$

The present value of the after-tax interest payments is approximately

$$100\left[\frac{0.12}{0.15}\left(1-\frac{1}{5\times 0.298}\right)\right]=\$26.31$$

Rule 26: Tax savings. The tax saving (tax shield) on the present value of the after-tax interest payment, as calculated in rule 25 is

$$PV\left(\frac{t}{1-t}\right)$$

where PV is the present value of after-tax interest payments and t is the income tax rate.
When the original, pretax interest is used for computing the present value of the interest payments, the tax saving is

$$PV(t)$$

where PV is the present value of pretax interest payments.

Example. The tax saving in the previous example is

$$26.31\times\frac{0.40}{1-0.40}=\$17.54$$

When the original pretax interest is used for calculations (that is, 20 percent), rather than after-tax interest, the present value of the interest payment is approximately

$$100\left[\frac{0.20}{0.15}\left(1-\frac{1}{5\times 0.298}\right)\right]=\$43.84$$

The tax saving is

$$43.84\times 0.40=\$17.54$$

Rule 27: Interest expenses in periodic payments. Because interest is charged on the outstanding balance of the principal, and because the balance changes each period, the periodic interest payments change as well.

Rule 27A. To compute the periodic interest charge in a given period, apply the loan's interest rate to the outstanding balance, as computed in rule 21.

Example. Consider example A for rule 21, where the exact outstanding balance of the loan at the end of year 2 is \$65.60 and the interest rate is 10 percent.
Solution: The interest expense in year 3 is

$$65.60\times 0.10=\$6.56$$

Rule 27B. To estimate the interest expenses for a series of loan repayments during a given year, apply the loan's interest rate to the average outstanding balance of principal (balance at the beginning and end of the year divided by 2).

Example. The outstanding principal for an installment loan on January 1 was \$882. The anticipated outstanding balance one year later is approximately \$808 (by using rule 21). The loan is repaid by monthly payments, at 1 percent monthly interest.
Solution: The interest payment for the 12 months is approximately

$$\frac{882+808}{2}\times 0.01\times 12=\$101$$

Inflation Adjustment of Interest Rates

During inflation the interest on a loan includes compensation for the reduction in the real value of the principal.

Rule 28: Interest rate to the borrower. Given the stated, nominal rate of interest of a loan, the real cost to the borrower is the inflation-free rate, which, under low inflation rates is approximated by

$$i - p$$

where i is the nominal interest rate and p is the inflation rate. The exact formula is

$$\frac{i - p}{1 + p}$$

When income tax exists, the after-tax interest rate is

$$i(1 - t)$$

where t is the income tax rate.

Example. A company intends to take out a \$100 loan for 1 year at 20 percent interest. The inflation rate in the coming year is expected to be 12 percent.
Solution: The pretax inflation-free rate of interest is approximately

$$0.20 - 0.12 = 0.08 = 8\%$$

The exact figure is

$$\frac{0.20 - 0.12}{1 + 0.12} = 0.0714 = 7.14\%$$

The actual interest payment on the loan will be \$20, but the real, inflation-free cost will be \$7.14. If the loan is invested in an asset, the returns of which will also rise because of inflation, the real cost of the loan in today's money terms is \$7.14. (This is because the borrower gains from the fact that he returns the \$100 principal with a reduced purchasing power).

Suppose the company's income tax rate is 46 percent. The after-tax interest on the loan is

$$0.20\ (1 - 0.46) = 0.108 = 10.8\%$$

The resultant inflation-free interest rate is

$$\frac{0.108 - 0.12}{1 + 0.12} = -0.0107 = -1.07\%$$

Because the \$20 interest payment is tax-deductible, the after-tax inflation-free cost of the loan is \$−1.07. Given that the company must pay income tax, the after-tax cost of the loan, in nominal terms, is \$10.80. When the effects of inflation are considered, the company benefits by \$1.07 from this loan.

Rule 29: Interest rate to the lender. Given the pre-inflation rate of interest on loans, the nominal rate that fully compensates for the effect of inflation is the inflation-compensated rate,which is approximated by

$$i + p$$

where i is the preinflation rate of interest and p is the inflation rate. The exact formula is

$$(1 + i)\ (1 + p) - 1$$

Example. You want to lend \$100 for one year. The pre-inflation rate of interest was 5 percent. You expect an inflation rate of 20 percent.
Solution: The inflation-compensated rate of interest is

$$(1 + 0.05)\ (1 + 0.20) - 1 = 0.26 = 26\%$$

The actual return on the loan should be \$26, of which \$20 provides inflation compensation to the principal. The remaining \$6 provides the 5 percent pre-inflation interest on the \$120 inflated principal.

Rule 30: Interest rate for computing gain on loans. The gain on a loan during inflation is computed in the same way as that shown in rule 15. Both the interest rate and the required rate of return to be used in the computations are the nominal rates.

Loan Indexation

Loan indexation is the procedure of stating past values in terms of today's money. In some countries where inflation is persistent and high (such as Brazil and Israel), loans are indexed.

Under this procedure, the loan is contracted by using the pre-inflation interest rate, but both principal and interest are indexed to safeguard against inflation and to keep the real interest intact. Indexation is usually carried out in each payment period.

Rule 31: Value of indexed contracts. The indexed value of a contracted amount is

$$M_t(P_t/P_0)$$

where M_t is the contracted amount, P_t is the price index at time of payment, and P_0 = price index when the loan was taken.

Rule 32: Indexing short-term loans. A short-term loan is safeguarded against inflation by using an inflation-compensated interest rate that provides indexation.

Example. A \$100 loan is taken for 1 year, at 5 percent interest. The loan is indexed. The price index rose from 110 to 132.
Solution: The contracted repayment is \$105 plus inflation compensation. Indexation is

$$105(132 / 110) = 105 \times 1.20 = \$126$$

This sum equals that resulting from using an inflation-compensated rate of interest (26 percent in the previous example.)

Indexing Long-Term Loans

Two procedures of indexing long-term loans are summarized in this section. These procedures are suitable for both installment and equal-principal-payments loans.

Rule 33: Indexing each contracted payment. This rule describes the most common procedure of indexation. The contracted payments, which are based on a pre-inflation interest rate, are indexed. From the accounting point of view, the outstanding loan balance is indexed as well.

Example. A loan of \$100 is taken for 4 years at a pre-inflation interest rate of 5 percent. The loan is indexed and the principal is to be paid by equal annual payments.

The price index was 110 when the loan was taken and increased to 132 and 158.4 after 1 and 2 years, respectively.

Solution: The contracted payments are

	Principal		*Interest*		*Payment*
Year 1	(100/4)	+	(100×0.05)	=	\$30.00
Year 2	(100/4)	+	(75×0.05)	=	\$28.75

the index payments are

Year 1	$30.00\ (132/110) = 30.00 \times 1.20 = \$36.00$
Year 2	$28.75\ (158.4/110) = 28.75 \times 1.44 = \$41.40$

The remaining principal at the end of the first year is also indexed:

$$75 \times (132/110) = 75 \times 1.20 = \$90$$

The second indexed payment can be alternatively calculated:

$$[(90\ /\ 3) + (90 \times 0.05)]\ (158.4\ /\ 132) = \$41.40$$

Rule 34: Payment of total indexed value. Indexation can also be calculated on the basis of the total indexed value. The inflation-compensation of the outstanding loan balance (as recorded at the beginning of the period) is paid at the end of each period with the interest payment at the pre-inflation rate. In other words, the long-term loan is implicitly considered as a one-period loan; after payment of interest and inflation-compensation on principal, the remainder of the original loan is automatically renewed for the next period.

Example. Consider the previous example using this technique.

Solution: Indexation of the principal, at the end of the first year, is

$$100\ (132\ /\ 110) = \$120$$

The interest payment of preinflation rate on the indexed value is

$$120 \times 0.05 = \$6$$

The payment on the loan is \$20 for inflation-compensation plus \$6 interest payment. This sum equals the solution in the example for rule 29 for the inflation-compensated interest rate. In addition, \$25 is repaid on the original principal. Thus, the total payment is

$$20 + 6 + 25 = \$51$$

The remaining principal at the end of the first year is \$75.

The total payments in the early years of the loan repayment under this procedure (\$51) are higher than under the former indexing procedure (\$36). Later payments will be lower, because the remaining principal is lower (\$75, as opposed to \$90 in the former case).

Rule 35: Indexing a standing loan. The principal of a standing loan is repaid at the end of the contract, whereas the interest is paid at the end of each period. Thus, each contracted payment of interest is indexed as shown in rule 33 and the principal repayment is indexed as well, for the period between the contract and the repayment.

Rule 36: Liquidity aspects of indexed loans. Inflation compensation of a loan can be carried out by indexing the contracted repayments or by setting the interest rate to be fully inflation-compensated and implicitly considering the loan as a one-period loan, as shown in the last example.

The periodic repayment on an installment loan, under indexation of the contracted payments at pre-inflation interest rate, is

$$E_t = (CR_{n,i})\,(P_t/P_0)$$

where E_t is the repayment in period t; i is the preinflation rate of interest; $CR_{n,i}$ is the capital recovery factor (rule 1, chapter 2); P_t is the price index at time of payment; and P_0 is the price index when the loan was taken. The periodic repayment, using the inflation-compensated interest rate, is

$$E = CR_{n,i_p}$$

where E is the periodic repayment; i_p equals $(1 + i)\,(1 + p) - 1$, which is the inflation-compensated rate of interest (rule 33, chapter 1); and p is the anticipated inflation rate.

If the anticipated inflation rate coincides with the actual inflation, both schemes of loan repayments are equal in present-value terms. From the aspect of liquidity, however, indexation of the contracted payments is superior, because the repayments in early periods are lower than those under the second scheme where the inflation-compensated interest rate is used.

Example. A $100 installment loan is taken for 3 years at a preinflation rate of 5 percent. Inflation is expected to be 10 percent annually.
Solution: The preindexed contracted payment is

$$100\ (CR_{3,0.05}) = 100 \times 0.3672 = \$36.72$$

If the loan is indexed, this repayment will be indexed every year. If the loan is not indexed, but the inflation compensation is via the interest rate, the inflation-compensated interest rate is

$$(1 + 0.05)\,(1 + 0.10) - 1 = 0.155 = 15.5\%$$

The annual repayment is

$$100\ (CR_{3,0.155}) = 100 \times 0.4416 = \$44.16$$

The annual repayments of both schemes are

Year, end:	1	2	3
Price index	110.0	121.0	133.3
Under indexation	$40.39	$44.43	$48.87
Under compensated rate	44.16	44.16	44.16

Under indexation the payment is lower in the first year and higher in the last year than the payment under the inflation-compensated rate of interest. During inflation, when prices increase, the investor's cash flow increases over time, thus meeting the increasing indexed loan repayments.

Price and Yield of Bonds

A bond is a long-term loan issued by public corporations and agencies to be sold to the public at large. It is a promise to pay stipulated sums of money on specified dates. Bonds are traded on the stock market.

The decision to buy or sell a bond depends mainly on the yield of the bond. The yield is the internal rate of return; that is, the discounting rate (cost of capital) required by the investor to equate the present value of the bond's future cash flow to its traded price. The traded price depends on the bond's stipulated cash flow and on the market conditions.

When the market price of a bond exceeds its face value, the bond is said to sell at a *premium,* and the excess of the price over the face value is called the premium. When the premium is negative, it is called the *discount.*

Bonds Paying Interest Periodically

The cash flow from a regular bond is the interest that is paid at the end of each period. This sum is the coupon. The principal is usually paid in a lump sum at the end of the last stipulated period.

Rule 37: Price of a regular bond. Interest is paid on the face value of the bond. The face value may be equal to or differ from the redemption value at the maturity date.

Rule 37A. When the redemption value equals the face value, the price of the bond on a coupon date, after the coupon has been cashed, is

$$F + F(i - r)\,(PVA_{n,r})$$

where F is the face value on coupon date; i is the interest rate of the bond; r is the yield rate or investor's discounting rate; $PVA_{n,r}$ is the present-value factor of annuity for n and r (rule 7, chapter 2); and n is the number of periods until maturity.

Example. A \$100 5 percent bond is redeemable in 5 years. The investor's discounting rate is 10 percent.
Solution: The price of the bond is

$$100 + 100\ (0.05 - 0.10)\,(PVA_{5,0.10})$$
$$= 100 - 100 \times 0.05 \times 3.7908 = \$81.05$$

Rule 37B. When the redemption value differs from the face value, the price of the bond on a coupon date, after the coupon has been cashed is

$$R + F\,(i - ar)\,PVA_{n,r}$$

where R equals aF, which is the redemption value, and a is the redemption ratio or R/F.

Example. Consider the previous example, but with the bond redeemable in 5 years at 110 percent of the face value.
Solution: The price of the bond is

$$100 \times 1.10 + 100\,(0.05 - 1.10 \times 0.10)\,(PVA_{5,0.10})$$
$$= 110 - 6 \times 3.7908 = \$87.26$$

Rule 38: Yield of a regular bond. Bond quotations often give the price of a bond without stating the corresponding yield rate. The yield rate can be determined tediously by using the formula in rule 37 for the price of the bond and solving for the appropriate rate, using annuity tables.

Approximation methods for calculating the yield are based on the principle of amortizing the premium over the bond's remaining period, in relation to the average investment.

The yield of a regular bond on a coupon date, after the coupon has been cashed, is approximated by

$$\frac{\text{Coupon} - \dfrac{\text{Premium}}{\textit{Period}}}{\text{Average investment}}$$

where premium equals price minus redemption value; coupon is $i \times$ face value; period is n number of periods until maturity; and average investment equals (0.4 × redemption value) + (0.6 × price).
Weighting the average investment by the factors 0.4 and 0.6 is based on the interest add-on factor (rule 2, chapter 2). This techique gives better results than the equal weights of 0.5 that are commonly used.

Example. A $100 5 percent bond is redeemable in 5 years at 110 percent of the face value. The price of the bond is $87.26 (see the previous example).
Solution: The coupon is

$$0.05 \times 100 = \$5$$

The premium is

$$87.26 - 100 \times 1.10 = \$-22.74$$

The yield is approximately

$$\frac{5 - \dfrac{(-22.74)}{5}}{0.4 \times 110 + 0.6 \times 87.26} = \frac{9.548}{96.356} = 0.099 = 9.9\%$$

Serial Bonds

A serial bond is essentially a long-term equal-principal-payment loan (rule 10). The principal is repaid in equal installments, starting with the period immediately following the issue date, and the interest is paid on the outstanding balance.

Rule 39: Price of a serial bond. The price of a serial bond, for which the redemption value equals the face value, can be found by using the formula for the economic cost of an equal-principal-payment loan (rule 19). However, the following rule is more general.

When the redemption value equals or differs from the face value, the price of a serial bond on the coupon date, after the coupon and the principal repayment have been cashed, is

$$R + Fk\,(i - ar)\,PVA_{n,r}$$

where F is the face value outstanding on coupon date; k is the interest add-on factor $\cong 0.6$ for $ni < 1$ (rule 2, chapter 2); R is the redemption value outstanding; a is the redemption ratio or R/F; and i, r is the interest rate and yield, respectively.

Example. Consider a $1,000 outstanding face value serial bond at 5 percent interest to be redeemed in five equal consecutive installments at 110 percent. The first installment is due at the end of the coming year. The investor's discounting rate is 10 percent.
Solution: The redemption value is

$$1{,}000 \times 1.10 = \$1{,}100$$

The price of the bond is

$$1{,}100 + 1{,}000 \times 0.6\,(0.05 - 1.1 \times 0.10)\,(PVA_{5,0.10}) =$$
$$1{,}100 + (-36)3.7908 = \$963.53$$

Rule 40: Yield of a serial bond. The yield rate of a serial bond can be determined tediously by using the previous formula and solving for the appropriate rate, using annuity tables. However, the following approximation rule provides very good results.

The yield of a serial bond, on a coupon date, after the coupon has been cashed, is approximated by

$$\frac{\text{Coupon} - \dfrac{\text{Premium}}{\textit{Average period}}}{\text{Price}}$$

where average period is kn; k is the interest add-on factor $\cong 0.6$ (rule 2, chapter 2); and n is the number of periods to maturity.

Example. Consider the previous example where the price was found to be \$963.53.
Solution: The coupon is

$$0.05 \times 1{,}000 = \$50$$

The average period is

$$0.6 \times 5 = 3 \text{ years}$$

The premium is

$$963.55 - 1{,}000 \times 1.10 = \$-136.47.$$

The yield is

$$\frac{50 - \dfrac{(-136.47)}{3}}{963.53} = 0.099 = 9.9\%$$

5 Investment Evaluation

There are many methods for evaluating investments. The main methods summarized in this chapter are payback period, discounted cash flow, internal rate of return, and periodic capital expense. Each method has some advantages and some limitations. The case of investment evaluation under uncertainty is discussed in chapter 6.

As a first step in investment evaluation, you should estimate in qualitative terms the pattern of the cash flow that will be generated by the proposed investment—that is, whether it is anticipated to be uniform, increasing, decreasing, or irregular. As a second step, screen the investment proposals in terms of the payback period, which is the simplest evaluation method.

The payback-period method provides satisfactory results for uniform and decreasing cash flows, but not for increasing and irregular cash flows. The latter cases should be evaluated by the discounted-cash-flow method. The periodic-capital-expense method provides accruate results for a uniform cash flow. It is also applicable to the other cash-flow patterns after the cash flow is adjusted by the discounting technique. The periodic-capital-expense method conforms to conventional business and accounting procedures.

During inflation, the evaluation of investments becomes more complicated because some cash-flow items are affected by inflation and others are not. Further, income tax on the future income (on net cash inflow) will be levied on nominal values. Thus, all cash-flow items, income tax, and the required rate of return must be adjusted correctly before the proposed investment can be evaluated.

Payback Period

The payback period of a proposed investment is the time needed for the accumulated anticipated net cash inflow to cover the cost of the investment.

Rule 1: Determining the payback period. In the case of a uniform annual net cash inflow, the payback period is

$$\frac{A}{W} = \frac{\text{Investment cost}}{\text{Annual net cash inflow}}$$

In the case of a varying annual net cash inflow, the payback period is derived by solving the following:

$$A = \sum_{t=1}^{m} W_t$$

where A is the cost of investment, W_t is the net cash inflow in year t, and m is the payback period.

Example. A proposed investment with a life span of 5 years costs \$100. Two alternative annual net cash inflows are analyzed: \$33 every year, and \$50, \$40, \$40, \$30, and \$15 for each of the years, respectively.
Solution: Under the uniform cash flow, the payback period is

$$\frac{100}{33} = 3 \text{ years}$$

Under the varying cash flow, the necessary period of net cash inflow to reach \$100 is 2.25 years; that is, the cash flow of the first year, second year, and the first quarter of the third year:

$$A = \sum_{1}^{2.25} = 50 + 40 + \frac{40}{4} = 100$$

which equals the investment cost; that is, the payback period is 2.25 years.

The major limitation of this method is that it ignores the interest (cost of capital). As a result, this method may not be reliable in comparing alternative investment proposals. It also ignores the salvage value and the financial leverage, but it suits the case of a lump-sum investment. However, this method emphasizes the liquidity and time-risk aspects of a proposed investment.

Rule 2: Profitability indicator. When the asset life span is relatively long, then the shorter the payback period, the more attractive the proposed investment.

Internal Rate of Return Derived from Payback

The internal rate of return (defined later in this chapter) of a proposed investment can be derived from the payback period when the anticipated life span is given.[1]

Rule 3: Rate of return, uniform cash flow. The internal rate of return, under anticipated uniform cash flow, is approximated by

$$\left(\frac{1}{m} - \frac{1}{n}\right) 1.5$$

where m is the payback period, and n is the life span, and 1.5 equals 1/k.

Example. Consider the previous example, where $m = 3$ and $n = 5$.
Solution: The internal rate of return is approximately

$$\left(\frac{1}{3} - \frac{1}{5}\right) 1.5 = 0.20 = 20\%$$

The exact figure is 19.9 percent.
The internal rate of return can be derived directly by using the entries in table 5–1. Suppose $m = 3$ and $n = 5$; the corresponding entry in table 5–1 is 19.9 percent.

Rule 4: Rate of return, declining cash flow. Often the anticipated net cash inflow is declining over time as a result of increased maintenance costs or decreased output. Alternatively, the anticipated net cash inflow may actually be uniform, but it is considered declining because the probability of receiving the net returns decreases over time (according to its remaining service life). This approach causes the present value of the net cash inflow to be reduced by about 25 percent, a sum that may be considered as a risk premium due to uncertainty.

Table 5–1
Internal Rate of Return, Constant Cash Flow (*percentages*)

Payback	*Service Life, Years (n)*							
(Years m)	*5*	*6*	*7*	*8*	*10*	*12*	*14*	*20*
2.5	28.7	32.7	35.2	36.8	38.5	39.2	39.6	40.0
3.0	19.9	24.3	27.1	29.0	31.2	32.2	32.7	33.3
3.5	13.2	18.0	21.1	23.1	25.6	27.0	27.7	28.3
4.0	7.9	13.0	16.3	18.6	21.4	22.9	23.7	24.7
5.0					15.1	16.9	18.1	17.5
6.0					10.6	12.8	14.0	15.8
7.0					7.1	9.5	11.0	13.1

The internal rate of return, under a declining cash flow, is approximated by

$$\frac{1}{m} - \frac{1}{n}$$

Example. Consider the uniform cash flow in the first example, where $m = 3$ and $n = 5$. However, assume a declining cash flow because of uncertainty. Solution: The internal rate of return is approximately

$$\frac{1}{3} - \frac{1}{5} = 0.13 = 13\%$$

The exact figure is 10.4 percent. This rate is lower than the rate (19.9 percent) for the uniform cash flow in the previous example.
The internal rate of return can be derived directly by using the entries in table 5–2. Suppose $m = 3$ and $n = 5$; the corresponding entry in table 5–2 is 10.4 percent.

Rule 5: Risk implications. Given that the cash flow is uniform, but is assumed as if it declines over time (assuming a total risk premium of about 25 percent), the payback period is roughly 1.25 times as long, and the internal rate of return is reduced by roughly 33 percent.

Rule 6: Payback for screening investment proposals. Usually, a company considers more investment proposals than it actually plans to undertake. An initial screening procedure may reduce the amount of work in analyzing the proposals and enable a more thorough analysis of the remaining proposals.

Table 5–2
Internal Rate of Return, Declining Cash Flow (*percentages*)

Payback	*Service Life (Years n)*							
(Years m)	*5*	*6*	*7*	*8*	*10*	*12*	*14*	*20*
2.5	17.5	21.5	24.5	26.8	30.0	32.1	33.5	35.9
3.0	10.4	14.2	17.2	19.6	22.9	25.1	26.6	29.1
3.5	6.4	9.8	12.6	14.8	18.1	20.3	21.8	24.3
4.0	3.0	6.1	8.7	10.9	14.2	16.4	18.0	20.6
5.0					8.8	11.0	12.6	15.4
6.0					5.4	7.4	9.0	11.9
7.0					3.0	4.9	6.4	9.3

The payback period can provide a simple method for quick evaluation of investment proposals. Therefore, it is useful for screening purposes.

Rule 6A: The larger the difference between the anticipated service life and the payback period, the more profitable the proposed investment. When the payback period is longer than half the service life (that is, when $m / n > 0.5$), discard the proposal.

Rule 6B. For a given service life, the payback period is inversely proportional to the present value of the net cash inflow.

Example. Consider two proposed projects with an equal service life, with payback periods of 5 and 4 years for investments A and B, respectively. Solution: The present value of the net cash inflow of project B is greater by $5/4 = 1.25$ (that is, by 25 percent) than that of project A.

Discounted Cash Flow

The discounted cash flow of a proposed investment is the present value of the anticipated annual net cash inflow that will be generated by the project. The present value provides the economic value of the proposed investment. When the economic value exceeds the cost of investment, the project is profitable.

Rule 7: Present value of a perpetual uniform cash flow. In the case of a constant annual net cash inflow, the present value of the perpetual net cash inflow is

$$\frac{W}{r}$$

(See the example for rule 8 in chapter 2.)

Rule 8: Present value of uniform cash flow. In the case of a constant annual net cash inflow, the present value of the net cash inflow is

$$W(PVA_{n,r})$$

where W is the annual net cash inflow; r is the rate of cost of capital; n is the life span, which equals the number of periodic inflows; and $PVA_{n,r}$ is the present-value factor of annuity for n and r (rule 7, chapter 2).

Rule 9: Present value of varying cash flow. In the case of varying annual cash inflow, the present value is

$$\sum_{t=1}^{n} \frac{W_t}{(1+r)^t}$$

where W_t is the net cash inflow in year t.

Example. A proposed investment that costs $100 has a service life of 5 years. Two alternative annual net cash inflows are analyzed: $33 in every year, and $50, $40, $40, $30, and $15 for each of the 5 years. The cost of capital is 15 percent per annum. No salvage value exists.
Solution: Under uniform cash flow, the present value of the cash inflow is

$$33(PVA_{5,0.15}) = 33 \times 3.352 = \$110.62$$

The factor $(PVA_{5,0.15})$ is the reciprocal of the capital recovery entry for five periods and 15 percent in appendix A.

Under varying cash flow, the present value is

$$\frac{50}{1+0.15} + \frac{40}{(1+0.15)^2} + \frac{40}{(1+0.15)^3}$$

$$+ \frac{30}{(1+0.15)^4} + \frac{15}{(1+0.15)^5} = \$124.58$$

This present value figure (under the varying cash flow) is higher than that under the uniform cash flow because the cash flow was higher in the earlier years and lower in the later years, compared to the uniform cash flow. The discounted cash flow is a function of the magnitude of the periodic net cash inflow and its duration. Therefore, a comparison between alternative investment proposals can be carried out only for equal life spans. This fact reduces the applicability of the method.

Rule 10: Comparing investments of different life spans. To compare alternative investment proposals, set a common time denominator for the investments that are analyzed.

Example. The two investment proposals are examined; the annual cost of capital is 15 percent, and there is no salvage value.

Investment	*Initial cost*	*Net annual cash inflow*	*Life span*
A	\$137	\$30	10
B	100	33	5

Solution: The common time denominator is 10 years; that is, investment B will be considered in year 0 and in year 5.
The net present value of investment A is

$$30(PVA_{10,0.15}) - 137 = 30 \times 5.019 - 137 = 150.57 - 137.00 = \$13.57$$

The net present value of investment B at both year 0 and at year 5 is

$$33(PVA_{5,0.15}) - 100 = 33 \times 3.352 - 100 = 110.62 - 100.00 = \$10.62$$

The net present value for year 0 of the investment in year 5 is

$$\frac{10.62}{(1 + 0.15)^5} = \$5.28$$

The total net present value of investment B is

$$10.62 + 5.28 = \$15.90$$

The resultant figures (\$13.57 for A and \$15.90 for B) are comparable.

Rating Investments

The profitability of a proposed investment is measured by the difference between or by the ratio of the present value of the net cash inflow (the economic value) and the initial cost. Two ways of rating investments are summarized in rules 11 and 12.

Rule 11: Net present value for rating investments. The net present value is the difference between the present value of the net cash inflow and the cost of investment.

Example. In the example for rule 9 the net present value for the first case (uniform cash flow) is

$$110.62 - 100.00 = \$10.62$$

Rule for profitability indicator. A high net present value does not always indicate a high profitability, except when the life span and the investment cost are the same for all proposals.

In evaluating investment projects, record the present value of the net cash inflow alongside the cost of the investment so as to shed light on the volume of the invested capital.

Rule 12: Profitability index for rating investments. The profitability index (also called the benefit-cost ratio) is the ratio of the present value of the net cash inflow to the initial cost of investment; that is

$$\frac{\text{Present value}}{\text{Investment cost}}$$

Example. In the example for rule 9 the profitability index for the first case (uniform cash flow) is

$$\frac{110.62}{100.00} = 1.106$$

Rule for profitability indicator. Whatever the life span, the higher the profitability index, the higher the profitability of the proposed investment.

Example. Consider the data in the example for rule 10, with the relevant data

			Present value	
Investment	Initial cost	Life span	One investment	Net for 10 years
A	$137	10	$150.57	$13.57
B	100	5	110.62	15.90

Solution: The profitability indexes are

$$\text{Investment A:} \quad \frac{150.57}{137} = 1.099$$

$$\text{Investment B:} \quad \frac{110.62}{100} = 1.106$$

Investment B is more profitable, which is verified by the comparable net present values in the example for rule 10.

The use of the profitability index is limited by the fact that it is not appropriate for investments that are not carried out in one lump sum. Further, it is often difficult to distinguish between investment cost and other outlays included in the cash flow from which the net cash inflow is calculated.

Internal Rate of Return

The internal rate of return of a proposed investment is the discounting rate that gives zero net present value; that is, it is the rate that equates the present value of the net cash inflow to the initial cost of investment.

The internal rate of return is usually estimated by trial and error. There are, however, short-cut procedures that provide good approximations.

Rule 13: Rate of return uniform cash flow. In the case of a uniform annual net cash inflow, the internal rate of return is approximated by

$$\left(\frac{W}{A} - \frac{1}{n}\right) 1.5$$

where W is the annual net cash inflow, A is the initial investment, and n is the life span.

Example. Consider the uniform cash flow in the example for rule 9.
Solution: The internal rate of return is approximately

$$\left(\frac{33}{100} - \frac{1}{5}\right) 1.5 = 0.195 = 19.5\%$$

The exact figure is 19.9 percent.

Given a uniform cash flow, the internal rate of return can be derived by using an annuity table. Compute the value of W/A and search for an equivalent entry in the line that matches the investment life span in the table of capital recovery factors (appendix A).

Example. Consider the example for rule 9, where

$$W / A = 0.33$$

Searching for such an entry (in line 5 years in appendix A), the entry 0.334 is found for $i = 20$ percent. Thus, the rate of return is a bit lower than 20 percent. Interpolation gives 19.9 percent.

Rule 14: Rate of return, varying cash flow. In the case of varying annual net cash inflow, the internal rate of return is approximated by

$$\frac{PV - A}{Akn} + \frac{PV}{A} r$$

where PV is the present value of net cash inflow, using the rate r; A is the initial investment; $k \cong 0.67$, which is the interest add-on factor (rule 2, chapter 2); r is the cost of capital used for discounting; and n is the life span. This rule also can be used for cases where the net cash inflow is negative in some periods.

Example. Consider the varying cash flow in the example for rule 9. Solution: The internal rate of return is approximately

$$\frac{124.58 - 100}{0.67 \times 5 \times 100} + \frac{124.58}{100} \times 0.15 = 0.2602 = 26.02\%$$

The exact figure is 26.87 percent.

Rule for derivation by interpolation. In the case of varying cash flow, the internal rate of return can be derived by solving the following:

$$\sum_{t=1}^{n} \frac{W_t}{(1 + r')} - A = 0$$

where A is the initial investment, W_t is the net cash inflow in year t, and r' is the internal rate of return. The solution must be found by means of trial and error. At least two calculations are required: one at rate r_1 which will give positive net present value (a_1), and a second at a higher rate r_2 which will give a negative net present value (a_2). The internal rate of return (r_0) that gives zero net present value falls between r_2 and r_1; that is

$$r_0 = r_1 + \frac{a_1}{a_1 + |a_2|} (r_2 - r_1)$$

where $|a_2|$ is the value of a_2 disregarding sign. When a_1 and a_2 are close to zero, r_0 will approach the true value. Otherwise, a second iteration is required using the value of a_0 which replaced either a_1 or a_2, depending upon whether r_0 is positive or negative, respectively. A good initial guess saves calculations (see rules 3, 4, 13 and 14).

Example. Consider the varying cash flow in the previous example and for rule 9.
Solution: For $r_1 = 0.24$, $a_1 = \$5.01$; for $r_2 = 0.28$, $a_2 = \$-1.91$.

$$r_0 = 0.24 + \frac{5.01}{5.01 + 1.91}(0.28 - 0.24) = 0.269 = 26.9\%$$

The internal rate of return is approximately 26.9 percent.

The internal rate of return method assumes that the cash flow earns (costs or yields) the resultant internal rate of return but, in practice, the cash flow earns the company's cost of capital. This fact impinges on the reliability of this method in comparing alternative investment proposals.

In practice, the anticipated rate of return of a proposed investment would fall between the internal rate of return and the company's cost of capital.

Sensitivity of Internal Rate of Return

After determining the internal rate of return of a proposed investment, management is often interested in checking the sensitivity of this rate to marginal changes in the net cash inflow or the initial cost of the investment.

Rule 15: Sensitivity to changes in cash inflow. Given a uniform net cash inflow over the investment's life, a 1 percent increase in the expected net cash inflow of a project will increase the internal rate of return by approximately 2 percent. A more accurate result in percentages can be reached by multiplying the percentage change in the net cash inflow by the factor:

$$\frac{1}{1 - \dfrac{n}{(1 + r)FVA_{n,r}}}$$

where n is the investment life span, r is the internal rate of return, and $FVA_{n,\,r}$ is the future value factor of annuity for n and r (rule 5, chapter 2).[2]

Example. The internal rate of return of a proposed investment, with an anticipated uniform net cash inflow over 12 years, is 10 percent. You want to know the effect of a 7 percent change in the anticipated annual net cash inflow.

Solution: A 7 percent increase in the net cash inflow will result in an approximately 14 percent increase in the internal rate of return. Thus, the rate of return will change from 10 percent to approximately 11.4 percent.

The more accurate figure is

$$7 \times \frac{1}{1 - \dfrac{12}{(1 + 0.10)21.3843}} = 7 \times 2.04 = 14.28\%$$

A 7 percent decrease in the expected net cash inflow will reduce the rate of return from 10 percent to approximately 8.6 percent.

Rule 16: Sensitivity to change in cost of investment. Given a uniform net cash inflow over the investment's life, a 1 percent increase in the cost of the investment will reduce the internal rate of return by approximately 2 percent. A more accurate result is given by the formula in rule 15.

Example. A proposed investment costs $1,000. It will generate a uniform net cash inflow for 12 years and yield a 10 percent internal rate of return. You want to know the effect of a 7 percent increase in the cost of the investment.

Solution: The 7 percent increase in the cost of investment will reduce the internal rate of return by approximately 14 percent—that is, from 10 percent to about 8.6 percent.

Periodic Capital Expense Method

The periodic-capital-expense method for investment evaluation conforms with common business practices and accounting procedures; it is based on capital recovery (rule 1, chapter 2). This method provides results in a form that can be compared easily with the future actual figures.

Rule 17: Capital expense on nondepreciable assets. The annual capital expense of a proposed investment in nondepreciable assets (such as land, permanent inventory, working capital, or securities) is the annual interest charge. This expense, which will exist indefinitely, is

$$E = Ar$$

where E is the annual capital expense, A is the cost of investment, and r is the rate of cost of capital.

Example. Consider a proposed investment of \$100 in land; the cost of capital is 12 percent per annum.
Solution: The annual capital expense is

$$100 \times 0.12 = \$12$$

Capital Expense on Depreciable Assets

The annual capital expense of a proposed investment in depreciable assets (such as buildings or equipment) is the annual charge for depreciation and interest. These expenses exist until the end of the asset's life.

The periodic-capital-expense method can be used for simple as well as more complicated cases. First, the general case is shown. Then, the cases of salvage value, varying cash flow, and continuing investment outlays are discussed.

Rule 18: Capital expense, general case. The annual capital expense of a proposed investment in a depreciable asset, assuming no salvage value, is approximated by

$$E = A\left(\frac{1}{n} + 0.67r\right)$$

where E is the annual capital expense, A is the cost of investment, n is the life span, r is the rate of cost of capital, and 0.67 is the interest add-on factor (rule 2, chapter 2). The exact formula for \$1 of investment is

$$CR_{n,r} = \frac{r}{1-(1+r)^{-n}}$$

where $CR_{n,r}$ is the capital recovery factor for n and r (rule 1, chapter 2; appendix A). The annual capital expense is

$$E = A(CR_{n,r})$$

Example. A proposed investment that costs \$100 will serve for 5 years. The anticipated annual net cash inflow is \$33. The annual cost of capital is 15 percent. No salvage value exists.
Solution: The annual capital expense is approximately

$$100\left(\frac{1}{5} + 0.67 \times 0.15\right) = \$30.05$$

The exact calculation is

$$100\frac{0.15}{1-(1+0.15)^{-5}} = 100 \times 0.2983 = \$29.83$$

Alternatively, the exact figure is

$$100(CR_{5,0.15}) = 100 \times 0.2983 = \$29.83$$

The factor $(CR_{5,0.15})$ is taken from appendix A; the entry for five periods and 15 percent. Given that the annual net cash inflow is \$33, the annual net return is

$$33.00 - 29.83 = \$3.17$$

Rule 19: Capital expense, salvage case. When there is a salvage value, its present value should be deducted from the initial investment. The resultant figure is then used for computing the annual capital expense; thus, the annual capital expense is

$$E = \left(A - \frac{L}{(1+r)^n}\right)(CR_{n,r})$$

where L is the salvage value in year n. An alternative formulation is

$$E = (A - L)(CR_{n,r}) + Lr$$

This formulation is easier to compute; it means that the annual capital expense is the capital recovery on the initial investment less the salvage value, plus interest on the salvage value.

Example. Consider the previous example, but suppose the salvage value at the end of 5 years is \$20.
Solution: The present value of the salvage value is

$$\frac{20}{(1+0.15)^5} = \$9.94$$

The annual capital expense is

$$(100.00 - 9.94)0.2983 = \$26.86$$

Alternatively, the capital expense is

$$(100 - 20)0.2983 + 20 \times 0.15 = \$26.86$$

Rule 20: Capital expense, varying cash flow. Any type of varying cash flow can be transformed into an equivalent uniform cash flow. A uniform cash flow is computed in two steps. First, compute the present value of the varying cash flow; that is

$$PV = \sum_{t=1}^{n} \frac{W_t}{(1 + r)^t}$$

where PV is the present value of net cash inflow (rule 9) and W_t is the net cash inflow in year t.

Second, multiply the result by the capital recovery factor; that is

$$PV(CR_{n,r})$$

where $CR_{n,r}$ is the capital recovery factor for n and r (rule 1, chapter 2). The resultant uniform cash flow is a weighted average (weighted by compounding) of the varying cash flow.

Example. Consider the example for rule 18, but with an anticipated net cash inflow of 50, 40, 40, 30, and 15 for each of the 5 years. The annual cost of capital is 15 percent.

Solution: The present value of this cash flow is \$124.58 (see the example for rule 9). The equivalent annual uniform cash flow is

$$124.58\ (CR_{5,0.15}) = 124.58 \times 0.2983 = \$37.16$$

Because the investment cost \$100 and the annual capital expense is \$29.83 (the example for rule 18), the annual net return is

$$37.16 - 29.83 = \$7.33$$

Rule 21: Capital expense, profitability index. The profitability index of an investment can be defined as

$$\frac{PV(CR_{n,r})}{A(CR_{n,r})}$$

where $PV(CR_{n,r})$ is the annual payment of the present value of the net cash inflow (rule 20) and $A(CR_{n,r})$ is the annual capital recovery of initial investment (rule 18). This formulation is identical to that in rule 12.

Example. Consider the data in the examples for rules 18 and 20.
Solution: The profitability index is

$$\frac{\text{Equivalent annual cash inflow}}{\text{Annual capital expense}} = \frac{37.16}{29.83} = 1.246$$

Using the formula in rule 12, the profitability index is

$$\frac{\text{Present value}}{\text{Investment cost}} = \frac{124.58}{100} = 1.246$$

Rule 22: "Averaging" (equivalent) annual physical units. The technique of "averaging" varying cash flow (rule 20) can also be used for transforming varying series of physical units into an "average" uniform series. This procedure can be used when the price level of the physical units is constant.

Example. The anticipated annual output of a proposed investment is 60, 100, and 120 units during the 3 years of the investment. The cost of capital is 15 percent per annum.
Solution: The "average" annual level of production (weighted by compounding at 15 percent, and using $CR_{3,0.15} = 0.438$) is

$$\left(\frac{60}{1+0.15} + \frac{100}{(1+0.15)^2} + \frac{120}{(1+0.15)^3}\right) 0.438 = 90.5 \text{ units}$$

The simple average level of production is 93.3 units; the weighted average is 90.5 units.

Rule 23: A case of continuing investment outlays. Most of the methods of investment evaluation assume that the initial investment is carried out as a lump sum. When the investment is carried out over several periods, the total costs should be compounded to the date in which the investment is completed.

When an investment project is constructed over several periods, the investment cost is determined by the future value of the periodic outlays. When some net inflows are generated during construction, they should be deducted from the respective periodic outlays.

Example. An investment in an orchard is carried out over 3 years before the orchard enters production. The respective outlays are \$50, \$150, and \$120. In the third year there is a net income of \$20. The cost of capital is 10 percent.
Solution: The net outlay in the third year is $120 - 20 = \$100$. The accumulated compounded cost of investment is

$$50(1 + 0.10)^3 + 150(1 + 0.10)^2 + 100(1 + 0.10)^1 = \$358.05$$

If the useful life of the orchard is 20 years, the annual capital expense, starting from the fourth year, is

$$358.05\ (CR_{20,010}) = 358.05 \times 0.1175 = \$42.07$$

Income Tax and Financial Leverage Considerations

Income tax and financial leverage should be taken into account in investment evaluation, regardless of which evaluation method is used. For this purpose, the after-tax periodic net cash inflow should be calculated, and the after-tax cost of capital should be used for discounting. The after-tax cash flow of the loan that is used to finance the investment should also be taken into account. Both depreciation expense and interest payments are tax-deductible (deductible from income before income tax is levied). The depreciation expense is charged only for computing the income tax; it is not a cash outlay. The interest, on the other hand, is a cash outlay, as is the repayment on the principal.

An investment that is financed by loans can be evaluated in two ways:

1. The cash flow associated with the physical project and the cash flow associated with the loan are analyzed separately and the results are combined.

2. The cash flow associated with both categories is analyzed jointly (as shown in rule 28).

Rule 24: Determining the after-tax cash inflow for an investment. The anticipated annual after-tax net cash inflow from a proposed investment is computed in two steps as follows, assuming 100 percent equity finance.

1. *Anticipated income statement*

Sales
− Direct costs
= Income before depreciation
− Depreciation expense

= Net income before tax
− Income tax
= Profit, after-tax

2. *Anticipated net-cash inflow*
Profit, after-tax
+ Depreciation expense
= Total

The net cash inflow can also be determined as follows:

Income before depreciation, multiplied by 1 minus the tax rate
+ Tax saving on depreciation expenses (= depreciation × tax rate)
= Total

The resultant total net cash inflow should be used for calculating the present value (see the earlier section on discounted cash flow); computing the internal rate of return (see the earlier section in this chapter); or comparing the annual capital expense (the previous section).

Example. A $100 investment is proposed with a life span of 2 years without a salvage value. The investment is financed solely by equity, and the after-tax cost of capital is 10 percent. Income tax is 40 percent. Additional data and the calculations of the profitability are presented in table 5–3.

The calculations in table 5–3 indicate a net present value of $12.53 on $100 of equity. When the periodic-capital-expense method is applied (rule 20), the "average" annual net cash inflow is

$$112.53\ (CR_{2,010}) = 112.53 \times 0.5762 = \$64.84$$

The annual capital expense is

$$100 \times 0.5762 = \$57.62$$

Thus, the annual net return on the $100 investment is

$$64.84 - 57.62 = \$7.22$$

Rule 25: Evaluating investment in a loan. The cash flow of a loan can be viewed similarly to that of a regular investment where the sign of the cash flow is reversed. The loan principal is equivalent to the initial cost of the investment and the loan repayments are equivalent to the net cash inflow.

The evaluation of the profitability of a loan is shown in chapter 4, where

Table 5–3
Investment Evaluation Financed by Equity

Year End	*0*	*1*	*2*
Income statement			
Sales		$150	$160
Direct costs		80	80
Income before depreciation		70	80
Depreciation expense ($100/2)		50	50
Net income before tax		20	30
Income tax (40%)		8	12
Profit after-tax		12	18
Net cash inflow[a]			
Profit, after-tax		$12	$18
Depreciation expense		50	50
Total		62	68
Discounting			
Present value factor (10%)		0.909	0.826
Present value, cash inflow	$112.53	$56.36	$56.17
Cost of investment	100.00		
Net present value	12.53		

[a] Alternative calculation:

Income before depreciation × (1 − 0.40)	$42	$48
Tax saving on depreciation = 50 × 0.40	20	20
	62	68

both the present value method and the periodic-capital-expense method are analyzed. Alternatively, the evaluation is performed by discounting the after-tax cash outflow, using the after-tax cost of capital as shown in rule 26.

Rule 26: Determining the after-tax cash outflow for a loan. The annual after-tax net cash outflow from the loan is computed in two steps:

1. *Loan repayment*
   Principal repayment
   \+ Interest payment
   = Total

2. *Net cash outflow*
   Principal repayment
   \+ Interest after-tax
   = Total

Interest after-tax equals interest payment multiplied by one minus tax rate. The net cash outflow can also be computed as follows:

Loan repayment
− Tax saving on interest (= interest × tax rate)
= Total

The resultant total net cash outflow should be used for calculating the gain (net present value).

Example. A $100 loan to be repaid in two annual equal principal payments is taken to finance an investment. The interest is 7 percent and the after-tax cost of capital is 10 percent. Income tax is 40 percent. Additional data and the calculations of the profitability are presented in table 5–4.

The result of the calculations in table 5–4 indicates a gain (net present value) of $7.70 on this loan.

Rule 27: Evaluating the investment plus its finance. An investment in an asset is usually partly financed by a loan. The profitability of each asset or loan should usually be evaluated separately, because an investment in an asset may be financed by several loans. The results of both analyses should be aggregated to provide the total net gain on the investment.

Example. Suppose the loan evaluated in table 5–4 is taken to finance the investment evaluated in table 5–3.
Solution: The gain on the loan is $7.70. The net present value of the investment in the asset is $12.53. Thus, the total gain is $20.23 in present-value terms. In periodic terms, the annual net return is

$$20.23(CR_{2,0.10}) = 20.23 \times 0.576 = \$11.65$$

Suppose only half the investment is financed by a loan (that is, a $50 loan). Then the gain on the loan is $3.85 (half of $7.70) and the total gain is $16.38 (3.85 + 12.53) in present-value terms on the $50 equity.

Rule 28: Evaluating the joint cash flow of investment and finance. The joint annual net cash flow from a proposed investment and its finance is

$$W(1 - t) + t(D) - \text{Loan repayment} + t(I)$$

where W is the annual income before depreciation and interest, D is the annual depreciation expense, I is the annual interest payment on loan, t is the income tax rate, $t(D)$ is the tax saving on depreciation expenses, loan

Table 5–4
Loan Evaluation

Year End	*0*	*1*	*2*
Loan repayment			
Principal repayment		$50.00	$50.00
Interest (7%)		7.00	3.50
Total		57.00	53.50
Net cash outflow[a]			
Principal repayment		$50.00	$50.00
Interest after-tax (40%)[b]		4.20	2.10
		54.20	52.10
Discounting			
Present-value factor (10%)		0.909	0.826
Present value, cash outflow	$92.30	$49.27	$43.03
Loan principal	100.00		
Gain (net present value)	7.70		

[a]Alternative calculation:

Loan repayment		$57.00	$53.50
Tax saving on interest	(7.00 × 0.40)	(2.80)	
	(3.50 × 0.40)		(1.40)
		54.20	52.10

[b]Where tax saving is calculated by 7.00 (1 − 0.40) = 4.20; 3.50(1 − 0.40) = 2.10

repayment is the principal plus interest, and $t(I)$ is the tax savings on interest payments.

Example. Consider the examples in tables 5–3 and 5–4. The relevant computations are applied to the joint annual net cash flow in table 5–5.

Rule 29: Evaluating the investment by present-value factors. In some cases the present value of the individual items can be determined easily by using present value factors rather than computing the periodic amounts for the cash flow—for example, in the case of depreciation according to an accelerated method or the repayment schedule of loans. The after-tax cost of capital should be used for discounting.

The following procedure is especially helpful when the life span of the investment proposal is long and the investment is composed of several types of assets and of several loans:

1. The net present value of a proposed investment, calculated by using present value factors, is

Table 5–5
Investment Evaluation Financed by Loan

Year End	*0*	*1*	*2*
$W(1-t)$		70(1 − 0.40) = $42.00	80(1 − 0.40) = $48.00
$t(D)$		0.40(50) = 20.00	0.40(50) = 20.00
Loan repayment		(57.00)	(53.50)
$t(I)$		0.40(7.00) = 2.80	0.40(3.50) = 1.40
Total		7.80	15.90
Discounting			
Present-value factor (10%)		0.909	0.826
Present-value cash flow	$20.22	$7.09	$13.13
Cost of investment	−100.00		
Loan principal	100.00		
Net present value	20.22		

(1 − t) PV of income before depreciation and interest
+ (t) PV of depreciation schedule (rules 30–33, chapter 8)
− Cost of investment
= Net present value of the investment

2. The gain on a loan (net present value), calculated by using present value factors, is

Initial principal
− PV of loan repayment schedule
+(t)PV of interest payments (rule 25, chapter 4)
= Gain = net present value of the loan

The net present value of the investment and its loan is the sum of the results of the first and second steps.

Rule 30: Present value of capital expenses. When the investment is fully financed by a loan, and the interest rate on the loan is used for discounting, the present-value of the depreciation expenses (whatever the depreciation method used) plus the present value of the interest payments (on the asset-depreciated values) equal the initial cost of the investment.[3]

The present value of the interest payments (on the asset depreciated values) is

$$1 - PV_{\text{depreciation}}$$

where $PV_{\text{depreciation}}$ is the present value of depreciation expenses on a $1 investment.

Investment Evaluation during Inflation

During inflation the various cash-flow items do not necessarily behave in the same way. Some items, such as sales and costs, are usually inflated over time; other items, such as depreciation expenses for income tax calculation and repayments of conventional loans, are stated in money terms of the date of acquisition.

The anticipated cash flow can be stated in either constant prices or nominal prices.

Rule 31: Evaluation, using constant prices. Constant prices imply that the anticipated cash flow is stated in a given date's (usually today's) money terms. A cash flow projected in constant prices is simple to compute and has an advantage of being meaningful to the decision-maker.

When the cash flow is stated in constant prices—that is, in real terms—it should be discounted by inflation-free cost of capital (rule 29, chapter 1).

The anticipated cash flow should be stated in constant prices in two cases. First, constant prices should be used when the payback-period method is used for screening purposes (rule 6), where the emphasis is on the simplicity of the method. In this case, the exact anticipated income tax cannot be determined. Second, constant prices should be used when there is no income tax and when the loans that finance the investment are evaluated separately.

Rule 32: Evaluation, using nominal prices. Nominal prices imply that the anticipated cash flow is stated in prices that are anticipated to prevail in each year in the future. A cash flow projected in nominal prices will be comparable in the future with actual events. Further, income tax is levied on nominal values, and loans are usually contracted in nominal terms. Finally, stating the cash flow in nominal terms makes it easier to incorporate specific price level changes into the projections.

When the cash flow is stated in nominal prices, it should be discounted by inflation-compensated cost of capital (rule 33, chapter 1).

The previous discussion indicates that both ways of projecting cash flows have advantages. As a result, both methods should be used to evaluate the investment.

Rule 33: Calculating the net PV during inflation. During inflation, the anticipated annual after-tax cash inflow from a proposed investment is computed in several steps:

1. Estimate the anticipated volume of production by estimating the magnitude of sales and direct costs in constant prices—that is, in the money terms of the date of analysis.

2. Transform the sales and cost data to nominal terms by inflating the various items by the anticipated specific prices indexes, and prepare the anticipated income statement (rule 24) using historical depreciation expense.

3. Prepare the anticipated net cash inflow by adding the depreciation expense to the after-tax income.

4. Deflate the total net cash inflow by the anticipated general price index (either the Consumer Price Index or the GNP Implicit Price Deflator).

The resulting figures indicate the periodic net cash inflow in constant prices—that is, in today's money terms. These figures should be discounted to evaluate the proposed investment, using the inflation-free, after-tax cost of capital (required rate of return).

Example. Consider a $100 investment proposal (which is analyzed in example 24 and table 5–3). The investment is financed solely by equity and the after-tax, inflation-free cost of capital is 10 percent. Additional data and the calculations of the profitability are presented in table 5–6. The price index of the direct costs is lower than the general index, indicating a relative decrease in the price level of the direct costs.

The result of the calculations in table 5–6 indicates a net present value of $9.41. This present value is lower than that arrived at in table 5–3 for the same data, for a noninflationary situation, despite the relative decrease in the price level of the direct costs. This is because only historical depreciation expenses are tax-deductible, hence there is over-taxation which causes the investment to be less profitable.

When the periodic-capital-expense method is applied, the "average" annual net cash inflow, in constant prices, is

$$109.41\ (CR_{2,0.10}) = 109.41 \times 0.5762 = \$63.04$$

The annual capital expense is

$$100 \times 0.5762 = \$57.62$$

Thus, the annual net return on the $100 investment, in today's money terms, is

$$63.04 - 57.62 = \$5.42$$

Rule 34: Evaluating "investment" in a loan during inflation. Following rule 25, a loan can be viewed as an investment. Because the loan repayment

Table 5–6
Investment Evaluation during Inflation Financed by Equity

Year End	*0*	*1*	*2*
(1) General price index	100.00	112.00	125.44
(2) Price index, of direct costs	100.00	110.00	121.00
Volume of activity, constant prices			
(3) Sales		$150.00	$160.00
(4) Direct costs		80.00	80.00
Income statement, nominal prices			
(5) Sales (3) × (1)		$168.00	$200.70
(6) Direct costs (4) × (2)		88.00	96.80
(7) Income before depreciation (5) − (6)		80.00	103.90
(8) Depreciation expense ($100 / 2)		50.00	50.00
(9) Net income (7) − (8)		30.00	53.90
(10) Income tax (40%)		12.00	21.56
(11) Profit after-tax		18.00	32.34
Net cash inflow, nominal prices			
(12) Profit after-tax		$18.00	$32.34
(13) Depreciation		50.00	50.00
(14) Total		68.00	82.34
Net cash inflow, constant prices			
(15) Total (14) / (1)		60.71	65.64
Discounting			
(16) Present-value factor (10%)		0.909	0.826
(17) Present-value, cash inflow (15) × (16)	$109.41	$55.19	$54.22
Cost of investment	100.00		
Net present value	9.41		

is usually stated in nominal terms, the net cash outlay should be discounted by the current nominal cost of capital, after tax, as shown in chapter 4. Alternatively, the profitability of the loan can be calculated in a similar way to that shown in table 5–6.

Example. Consider a $100 loan (which is analyzed in the example for rule 26 and table 5–4). Because of inflation, the interest rate is 14 percent; the inflation-free cost of capital is 10 percent. Additional data and the calculations of the profitability are presented in table 5–7.

The result of the calculations in table 5–7 indicates a gain (net present value) of $16.91 on this loan. This gain is higher than that on a comparable loan under stable price level ($7.70 gain on $100 loan at 7 percent, in table

Table 5–7
Loan Evaluation during Inflation

Year End	*0*	*1*	*2*
General price index	100.00	112.00	125.44
Loan repayment			
Principal repayment		$50.00	$50.00
Interest (14%)		14.00	7.00
Total		64.00	57.00
Net cash outflow, nominal prices			
Principal repayment		$50.00	$50.00
Interest after-tax (40%)[a]		8.40	4.20
Total		58.40	54.20
Net cash outflow, constant prices			
Total nominal / price index		$52.14	$43.21
Discounting			
Present-value factor (10%)		0.909	0.826
Present-value cash outflow	$83.09	$47.40	$35.69
Loan principal	100.00		
Gain (net present value)	16.91		

[a]14.00(1 − 0.40) = 8.40; 7.00(1 − 0.40) = 4.20

5–4), because the interest rate on the loan does not provide the full inflation-compensation (rule 29, chapter 4).

Notes

1. Based on L. Shashua and Y. Goldschmidt, "Internal Rates of Return Derived from the Pay-Back Period," *Omega* 8 (1980), pp. 695–696.
2. Based on W.D. Whisler, " Sensitivity of Rates of Returns," *Journal of Finance* (March 1976), pp. 63–69.
3. Based on W.T. Morris, *Engineering Economics* (Homewood, Ill.: Irwin, 1960), pp. 51–52.

6 Investment Evaluation under Uncertainty

Investment evaluation, assuming certainty regarding the future returns, has been discussed in chapter 5. Among the several methods used in evaluating the profitability of an investment, the discounting techniques (net present value of the cash flow and periodic capital expense) are the most powerful. The investor's after-tax cost of capital, which takes into account the company's average financial risk level, is used for discounting. No consideration has been given, however, to the size of the investment, which is an important factor in cases where conditions are uncertain.

The analysis of investments with uncertain returns is conducted using the same tools as those used under certainty. The uncertain cash flow is either adjusted for risk and then discounted using the company's after-tax cost of capital, or it is left unadjusted but discounted using a risk-adjusted rate. Both procedures ignore the risk of failure resulting from a possible large loss from an adverse outcome. The procedures implicitly assume that the investment is one among many, so that a possible large loss can be borne by the company without endangering its financial position.

When a sizeable investment with uncertain returns is to be undertaken by the company, the analysis should be supplemented by a sensitivity analysis. The sensitivity analysis lists the probability of adverse outcomes and is submitted to management for evaluation.

Analysis Using Risk-Adjusted Cash Flow

When the returns are uncertain, the investment can be analyzed in terms of the certainty equivalent of the net cash inflow. The certainty equivalent of a net cash inflow (see chapter 18) is given by

$$\text{Certainty}(F)_t = F_t - bS_t$$

where certainty $(F)_t$ is the certainty equivalent of cash inflow in year t, F_t is the expected cash inflow in year t, b is the unit-risk premium factor, S_t is the standard deviation of cash inflow in year t, and bS_t is the risk premium of the cash inflow in year t.

Rule 1: Calculating the certainty equivalent for investment evaluation. The certainty equivalent of a net cash inflow in each year is estimated by the following steps.

1. Estimate the expected net cash inflow in each year (year *t*). An average value from past experience or from the industry can serve as an estimate. For a new production process, the net cash inflow in year *t* can be estimated by

$$\frac{\text{Optimistic} + \text{pessimistic}}{2}$$

where optimistic is high returns minus low costs and pessimistic is low returns minus high costs.

2. Estimate the standard deviation of the net cash inflow in each year by

$$\frac{\text{Optimistic} - \text{pessimistic}}{4}$$

3. Estimate the unit-risk premium coefficient of the investor, *b*, as explained in rule 5, chapter 18. Note that *b* should not exceed a value of one.

4. Calculate the annual certainty-equivalent values.

5. Calculate the present value of the investment, using the company's after-tax cost of capital, either on the expected net cash inflow values and the risk premium separately or on the certainty equivalent values. When the present value of the certainty equivalent cash flow is greater than the investment cost, the investment is profitable, taking into account the disutility of risk.

Example. Consider the investment that is evaluated under certainty conditions in table 5–3. Suppose the estimated optimistic and pessimistic net cash flows are presented in the upper section of table 6–1. These figures have been arrived at by first estimating the highest and lowest sales values in each year, then estimating the lowest and highest cost level of each input in each year, and finally summing the lowest levels of all costs of input in a given year to arrive at the optimistic level and summing the highest levels of all costs of input in a given year to arrive at the pessimistic level. The investor unit-risk premium is 0.364 (see chapter 18) and the aftertax cost of capital is 10 percent.

Solution: The annual risk premium and its present value are calculated in the

Table 6–1
Risk Premium of an Investment

	Year 1	Year 2
Investment, optimistic scenario		
Sales	\$175	\$185
Costs	75	70
	100	115
Investment, pessimistic scenario		
Sales	120	135
Costs	80	90
	40	45
Computations		
Expected net cash inflow	$\frac{100 + 40}{2} = \$70.00$	$\frac{115 + 45}{2} = \$80.00$
Standard deviation	$\frac{100 - 40}{4} = \$15.00$	$\frac{115 - 45}{4} = \$17.50$
Risk premium	$15.00 \times 0.364 = \$5.46$	$17.50 \times 0.364 = \$6.37$
Present-value factor (10%)	0.909	0.826
Present value of risk premium	$5.46 \times 0.909 = \$4.96$	$6.37 \times 0.826 = \$5.26$
Total risk premium	$4.96 + 5.26 = \$10.22$	

lower section of table 6–1. The present value of the certainty equivalent cash flow is

Present value of the average net cash inflow (table 5–3)	\$112.53
Present value of the risk premium (table 6–1)	10.22
	102.31

Alternatively, the annual certainty equivalent values are

	Year 1	Year 2
Expected net cash inflow	\$70.00	\$80.00
Income tax (table 5–3)	8.00	12.00
After tax net cash inflow	62.00	68.00
Risk premium (table 6–1)	5.46	6.37
	56.54	61.63

The present value (10 percent) of these is \$102.31.

The present value of the certainty equivalent net cash inflow is larger than the cost of the investment (\$100), hence the investment is profitable, taking into account the disutility of risk. The $10.22 risk premium (which is 10.22 percent as the investment is $100) can be viewed as a premium for self-insurance against all possible outcomes that diverge from the average return. This procedure would be correct in the case where the investment is one of several investments that are undertaken by the investor.

Analysis Using Risk-Adjusted Discounting Rate

A common business procedure used to take account of uncertainty is to incorporate the risk into the discounting factor. The idea behind the risk-adjusted discounting rate is that, by raising the discounting rate, the present value of the expected cash flow is reduced by the uncertainty cost. The method is equivalent to the certainty equivalent approach under two assumptions. First, the risk levels of the anticipated annual net cash inflow, as measured by the coefficients of variation, are more or less equal in magnitude. Second, the cash-flow stream is more or less uniform. Under these conditions the arithmetic average of the periodic coefficients of variation is a good estimate of the average risk level of the whole investment.

Rule 2: Determining the risk-adjusted rate. Given that the annual net cash inflows and their coefficients of variation are more or less constant, the risk-adjusted discounting rate is approximated by

$$r = \frac{i + \dfrac{bC}{nk}}{1 - bC}$$

where i is the cost of capital; b is the unit-risk premium factor; C is the average coefficient of variation, which equals the average of standard deviation divided by the expected value; n is the investment's life span; and $k \cong 0.67$, which is the add-on factor (rule 2, chapter 2) for n and r.[1] For approximation, use $k = 0.67$; for a more accurate result recalculate, using k for the resultant r.

Example. Consider an investment proposal with a life span of 12 years ($n = 12$). The unit risk premium is 20 percent ($b = 0.20$); the cost of capital is 10 percent ($i = 0.10$); and the average coefficient of variation is one ($C = 1$).

Solution: The risk-adjusted discounting rate is approximately

$$\frac{0.10 + \dfrac{0.20 \times 1}{12 \times 0.67}}{1 - (0.20 \times 1)} = 0.1561 = 15.61\%$$

The value of k for $r = 0.1561$ is about 0.678 (see appendix B), which is very close to the 0.67 used in the previous example. Thus, there is no need to recalculate the risk-adjusted rate, using the new value of k.

Rule 3: Risk-adjusted rate for one-period investment. Given the relation between the cost of capital and the risk-adjusted discounting rate, the risk-adjusted rate for a one-period investment ($n = 1$, hence, $k = 1$ as shown in rule 2, chapter 2), is approximated by

$$\frac{i + bC}{1 - bC}$$

Example. Consider the data in the previous example, but with $n = 1$ and $C = 0.2$. Then, the risk-adjusted discounting rate is approximately

$$\frac{0.10 + 0.20 \times 0.2}{1 - (0.20 \times 0.2)} = 0.146 = 14.6\%$$

Rule 4: Risk-adjusted rate for perpetuity investment. Using the relation between the cost of capital and the risk-adjusted rate for depreciable assets (rule 2) and setting n very large, the risk-adjusted rate for perpetuity investment is approximated by

$$\frac{i}{1 - bC}$$

Example. Consider the data in the example for rule 2, but with $n = \infty$. Then, the risk-adjusted discounting rate is approximately

$$\frac{0.10}{1 - (0.20 \times 1)} = 0.125 = 12.5\%$$

Rule 5: Effect of life span on risk-adjusted rate. For a given unit risk-premium coefficient, and given that the coefficient of variation is constant over time, the longer the life span of the investment, the lower the risk-adjusted discounting rate. This outcome can be seen in the second and fourth examples. In practice, however, the assumption of a constant coefficient of variation does not hold. Usually, the coefficient of variation is expected to be larger the longer the investment's life span because the farther we look into the future, the greater our level of ignorance.

Rule 6: Investment evaluation with risk-adjusted discounting rate. Investments can be evaluated by using risk-adjusted discounting rate, following three steps:

1. Estimate the coefficient of variation for each year, by dividing the standard deviation by the expected net cash inflow (rule 10, chapter 3).
2. Calculate the risk-adjusted rate, using the average coefficient of variation (rule 2).
3. Calculate the present value of the investment, using the risk-adjusted discounting rate.

This procedure will provide similar results to those arrived at using the risk-adjusted cash flow (rule 1), given that the annual cash flow and coefficients of variation are more or less uniform.

Example. Consider the first example, where the investor's unit risk premium is 0.364, and the after-tax cost of capital is 10 percent.
Solution: The coefficients of variation (using data from table 6–1) are

Year 1: $$\frac{S_1}{F_1} = \frac{15.00}{70} = 0.21$$

Year 2: $$\frac{S_2}{F_2} = \frac{17.50}{80} = 0.22$$

where S_1, S_2 are standard deviations in years 1 and 2, and F_1, F_2 are expected cash flows in years 1 and 2.
The average coefficient of variation is

$$(0.21 + 0.22) \div 2 = 0.215$$

The risk-adjusted discounting rate is approximately (rule 2).

$$\frac{0.10 + \dfrac{0.364 \times 0.215}{2 \times 0.67}}{1 - (0.364 \times 0.215)} = 0.1719 = 17.19\%$$

The resultant risk-adjusted rate is used for discounting the net cash inflow (data from table 5–3). The present value is

$$\frac{62}{1 + 0.1719} + \frac{68}{(1 + 0.1719)^2} = \$102.42$$

This is the certainty-equivalent net cash inflow,which is very close to that arrived at in the example for rule 1, because the coefficients of variation in both years do not differ considerably.

Rule 7: Comparing risk-adjusted rate with rate of return. The risk-adjusted discounting rate may also be used as a standard against which to judge the internal rate of return of the investment (calculated using the expected value of the cash flow as shown in chapter 5). If the internal rate is higher than the risk-adjusted rate, the investment is profitable, taking into account the disutility of risk.

Example. Consider the previous example and the data in table 5–3, where the net cash inflow is \$62 and \$68 in years 1 and 2, respectively.
Solution: The internal rate of return is computed to be 19.1 percent. The risk-adjusted rate was computed to be 17.19 percent. Because the latter rate is lower than the former, the investment is profitable, taking into account the disutility of risk.

Sensitivity Analysis

When several investments are undertaken by the company in the natural course of its current operations, the probability of failure because of the adverse outcome of one investment is small. The utility approach (certainty-equivalent cash flow or risk-adjusted discounting rate) is adequate for correct decisions under uncertainty conditions. However, when the proposed investment is sizeable relative to the total operation of the company, all the possible adverse outcomes and their probability of occurrence should be duly studied, even though the utility approach indicates high profitability.

Sensitivity analysis is a procedure for providing answers to the question "what if?" For example, what would be the present value of a proposed investment if the net cash inflow is reduced? Sensitivity analysis investigates the effect of a change in a given factor (present value, annual net income, rate of return) on the final outcome, while holding the other factors at a constant level. Special attention should be given to those factors which most affect the final results.

The sensitivity of the final outcome can be studied by simulation. Simulation is the systematic calculation of the outcomes under alternative assumptions regarding sales, prices, costs, and their probabilities. The outcomes of the simulation are then distributed to show the probability of occurrence of each outcome. This process is usually done by computing the average and the standard deviation of the simulated outcomes. The areas under the normal table or the empirical distribution curve (see rules 12–15, chapter 3) are used to find the probability of occurrence of each outcome The disadvantage of this appraoch is that management has no way to check the final outcomes because the final outcome of the simulation is a result of many factors, each one described by an hypothesized probability distribution.

Sensitivity to Overall Risk

Conventional sensitivity analysis is carried out by investigating the effect of various factors on the final outcome. Alternatively, the sensitivity of the returns of a proposed investment can be analyzed with respect to the overall risk. The sensitivity can be inferred directly from the certainty-equivalent analysis by calculating the standard deviation of the investment's expected present value. This procedure is efficient, because it is simple to apply, and effective, because it measures the degree of sensitivity of the final outcome to the overall risk through a procedure that can be comprehended by management.

Rule 8: Measuring the risk level. An investment's risk is measured by the standard deviation of the expected present value of the anticipated cash flow.

The standard deviation of a proposed investment is calculated by

$$\frac{\text{Investment-risk premium}}{\text{Investor's unit-risk premium}}$$

where the investment-risk premium is the difference between the present value of the expected cash flow and that of the certainty equivalent. Investor's unit-risk premium is determined by rule 5 in chapter 18.

Example. Consider the first example, where the present value of the risk premium is \$10.22 and the investor unit risk premium is 0.364.

Solution: The standard deviation of the investment is

$$\frac{10.22}{0.364} = \$28.08$$

Rule 9: Determining the sensitivity to risk. The sensitivity of the returns from a proposed investment to the overall risk is measured by the probabilities of receiving various levels of return (gains). The probabilities of various levels of net present values from a proposed investment are derived as follows:

1. Calculate the expected net present value (ENPV) by subtracting the cost of investment from the present value of the average net cash inflow (rule 11, chapter 5).
2. Calculate the standard deviation (S) of the investment as shown in rule 8.
3. Determine a short series of levels of possible outcomes of net present values (NPV) below the ENPV, to be checked for sensitivity, such as one-half of the ENPV, zero, loss at one-half of the ENPV, and calculate

$$\text{ENPV} - \text{NPV}$$

4. Calculate the level (z) of each of the values in the previous steps in terms of standard deviations by

$$z = \frac{\text{ENPV} - \text{NPV}}{S}$$

5. Use the resultant z's to find the probabilities of occurrence by inspecting the first two columns in table 6–2.
6. Record the pairs of figures in a sensitivity table.

Example: Investment evaluation. An investment that cost $100,000 yields present value of the average net cash inflow of $112,530 and present value of the certainty equivalent net cash inflow of $102,310. The unit-risk premium is 0.364. Because the investment is considered to be very large, a sensitivity to risk is carried out.

Solution:

1. The expected net present value is

$$112{,}530 - 100{,}000 = \$12{,}530$$

2. The standard deviation is

Table 6–2
Probabilities and Loss Integral: Normal Distribution

Number of Standard Deviations below the Average (z)	*Percentage of Probability* $F(z)$	*Percentage of Unit-Normal Loss Integral* $N(z)$
0.0	50.0	39.9
0.2	42.1	30.7
0.4	34.5	23.0
0.6	27.4	16.9
0.8	21.2	12.0
1.0	15.9	8.3
1.2	11.5	5.6
1.4	8.1	3.7
1.6	5.5	2.3

$$\frac{112{,}530 - 102{,}310}{0.364} = \frac{10{,}220}{0.364} = \$28{,}080$$

3. The series for possible outcome of net present values is $12,530, $6,250, $0, $−6,250.

4. These levels in terms of standard deviation are as follows:

NPV	z Values
$12,530	(12,530 − 12,530) / 28,080 = 0
6,250	(12,530 − 6,250) / 28.080 = 0.22
0	(12,530 − 0) / 28,080 = 0.45
− 6,250	[12,530 − (−6,250)] / 28,080 = 0.67

5. The resultant figures are used to find the probabilities of occurrence in table 6–2. For the first outcome ($z = 0$) the probability is 50 percent; for the second outcome ($z = 0.22$) the probability is about 41 percent; and so on.

6. The sensitivity of the investment to risk is

Level of NPV	Probability (%)
$12,530	50
6,250	41
0	33
−6,250	26

Although the investment is found to be profitable (expected NPV of \$12,530, and certainty equivalent of \$2,310), there are significant probabilities for loss. For example, in the last line, the probability of losing \$6,250 or more is 26 percent.

Sensitivity to Marginal Changes

The previous risk analyses are carried out for a given life span and a given discounting rate. The sensitivity of the present value of the anticipated net cash inflow to marginal changes in these factors provides important information.[2]

Rule 10: Sensitivity to changes in life span. Given a uniform net cash inflow over the investment's life, a 1 percent change in the investment's life span will affect the present value of the net cash inflow in percentages by approximately

$$\frac{n}{FVA_{n,r}}$$

where n is the life span; and r is the discounting rate. $FVA_{n,r}$ is the future value factor for annuity for n and r (rule 5, chapter 2).

Example. The present value of the anticipated uniform net cash inflow from a proposed investment is \$1,000. The life span is 12 years and the discounting rate is 8 percent. You want to know the effect of a change of 10 percent in the investment life span.

Solution: The percentage change in the present value for a 1 percent change in the life span is approximately

$$\frac{12}{\mathrm{FVA}_{12,\,0.08}} = \frac{12}{18.977} = 0.63\%$$

A 10 percent decrease in the life span will reduce the present value by approximately 6.3 percent; that is, from \$1,000 to about \$937, and vice versa.

Rule 11: Sensitivity to changes in discounting rate. Given a uniform net cash inflow over the investment life, a 1 percent decrease in the discounting rate that has been used will increase the present value of the net cash inflow by approximately 0.5 percent. A more accurate result in percentages is given by

$$1 - \frac{n}{(1 + r)\, FVA_{n,r}}$$

The notations are explained in rule 10.

Example. Consider the previous example, but you want to know the effect of a 10 percent change in the discounting rate.
Solution: A 10 percent increase in the discounting rate will reduce the present value by approximately 5 percent; that is, from \$1,000 to about \$950, and vice versa.

The more accurate figure is

$$-10 \times \left[1 - \frac{12}{(1 + 0.08)18.977} \right] = -4.14\%$$

Cost of Failure

The cost of uncertainty is defined as the difference between the expected value and the certainty equivalent value. The latter is based on the investor's degree of risk aversion regarding all possible outcomes. In practice, cautious investors are not interested in all possible outcomes; to them the cost of uncertainty is the expected damage resulting from adverse outcomes; that is, the damage from receiving less than a minimum level of income. This attitude is of special importance when the proposed investment is sizeable relative to the investor's total operation. The minimum level is set by the investor according to his financial condition; it may be the ruin level, the breakeven level of the investment, or any other level.

Rule 12: Determining the probability of failure. The probability of failure is the probability of receiving net returns from a proposed investment that are below the failure level, as set by the minimum level of returns derived by the investor.

Given the present value of the average net cash inflow (that is, expected present value = EPV) and its corresponding certainty equivalent, the probability of failure is calculated as follows:

1. Calculate the level of failure (f) by deducting from the investment cost (A) the loss (L) that the investor can bear before failure, that is

$$f = A - L$$

2. Calculate the level of loss with respect to the expected present value (EPV), by deducting the level of failure (f) from the expected present value, that is,

$$\text{EPV} - f$$

3. Calculate the standard deviation of the investment (S) by dividing the total risk premium by the unit risk premium (rule 8).

4. Calculate the level of loss in terms of standard deviations (z) by dividing the result of step 2 by that of step 3, that is,

$$z = \frac{\text{EPV} - f}{S}$$

5. Use the resultant z to find the probability of occurrence by inspecting the first two columns in table 6–2.

Example. An investment that costs $1 million yields an expected present value of $1.1 million and a certainty equivalent of $1.05 million. The risk premium is thus $50,000 (1,100 − 1,050 million), which is 5 percent of the cost of investment. The investor's unit risk premium is 0.10.

The total loss the company can bear before failure is $0.3 million. Although the investment is found to be profitable, what is the probability of failure if this investment is undertaken?

Solution: Given that the investment cost $1. million, the level of returns before failure is

$$1.000 - 0.300 = \$0.700 \text{ million}$$

That is, the realized present value of the net cash inflow should not be lower than $0.7 million.

The level of loss is

$$1.100 - 0.700 = \$0.400 \text{ million}$$

The standard deviation is

$$\frac{1.100 - 1.050}{0.1} = \$0.500 \text{ million}$$

The level of loss in terms of standard deviations is

$$\frac{0.400}{0.500} = 0.8$$

Looking in table 6–2, the probability of receiving a level of 0.8 standard deviations below the average is 21.2 percent. Thus, if the investment is undertaken, the probability of failure will be 21.2 percent, which is quite high. Hence, management may reject this investment proposal, even though it could be profitable in the long run.

Expected Cost of Failure

The expected cost of failure is the sum of the differences between the minimum acceptable level of returns (failure level) and all the outcomes whose values are less than the failure level, that is

$$\sum (f - f_i)p_i$$

where f is the failure level, f_i is an outcome with a value below f, p_i is the probability of receiving the level f_i.

Suppose the investor can find an agency that insures him against the risk of receiving less than a minimum level of returns, called the failure level. In the previous example, this level was set at \$0.7 million. If the realized outcome happens to be less than the failure level, say \$0.6 million, then the agency will compensate him up to the failure level; that is, the investor will receive \$0.1 million. The sum that the investor is ready to pay for such insurance is the cost of uncertainty or the risk premium, which is equal to the expected cost of failure.

Rule 13: Calculating the cost of failure. Based on the normal distribution, the expected cost of failure is

$$NS \text{ in dollars}$$

where S is the standard deviation of the expected present value (rule 8) and N is the unit normal loss integral $= f(z) + zF(z)$. $f(z)$ and $F(z)$ are the ordinates and areas (probabilities) of the normal curve (see chapter 3). Values of N are listed in the right-hand column of table 6–2, under $N(z)$.

The expected cost of failure is computed as follows:

1. Set the failure level in terms of standard deviations below the average (z), that is

$$z = \frac{\text{EPV} - f}{S}$$

where EPV is the expected present value, which equals present value of average cash inflow; f is the failure level (rule 12); and S is the standard deviation of the expected present value (rule 8).

2. Use the resultant z to find the unit normal loss integral (N) by inspecting the first and last columns in table 6–2.

3. Multiply the resultant figure of step 2 by the standard deviation to arrive at the expected cost of failure, that is,

$$NS \text{ in dollars}$$

where N is the unit normal loss integral (table 6–2).

Example. Consider the previous example, where the failure level is \$0.7 million.

Solution: The failure level in terms of standard deviations below the average is

$$z = \frac{1.100 - 0.700}{0.500} = \frac{0.400}{0.500} = 0.8$$

In table 6–2, the unit normal loss integral (N) corresponding to 0.8 standard deviations below the average is 12 percent.
The total cost of failure is

$$0.12 \times 0.500 = \$0.060 \text{ million} = \$60{,}000$$

If the investor can find an agency that insures him against the risk of receiving less than his failure level (\$0.7 million), he should pay this agency \$60,000 as an insurance premium.

The expected cost of failure, as a percentage of the expected returns, in present value terms, is

$$0.060 / 1.100 = 0.0545 = 5.45\%$$

Rule 14: Approximating the cost of failure. The cost of failure can be approximated by

$0.7FS$ in dollars
$0.7FC$ in percentage of expected returns

where F is the probability of receiving not more than the failure level, S is the standard deviation, and C is the coefficient of variation.

Example. In the example for rule 12, where $F = 21.1$ percent, the cost of failure is approximately

$$0.7 \times 0.211 \times 0.500 = \$0.07385 \text{ million} = \$73{,}850$$

The accurate result in the previous example is $60,000.

Notes

1. This formula is derived by equating the present value of the expected cash flow, using the unknown discounting rate, to the present value of the certainty equivalent value, that is

$$\text{PV of certainty } (F_t) \text{ at } i = \text{PV of } F_t \text{ at } r$$

where PV is the present value, F_t is the expected cash inflow in year t, i is the after-tax cost of capital, and r is the risk-adjusted discounting rate and solving for r.

2. Based on W.D. Whisler, "Sensitivity of Rates of Return," *Journal of Finance* (March 1976), pp. 63–69.

7 Rate of Return and Cost of Capital

The cost of capital is an important concept in financial and investment management. It is used as a criterion for evaluation purposes, for determining the optimal mix of funds, and for evaluating the performance of existing assets and new investments.

Capital is a major factor in most production processes. As such it has a price and contributes to total revenue and profit. The price of capital is the average cost paid to suppliers of funds—that is, shareholders and creditors. Revenue is the average return on assets financed by the capital funds. However, unlike any other factor of production, where average cost need not be equal to average revenue, these two averages are equal in the case of capital. This anomaly results from the fact that shareholders are being paid the residue of capital revenue—that is, they are paid after the payments of interest on debts have been met. Thus the terms "rate of return on capital" and "cost of capital" are often used synonymously.

The rate of return on capital is derived from the financial statements; this rate is the actual (ex-post) cost of capital. It should be used for performance evaluation regarding the use of assets (invested capital). This rate is different from the cost of capital that should be used in capital budgeting (ex-ante), for discounting cash flows and evaluating new investments.

Inflation considerably affects the cost of capital of a company. The treatment of the effect of inflation on the cost of capital from the lender's and borrower's points of view is discussed in this chapter; the effect of equity erosion on the cost of capital is discussed in chapter 19.

Accounting-Derived Rates of Return

Financial information is often used for deriving actual (ex-post) rates of return on capital. There are many procedures for deriving the actual rate of return, depending on the items excluded or included in the numerator (such as returns or income) and the denominator (such as capital or assets). This section discusses two measures of the return on capital.

Rate of Return on Company's Market Value (ROR)

A company's actual (ex-post) rate of return on capital (ROR, often called cost of capital) is the weighted average of the company's after-tax return on owners' equity and the interest on debt.

Rule 1: Determining ROR. The company's after-tax rate of return on capital (ROR) equals

$$\frac{\text{Net earning} + \text{interest}}{\text{Equity} + \text{debt}} = \frac{\text{EBIT} - \text{income tax}}{\text{Equity} + \text{debt}}$$

where EBIT is earnings before interest and tax, and equity is the market value of owners' equity.

The after-tax return on market value of equity is

$$\frac{\text{EBIT} - \text{interest} - \text{income tax}}{\text{Equity}}$$

Example. The following data are taken from a company's financial statements: Equity at market value, \$2,500; debt, \$1,500; EBIT, \$650; interest expenses, \$150; income tax, \$200.

Solution: The company's after-tax rate of return on capital is

$$\frac{650 - 200}{2{,}500 + 1{,}500} = 0.1125 = 11.25\%$$

The after-tax rate of return on equity is

$$\frac{650 - 150 - 200}{2{,}500} = 0.12 = 12\%$$

The pre-tax rate of return on capital is

$$650 / 4{,}000 = 0.1625 = 16.25\%$$

The average interest rate is

$$150 / 1{,}500 = 0.10 = 10\%$$

The average tax rate is

$$200 / 500 = 0.40$$

The financial leverage is

$$1{,}500 / 4{,}000 = 0.375$$

Rule 2: ROR during inflation. During inflation, EBIT used for calculating the return on capital should be computed on the basis of current prices; that is, after the depreciation expense and cost of materials have been revalued. The resultant rate of return thus derived is in real terms.

Rule 3: ROR as an indicator of risk. The company's rate of return is used to evaluate the company's risk by comparing its return to those of other companies. The higher the company's return compared to the returns of similar companies in the same line of business, the higher the risk class to which it belongs because the return is related to the market value of the company and not to the book value of the assets.

Rate of Return on Company's Assets (ROI)

The actual rate of return on assets (often called rate of return on investment or ROI) is the return on the book value of the assets.

Rule 4: Calculating ROI. The rate of return on the company's assets (ROI) is

$$\frac{\text{Returns}}{\text{Assets book value}}$$

The figures in this ratio may be calculated in various ways. Thus, the returns may include or exclude income tax and administration and selling expense. The assets book value may include or exclude working capital and unemployed assets.

Rule 5: ROI during inflation. During inflation the returns should be computed on the basis of current prices; that is, after the depreciation and the cost of materials have been revalued. The value of assets should also be revalued. The resultant rate of return thus derived is in real term.

Rule 6: ROI derived from financial ratios. The return on assets (ROI) is often measured by using two additional ratios, as follows:

$$\frac{\text{Sales}}{\text{Assets}} \times \frac{\text{Net earnings}}{\text{Sales}} = \frac{\text{Net earnings}}{\text{Assets}}$$

The first term is the so-called assets turnover; the second term is the so-called profit margin (see chapter 15).

Example. The following data are taken from a company's financial statement: sales, $150; assets book value, $100; net earnings, $12.
Solution: The return on assets is

$$\frac{150}{100} \times \frac{12}{150} = 0.12 = 12\%$$

Rule 7: Limitations of ROI for performance evaluation. ROI is often used to measure performance of company subunits (for example, divisions, departments, or production lines). Comparing this measure for different subunits has a drawback because it ignores the total return.

Example. Consider the following data:

	Department A	Department B
Rate of return	10%	6%
Assets book value	$10,000	$100,000
Total returns	1,000	6,000

The figures show that the performance of these departments cannot be evaluated by the criterion of the rate of return.

Using the return on assets as a measure of performance of a company's subunits will induce the respective managers to try to maximize the reported figure of the return on assets. These efforts may, however, be in an erroneous direction. For example, investment projects that yield a lower return on assets may be rejected even though they yield higher returns than the company's cost of capital. In addition, assets may not be replaced because returns are related to (divided by) the depreciated book value; the replacing assets, which are recorded at their acquisition cost, will reduce the average ratio of return on assets.

Required Rate of Return for Capital Budgeting

The cost of capital for purposes of decisions regarding capital budgeting (ex-ante) must represent the opportunity that the investor has for his capital. Having in mind a particular opportunity for investment, the investor sets a desired rate of return (cost of capital). This rate of return should be used for decisions regarding volume and mix of both investment and finance and for discounting cash flows.

Rule 8: The required rate of return under equity. Consider a case where the investor invests his equity capital. His objective is to receive a desired rate of return on his capital, assuming that only equity capital is invested.

The amount to be considered as return on the invested capital is the after-tax net income. This amount (rate) on \$1 of equity, is

$$i_e = r(1 - t)$$

where i_e is the desired rate of return on equity, after-tax; r is the rate of return on investment, before tax; and t is the income tax rate. This formula provides the basis for deriving the required rate of return on invested capital.

Rule 8A. Given the desired rate of return on equity, the required after-tax rate of return on investment to be used in capital budgeting is

$$r_t = i_e$$

where $r_t = r(1 - t)$, which is the after-tax rate of return on invested capital.

Rule 8B. Given the required after-tax rate of return on equity (i_e) the required pretax rate is

$$r = \frac{i_e}{1 - t}$$

Example. An investor sets his desired after-tax rate of return as 4 percent ($i_e = 0.04$). He does not employ debt, and his income tax rate is 50 percent.

Solution: The required pretax rate of return on the investment, which the investor wants to finance, is

$$\frac{0.04}{1 - 0.50} = 0.08 = 8\%$$

Rule 9: The required rate of return under leverage. Consider a company that borrows money and invests its equity and the borrowed funds. The company's objective is to pay the owners a desired rate of return on their equity. Alternatively stated, the company's cut-off rate on new investments is that rate that will keep net earnings per share from falling.

The amount to be paid to the owners on their equity is the after-tax net income. Given that the company employs financial leverage, the amount (rate) to be paid to the owners, per $1 of equity, is

$$i_e(1 - f) = (r - if)\,(1 - t)$$

where i_e is the desired rate of return on equity, after-tax; f is the financial leverage which is the proportion of debt to total capital; r is the rate of return on total invested capital, before tax; i is the interest rate on debt; and t is the income tax rate. This formula provides the basis for deriving the required rate of return on invested capital.

Rule 9A. Given the desired rate of return on equity, the required after-tax rate of return on total invested capital, to be used in capital budgeting, is

$$r_t = i_e(1 - f) + if(1 - t)$$

where $r_t = r(1 - t)$, which is the rate of return on total capital, after-tax.

Rule 9B. Given the previous rates on equity and debt, and the financial leverage, the required pretax rate of return on total invested capital is

$$r = \frac{i_e}{1 - t}(1 - f) + if$$

Example. A company sets its desired after-tax rate of return on equity to be 4 percent ($i_e = 0.04$). The borrowed funds comprise 40 percent of total capital, at 5 percent average interest rate. The income tax rate is 50 percent.

Solution: The required after-tax rate of return on total invested capital is

$$r_t = 0.04\,(1 - 0.40) + 0.05 \times 0.40\,(1 - 0.50) = 0.034 = 3.4\%$$

The required pretax rate of return on total invested capital is

$$r = \frac{0.04\ (1 - 0.40)}{1 - 0.50} + 0.05 \times 0.40 = 0.068 = 6.8\%$$

Alternatively, given $r = 0.068$, then

$$r_t = 0.068\ (1 - 0.50) = 0.034 = 3.4\%$$

Actual Versus Required Rates of Return

There is sometimes confusion between the actual rate of return on capital (ex-post), as derived from the financial statements (rule 1), and the required rate of return on investment (ex-ante), which should be used for capital budgeting (rules 8 and 9).

Actual Rate of Return

A company's actual after-tax rate of return on capital is measured by dividing the after-tax net earnings plus the interest expense by the total capital employed (equity at market value plus debt). The after-tax net earnings are allocated between dividends and retained earnings; that is, they are attributed to the owners' equity. Note that the owners will pay regular income tax on the dividends.

Rule 10: Calculating the actual ROR. The company's actual rate of return (ROR) on $1 of capital is

$$\bar{r}_t = i_e\ (1 - f) + if$$

where $\bar{r}_t$ is the actual rate of return on capital, after-tax; i_e is the rate of net earnings (dividends and retained earnings) on equity, after corporate tax; f is the financial leverage, which is the proportion of debt to total capital; $(1 - f)$ is the proportion of equity to total capital; i is the average interest rate on debt; and if is the total interest expense.

Example. Consider the data in the first example, where $i_e = 12$ percent, $f = 37.5$ percent, and $i = 10$ percent.
Solution: The company's actual after-tax rate of return is

$$0.12\ (1 - 0.375) + 0.10 \times 0.375 = 0.1125 = 11.25\%$$

Rule 11: Meaning of the actual ROR. The company's actual after-tax rate of return (ROR) is the weighted average of the after-tax return on owners' equity and the interest on debt (see the previous example).

Tax Saving (Tax Shield)

When a company finances part of its investments by loans, the total tax paid is lower than a similar situation where the investment is financed by 100 percent equity. The rate is lower because the interest payments are tax-deductible; that is, they are deductible from income before income tax is levied. The difference in tax saving between these two cases is added to the return on the investment. Hence, if the pretax rate of return on investment is equal in the two cases, the levaraged company will show a higher after-tax ROI.

Rule 12: Calculating the tax savings. Tax savings is the amount of tax that is not paid because the interest expenses are tax-deductible. The amount of tax savings on \$1 of investment, which is financed partially by loans, is

$$tif$$

where t is the income tax rate, i is the interest rate, and r is financial leverage.

Example. Consider a \$100 investment financed by 37.5 percent debt at 10 percent interest. The income tax is 40 percent.
Solution: The tax saving on this investment is

$$100 \times 0.40 \times 0.10 \times 0.375 = \$1.50$$

Rule 13: Divergence between actual and required rates. The divergence between the actual rate of return on capital (ex-post) and the required rate of return on investment (ex-ante) is the tax saving, that is

$$\text{Actual rate} = \text{Required rate} + \text{Tax saving}$$

To recapitulate, there are two formulations for after-tax rates of return. The actual rate of return on capital (rule 10) is

$$\bar{r}_t = i_e (1 - f) + if$$

The required rate of return on \$1 of investment (rule 9) is

$$r_t = i_e (1 - f) + if(1 - t)$$

where i_e is the rate of actual net earnings on equity, after tax, which equals the desired rate of return on equity, after-tax; f is the financial leverage, which equals proportion of debt to total capital; $(1 - f)$ is the proportion of equity to total capital; i is the interest rate on debt, average; and t is the income tax rate.

Example. Consider the following data derived from the financial statements of a company (the first example): $i_e = 12$ percent, $f = 37.5$ percent, $i = 10$ percent, and $t = 40$ percent. Assume that these figures are also applicable to a proposed investment. The desired after-tax rate of return on equity (i_e) is set at the same level as it actually was in the past—that is, $i_e = 12$ percent.
Solution: The company's actual rate of return on capital is

$$0.12\,(1 - 0.375) + 0.10 \times 0.375 = 0.1125 = 11.25\%$$

The required rate of return on the new investment is

$$0.12\,(1 - 0.375) + 0.10 \times 0.375\,(1 - 0.40) = 0.0975 = 9.75\%$$

The difference between these two rates is 1.5 percent, which is equal to the tax saving on the investment; that is

$$0.40 \times 0.10 \times 0.375 = 0.015 = 1.5\%$$

Cost of Capital and Financial Leverage

The company's cost of capital is determined by the desired rate of return on equity, the cost of debt, and its financial leverage (proportion of debt to total capital). The relationships among these variables, as shown by the last formula in rule 9, can be used to determine the required volume of debt or the maximum interest rate given the other parameters in the formula.

Two types of interrelated decisions are often made in regard to debt: the decision to borrow and the decision on the amount to be borrowed.

When raising new funds, it is profitable to take loans as long as the interest rate on the loan is lower than the company's cost of capital.

However, increasing the volume of debt raises the company's risk. Thus, the company sets a desired level of financial leverage, taking into account related aspects, as shown in the following analysis.

Loans can be taken for investment as long as their after-tax rate of interest is lower than the desired rate of return on equity. This rule will give an undetermined level of loans; that is, if it pays to take a loan then the rule leads you to the result that the whole investment should be financed by loans.

In practice, however, the investor sets a maximum level of financial leverage. Hence, the amount of the loan on new investments depends on the maximum level of leverage.

The level of financial leverage is determined by comparing the risk involved in taking an additional loan with the return from the loan (as long as the interest rate on the loan is lower than the company's cost of capital).

Rule 14: Determining financial leverage. The minimum financial leverage (f) to break even on new investment, given the interest on the new loan (i), the desired rate of return on equity (i_e), and the expected return on the investment (r) is

$$f \geq \frac{i_e - r(1 - t)}{i_e - i(1 - t)}$$

This formula is derived from the last formula in rule 9. When the numerator is negative, the denominator is also negative.

Example. Consider the following data: $i_e = 12$ percent, $r = 20$ percent, $t = 50$ percent, and $i = 7$ percent.
Solution: The minimum financial leverage to break even on additional investment is

$$\frac{0.12 - 0.20(1 - 0.50)}{0.12 - 0.07(1 - 0.50)} = 0.235 = 23.5\%$$

Rule 15: Determining the maximum interest rate. The maximum interest rate (i) that can be paid on a loan to finance a new investment that satisfies the maximum level of leverage (f), the desired rate of return on equity (i_e), and the expected return on the investment (r), is

$$i \leq \frac{r(1 - t) - i_e(1 - f)}{f(1 - t)}$$

where i is the interest on additional loan; r is the pretax rate of return on total investment; i_e is the desired rate of return on equity, after-tax; f is the proportion of debt to total capital, as determined by the company; and t is the income tax rate. This formula is derived from the last formula in rule 9.

Example. Consider the following data: $i_e = 12$ percent, $r = 20$ percent, $t = 50$ percent, and $f = 40$ percent.
Solution: The interest on additional loans should be less than

$$\frac{0.20(1-0.50)-0.12(1-0.40)}{0.40(1-0.50)} = 0.14 = 14\%$$

Lenders' Cost of Capital during Inflation

During inflation, the purchasing power of money declines. To prevent loaned capital from deteriorating, the actual returns must provide inflation-compensation to the principal capital. This rule implies that during inflation the required rate of return should provide both return on principal in real (preinflation) terms and inflation-compensation to maintain the real value of the loaned capital.

Income tax authorities treat the inflation-compensation of equity capital as regular income. Thus, to maintain the real value of equity, the pretax return on total loaned capital should be high enough to cover income tax, preinflation return on equity, and inflation-compensation.

Funds that the lender borrows are treated differently, because he does not have to maintain the real value of the debt that he utilizes. The interest that the lender pays includes inflation-compensation to the debt capital, which is a tax-deductible cost.

Because loaned capital is stated in nominal prices, the required rate of return on capital should also be stated in terms of nominal prices. The resulting rates of return (cost of capital) should be used to set the rates on loaned capital and to discount cash flows.

Rule 16: Lender's required rate of return under equity. Consider a case where a lender lends his equity capital. His objective is to keep net earnings during inflation at the preinflation rate.

Rule 16A. Given the preinflation desired rate of return on equity, the inflation-compensated rate of return, per \$1 of equity, is

$$i_{e,p} = (1 + i_e)(1 + p) - 1 = i_e(1 + p) + p$$

where $i_{e,p}$ is the inflation-compensated desired rate of return on equity, after-tax, in nominal terms; i_e is the preinflation desired rate of return on equity, after-tax; and p is the inflation rate.

Rule 16B. Given the inflation-compensated rate, the required after-tax rate of return on the loaned equity capital is

$$r_t = i_{e,p}$$

where $r_t = r(1 - t)$, which is the after-tax rate of return on loaned equity in nominal terms.

If the actual returns are lower than r_t, the real return on the lender's equity will drop below the preinflation rate.

Rule 16C. Given the required after-tax rate of return on equity, the required nominal pre-tax rate is

$$r = \frac{i_{e,p}}{1 - t}$$

Some illustrative rates for various levels of the variables are presented in table 7–1. The high rates result from the fact that income tax is levied on returns that are meant to maintain the real value of the loaned equity.

Example A. An investor requires that the preinflation after-tax return on his equity be 4 percent. His income tax rate is 50 percent, and the inflation rate is 18 percent.
Solution: The desired real rate of return on equity is

$$i_{e,p} = (1 + 0.04)(1 + 0.18) - 1 = 0.2272 = 22.72\%$$

The nominal pretax rate of return, which the loaned equity should yield, is

$$r = \frac{0.2272}{1 - 0.50} = 0.4544 = 45.44\%$$

This result can be found in table 7–1.

Example B. Consider the investor in example A, but assume that he requires only that his equity capital maintain its real value, without earning

Table 7–1
Nominal Pretax Required Rates of Return on Loaned Equity (r)

Tax Rate (t)	*0.35*	*0.50*	*0.35*	*0.50*
	Desired Real Return on Equity ($i_{e,p}$)			
Inflation Rate (p)	*0*		*0.04*	
0.06	0.092	0.120	0.158	0.205
0.12	0.185	0.240	0.254	0.330
0.18	0.277	0.360	0.350	0.454
0.24	0.369	0.480	0.446	0.579

any real return; then the nominal pretax rate of return on the investment should be

$$\frac{0.18}{1-0.50} = 36\%$$

Lender's Required Rate of Return under Leverage

Consider a case where the lender (a bank) borrows money (such as deposits or bonds) and lends both its equity and the borrowed funds. The lender's objective is to keep the net earnings on the equity during inflation at the preinflation rate.

Rule 17: Determining the lender's after-tax required rate of return. Given the preinflation desired rate of return on the lender's equity, the required after-tax rate of return on total loaned capital, per $1 of loan, is

$$r_t = i_{e,p}\,(1-f) + if(1-t)$$

where $r_t = r(1-t)$, which is the after-tax inflation-compensated rate of return on loaned capital, in nominal terms; $i_{e,p}$ is the inflation-compensated desired rate of return on equity, after-tax (rule 16); f is the proportion of lender's borrowed funds to total capital; i is the nominal rate of interest on lender's borrowed funds; and t is the income tax rate. If the actual returns are lower than r_t, the real return on the bank's equity will drop below the preinflation rate.

Example. Consider the investor in example A for rule 16 but assume that he finances 40 percent of the loaned capital by debt at 20 percent interest.
Solution: The required after-tax rate of return on total loaned capital is

$$r_t = 0.2272(1 - 0.40) + 0.20 \times 0.40(1 - 0.50) = 0.1763 = 17.63\%$$

The required rate here is lower than that under total equity (22.72 percent in example A for rule 16) because the interest rate on the debt is lower (20 percent).

Rule 18: Determining the lender's required interest rate. Given the required after-tax rate of return on the lender's total capital, the required pretax rate to charge his customers is

$$r = \frac{i_{e,p}}{1 - t}(1 - f) + if$$

Some illustrative rates, for various levels of the variables, are presented in table 7–2.

Example. A lending institution requires a preinflation after-tax return on owner's equity to be 4 percent. The borrowed funds comprise 40 percent of total capital, at 20 percent average interest rate. The income tax rate is 50 percent and the inflation rate is 18 percent.
Solution: The desired rate of return on equity is

$$i_{e,p} = (1 + 0.04)(1 + 0.18) - 1 = 0.2272 = 22.72\%$$

The nominal after-tax rate of return, which the loaned capital should yield, is

$$r_t = 0.2272(1 - 0.40) + 0.20 \times 0.40(1 - 0.5) = 0.1763 = 17.63\%$$

The pretax rate is

$$r = \frac{0.2272}{1 - 0.50}(1 - 0.40) + 0.20 \times 0.40 = \frac{0.1763}{1 - 0.50} = 0.3526 = 35.26\%$$

This rate is the interest rate that the institution should charge for the capital that it lends to provide the 4 percent real return on its equity.

Table 7–2
Nominal Pretax Required Rates of Return on Loaned Capital (r)[a]

Interest Rate (i)	*0.10*	*0.20*	*0.30*	*0.10*	*0.20*	*0.30*
			Tax Rate (t)			
Inflation Rate (p)		*0.35*			*0.50*	
0.06	0.135	0.175	0.215	0.163	0.203	0.243
0.12	0.192	0.232	0.272	0.238	0.278	0.318
0.18	0.250	0.290	0.330	0.313	0.353	0.393
0.24	0.307	0.347	0.387	0.388	0.428	0.468

[a]Given the desired real return on equity ($i_{e,p}$) of 4 percent, and financial leverage (f) of 40 percent.

Suppose the institution lends \$100 and charges \$35.26 as interest. The returns are

Gross return	\$35.26
Interest, 20% on \$40	8.00
Net income, before tax	27.26
Income tax, 50%	13.63
Net income	13.63

The net income equals the required return on the \$60 equity, that is,

$$60[(1 + 0.04)(1 + 0.18) - 1] = \$13.63$$

The resultant rates here (17.63 percent and 35.26 percent) are lower than those for the case of 100 percent equity (22.72 percent and 45.44 percent in example A), because the institution borrowed money at a lower rate (in real, after-tax terms) than the required rate of return on equity.

Rule 19: Lender's marginal markup. On the margin, the cost of the lender's funds is more or less equal to the desired rate of return on his equity. The required markup on his cost of capital ($i_{e,p}$) is

$$\left(f + \frac{1-f}{1-t}\right) - 1$$

Example. A lender's financial leverage is 90 percent ($f = 0.90$) and his income tax is 50 percent ($t = 0.50$).
Solution: The required markup is

$$\left(0.90 + \frac{1 - 0.90}{1 - 0.50}\right) - 1 = 0.10 = 10\%$$

If his after-tax cost of capital is 20 percent, the minimum rate of interest to charge his customers is 20 percent plus 10 percent markup; that is

$$0.20\,(1 + 0.10) = 0.22 = 22\%$$

Rule 20: Uses of lender's cost of capital. The pretax rate of return on total capital (rule 18) should be used for setting the lending rate. The pretax and after-tax rates (rules 18 and 17) should be used for discounting cash flows (pretax and after-tax, respectively), given that the various variables are anticipated to remain at the same level of magnitude in the future.

Part III
Assets Accounting and Analysis

8 Single Assets Valuation and Accounting

Interest and depreciation constitute the costs of holding assets and inventory. These costs depend on the value of the assets and the method of accounting. Understanding the proper procedures for determining assets and inventory values is important to various aspects of financial management.

The choice of the accounting method for depreciation and inventory valuation affects both the value of assets as recorded in the balance sheet and the level of expenses as recorded in the income statement or in the cost statement (chapter 12). Thus, the choice of accounting method has implications for costing, pricing, taxation, and financial statement analysis. The use of the present value of a depreciation-expense flow (schedule) simplifies the analysis of the effect of income tax on investment evaluation.

Valuation of Fixed Assets

Calculation of an asset's value may be required for various purposes, such as measuring returns on investment, decisions regarding purchase or sale of assets, determining the appropriate financial leverage, and costing the asset's services.

Assets Valuation Procedures

Each of the various valuation procedures is applicable for a different purpose. The valuation procedures in this section are for a noninflationary situation.

Rule 1: Accounting valuation. According to the accounting discipline, the value of an asset is the historical acquisition cost minus the accumulated depreciation expenses. Thus, the book or depreciated value is the accounting value. This value is affected by the method of depreciation that is used (see table 8–1) and by the expected life span of the asset.

Rule 2: Economic valuation. According to the economic discipline, the value of an asset is determined by the present value of the future net receipts that the asset will generate. This value is affected by the estimates of the level and duration of the net receipts and by the discounting factor that is used.

Example. A given asset is expected to generate net receipts of $40 at the end of the first year and $30 at the end of the second year. The discounting factor is 15 percent per annum.

Solution: The economic value at date of valuation is

$$\frac{40}{(1+0.15)} + \frac{30}{(1+0.15)^2} = \$57.47$$

and at the beginning of the next year it is

$$\frac{30}{(1+0.15)} = \$26.09$$

Rule 3: Replacement-cost valuation. For a business to survive in the long run, the revenue from sales must cover the replacement of all inputs used in production, including replacement of the fixed assets. Therefore, the replacement cost should serve as a basis for costing and pricing the services of the assets. Replacement cost is the amount of money that would be needed to replace an existing asset with one that would produce the same quantity, quality, and cost of service. The replacement-cost value is determined by the present acquisition cost of an equal or similar asset and either equally depreciated or multiplied by the estimated service potential of the existing asset relative to the new one. This value is affected by the judgment of the appraiser. This method of valuation is appropriate for both non-inflationary and inflationary periods.

Example. The acquisition cost of an asset that can be substituted for the existing asset is $1,000. If the existing asset is half-depreciated, the replacement value is set at $500. However, if the service potential of the existing asset over its remaining life is estimated to be 70 percent, the replacement value is set at $700.

Rule 4: Market valuation. The market net realizable value is the amount that can be received from the sale of an asset, less the cost that would be incurred in selling it. This valuation method can be applied only to assets that are traded in the market—for example, liquid assets such as securities, land, livestock, or trucks.

Rule 5: Implications of the valuation methods. Comparing the values of a given fixed asset that are derived by various valuation procedures can provide interesting information.

1. If the economic value of an asset exceeds its acquisition cost, it is profitable to buy the asset. If the market (sale) value of an existing asset exceeds its economic value, it is profitable to sell the asset.

2. If the market value exceeds the book value, there would be a capital gain tax on the difference at the time the asset is sold. The real value of the asset is the after-tax value.

3. If the replacement value of an asset exceeds its inflation-adjusted book value, the asset has been overdepreciated. For example, a machine that has been completely depreciated but can still provide some service has a replacement value.

4. If the inflation-adjusted book value of an asset that is correctly depreciated exceeds its replacement value, the investment is not as effective as was originally planned when it was acquired, because of such factors as obsolescence or errors in planning.

Example. A machine with an inflation-adjusted book value of $800 can be replaced by a newly designed machine that costs $500. Given that the old machine is half-depreciated, its replacement value is estimated at $250. This value indicates that the old machine is obsolete.

Rule 6: Average value of a depreciable asset for costing. As a result of the annual depreciation charges, the book value of a given asset declines over time. For various purposes, the average value over the asset's whole life span is required, for example, to compute the returns on investment and to charge interest on the investment.

The average value of an asset computed over its life span is approximately two-thirds of its acquisition cost. The exact figure for a $1 investment is the interest add-on factor (rule 2, chapter 2). This rule is a better approximation than the average between the acquisition cost and the last year's book value.

Example. The annual return from a depreciable asset is $100. The acquisition cost was $1,000, and the life span is 5 years. The straight-line method of depreciation is used.
Solution: The average value of the investment is $670, and the average return is

$$\frac{100}{670} = 0.15 = 15\%$$

If the return on the book value was computed, then the return in the first year was 10 percent (100 / 1,000) and in the last year 50 percent (100 / 200).

Depreciation Methods

Because the asset is expected to serve many production periods, the acquisition cost is distributed over those periods in the form of depreciation expenses. There are many depreciation methods; the main ones are summarized in this section. The annual depreciation expenses and the resulting book values, under the various methods, are presented as factors on a $1 investment or on a $1 depreciable base.

Example. Consider an investment of $1,000 with a service life of 5 years and no salvage value. The annual depreciation expenses and the book values for each year, according to the various depreciation methods, are presented in table 8–1. The computations are explained in the text describing each method.

The Straight-Line Method (SL)

According to the straight-line method, the annual depreciation expenses are equal throughout the asset's life span.

Table 8–1
Depreciation and Book Value under Various Depreciation Methods
(Acquisition Value $1,000, No Salvage Value)

				DDB	
Year	*SL*	*SYD*	*DB*	*Regular*	*Switch*
Annual depreciation expenses, end of year					
1	$200.00	$333.30	$369.00	$400.00	$400.00
2	200.00	266.70	232.80	240.00	240.00
3	200.00	200.00	146.90	144.00	144.00
4	200.00	133.30	92.70	86.40	108.00
5	200.00	66.70	58.50	51.80	108.00
Salvage	0	0	100.10	77.80	0
	1,000.00	1,000.00	1,000.00	1,000.00	1,000.00
Book value, end of year					
0	$1,000.00	$1,000.00	$1,000.00	$1,000.00	$1,000.00
1	800.00	667.70	631.00	600.00	600.00
2	600.00	400.00	398.20	360.00	360.00
3	400.00	200.00	251.30	216.00	216.00
4	200.00	66.70	158.60	129.60	108.00
5	0	0	100.00	77.80	0

Note: SL = straight-line; SYD = sum-of-the-years' digits; DB = declining balance corresponding to 10 percent salvage; and DDB = double-declining balance.

Rule 7: Depreciation rate, SL. The annual depreciation rate on a $1 investment is

$$d = \frac{1}{n}$$

where d is the depreciation rate, applied to acquisition cost, and n is the asset's life span in years.

Example. In the previous example, the depreciation rate is

$$\frac{1}{5} = 20\%$$

The annual depreciation expense is

$$1{,}000 \times 0.2 = \$200$$

Rule 8: Book value, SL. The book value at the end of a given year is equal to the acquisition cost less the accumulated depreciation expenses; on a $1 investment, the book value is

$$B_t = \frac{n - t}{n}$$

where B_t is the book value at the end of year t, of $1 depreciable base.

Example. In the first example in this section, the book value at the end of year 4 is

$$1{,}000 \times \frac{5 - 4}{5} = \$200$$

Rule 9: Salvage value, SL. When there is a salvage value, it should first be deducted from the acquisition cost to find the depreciable base. Depreciation should be calculated on this base. The book value is the depreciated value (computed from the depreciable base) plus the salvage value.

The Sum of The Years' Digits (SYD) Method

According to the SYD method, the annual depreciation expenses are proportional to the remaining life span of the asset, and therefore, decline over time. The case of salvage follows rule 9.

Rule 10: Depreciation rate, SYD. The depreciation rate on a \$1 investment in a given year is

$$d_t = \frac{n - t + 1}{c}$$

where d_t is the depreciation rate in year t, applied to acquisition cost; c is $n(n + 1)/2$, and n is the asset's life span in years.

Example. In the first example in this section

$$c = \frac{5(5 + 1)}{2} = 15$$

The depreciation in year 4 is

$$1{,}000 \times \frac{5 - 4 + 1}{15} = \$133.30$$

Rule 11: Book value, SYD. The book value at the end of a given year, on a \$1 investment, is

$$B_t = \frac{(n - t)(n - t + 1)}{2c}$$

where B_t is the book value at the end of year t of \$1 depreciable base.

Example. In the first example in this section, the book value at the end of year 4 is

$$1{,}000 \times \frac{(5 - 4)(5 - 4 + 1)}{2 \times 15} = \$66.70$$

The Declining-Balance (DB) Method

According to the declining-balance method, the annual depreciation expense is a constant percentage of the book or depreciated value at the beginning of the year. Because the book value (the balance) is declining, the annual expenses decline over time.

Rule 12: Depreciation rate, DB. The declining-balance method implies an inherent salvage value, given by

$$s = (1 - d)^n$$

where d is the depreciation rate, constant for all years; s is the salvage value / acquisition cost; and n is the asset's life span in years. The depreciation rate is derived from this formula, that is,

$$d = 1 - \sqrt[n]{s}$$

Example. In the first example in this section, assuming that the salvage value is \$100, then

$$d = 1 - \sqrt[5]{\frac{100}{1,000}} = 0.369$$

Rule 13: DB depreciation rate in practice. For practical uses the depreciation rate is determined arbitrarily by

$$d = \frac{a}{n}$$

where a equals 2.00 under the 200 percent accelerated method, or double-declining balance; a equals 1.50 under the 150 percent accelerated method; and a equals 1.25 under the 125 percent accelerated method.
The case of double-declining balance is discussed in the following subsection. The other methods are applicable by changing the factor from 2 to 1.50, 1.25, or any other factor.

Rule 14: Switch-over, DB to SL. When there is no salvage value it is profitable to switch over to the straight-line method at a certain year. The date to switch over is when the straight-line depreciation for the remaining life of the asset would be higher than that determined by the corresponding declining method. The data for the switch-over is after the year:

$$\frac{n(a - 1)}{a}$$

Example. The date of switch-over from the 150 percent accelerated method to the straight-line method is at the year following

$$\frac{n(1.5 - 1.0)}{1.5} = \frac{n}{3}$$

That is, switch at the year following one-third of the life span.

The Double-Declining Balance (DDB) Method

According to the DDB method, which is also called the 200 percent accelerated method, the annual depreciation expense is a constant rate (percentage) which equals twice the straight-line rate applied to the book value at the beginning of the year. given that the straight-line depreciation rate is $1 / n$, the DDB rate is $2 / n$. This rate is applied every year to the book value to determine the depreciation expense.

Rule 15: Depreciation rate, DDB. The depreciation rate on a $1 book value in a given year is

$$d_t = \frac{2}{n}(B_{t-1})$$

where d_t is the depreciation rate in year t, B_{t-1} is the book value at the beginning of year t, n is the asset's life span in years.

Example. In the first example in this section, the depreciation expense in year 1 is

$$d_1 = \frac{2}{5} \times 1{,}000 = \$400$$

The depreciation expense in year 4 is

$$d_4 = \frac{2}{5} \times 216 = \$86.40$$

(The value 216 is taken from table 8–1 for end of year 3 or from the following example).

Rule 16: Book value, DDB. The book value at the end of a given year on a $1 investment is

$$B_t = \left(1 - \frac{2}{n}\right)^t$$

where B_t is the book value at end of year t.

Example. In the first example in this section, the book value at the end of year 3 is

$$1{,}000 \times \left(1 - \frac{2}{5}\right)^3 = \$216$$

Rule 17: Switch-over, DDB to SL. The date for switch-over from the DDB to straight-line is at the year following half the useful life; that is

$$\frac{n(2 - 1)}{2} = \frac{n}{2}$$

Example. In the first example in this section, the switch-over is after the third year. The new annual depreciation rate for the remaining 2 years is

$$\frac{\text{Book value at end of 3 years}}{2} = \frac{216}{2} = \$108$$

Rule 18: Depreciation expense, DDB. The depreciation expense in any year is $(1 - d)$ of the last year's depreciation (where d = depreciation rate = $2/n$)

Example. Last year's depreciation on a given asset amounted to $1,000; the depreciation rate is two-fifths = 0.40.
Solution: The depreciation in the present year is

$$1{,}000\ (1 - 0.40) = \$600$$

Rule 19: The double straight-line method (DSL). This method splits the life span into two periods, each of which is depreciated according to the straight-line method. In the first half of the life of the asset, depreciate at the rate of four-thirds the straight-line rate; in the second half, depreciate at the rate of two-thirds the straight-line rate. The rate is applied to the acquisition cost. This method is a good approximation of the DDB method.

Example. An asset's acquisition cost is \$1,000 and the life span is 10 years.
Solution: In the first 5 years the annual depreciation rate is

$$\frac{4/3}{10} = 0.1333 = 13.33\%$$

and the depreciation expense is

$$1{,}000 \times 0.1333 = \$133$$

In the last 5 years, the annual depreciation rate is 6.67 percent.

Rule 20: Salvage value, DSL. When the asset has a salvage value, the annual depreciation in the first half of its life is not affected; in the second half of its life the annual depreciation rate is

$$\frac{2/3}{n} - \frac{s}{0.5n}$$

where s is the salvage rate, which is the salvage value / acquisition cost.

Example. Suppose the salvage value is 10 percent of the acquisition cost.
Solution: The depreciation rate in the second half of its life is

$$\frac{2/3}{10} - \frac{0.10}{0.5 \times 10} = 0.0467 = 4.67\%$$

Implications of Depreciation Methods

The choice of the depreciation method to be used affects the level of the annual expenses and the level of the asset's book value. The choice affects, therefore, the reported financial statements; as discussed later in this chapter, it has income tax implications and affects the costing of the asset's service. From the economic point of view, depreciation is the annual decrease in the value of the asset.

Rule 21: Depreciation according to economic valuation. The economic value of an asset is determined by the series of future net receipts which the asset will generate (rule 2). From one accounting year to the next, this series of net receipts is shortened by one year, hence the economic value decreases. The decrease in the economic value determines the true depreciation.

Example. Consider the first example in this chapter, where the economic values are

At date of valuation	\$57.47
At the beginning of next year	26.09

The depreciation in the first year is the difference between these values, that is, \$31.38.

Rule 22: Depreciation according to market valuation. The correct annual depreciation expense for a liquid asset (that is, an asset which can be traded in an active market) is the difference in the market value of the asset at the beginning and end of the year, given that the values are stated in constant prices.

Rule 23: Effect of accelerated depreciation on balance sheet. Under accelerated depreciation, the book value of a single asset is lower than under the straight-line method. (This does not hold for a stock of assets the age of which is evenly distributed; see chapter 9.) When the value of a single asset provides a large share of the total value of all the company's assets (for example, a new plant), the choice of an accelerated depreciation method would affect the level of the total value as recorded in the balance sheet. In this case, the total value may be understated and thus affect the results of the various uses of these data, such as in calculating financial ratios.

Rule 24: Choosing the appropriate depreciation method. For information about the desired depreciation policy for a given type of asset, compare its market price with the depreciated value calculated according to various methods. The book values for various life spans are summarized in table 8–2.

Example. The life span of a truck is 10 years and its market value after 3 years is 50 percent of the acquisition cost.
Solution: The time elapsed is $3/10 = 0.3 = 30$ percent. At the 30 percent level in the first column of table 8–2, the column for the SYD shows 49 percent. Because this level is close to the 50 percent market value, the SYD method is the best depreciation method. The DDB is also a good method, as it shows 55 percent.

Table 8–2
Book Value as a Percentage of Acquisition Cost

	Depreciation Method				
			Declining Balance		
Time Elapsed (Percentage of n)	*SL*	*SYD*	*150%*	*200%*	*DDB, 200% with Switch*
10	90%	81%	86%	82%	82%
20	80	64	74	67	67
30	70	49	64	55	55
40	60	36	55	45	45
50	50	25	47	36	36
60	40	16	40	30	29
70	30	9	35	24	22
80	20	4	30	20	15
90	10	1	26	16	8
100	0	0	22	13	0

Note: SL = straight line; SYD = sum of the years' digits; DDB = double declining balance; and n = life span.

Rule 25: Examining the suitability of depreciation method. For information about the suitability of the depreciation method used by a company, compute the following rate for the various assets for which there is an active market:

$$\frac{\text{Market value}}{\text{Book value}}$$

Both figures should be stated in terms of the same price level.

If the resulting ratio differs from one, the depreciation method which is used does not represent the correct value of the asset.

Example. A machine was acquired 2 years ago for $1,000. Its life span is 10 years with no salvage value. The machine is straight-line depreciated. Its market value at present is 60 percent of its original value.
Solution: The book value of the machine is $800 and the market value is $600. Thus, the ratio is

$$\frac{600}{800} = 0.75$$

The low ratio implies that the depreciation method is not adequate; an accelerated depreciation method is better in this case.

Depreciation and Interest Charges for Costing

Costing the asset's services implies charging direct costs (such as maintenance, repairs, or insurance) and imputed capital charges (such as depreciation and interest as a cost of capital). The capital charges are determined as standards that should be charged to the users of the asset service (chapter 13).

For a stock of assets that includes assets of all ages, the depreciation method does not affect the total annual charges (chapter 9). But if a given asset provides the service, the depreciation method affects considerably the annual charges.

Rule 26: Capital charges under constant service. When the service of an asset remains more or less constant over its life span, the annual capital charges for costing purposes should be equal as well.

The standard for the annual capital charge for costing the service of an asset, on \$1 of investment, should be the straight-line depreciation plus the average interest on asset value; that is, the capital recovery factor (rule 1, chapter 2) which is approximated by

$$\frac{1}{n} + 0.67i$$

where n is the asset life span, 0.67 is the interest add-on factor (rule 2, chapter 2), and i is the rate of interest or cost of capital.

Example. the acquisition cost of a machine was \$1,000; it will serve for 5 years. The salvage value is zero. The annual cost of capital is 10 percent. Solution: The standard for the annual charge for the service of the machine, in addition to the direct costs, should be

$$1{,}000 \left(\frac{1}{5} + 0.67 \times 0.10 \right) = \$267$$

Rule 27: Capital charges under increasing costs. When the service costs of an asset increase over time (for example, as a result of increased maintenance), it is common to use an accelerated depreciation method.

Rule 27A. When there are several units of the same type, the ages of which are evenly distributed, and the service of each declines over time, the use of the last rule—the capital recovery factor—still holds.

Rule 27B. The annual capital charge for an asset whose service declines over time is calculated by using an accelerated depreciation and an average interest charge. For the SYD depreciation method (rule 10), this charge in a given year, on a \$1 investment, is

$$d_t + ki - \left(\frac{2k}{n+1} - \frac{1}{n}\right)$$

where d_t is the depreciation rate in year t and $k \cong 0.67$, which is the interest add-on factor (rule 2, chapter 2).

Example. Consider the example under rule 10, where the depreciation in year 4 is \$133.30, for a \$1,000 asset (that is, $d = 0.1333$), with a life span of 5 years.
Solution: The total capital charges for year 4 are

$$1{,}000\left[0.1333 + 0.67 \times 0.10 - \left(\frac{2 \times 0.67}{5+1} - \frac{1}{5}\right)\right] = \$176.97$$

Rule 28: Capital charges under decreasing output. When the service of an asset declines over time as a result of decreased output, use the capital recovery factor (rule 26) and divide by the level of output.

Example. Consider the example under rule 26 for the even service over time, where the annual capital charge is \$267. Suppose the output in year 2 is 1,000 units and in year 3 is 500 units.
Solution: The per unit capital charges are

Year 2:	267 / 1,000 = \$0.27
Year 3:	267 / 500 = \$0.53

Present Value (PV) of Depreciation Schedules

The present value of the future annual depreciation expenses (the depreciation schedule) should be used to compare the various depreciation methods. The higher the present value, the better the method for tax purposes. The present value of the appropriate depreciation method is used in investment evaluation (rule 29, chapter 5).

For every depreciation method there is a formula to provide the present-value factor of the depreciation schedule for a \$1 investment.

Rule 29: PV of a depreciation schedule. The present value of a depreciation schedule is computed by discounting each anticipated depreciation expense by the corresponding discounting rate.

Example. The depreciation schedule of a \$100 machine with a life span of 2 years is: year 1, \$50; year 2, \$50. The discounting rate is 10 percent. Solution: The present value of the depreciation schedule is

$$\frac{50}{(1+0.10)^1}+\frac{50}{(1+0.10)^2}=\$86.78$$

Rule 30: PV of straight line. The present value of the future annual depreciation expenses on a \$1 investment is approximated by

$$\frac{1}{1+knr}$$

where $k \cong 0.67$, which is the interest add-on factor (rule 2, chapter 2); n is the life span, and r is the investor's discounting rate. The exact formula is

$$PVA/n$$

where PVA is the present value factor of annuity (rule 7, chapter 2).

When there is a salvage value, multiply the formula by

$$(1-s), \text{ and add } s/(1+r)^n$$

where s is the salvage rate, which is determined by salvage value / acquisition cost.

Example. Consider an investment of \$100 with a life span of 5 years, without a salvage value. The investor's discounting rate is 10 percent. Solution: The present value of the depreciation schedule is approximately

$$100 \times \frac{1}{1+(0.67\times 5\times 0.10)}=\$74.91$$

The exact figure is \$75.82.

Rule 31: PV of sum-of-the-years' digits. The present value of the future annual depreciation expenses on a \$1 investment is

$$(PVA)\frac{2k}{n+1}$$

An alternative formula is

$$\frac{n - PVA}{rc}$$

where c equals $n(n+1)/2$. When there is a salvage value, multiply the above formula by

$$(1 - s), \text{ and add } s/(1+r)^n$$

where s is the salvage value / acquisition cost.

Example. Consider the previous example, where the investment is \$100, $n = 5$, and $r = 0.10$, and assume the SYD is used.
Solution: The present value of the depreciation schedule, given $PVA_{5,0.10} =$ 3.791, is approximately

$$100 \times 3.791 \frac{2 \times 0.67}{5+1} = \$84.67$$

The exact figure is \$80.60. Table 8–3 illustrates some present values of a \$1 investment.

Rule 32: PV of declining balance. The present value of the future annual depreciation expenses on a \$1 investment is

$$\frac{d}{d+r}\left[1 - \left(\frac{1-d}{1+r}\right)^n\right]$$

When n is relatively large, the present value is

$$\frac{d}{d+r}$$

where d is the depreciation rate of declining balance (rule 12).

Example. Consider the example under rule 30, when the investment is \$100, $n = 5$, and $r = 0.10$, and assume DDB is used; that is

Table 8–3
Present-Value Factors of Depreciation Schedule (SYD)

	Discounting Rate (%)			
Life Span (Years)	*6*	*12*	*18*	*24*
5	0.875	0.775	0.694	0.626
10	0.800	0.659	0.556	0.479
15	0.734	0.569	0.459	0.382

$$d = 2 / 5 = 0.4$$

Solution: The present value of the depreciation schedule is

$$100 \times \frac{0.4}{0.4 + 0.10}\left[1 - \left(\frac{1 - 0.4}{1 + 0.10}\right)^5\right] = \$76.14$$

This amount is lower than that in the last example for the SYD because this example assumes a salvage value.

Rule 33: PV of double-declining balance with switch. The present value of the DDB method with switch-over is very close to that of the SYD method. Table 8–4 illustrates some present values of a $1 investment.

Rule 34: PV of accelerated to straight-line. The present value of the depreciation schedule of accelerated depreciation methods is always higher than that of the straight-line method. Table 8–5 illustrates the ratio of accelerated depreciation (the SYD, which is very close to DDB with switch-over) to the straight-line method.

Rule 35: PV of DDB to SYD, no salvage. The DDB method with switch-over is preferable to the SYD for assets with a life span of less than 6 years (the difference is about one percentage point). For assets with a life span of 6 years and over, the SYD is preferable (the difference is about 2–5 percentage points). The longer the life span and the higher the discounting rate, the more preferable is the SYD. Its advantage can be seen by comparing the entries in tables 8–3 and 8–4.

Rule 36: PV of DDB to SYD, with salvage. When there is a salvage value (at least at the level of the DDB inherent salvage), the DDB method is preferable to the SYD (the difference is about one to six percentage points). The higher the discounting rate, the higher the difference in preferability.

Table 8–4
Present-Value Factors of Depreciation Schedule (DDB with Switch)[a]

Life Span (Years)	*Discounting Rate (%)* 6	12	18	24
5	0.878	0.781	0.702	0.637
10	0.787	0.642	0.505	0.465
15	0.711	0.542	0.436	0.363

[a] The present value of DDB with switch is

$$\frac{f\left[1-\left(\frac{1-f}{1+i}\right)^{h}\right]}{f+i}+\frac{\left(\frac{1-f}{1+i}\right)^{h} a_{(n-h),i}}{n-h}=\text{PVD}$$

where f is $2/n$, i is the nominal growth rate, h is the integer of $(n+1)/2$, n is the asset's life span, and $a_{n,\,i}$ is the present value factor of annuity (rule 7, chapter 2).

Rule 37: Prefered depreciation schedule. When there is no salvage value, the declining-balance method with switch-over (rule 14) is preferable to no switch-over. The depreciation schedule where the DDB method is used for the first year and switched to the SYD for all other years provides the highest present value and therefore is preferred. In the United States, the asset depreciation range system allows using this procedure for income tax purposes.

Table 8–5
Ratio of Present Value of SYD to Straight-Line Schedules[a]

Life span (Years)	*Discounting rate* (%) 6	12	18	24
5	1.039	1.075	1.109	1.141
10	1.087	1.166	1.238	1.300
15	1.134	1.253	1.351	1.432

[a] The ratio of present value of SYD to straight-line is

$$\frac{2kn}{n+1}=\frac{n(n-a_{n,i})}{ica_{n,i}}$$

where k is the interest add-on factor $\cong 0.67$ (rule 2, chapter 2), and $c = n(n+1)/2$.

Inventory Valuation

Inventories (raw materials, work in progress, and finished goods) are held for carrying out regular production and merchandising activities. Because inventories are constantly changing (receiving and issuing items), the monitoring of inventory valuation is both important and troublesome.

Inventory Valuation Methods

Rule 38: Conventional inventory valuation methods. There are many valuation methods; the main ones are summarized below.

1. *FIFO (first in, first out):* This method assumes, for the purpose of valuation, that the earliest acquired batch is used first, then the next acquired batch, and so on. The latest acquired stock is on hand.
2. *LIFO (last in, first out):* This method assumes, for the purpose of valuation, that latest acquired batches are used first, whereas the earliest acquired stock is kept on hand.
3. *Moving average:* The moving average method assumes that each acquired batch is added to the existing stock, and a new average unit price is used for valuation.

Example. Consider the following movement of inventories during January of year 1:
January 1—200 units @ $2.00; received January 5—200 units @ $3.00 and January 25—100 units @ $4.00; issued January 10—300 units. The value of inventory and number of units used under the various valuation methods are presented in table 8–6.

Rule 39: The retail method of inventory valuation. This method is widely used in retailing, which is characterized by wide variety, large volume, and low-priced items. The marked selling price of the merchandise is the value used for control purposes. The cost value for inventory valuation is arrived at by discounting the selling price by the average markup for the corresponding period, as follows:

$$\text{Cost} = \frac{\text{Retail value}}{1 + \text{markup}}$$

where markup is the percentage of added-on cost. The resultant cost value is used in the United States for tax purposes.

Example. The end of the period count showed $1,000 inventory at marked retail price. The average markup is 25 percent.

Table 8–6
Value of Inventory and Units Used under Various Valuation Methods

		Received			*Issued*			*Balance*		
Date	*Details*	*Quantity*	*Price*	*Sum*	*Quantity*	*Price*	*Sum*	*Quantity*	*Price*	*Sum*
FIFO										
1/1	Beginning							200	$2.00	$400
1/5	Received	200	$3.00	$600				200	3.00	600
1/10	Issued				200	$2.00	$400			
					100	3.00	300	100	3.00	300
1/25	Received	100	4.00	400				100	4.00	400
	Total	300		1,000	300		700	200		700
LIFO										
1/1	Beginning							200	$2.00	$400
1/5	Received	200	$3.00	$600				200	3.00	600
1/10	Issued				200	$3.00	$600			
					100	2.00	200	100	2.00	200
1/25	Received	100	4.00	400				100	4.00	400
	Total	300		1,000	300		800	200		600
Moving average										
1/1	Beginning							200	$2.00	$400
1/5	Received	200	$3.00	$600				400	2.50	1000
1/10	Issued				300	$2.50	$750	100	2.50	250
1/25	Received	100	4.00	400				200	3.25	650
	Total	300		1,000	300		750	200		650

Solution: The cost value of this inventory is

$$\frac{1{,}000}{1 + 0.25} = \$800$$

Rule 40: Standard price for inventory valuation. This method assigns a predetermined price to all units added to inventory and issued. It eliminates the detailed record-keeping and computations inherent in the conventional inventory valuation methods, but it is usually not used for financial statements. The cost per unit of both inventory and units used does not fluctuate as it does in the former methods.

Rule 41: Replacement value for inventory valuation. The accounting value of inventory is the historical acquisition cost computed by one of the valuation methods. An alternative method of inventory valuation is the replacement cost. If a given inventory is in use, the replacement cost is its current acquisition cost. If the inventory is not in use, it would not be replaced and its replacement value is its alternative usage: the value determined by an internal use, selling price, or zero value.

Perpetual and Periodic Inventory Accounting

There are two methods of accounting for inventory for the purpose of preparing financial statements.

Rule 42: Perpetual inventory accounting. This method requires recording each addition to and usage of stock; that is, a strict adherence to the perpetual updating calculations implied by one of the three valuation methods just discussed (FIFO, LIFO, or moving average) and as illustrated in table 8–6.

Rule 43: Periodic inventory accounting. This method requires physical counting and calculations once in a period, rather, than carrying out perpetual updating of amounts and values. The retail and standard-cost methods are in essence based on the periodic inventory method. The LIFO methods are designed for use with perpetual inventory. To use these methods with periodic inventory accounting, the value of inventory and the cost of units are calculated by using the period's purchases and the change in stock, as explained in the following rules.

Rule 44: FIFO under periodic inventory accounting. The value of ending inventory is determined by the value of the latest invoices that correspond to the counted amount of stock in storage (c, in the following equation). The cost of units used is determined by the beginning inventory (a) plus the period's total invoices (b) minus the invoices assigned to the ending inventory (c). That is

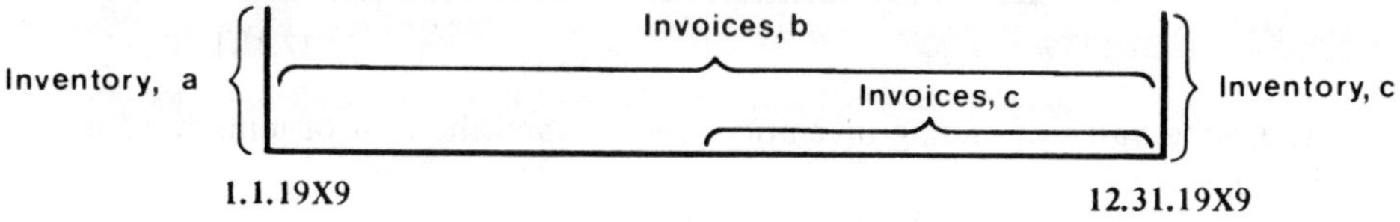

where the value of ending inventory is c and cost of units used is $a + b - c$.

Example. The count of the ending inventory was 200 units. The value of the beginning inventory was $500, and purchases during the year amounted to $1000.

Solution: The latest invoices, which correspond to 200 units of the inventory, amount to \$700. Thus, the value of the ending inventory is \$700. The cost of units used is

$$500 + (1{,}000 - 700) = \$800$$

Rule 45: LIFO under periodic inventory accounting. There are three cases of LIFO under the periodic inventory accounting: constant, increasing, and decreasing levels of inventory.

1. *LIFO, constant inventory:* When the value of ending inventory equals the value of the beginning inventory, the cost of units used is equal to the period's invoices.

Example. Consider the example for rule 38, where the ending inventory (200 units) equals the beginning inventory.
Solution: The value of the ending inventory is \$400, just as it was at the beginning inventory. The cost of units used is \$1,000.
Note: The data in the example for rule 38 are also used in table 8–6 applying the perpetual inventory method. However, here the periodic inventory method is used and therefore the results differ (\$800 versus \$1,000).

2. *LIFO, increasing inventory:* When purchases exceed usage, the level of inventory increases. The value of the ending inventory is determined by the value of the beginning inventory, plus the value of the earliest invoices that correspond to the increased amount of the ending inventory (d in the follow equation). The cost of units used is determined by the rest of the period's invoices (the period's total invoices, b, minus the invoices assigned to ending inventory, d). That is

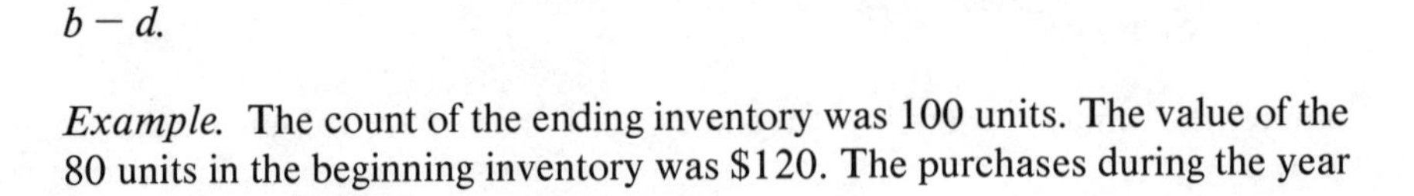

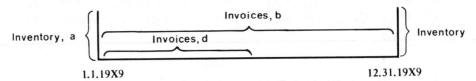

where the value of ending inventory is $a + d$ and the cost of units used is $b - d$.

Example. The count of the ending inventory was 100 units. The value of the 80 units in the beginning inventory was \$120. The purchases during the year amounted to \$1,200.
Solution: The increase in inventory is

$$100 - 80 = 20 \text{ units}$$

The earliest invoices, which correspond to 20 units (of the increase in inventory), amounted to \$60. Thus, the value of the ending inventory is

$$120 + 60 = \$180$$

The cost of units used is

$$1{,}200 - 60 = \$1{,}140$$

3. *LIFO, decreasing inventory:* When purchases are lower than usage, the level of inventory decreases. The cost of units used is determined by the period's total invoices plus the value of the reduced amount of the beginning inventory. The value of the reduced inventory is determined by calculating the value of the latest layers that have been added to the beginning inventory. That is

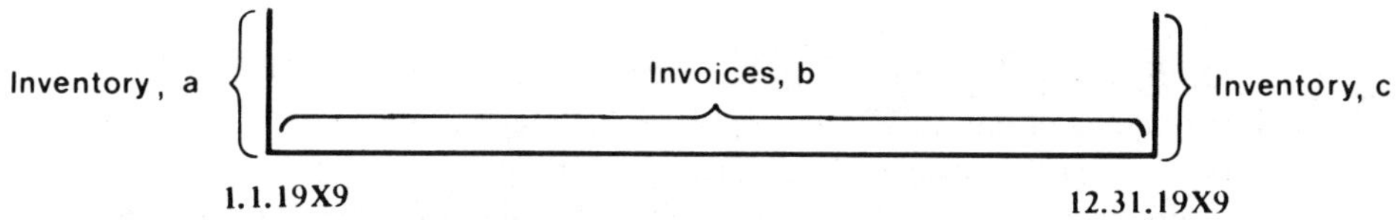

where the value of ending inventory is c from the lower layers of a and the cost of units used is $b + (a - c)$.

Example. The count of the ending inventory was 80 units. Purchases during the year amounted to \$1,200. The beginning inventory was 100 units, valued at \$120. The transactions relevant to the beginning inventory are:

	May	July	August	September	Total
Units in order of acquisition	45	35	10	10	100
Acquisition cost (\$)	45	40	20	15	120

Solution: The decrease in inventory is

$$100 - 80 = 20 \text{ units}$$

The value of the 80 units of ending inventory (45 and 35 acquired in May and July) is

$$45 + 40 = \$85$$

The cost of units used is

$$1{,}200 + (120 - 85) = \$1{,}235$$

Effect of Inflation on Inventory Accounting

The choice of the inventory valuation method to be used affects the level of the annual expenses and the level of inventory value. The choice affects, therefore, the reported financial statements; it has tax implications and affects the costing of products. During inflation, these effects are magnified considerably. For example, a rise in the price level of materials affects the valuation of inventories differently under the various valuation methods. The value of inventory and cost of units used are affected in opposite directions under the FIFO and LIFO methods, whereas the moving-average method provides in-between results.

Rule 46: Effect of LIFO on reported income. When the LIFO method is used, management can affect the reported net income directly by timing of purchases, given that prices are changing. When prices rise, the effect is to reduce reported net income; when prices decline, the effect is to raise reported net income.

Rule 47: Effect of inflation on the value of inventory. During inflation the value of inventories is lower under the LIFO method than it is under the FIFO method. Thus, the LIFO method provides less representative figures regarding current values. The LIFO method provides understated inventory values, compared to current market prices. The longer the method is practiced, the higher the bias. As a result, the value of inventory determined by the LIFO method should not be used for insurance and other managerial uses. This value may be of benefit for reducing property tax. Furthermore, this understated value would affect the results of the various uses of these data, such as financial ratios.

Rule 48: Effect of inflation on the cost of materials. During inflation the cost of materials used is higher under the LIFO method than it is under the FIFO method. Thus, the LIFO method provides more representative figures regarding current prices. As prices are rising, the LIFO method provides higher cost of goods and lower reported net income and thus, lower income tax.

Rule 49: Standard price for valuation during inflation. During inflation, when the standard price is updated, the standard price method provides the most reliable figures of both inventory value and cost of units used.

Income Tax Considerations

The depreciation expense and the cost of materials drawn from inventory are charged against income before income tax is levied. Thus, the methods of depreciation and inventory valuation you use affect the reported net income and, in turn, the level of income tax.

Rule 50: Life span for depreciable assets. For income tax purposes, the shorter the life span of a depreciable asset, the higher the tax saving. In the United States, the asset depreciation range system allows you to deviate 20 percent from the guideline life span for income tax purposes.

The U.S. investment tax credit system encourages the adoption of a longer life span so as to obtain the maximum credit. (In 1979, the 10 percent credit that is charged against the income tax liability is applied to one-third of the acquisition cost for personal tangible assets with a life span of 3 to 5 years, to two-thirds of the cost for a life span of 5 to 7 years, and to the full cost of the investment for a life span of 7 years or more.)

Rule 51: Timing of depreciation expense. For tax purposes, the more accelerated the depreciation pattern, the higher the tax savings, given that there is time preference for money. This savings is the result of the fact that the steeper the depreciation pattern, the earlier is the tax deduction (see the earlier section in this chapter on the implications of various depreciation methods). For example, the 200 percent (double) declining balance is steeper than the 150 percent method; therefore, the former is preferable.

The U.S. Internal Revenue Service allows the 200 percent and 125 percent declining-balance methods. Using these methods for income tax purposes does not require using the same methods in the official financial statements.

Rule 52: Present value of tax saving on depreciation. The tax saving (shield) on a given investment, in present-value terms, is the present value of the depreciation schedule times the tax rate.

Example. A proposed investment of $1,000 with a life span of 10 years will be depreciated by the straight-line method. The relevant tax rate is 40 percent, and the discounting rate is 12 percent.

Solution: The present value of the annual depreciation schedule (rule 30) is approximately

$$1{,}000 \times \frac{1}{1 + (0.67 \times 5 \times 0.12)} = \$713$$

The exact figure is $721.
The tax saving is

$$721 \times 0.40 = \$288.40$$

If the sum-of-the-years'-digits method is used, the corresponding present value is $775 and the tax saving is $310.

Rule 53: Effect of salvage value on tax saving. For income tax purposes, reducing or ignoring the salvage value increases the tax saving. In the United States, the asset depreciation range system allows you to apply depreciation without deducting the anticipated salvage value from the asset cost.

Rule 54: Additional first-year depreciation. The U.S. tax authorities recognize additional first-year depreciation in the following manner. For personal tangible assets with a life span of 6 years or more, 20 percent of the acquisition cost (with a limitation of $10,000 in 1979) can be allowed as tax-deductible expenses in the year of acquisition, even if purchased on the last day of the tax year. The remaining 80 percent is depreciated by one of the regular methods.

Example. Equipment is acquired for $1,000 on June 1, 1980, with an expected life span of 10 years, and without a salvage value. The DDB method is used.
Solution: The depreciation for tax purposes is

First-year depreciation	$1{,}000 \times 0.20 = \$200$
Depreciable base	$1{,}000 - 200 = \$800$
Depreciation in 1980	$800\ (2/10) = \$160$
Total depreciation in the first year	$200 + 160 = \$360$

Rule 55: Tax saving with LIFO during inflation. As shown in rule 46, management can affect the reported net income directly by timing of purchases, given that prices do change. This procedure, when allowed, has some implications for income tax purposes.

During inflation, the use of the LIFO method is preferable to FIFO and to the moving average method (rules 47, 48). In the United States, the tax authorities allow a switch to the LIFO method. However, if the LIFO method is adopted, it must also be used in the official financial statements. Furthermore, the U.S. tax authorities allow obsolescence and decline in value of inventory to be recognized without disposition, under the LIFO method.[1]

Note

1. W.L. Raby, *The Income Tax and Business Decisions,* 4th ed. (Englewood Cliffs, N.J.: Prentice-Hall, 1978).

9 Stock of Assets Analysis

The financial statements record aggregate data on the stock of fixed assets and inventories, including acquisition cost, depreciated value, current and accumulated depreciation, inventory value, and cost of materials. These data are often the only ones available to an analyst. Therefore, tools and rules of thumb that enable the analyst to learn about the relationships among the various aggregate items and to find the magnitude of some missing data will help him in his work.

The relations among the various values of a stock of assets do not necessarily follow the corresponding relationships among the values of an individual asset. For one reason, the stock of assets is composed of a mixture of assets, each with a different age.

The tools in this chapter have been developed for a stock of assets under the assumption that the assets are of the same type and that their ages are evenly distributed; that is, the stock includes assets of all ages. In practice, even when these conditions do not hold exactly, the application of the rules may still be a good and convenient way to estimate the actual values. Of course, the closer the actual conditions are to the assumed ones, the better will be the approximations. The rules may be applied for separate groups of assets of a similar type, such as buildings, machinery, and equipment. In the case of inflation or growth, an even annual rate has been assumed in developing the rules.

The rules are developed for both constant and growth conditions regarding the value of the stock of assets. Constant conditions imply that both the volume of assets and the price level do not change, whereas growth conditions imply that either or both increase over time.

The financial statements also record aggregate data on the stock of debt; these can be analyzed in a manner similar to that used for the stock of assets.

Depreciation of a Stock of Assets

Annual depreciation expenses recorded in profit-and-loss statements are in aggregate form. Under the straight-line depreciation method the depreciation expense of the stock of assets follows the same pattern as that of an individual asset. This pattern holds for both constant and growth conditions.

On the other hand, under the accelerated depreciation method, the aggregate expenses follow a different pattern than that of the individual asset because the aggregate depreciation expenses are composed of depreciation expenses for both, old and young assets.

Rule 1: Depreciation of a constant stock. Under noninflationary conditions, the value of the stock of assets is constant when a mature company reinvests the whole amount of its depreciation expenses and thus renews the aging stock. The annual depreciation expense for an individual young asset is higher than that of a old asset under accelerated depreciation. But for a stock of assets whose age is evenly distributed (that is, the stock includes assets of equal acquisition value for all ages), the aggregate expenses for the young and old assets compensate for each other.

Rule 1A. The annual depreciation expenses of a stable stock of fixed assets, whose age is evenly distributed, is the same for all the depreciation methods.

Rule 1B. The annual depreciation expense of a stable stock of assets for all the depreciation methods is equal to

$$\frac{1}{n} \text{ of the investment value}$$

where n is the life span.

Example. You want to know the depreciation expenses on a stock of equipment with a service life of 10 years.

Solution: The depreciation expenses, regardless of the depreciation method, will be one-tenth (10%) of the investment acquisition value.

Rule 2: Depreciation under inflation and growth. When the current value of the stock of depreciable assets is growing as a result of inflation or because of real growth, the relative share of young assets in the stock is high and affects the depreciation expenses on the stock of such assets in the case of accelerated methods.

Rule 2A: Straight-line. When the current value of the stock of fixed assets is growing as a result of inflation or real growth, the annual depreciation expense under the straight-line (SL) method is $1/n$ of the current value of the investment.

Rule 2B: Accelerated depreciation. When the current value of the stock of fixed assets is growing, the annual depreciation expenses under accelerated methods are higher than under the straight-line method, approximately by the factor

$$\frac{2kn}{n+1}$$

where $k \cong 0.67$, which is the interest add-on factor (rule 2, chapter 2; appendix B), and n is the average life span.

This rule has been developed for the sum-of-the-years-digits method. For the double-declining method with switch-over, the results change slightly.

The annual depreciation expenses are computed in two steps. First, compute the depreciation expenses with the straight-line method (rule 2A). Next, multiply the result by the factor in rule 2B.

Example. Consider the first example, where the life span is 10 years and the depreciation expenses are 10 percent of the investment, but the annual inflation rate is 12 percent and the accelerated-depreciation method is used.

Solution: The depreciation expenses are approximately

$$\frac{1}{10} \times \frac{2(0.67)\,10}{10+1} = 0.122$$

That is, 12.2 percent of the investment. For a more exact solution, use the value of k for 10 years and 12 percent in appendix B:

$$\frac{1}{10} \times \frac{2(0.642)10}{10+1} = 0.1167$$

This result can be found in table 9–1.

Table 9–1
Factors for the Sum-of-the-Years' Digits (SYD)[a]

	Nominal Growth (%)			
Life Span (Years)	*6*	*12*	*18*	*24*
5	1.039	1.075	1.109	1.141
10	1.087	1.166	1.238	1.300
15	1.134	1.253	1.351	1.432

[a]See rule 2B.

Rule 2C: Use of tables for SYD and DDB. When the stock of depreciable assets is growing, the annual depreciation expenses are estimated by multiplying the expenses assuming the straight-line method (rule 2A) by the relevant factor from tables 9–1 or 9–2.

Example. The financial statements of a company that uses the straight-line method record \$100 depreciation expenses. You want to estimate the annual depreciation expenses resulting from a switch to the double-declining method. The average life span of the assets is 15 years and the nominal growth in assets value is 18 percent per annum.
Solution: Using table 9–2, the approximate factor is 1.283. The annual depreciation expense will be approximately

$$100 \times 1.283 = \$128.30$$

Life Span of a Stock of Depreciable Assets

The average life span of a stock of depreciable assets is of interest for various policy decisions. It is also required for financial statements analysis, assets accounting and revaluation. The rules in this section provide an estimate of the average life span, weighted by the acquisition cost of each asset in the stock.

Rule 3: Average life span of a constant stock. The average life span of a constant stock of depreciable assets, in terms of years, under all the depreciation methods, is approximated by

Table 9–2
Factors for the Double-Declining Balance (DDB) with Switch[a]

	Nominal Growth (%)			
Life Span (Years)	*6*	*12*	*18*	*24*
5	1.042	1.083	1.122	1.160
10	1.070	1.138	1.203	1.263
15	1.098	1.195	1.283	1.362

[a]The ratio of DDB with switch to straight-line depreciation, using the notations from table 8–4, is

$$\frac{n}{a_{n,i}}(\text{PVD})$$

$$\frac{\text{Acquisition cost}}{\text{Depreciation expense}}$$

Example. A company's financial statements record \$1,700 total acquisition costs of depreciable assets and \$100 depreciation expenses. No growth is recorded.
Solution: The average life span of the assets is approximately

$$\frac{1{,}700}{100} = 17 \text{ years}$$

Rule 4: Assets life span under inflation and growth. In conditions of inflation or growth the previous rule still holds for the straight-line depreciation method but not for the accelerated-depreciation methods.

When the stock of depreciable assets is growing, the average life span of a stock of fixed assets is computed in two steps. First, compute the life span assuming the straight-line method (rule 3). Then, multiply the results by

$$\frac{2kn}{n+1}$$

where $k \cong 0.67$, which is the interest add-on factor (rule 2, chapter 2), and n is the average life span derived by rule 3.
This formula has been developed for the sum-of-the-years'-digits method. For the double-declining method with switch-over, the results change slightly.

Example A. A company's financial statements record \$1,700 total acquisition costs of depreciable assets and \$130 depreciation expenses. The growth in assets value is 10 percent per annum. The sum-of-the-years'-digits method is used.
Solution: The average life span, assuming the straight-line method, is approximately

$$\frac{1{,}700}{130} = 13.1 \text{ years}$$

In appendix B we find for 10 percent and 13 years that $k = 0.639$. The average life span is approximately

$$13.1 \times \frac{2\,(0.639)\,13}{13+1} = 13.1 \times 1.186 = 15.5 \text{ years}$$

The previous rule can also be applied by using the relevant factor from tables 9–1 or 9–2, rather than using the formula.

Example B. Consider example A, but the double-declining method is used.
Solution: In table 9–2, for a 12 percent growth rate and a 13.1-year life span, the factor is approximately 1.175 (between 1.138 and 1.195). The average life span of the assets is approximately

$$13.1 \times 1.175 = 15.4 \text{ years}$$

Rule 5: Remaining average life span of a stock. A stock of depreciable assets maintains its value when the depreciation expenses are reinvested in asset renewal. When investment in asset renewal stops, the value of the stock will decrease until the end of the last unit's life span (that is, n years). Also, the annual depreciation expense will decline over time as old assets are discarded. The figure of the value-weighted average of the remaining life span of such a stock is required for assets accounting and revaluation.

Rule 5A. The average remaining life span of a stock of depreciable assets that is not renewed and is depreciated using the straight-line method is roughly 0.7 of the average life span. It is approximated by

$$\frac{\text{Book value}}{\text{Depreciation expense}}$$

Rule 5B. When the accelerated depreciation method is practiced, the average remaining life span is computed in two steps: compute the average remaining life span assuming the straight-line method (the previous rule) and multiply the results by

$$\frac{2k}{n+1}$$

where $k \cong 0.67$, which is the interest add-on factor (rule 2, chapter 2), and n is the average remaining life span derived by the previous rule.

Turnover of Stock of Inventory

The time a stock of materials is held in inventory (turnover) is of interest for various policy decisions and control purposes. It is also required for financial statement analysis, assets accounting, and revaluation. The rules in this section provide an estimate of the average holding time, weighted by the value of each type of material or product in the stock.

Rule 6: Turnover of a constant stock of raw materials. The average time an inventory of raw materials is held in storage, expressed in months, under all methods of calculation, is approximated by

$$\frac{\text{Average inventory value}}{\text{Costs of materials used}} \times 12$$

The average inventory value is derived from the sum of the balance sheet values at the beginning and end of the period divided by 2.

Example. The financial statements of a company record \$95 and \$105 of materials inventory in the opening and closing balance sheets, respectively, and \$400 cost of materials used.
Solution: The average time that a stock of materials is held in storage is approximately

$$\frac{(95 + 105)/2}{400} \times 12 = 3 \text{ months}$$

This equation means that the company keeps an inventory of raw materials for an average of three months of production.

Rule 7: Turnover of inventory under inflation and growth. The average time an inventory of raw materials is held in storage depends on the accounting method of calculations. Under the FIFO and average methods the previous rule still holds; under the LIFO method, the average time an inventory of raw materials is held in storage, expressed in months, is approximated by

$$\frac{\text{Average revalued inventory}}{\text{Cost of materials used}} \times 12$$

The revalued figures for the opening and closing balances can be approximated by the rules in chapter 10.

Example. The financial statements of a company record \$145 and \$155 of raw materials inventory in the opening and closing balance sheets, respectively, and \$600 cost of materials used. The LIFO method is used. The value

of the average restated opening and closing inventory (at the respective current price levels) is estimated to be $200.
Solution: The average time the stock of materials is held in storage is approximately

$$\frac{200}{600} \times 12 = 4 \text{ months}$$

This means that storage is sufficient for an average of 4 months of production.

Rule 8: Turnover of work in process and finished goods. The previous rules can be applied also to the stock of work in process or finished goods for estimating the holding time of these items. However, in this case the cost of goods sold should be used for the denominator of the formula.

Example. A company's financial statements record $100 of goods in process and $80 of finished goods, and $800 cost of goods sold. The FIFO method is used.
Solution: The average time the goods in process are held in storage is approximately

$$\frac{100}{800} \times 12 = 1.5 \text{ months}$$

The finished goods are held in storage approximately

$$\frac{80}{800} \times 12 = 1.2 \text{ months}$$

Ratio of Book Value to Acquisition Cost

The balance sheet usually records the book value (that is, the depreciated value) of depreciated assets. However, information on the total acquisition costs is sometimes needed, for example to derive the average life span of the stock of assets (rules 3 and 4) or to estimate the required gross investment in a similar company.

In some cases, the acquisition costs of a stock of assets are provided, (for example, a proposed investment or a balance sheet for a new plant). Information on the average book value of a similar stock of assets is required.

Value of Assets under Constant Stock

Under noninflationary conditions, when the value of the assets is constant, a mature company reinvests the whole amount of its depreciation expenses.

Rule 9: Deriving the acquisition cost, SL. Given the book value of a constant stock of depreciable assets, the corresponding acquisition cost under the straight-line (SL) method is approximated by

$$A = B\frac{2n}{n+1}$$

where A is the acquisition costs, B is the book (depreciated) value, and n is the average life span.

Example. A company's financial statements record \$550 depreciated assets. The assets' average life span is 10 years, and the straight-line method is used.
Solution: The acquisition cost of the assets is approximately

$$550 \times \frac{2 \times 10}{10 + 1} = \$1{,}000$$

Rule 10: Deriving the book value, SL. Given the acquisition costs of a constant stock of depreciable assets, the corresponding depreciated value under the straight-line (SL) method is approximated by

$$B = A\frac{n+1}{2n}$$

Example. A proposed investment in a new plant amounts to \$1,000, the assets' average life span is 15 years, and the straight-line method is used.
Solution: The corresponding depreciated value (the average value over the life span) is approximately

$$1{,}000 \times \frac{15 + 1}{2 \times 15} = \$533$$

Rule 11: Book value and acquisition cost, accelerated depreciation. Given the book value of a constant stock of depreciable assets, the corresponding acquisition cost under accelerated depreciation is roughly 40 percent higher than under the straight-line method.

Given the acquisition costs of a constant stock of depreciable assets, the corresponding book value under accelerated depreciation is roughtly 70 percent of the value arrived at under the straight-line method.

Rule 12: Deriving the acquisition cost, SYD. Given the book value of a constant stock of depreciable assets, the corresponding acquisition cost under the sum-of-the-years'-digits (SYD) method is approximated by

$$A = B \frac{3n}{n + 2}$$

Example. Consider the example for rule 9, but the SYD method is used. Solution: The corresponding acquisition cost is approximately

$$550 \times \frac{3 \times 10}{10 + 2} = \$1{,}375$$

The resultant value is 37.5 percent higher than under the straight-line method.

Rule 13: Deriving the book value, SYD. Given the acquisition costs of a constant stock of fixed assets, the corresponding depreciated value under the SYD method is approximated by

$$B = A \frac{n + 2}{3n}$$

Example. Consider the example for rule 10, but the SYD method is used. Solution: The corresponding depreciated value is approximately

$$1{,}000 \times \frac{15 + 2}{3 \times 15} = \$377$$

The resultant value is 31 percent lower than under the straight-line method.

Rule 14: Book value and acquisition cost, DDB. When the double-declining balance (DDB) method is practiced, the application of rules 12 and 13 (for the SYD) will provide good approximations.

Assets under inflation and growth conditions

When the value of assets increases over time because of inflation or real growth, the ratio of book value to acquisition will also increase. This increase occurs because the weight of the young assets, which are only partially depreciated, is larger than that of the older assets, which are more depreciated.

Rule 15: Deriving the acquisition cost under growth, SL. Given the book value of a growing stock of depreciable assets, the corresponding acquisition cost is derived by dividing the book value by the relevant factor in table 9–3.

The figures in the first column in table 9–3 are derived by rule 10; the other figures are derived by

$$1 - \frac{(FVA_{n,g}) - n}{ng(FVA_{n,g})}$$

where g is the annual rate of growth in assets value and $FVA_{n,g}$ is the future value factor of annuity, compounded at g (rule 5, chapter 2).

Example. A company's financial statements record \$550 of depreciated assets; the life span is 10 years and the volume of assets grew in the last 10 years by 5 percent per annum. The straight line method is used.

Solution: Using table 9–3, we find, for 10 years and 5 percent, a ratio of about 0.59 (between 0.550 and 0.598). The acquisition cost of the assets is

$$550 / 0.59 = \$932$$

Table 9–3
Ratio of Book Value to Acquisition Cost (SL)

	Nominal Growth (%)				
Life Span (Years)	*0*	*6*	*12*	*18*	*24*
5	0.600	0.623	0.645	0.665	0.684
10	0.550	0.598	0.642	0.681	0.715
15	0.533	0.605	0.668	0.721	0.764

Rule 16: Deriving the book value under growth, SL. Given the acquisition cost of a growing stock of depreciable assets, the corresponding depreciated value is approximated by multiplying the acquisition costs by the relevant factor shown in table 9–3.

Example. A company's financial statements record \$1,000 of acquisition cost, the life span is 10 years, and the volume of assets grew in the last 10 years by 5 percent per annum. The straight-line method is used.
Solution: The respective book value is

$$1{,}000 \times 0.59 = \$590$$

Rule 17: Deriving the acquisition cost accelerated depreciation. Given the book value of a growing stock of depreciable assets, the corresponding acquisition cost calculated under accelerated depreciation is roughly 25 percent higher than under the straight-line method. For a better approximation, the corresponding acquisition cost is derived by dividing the book value by the relevant factor in table 9–4 or 9–5.

Rule 18: Deriving the book value, accelerated depreciation. Given the acquisition cost of a growing stock of depreciable assets, the corresponding book value calculated under accelerated depreciation is roughly 80 percent of the value arrived at under the straight-line method. For a better approximation, the corresponding book value is derived by multiplying the acquisition cost by the relevant factor in tables 9–4 or 9–5.

Table 9–4
Ratio of Book Value to Acquisition Cost (SYD)[a]

	Nominal Growth (%)				
Life Span (Years)	*0*	*6*	*12*	*18*	*24*
5	0.467	0.494	0.520	0.544	0.567
10	0.400	0.453	0.503	0.549	0.590
15	0.378	0.456	0.528	0.591	0.644

[a]The ratio of book value to acquisition cost, under SYD, is

$$\frac{S_{n,i}(i^2c + 1 - in) + ic - n}{i^2cS_{n,i}}$$

where $S_{n,i}$ is the future value factor for annuity (rule 5, chapter 2), and c equals $n(n + 1)/2$. When $i = 0$, then the ratio is equal to $(n + 2)/3n$.

Table 9–5
Ratio of Book Value to Acquisition Cost (DDB)[a]

	Nominal Growth (%)				
Life Span (Years)	*0*	*6*	*12*	*18*	*24*
5	0.461	0.486	0.510	0.533	0.554
10	0.446	0.491	0.534	0.574	0.610
15	0.442	0.507	0.567	0.621	0.666

[a]The ratio of book value to acquisition cost, under DDB with salvage inherent, is

$$\frac{(1+i)^n - (1-f)^n}{(1+f)S_{n,i}}$$

where f is $2/n$.
When $i = 0$, then the ratio is equal to

$$\frac{1-(1-f)^n}{nf}$$

Ratio of Accumulated to Current Depreciation

You want to know the accumulated depreciation of the stock of assets when only figures on the current depreciation expenses are available, and vice versa. These figures can be derived from one another.

Rule 19: Deriving the accumulated depreciation of a constant stock. The accumulated depreciation of a constant stock of assets is approximated by

$$D = d\frac{n-1}{2}$$

where D is the accumulated depreciation and d is the current depreciation.

Example. The depreciation expenses in year 1 are \$100, and the average life span of the assets is 10 years.
Solution: The accumulated depreciation is approximately

$$100 \times \frac{10-1}{2} = \$450$$

Rule 20: Deriving the accumulated depreciation under inflation and growth. Given that the value of assets increases over time, the accumulated depreciation of a stock of assets is approximated by

$$D = dn\left(1 - \frac{B}{A}\right)$$

where B/A is the ratio of book value to acquisition cost (rule 15).

Example. Consider the previous example where $d = 100$, but with an annual growth in the volume of assets over the last 10 years of 5 percent.
Solution: Using table 9–3, the appropriate value for B/A is about 0.59 (between 0.550 and 0.598). The accumulated depreciation is approximately

$$100 \times 10\ (1 - 0.59) = \$410$$

Analysis of Outstanding Debt

The outstanding loans are recorded in the balance sheet in the form of aggregate amounts. The aggregate stock of debt is composed of a mixture of loans, each at a different age. It can be assumed that the age of the loans is evenly distributed; that is, the stock includes loans of all ages. Therefore, the aggregate long-term debt can be analyzed in a similar way to that used for a stock of assets. The retirement of loans is considered as depreciation and the analysis follows the same procedures.

Example. A company owes only equal-principal-payment loans (see chapter 4), the retirement of which resembles straight-line depreciation. Suppose the outstanding balance of the stock of loans is \$550 and the average repayment term is 10 years.
Solution: Following rule 9, the original amount of the stock of loans is approximately

$$550 \times \frac{2 \times 10}{10 + 1} = \$1{,}000$$

Following rule 1, the annual retirement amount is approximately

$$\frac{1000}{10} = \$100$$

Thus, to keep the outstanding balance at a constant level the annual renewal of loans by new loans is approximately \$100.

In practice, the stock of loans is composed of various types of loans, such as installment loans and equal-principal-payment loans (see chapter 4), and the stock is usually growing over time. Therefore, the following rules provide only rough approximations. Further, they are applicable only to long-term loans.

Rule 21: Deriving the original amount of debt. The original amount of the outstanding aggregate long-term debt, as recorded in the balance sheet, is approximately 1.5 times the outstanding debt (the outstanding aggregate debt is roughly 0.67 of the original sum).

Example. The outstanding debt (long-term loans) of a company, as recorded in the balance sheet, is \$1.37 million.
Solution: The original amount was roughly

$$1.37 \times 1.5 = \$2 \text{ million}$$

Rule 22: Deriving the amount of debt retirement. The annual retirement of long-term loans is approximated by dividing the original amount of the stock of loans by the average repayment term.

Example. Consider the previous example, and suppose the average period of debt repayment is 5 years.
Solution: The annual loan retirement is approximately

$$\frac{2{,}000{,}000}{5} = \$400{,}000$$

Rule 23: Deriving the remaining life span. The weighted average remaining repayment term of the outstanding aggregate long-term debt, assuming that the retired loans are not renewed, is approximated by

$$\frac{\text{Outstanding debt}}{\text{Retirement of loans}}$$

Example. For the last two examples, the remaining repayment term is approximately

$$\frac{1{,}370{,}000}{400{,}000} = 3.4 \text{ years}$$

10 Inflation Adjustment of Stock of Assets

During a period of inflation, the values of assets and the costs deduced from them as recorded in financial statements tend to be understated. To provide sound information, these figures should be revalued. The distortions that inflation causes in conventional financial statements can be remedied by revaluing the company's assets in current monetary terms. Revaluation is carried out by inflating the acquisition cost of each unit of fixed asset or batch of raw material by the appropriate price index. This procedure is tedious, especially when used to revalue the inventory of raw materials. Short-cut rules can provide approximate revalued figures.

Asset revaluation is required for the analysis of financial statements and for measuring both the current profit figure and the minimum sum required for the replacement of assets. Further, the proposed rules enable an external party to arrive at the revalued figures when analyzing a company's official financial statements without having access to the detailed data.

The rules in this chapter have been developed for a stock of assets under the following assumptions. The assets are of the same type and their age is evenly distributed; that is, the stock includes assets of all ages. The inflation rate and the real growth rate are constant over the time involved.[1] In practice, when the conditions are somewhat different, the application of the rules may still be a convenient and useful way to estimate the revalued figures. The closer the actual conditions are to the assumed ones, the better the approximation. The rules may be applied for separate groups of assets of a similar type, such as buildings, machinery, and equipment.

The rules are developed for both constant and increasing volumes of the stock of assets. Constant volume implies that the increase in recorded values is only a nominal growth resulting from inflation.

Revaluing Depreciation Expenses

Depreciation expenses are derived from historical asset values. During a period of inflation these expenses are usually understated and therefore should be revalued.

Rule 1: Revaluing depreciation of a constant stock, SL. Constant volume of a stock of assets implies that the increase in the recorded values results only from inflation. Given that the straight-line (SL) method is used, the factor for revaluing $1 of historical depreciation, as recorded in the profit and loss statement, is approximated by

$$1 + (n \times p \times 0.6)$$

where n is the average life span of assets in years, and p is the annual rate of inflation, average over n.
The exact formula is

$$\frac{(1 + p)^n np}{(1 + p)^n - 1}$$

Example. A company's income statement for 1980 records $100 depreciation expenses. The average life span of the fixed assets is 10 years, and the straight-line method is used. The average annual inflation rate during the 1970–1980 period was 7 percent.
Solution: The revalued depreciation is approximately

$$100[1 + (10 \times 0.07 \times 0.6)] = \$142$$

The exact figure is $142.38.
Table 10–1 illustrates some revaluation factors.

An alternative formula for the factor for revaluation is

$$\frac{\text{Price index at date of analysis}}{\text{Sum of } t \text{ indexes for } n \text{ prior years} / t}$$

where $t = n + 1$, which is number of indexes from beginning to end of n periods

Example. The asset's life span is 4 years. The relevant price indexes for the last years are 170, 180, 195, 215, and 238; implying an 8.8 percent average annual inflation.
Solution: The revaluation factor is

$$\frac{238}{998 / 5} = 1.19$$

The approximated factor is

$$1 + (4 \times 0.088 \times 0.6) = 1.21$$

Table 10–1
Revaluation Factors for Depreciation and Acquisition Cost (SL)

	Annual Inflation Rate (%)				
Life Span (Years)	*6*	*12*	*18*	*24*	*30*
5	1.187	1.387	1.599	1.821	2.053
10	1.359	1.770	2.225	2.716	3.235
15	1.544	2.202	2.946	3.748	4.590

Rule 2: Revaluing depreciation under growth, SL. A real growth of the volume of assets increases the relative share of young assets in the asset stock. Thus, the larger the rate of real growth, the lower the revaluation factor.

The factor for revaluing $1 of historical depreciation, when the volume of assets increases over time, is approximated by the rule for constant volume. However, the resultant factor should be reduced by about 2 percent for a life span of 10 years, and by about 5 percent for a life span of 15 years.

The exact formula is

$$\frac{(1+p)^n\,(FVA_{n,g})}{FVA_{n,(g+p)}}$$

where FVA is the future value factor of annuity for n years and g or $(g+p)$ percentages (rule 5, chapter 2), and g is the rate of real growth.

Example. Consider the first example, where the revalued depreciation was $142; however, suppose the volume of assets grew by 5 percent annually during the last 10 years.
Solution: The revalued depreciation is approximately

$$142 - (142 \times 0.02) = \$139.16$$

The exact figure is $140.

Rule 3: Revaluation factor for accelerated depreciation. During a period of inflation, the historical depreciation expenses under an accelerated method are higher than under the straight-line method, but the revaluation factor is smaller.

Rule 4: Revaluing depreciation of a constant stock, accelerated depreciation. Under accelerated depreciation methods, the revaluation of the depreciation expenses is carried out in two steps:

1. Revalue the historical depreciation expenses by the rule for the straight-line method (rule 1).

2. Multiply the results by

$$\frac{n+1}{2kn}$$

where $k \cong 0.67$, which is the interest add-on factor (rule 2, chapter 2; appendix B).

This formula has been developed for the sum-of-the-years'-digits (SYD) method. For the double-declining method with switch-over, the results change slightly.

Example. Consider the first example, where the revalued depreciation was \$142; however, an accelerated depreciation method is now used.
Solution: In appendix B we find for 7 percent and 10 years that $k = 0.605$. The revalued depreciation is approximately

$$142 \times \frac{10+1}{2 \times 0.605 \times 10} = \$129$$

Rule 5: Revaluing depreciation under growth, accelerated depreciation. When the stock of assets is growing in real terms and is depreciated under accelerated methods, the revaluation is carried out in two steps:

1. Revalue the historical depreciation expenses by using the rule for the straight-line method (rule 2).

2. Multiply the results by

$$\frac{k_g}{k_{(g+p)}}$$

where k is the interest add-on factor for rate g or $(g+p)$—see appendix B; and g is the rate of real growth.

This formula has been developed for the SYD method. For the double-declining method with switch-over, the results change slightly.

Example. Consider the example for rule 2, where the average life span was 10 years, the inflation rate was 7 percent, the real growth in the volume of assets was 5 percent, and the revalued depreciation was \$140; however, an accelerated depreciation method is now used.
Solution: In appendix B we find for 7 percent and 10 years that $k = 0.605$,

and for 12 percent and 10 years that $k = 0.642$. The revalued depreciation is approximately

$$140 \times \frac{0.605}{0.642} = \$132$$

Revaluing Fixed-Assets Acquisition Cost

The value of the assets that are recorded in the balance sheet is usually understated during a period of inflation and therefore should be revalued.

Rule 6: Revaluing acquisition cost of a stock of depreciable assets. The factor for revaluing \$1 of acquisition cost of a stock of depreciable assets as recorded in the balance sheet, and under all the depreciation methods, is approximated by

$$1 + (n \times p \times 0.6)$$

The exact formula is shown in rule 1 and revaluation factors are listed in table 10–1.

Example. A company's balance sheet records \$1,000 total acquisition costs for depreciable assets. The assets' average life span is 10 years, and the annual average inflation rate during the last 10 years was 5 percent.
Solution: The revalued acquisition cost is approximately

$$1{,}000[1 + (10 \times 0.05 \times 0.6)] = \$1{,}300$$

The exact figure is \$1,295.
In the case of growth in the volume of assets rule 2 should be applied.

Rule 7: Revaluing nondepreciable assets. The factor for revaluing \$1 of acquisition cost of nondepreciable assets is

$$\frac{\text{Index at date of analysis}}{\text{Index at date of acquisition}}$$

This factor should be applied to the recorded values for each year, rather than to the aggregate stock of nondepreciable assets.

Example. A company's balance sheet records $1,000 of land value at the end of 1979.
Solution: Revaluation can be carried out only when the dates of acquisition of the land are known. Suppose $800 was invested in 1960 and $200 in 1975. The relevant price indexes for land are: 1960, 68.4; 1975, 212.7; and 1979, 351.0
The revalued land at the end of 1979 is

$$800 \times \frac{351}{68.4} + 200 \times \frac{351}{212.7} = \$4{,}435$$

Revaluing Book (Depreciated) Value

The revaluation factor for the book (depreciated) value of a stock of assets is lower than that for the acquisition cost. The difference results from the fact that the share of new assets (which are only partially depreciated) in the stock is larger than that of the older assets (which are more fully depreciated).

Rule 8: Revaluing book value, SL. Given that the straight-line (SL) method is used, the factor for revaluing $1 of aggregate-depreciated value of a constant stock of assets, as recorded in the balance sheet, is approximated by

$$1 + (n \times p \times 0.4)$$

The exact formula is

$$\frac{(1+p)^n\ (n+1)\ 0.5np^2}{[(1+p)^n - 1]\,(np - 1) + np}$$

Example. A company's balance sheet records $550 depreciated assets. The assets' average life span is 10 years and annual average inflation over the last 10 years has been 5 percent. No real growth is recorded.
Solution: The revalued figure for the depreciated assets is approximately

$$550[1 + (10 \times 0.05 \times 0.4)] = 550 \times 1.2 = \$660$$

The exact figure is

$$550 \times 1.207 = \$664$$

Table 10–2 illustrates some revaluation factors. When the volume of assets increases over time, the revaluation factor will be slightly smaller, especially when the average life span is large. For an average life span of over 15 years, the factor is smaller by about 2 percent for relatively low growth rates and by about 4 percent for relatively high growth rates.

Rule 9: Revaluing book value, accelerated depreciation. For a given stock of depreciable assets, the book value under an accelerated depreciation method is lower than that under the straight-line method (rule 11, chapter 9). The revaluation factor is also lower.

When the stock of assets is growing in real terms and is depreciated under the accelerated method, the revaluation is carried out in two steps:

1. Revalue the book value by the rule for the straight-line method (rule 8).
2. Multiply the results by

$$\frac{F_g}{F_{(g+p)}}$$

where F is the factor from tables 10–3 or 10–4 for rate g or $(g+p)$ and g is the rate of real growth.
Tables 10–3 and 10–4 illustrate factors for the SYD and the DDB methods.

Example: Consider the previous example, where the average life span was 10 years, the inflation rate was 5 percent, and the revalued depreciated assets were $664; however, the double-declining-balance method is now used.
Solution: Because there was no real growth in assets, in table 10–4 provides for 0 percent and 10 years the factor 0.812 and for 5 percent and 10 years an

Table 10–2
Revaluation Factors for Book Value (SL)

	Annual Inflation Rate (%)				
Life Span (Years)	*6*	*12*	*18*	*24*	*30*
5	1.143	1.290	1.442	1.597	1.755
10	1.250	1.517	1.798	2.089	2.388
15	1.362	1.758	2.180	2.619	3.069

Table 10–3
Factors for the SYD Method[a]

	Growth (%)				
Life Span (Years)	*0*	*6*	*12*	*18*	*24*
5	0.778	0.793	0.806	0.818	0.829
10	0.727	0.758	0.784	0.806	0.825
15	0.708	0.753	0.790	0.819	0.843

[a]The factor for the book value under SYD is

$$\frac{\text{Book value, SYD}}{\text{Book value, SL}} = \frac{\dfrac{S_{n,\alpha}(\alpha^2 c + 1 - \alpha n) + \alpha c - n}{\alpha^2 c}}{S_{n,\alpha} - \dfrac{S_{n,\alpha} - n}{n\alpha}}$$

where $\alpha = g$ or $g + p$, and $c = n(n+1)/2$.
When $\alpha = 0$, then the factor is equal to

$$\frac{\dfrac{n+2}{3}}{\dfrac{n+1}{2}}$$

approximate factor of 0.820. The revalued figure for the depreciated assest is approximately

$$664 \times \frac{0.812}{0.820} = \$658$$

Timeseries Revaluation

Application of the revaluation rules in the previous section provides only a crude approximation of the correct current value of depreciable assets, especially when the actual conditions differ from those assumed in developing the rules (see the introduction to this chapter).

The procedure suggested in this section can be used to arrive at a better estimate of the revalued figures for a given date of analysis and to provide revalued figures for a series of years. The procedure for the first purpose is delineated and illustrated first; the application of the procedure for the second purpose is shown at the end of the section.

Table 10–4
Factors for the DDB Method[a]

	Growth (%)				
Life Span (Years)	*0*	*6*	*12*	*18*	*24*
5	0.769	0.780	0.791	0.800	0.810
10	0.812	0.822	0.832	0.843	0.853
15	0.828	0.837	0.849	0.861	0.873

[a]The factor for the book value, under DDB with salvage inherent, is

$$\frac{\text{Book value, DDB}}{\text{Book value, SL}} = \frac{\dfrac{(1+\alpha)^n - (1-f)^n}{\alpha + f}}{S_{n,\alpha} - \dfrac{S_{n,\alpha} - n}{n\alpha}}$$

When $\alpha = 0$, then the factor is equal to

$$\frac{\dfrac{1-(1-f)^n}{f}}{\dfrac{n+1}{2}}$$

where $f = 2/n$ and $\alpha = g$ or $g + p$.

Rule 10: Improved revaluation. A procedure for improved revaluation partitions the assets into "old stock" and "recent investments"; the date of partitioning is called the "starting date." Each set of assets is treated differently: the old stock is revalued by the rules in previous sections, while recent investments are revalued by indexing (rule 36, chapter 1).

Rule 11: Determining the starting date for improved revaluation. The length of the period from the starting date to the date for which the analysis is carried out should be at least 0.3 of the average-assets' life span, and should not exceed the average life span; that is

$$0.3n < m < n$$

where m is the number of years elapsed between analysis and starting dates, n is average life span, and 0.3 is the accumulated depreciation of old stock, on the average (rule 5, chapter 9). The larger m is, the more reliable the result.

Rule 12: Revaluing book value, SL. Given that the straight-line (SL) method is used, a relatively good estimate of the revalued figure of the book (depreciated) value can be arrived at by four steps:

1. Revalue the book value of the stock of assets at the determined starting date (rule 11) by using rule 8.

2. To arrive at the depreciated value of this old stock at the date of analysis, multiply the result of step 1 by

$$\left(\frac{n_0 - T}{n_0}\right)\frac{p_T}{p_0}$$

where n_0 is the average-value-weighted life span of the stock of assets at the starting date (rule 5, chapter 9) or approximately $0.7n$; n is the average life span; T is the number of years between starting and analysis dates; p_T is the price index at the date of analysis; and p_0 is the price index at the starting date.

3. To arrive at the depreciated value of each of the annual investments between the starting and analysis dates, stated in date-of-analysis prices, compute the following for every year:

$$I_t\left(\frac{n - T + t - 0.5}{n}\right)\frac{p_T}{p_t}$$

where I_t is the investment in depreciable assets in year t and p_t is the price index for year t.

4. Sum the figures for the recent investments and add to the results of step 2 (for the old stock) to arrive at the revalued depreciated stock of assets for the date of analysis.

Example. You want to estimate the book value of a company's depreciable assets in terms of 1980 current price level. In 1975 the balance sheet records \$1,500 book value. The average life span of the assets is 10 years, the straight-line method is used, and the average annual inflation rate over the last 10 years has been 5 percent. The following data are available:

	1975	1976	1977	1978	1979	1980
t	0	1	2	3	4	5
Investment		200	—	300	150	500
Price index	156	170	180	195	215	238

Solution:

1. Applying rule 8, the revalued depreciated stock in 1975 is approximately

$$1{,}500[1 + (10 \times 0.05 \times 0.4)] = 1{,}500 \times 1.2 = \$1{,}800$$

2. The depreciated value of this stock in 1980, stated in 1980 prices, is approximately

$$1{,}800 \times \frac{(0.7 \times 10) - 5}{(0.7 \times 10)} \times \frac{238}{156} = 785$$

3. The depreciated values of the annual investments in the period 1976–1980, stated in 1980 prices, are

For 1976 investment: $200 \times \frac{10 - 5 + 1 - 0.5}{10} \times \frac{238}{170} =$ \$154

For 1977 investment: 0

For 1978 investment: $300 \times \frac{10 - 5 + 3 - 0.5}{10} \times \frac{238}{195} =$ 275

For 1979 investment: $150 \times \frac{10 - 5 + 4 - 0.5}{10} \times \frac{238}{215} =$ 141

For 1980 investment: $500 \times \frac{10 - 5 + 5 - 0.5}{10} \times \frac{238}{238} =$ 475

Total 1,045

4. The revalued depreciated stock of assets in 1980 is approximately

$$785 + 1045 = \$1{,}830$$

Rule 13: Revaluing depreciation expenses, SL. Given that the straight-line (SL) method is used, a relatively good estimate of the revalued annual depreciation expenses can be arrived at by the following steps:

1. To arrive at the annual depreciation expense of the old stock, divide its

revalued book value at the date of analysis (the preceding rule) by the remaining average life span, that is, by $(n - T)$.

2. To arrive at the annual depreciation expense for every annual investment between the starting and analysis dates, stated in date-of-analysis prices, compute the following for each year:

$$\frac{I_t}{n} \times \frac{p_T}{p_t}$$

3. Sum the figures for the recent investments and add to the results in step 1 (for the old stock) to arrive at the revalued depreciation expenses for the date of analysis.

Example. Consider the data in the previous example.
Solution:

1. The depreciation expense in 1980 for the old stock (acquired before 1975), stated in 1980 prices, is approximately

$$\frac{785}{17 - 5} = \$392$$

2. The depreciation expenses for the annual investments in the period 1976–1980, stated in 1980 prices, are:

For 1976 investment:	$\frac{200}{10} \times \frac{238}{170} =$	\$28
For 1977 investment:		0
For 1978 investment:	$\frac{300}{10} \times \frac{238}{195} =$	37
For 1979 investment:	$\frac{150}{10} \times \frac{238}{215} =$	17
For 1980 investment:	$\frac{500}{10} \times \frac{238}{238} =$	50
Total		132

3. The revalued depreciation expenses of the whole stock of assets in 1980 is approximately

$$392 + 132 = \$524$$

Rule 14: Revaluing book value, accelerated depreciation. This procedure assumes (in addition to the assumptions in the introduction to this chapter) that, when accelerated depreciation is used, the annual depreciation is determined by a rate that is the same for all the assets. This process provides approximations for all the accelerated depreciation methods.

A relatively good estimate of the revalued figure for the book (depreciated) value can be arrived at by the following steps:

1. Revalue the book value of the stock of assets at the determined starting date (rule 11), by using rules 8 or 9.

2. To arrive at the depreciated value of this old stock at the date of analysis, multiply the result of step 1 by

$$(1 - d)^T \left(\frac{p_T}{p_0}\right)$$

where d is the depreciation rate, assuming the declining balance method (for the double declining method, $d = 2 / n$; this rate can also be used when the sum-of-the-year's-digits method is used); n is the average life span; T is the years between starting and analysis dates; p_T is the price index at the date of analysis; and p_0 is the price index at the starting date.

3. To arrive at the depreciated value of each of the annual investments between the starting and analysis dates, stated in date-of-analysis prices, compute the following for every year:

$$I_t(1 - d)^{T-t+0.5} \left(\frac{p_T}{p_t}\right)$$

where I_t is the investment in depreciable assets in year t, p_t is the price index for year t

4. Sum the figures for the recent investments and add to the results of step 2 (for the old stock) to arrive at the revalued depreciated stock of assets for the date of analysis.

Example. Consider the data in the example for rule 12, but using the double-declining-balance depreciation method.

Solution:

1. Applying rules 8 and 9, the revalued depreciated stock in 1975 is approximately

$$1{,}500[1 + (10 \times 0.05 \times 0.4)] \times \frac{0.812}{0.820} = \$1{,}782$$

2. The depreciation rate is approximately two-tenths = 0.20. The depreciated value of this stock in 1980, stated in 1980 prices, is approximately

$$1{,}782\,(1 - 0.2)^5 \times \frac{238}{156} = \$891$$

3. The book values of the annual investments in the period 1976–1980, stated in 1980 prices, are

For 1976 investment:	$200\,(1 - 0.2)^{5-1+0.5} \times \frac{238}{170}$	= \$103
For 1977 investment:		0
For 1978 investment:	$300\,(1 - 0.2)^{5-3+0.5} \times \frac{238}{195}$	= 210
For 1979 investment:	$150\,(1 - 0.2)^{5-4+0.5} \times \frac{238}{215}$	= 119
For 1980 investment:	$500\,(1 - 0.2)^{5-5+0.5} \times \frac{238}{238}$	= 447
Total		879

4. The revalued depreciated stock of assets in 1980 is approximately

$$891 + 879 = \$1{,}770$$

Rule 15: Revaluing depreciation expenses, accelerated depreciation. A relatively good estimate of the revalued annual depreciation expenses can be arrived at by multiplying the revalued depreciated stock of assets, as computed above, by

$$\frac{d}{1-d}$$

where d is the depreciation rate.

Example. Consider the solution for the previous example.
Solution: The revalued depreciation expenses of the whole stock of assets in 1980 is approximately

$$(891 + 879)\frac{0.2}{1-0.2} = 222.75 + 219.75 = \$442.50$$

Timeseries Revaluation of Assets for Comparisons

The procedures in rules 12–15 can be applied for revaluing the book values and depreciation expenses for a series of years to facilitate comparisons.

Rule 16: Determining the starting date of the timeseries. The length of the period from the starting date to the last date of the analyzed series should be at least one-half of the assets' average life span. That is

$$m > 0.5n$$

where m is the number of years elapsed between analysis and starting dates and n is the average life span. The larger m is and the further away the years are from the starting date, the more reliable the results.

Rule 17: Revaluing book value for timeseries. A series of revalued book (depreciated) values can be arrived at for either method of depreciation by two steps:

1. Revalue the book value for each current year (rule 12 or 14 as the case may be).
2. Inflate the values arrived at in step 1 to current values of last year.

Example. Consider the date in the example under rule 14. Compare the revalued depreciated stocks for 1979 and 1980.
Solution: Applying steps 2–4 of rule 14 to arrive at the book value for 1979 provides the following figures:

For the old stock:	$1{,}782(1-0.2)^4 \times \frac{215}{156} =$	\$1,006
For 1976 investment:	$200(1-0.2)^{4-1+0.5} \times \frac{215}{170} =$	116
For 1977 investment:		0
For 1978 investment:	$300(1-0.2)^{4-3+0.5} \times \frac{215}{195} =$	237
For 1979 investment:	$150(1-0.2)^{4-4+0.5} \times \frac{215}{215} =$	134
Total		1,493

In 1980 prices

$$1{,}493 \times \frac{238}{215} = 1{,}653$$

The revalued figures (the one just given and the one from the solution of the example for rule 14 in 1980 prices are \$1,653 for 1979 and \$1,770 for 1980.

Rule 18: Revaluing depreciation expenses for timeseries. A series of revalued annual depreciation expenses can be arrived at by applying the same procedure used in rule 17 for the book value.

Revaluing Cost of Materials Used

The costs of materials recorded in the income statement can be stated at the end of the year's price level for costing purposes.

Rule 19: Revaluing cost of materials, FIFO. Under the FIFO method, the factor for revaluing \$1 of cost of materials drawn from inventory is approximated by

$$1 + (n \times p \times 0.6)$$

where n is the holding time of inventory, in months, and p is the inflation rate per month. The exact formula is

$$\frac{(1+p)^n np}{(1+p)^n - 1}$$

Example A. A company's income statement records \$400 as the costs of materials used. The FIFO method is used and the materials are held 3 months in inventory. The inflation rate prior to the date of the income statement was 2 percent per month.
Solution: The revalued cost of materials is approximately

$$400[1 + (3 \times 0.02 \times 0.6)] = \$414$$

The exact figure is \$416.
Table 10–5 illustrates some revaluation factors.

An alternative formula for the factor for revaluation is

$$\frac{\text{Price index at date of analysis}}{\text{Sum of } t \text{ indexes for } n \text{ prior months}/t}$$

where t equals $n + 1$, which is the number of indexes from beginning to end of n periods.

Example B. Materials are held 2 months in inventory. The relevant price indexes for the period under analysis are 125, 126, and 129; the implied average monthly inflation rate is 1.6 percent.
Solution: The relevant factor is

$$\frac{129}{(125 + 126 + 129)\,/\,3} = 1.0184$$

The approximated factor is

$$1 + (2 \times 0.016 \times 0.6) = 1.0192$$

Rule 20: Revaluing cost of materials average method. The factor for revaluing \$1 of cost of materials that are drawn from inventory, under the average valuation method, is approximated by

$$1 + (n \times p \times 0.4)$$

Table 10–5
Revaluation Factors for Inventories under FIFO

	Monthly Inflation Rate (%)				
Turnover (Months)	*0.5*	*1.0*	*1.5*	*2.0*	*2.5*
3	1.010	1.020	1.030	1.040	1.050
6	1.018	1.035	1.053	1.071	1.089
9	1.025	1.051	1.077	1.103	1.129

Example. Consider example A for rule 19, but with the average method of valuation.
Solution: The revalued cost of materials is approximately

$$400[1 + (3 \times 0.20 \times 0.4)] = \$410$$

Table 10–6 illustrates some revaluation factors under the average method.

Rule 21: Revaluing cost of materials, LIFO. The cost of materials that are drawn from inventory under the LIFO method usually should not be revalued.

Revaluing Stock of Inventory

The value of inventories (raw materials, goods in process, and finished goods) recorded in the balance sheet is usually understated during a period of inflation and therefore should be revalued

Rule 22: Revaluing stock of inventory, FIFO. The factor for revaluing \$1 of a stock of any type of inventory, under the FIFO method, is approximated by

$$1 + (n \times p \times 0.6)$$

The exact formula is given in rule 1 and revaluation factors are listed in table 10–5.

Example. A company's balance sheet records \$1,000 in raw materials inventory. The FIFO method is used and the materials are held 3 months in inventory. The inflation rate prior to the date of the balance sheet was 2 percent per month.

Table 10–6
Revaluation Factors for Inventories under the Average Method

	Monthly Inflation Rate (%)				
Turnover (Months)	*0.5*	*1.0*	*1.5*	*2.0*	*2.5*
3	1.008	1.017	1.025	1.033	1.042
6	1.013	1.027	1.040	1.054	1.067
9	1.018	1.037	1.056	1.074	1.093

Solution: The revalued inventory is approximately

$$1{,}000[1 + (3 \times 0.02 \times 0.6)] = \$1{,}036$$

Rule 23: Revaluing stock of inventory, LIFO. The revaluation of a stock of any type of inventory under the LIFO method can be estimated when the switch from FIFO to LIFO has been carried out in a recent year. Revaluation estimates require several steps:

1. Revalue the stock of inventory at the date when the company switched from FIFO to LIFO by using rule 22 for FIFO. When the inflation rate at that year was low, skip this step.

2. To state this value in terms of the prices at the date of analysis, multiply the result by

$$\frac{p_T}{p_O}$$

p_T is the price index at date of analysis, and p_O is the price index at switch date.

3. Revalue the change in inventory between the two dates—that is,

$$(A_{\text{analysis}} - A_{\text{switch}}) \frac{\text{Sum of } t \text{ indexes for } T \text{ years} / t}{\text{Price index at date of switch}}$$

where A is the recorded stock value at dates of analysis and switch-over, and t equals $T + 1$ which is number of indexes from the beginning to end of T periods.

4. Add the results of steps 2 and 3.

Example. A company's balance sheet records \$1,500 materials inventory for 1980 and \$1,000 for 1975. In 1976 the company switched from the

FIFO to the LIFO method. Inventory is held 6 months and the monthly inflation rate in 1975 was 2 percent. The end-of-the-year price indexes for the period 1976–1980 are: 170, 180, 195, 215, and 238.
Solution:

1. The revalued 1975 stock of materials is approximately

$$1{,}000[1 + (6 \times 0.02 \times 0.6)] = \$1{,}072$$

2. This value, in 1980 prices, is

$$1{,}072(238 / 170) = \$1{,}501$$

3. The sum of the price indexes for the 1976–1980 period is 998. The revalued change in inventory is approximately

$$(1{,}500 - 1{,}000)\frac{998 / 5}{170} = \$587$$

4. The revalued stock of materials in 1980 is approximately

$$1{,}501 + 587 = \$2{,}088$$

Notes

1. Rules 1, 2, 6, 8, 19, 20, and 22 are based on these assumptions. These rules are drawn from L. Shashua and Y. Goldschmidt, "A Tool for Inflation Adjustment of Financial Statements," *Journal of Business and Accounting* (Spring 1976), pp. 33–42.

11 Profit Measurement during Inflation

During inflation the price level increases and the purchasing power of money declines. To enable meaningful comparisons of financial activities that occurred at different times, you must restate the monetary values in constant units. This procedure is done by using price indexes.

The objective of this chapter is to summarize the main features of inflation accounting: revaluation of assets, adjustment of balance sheet and income statement items, and profit measurement.

Asset Revaluation in Financial Statements

The historical value of an asset is usually understated in inflationary periods. This value should be adjusted or revalued to correct the distortion caused by inflation. The main procedures for price level adjustment or revaluing are summarized in rules 1 and 2.

Rule 1: Revaluation by price index. Revaluation of assets by the use of indexing is carried out by multiplying the historical value by the price level index. That is,

$$\frac{\text{Price index at date of analysis}}{\text{Price index at acquisition date}}$$

General price index adjustment. To state the historical value in terms of the current purchasing power of money (that is, adjusted for the effect of inflation), revaluation should be carried out by using a general price index, usually the Consumer Price Index (CPI).

Specific price index adjustment. To arrive at the estimated current cost of a given asset (or group of assets), revaluation should be carried out by using the specific price index for the given type of asset.

Example. A piece of equipment was acquired in January 1975 for $2,000; in January 1980 its book value is $1,000. The following price indexes were recorded:

	1975	1980
CPI	113.3	232.0
Equipment price index	115.0	270.0

Solution: The book value adjusted for the effects of inflation using the CPI is

$$1{,}000 \times \frac{232.0}{113.3} = \$2{,}048$$

The book value, adjusted for the effect of specific price changes using the equipment price index, is

$$1{,}000 \times \frac{270}{115} = \$2{,}348$$

Rule 2: Revaluation by replacement cost. For a company to survive in the long run, the revenue from sales must cover the replacement of all inputs used in production, including the replacement of assets. Therefore, the assets should be revalued to represent their market price (in the case of liquid assets) or their replacement costs (in the case of fixed assets and inventories).

Price level adjustment by the specific price index (as explained in rule 1) approximates the value of the replacement cost of the assets. Alternatively, the replacement cost of each asset can be evaluated by reference to market prices and checking the service potential of the asset (see the first section of chapter 8).

Rule 3: Required adjustments for financial analysis. Before analyzing a financial statement, two types of price level adjustments should be carried out.

1. *Revaluation of distorted values:* Various items in the financial statement should be revalued, including assets in the balance sheet and lagged costs (depreciation and materials from opening inventory) in the income statement. Revaluation may be carried out by indexing each type or group of assets or by applying the tools and short-cut procedures in chapter 10.

Revaluation of the distorted values is applied for various purposes, mainly for adjusting the conventional financial statements before analyzing these statements (chapter 15); adjusting an opening balance sheet to be used as a basis for preparing annual price-level–adjusted financial statements; and annual end-of-the-year adjustments when these are required.

2. *Indexation of revalued items:* A financial statement adjusted for the

effects of inflation is stated in terms of the money values of the year for which it is published. To enable timeseries comparisons of financial statements, figures must be stated in constant money—for example, in terms of the price level of the last year in the series. This process is done by indexing the items that are analyzed. Indexation is carried out by multiplying each reported figure by the price level index. That is,

$$\frac{\text{Price index at date of analysis}}{\text{Price index at reported date}}$$

This procedure is illustrated in the example for rule 16 later in this chapter.

Financial Statement Adjustments

The profit of a going concern is defined as the sum that may be withdrawn from the company during a period without impairing its equity funds in comparison with the beginning of the period. Profit is measured by the change in the equity value plus dividends. For measuring the correct change in equity value and profit in time of inflation, distorted values in the conventional financial statements must be adjusted.

Adjusting Balance Sheet Items

The first step in measuring the profit correctly is to adjust the balance sheet of a given year to provide an opening balance sheet. This balance sheet enables year-to-year adjustments and profit measurement.

Rule 4: Adjusting opening balance sheet. The opening balance sheet is adjusted by revaluing the assets to represent their replacement cost, for example, by applying the specific price index to each group of assets. This procedure can be done by detailed revaluation (of each asset or group of assets) or by using the short-cut procedures in chapter 10. The difference between the adjusted value and the historical value is added to the equity.

Rule 5: Yearly adjustment of balance sheet. Given that the opening balance sheet is adjusted to current prices, yearly adjustment of the balance sheet is required as long as inflation persists. At the end of the year the nonmonetary assets (fixed assets and inventories) should be revalued to represent their replacement cost by using the specific price indexes. The resultant value provides the assets value in the closing balance sheet. The nominal value of monetary assets (such as cash and accounts receivable) and debt (current and long-term liabilities) usually is not affected by inflation.

Rule 6: Adjusting nonmonetary assets. Adjusted nonmonetary assets (fixed assets and inventories) is the current value of the stock of assets at the end of the year. It is computed as follows.
Depreciable assets:

$$(A_b - d)\,(I_{\text{specific}}) + NA(I_{\text{specific},1/2})$$

Land and inventories:

$$A_b(I_{\text{specific}}) + NA(I_{\text{specific},1/2})$$

where A_b is the nonmonetary assets' adjusted value, beginning of year (opening balance sheet); d is the recorded depreciation expense, based on opening balance sheet; NA is the new nonmonetary assets acquired during the year; I_{specific} = Index at end of year/Index at beginning of year; and $I_{\text{specific},1/2}$ = average index = $1 + (I_{\text{specific}} - 1)/2$.

Example. Consider the balance sheet of Company X in table 15–2. Suppose the balance sheet for 1979 is an adjusted opening-balance sheet and the sheet for 1980 is a conventional balance sheet that is based on the 1979 adjusted opening-balance sheet. The relevant data for arriving at an adjusted balance sheet for 1980 are presented in table 11–1. It is assumed that the company is using the LIFO method for inventory accounting.
Solution: The adjustment of the nonmonetary assets (in $000) is

Inventories	$(80 \times 1.20) + (20 \times 1.10) =$	$ 118
Equipment	$(350 - 50)\,1.24 + (100 \times 1.12) =$	484
Buildings	$(450 - 50)\,1.20 + (100 \times 1.10) =$	590
Land	$300 \times 1.30 =$	390
		1,582

These figures, plus $200 monetary assets, provide the closing balance sheet ($1,782) as shown in the next to the last column in table 11–1.

Adjusting Income Statement

To arrive at a meaningful annual profit in time of inflation, two cost items should be adjusted:

Table 11–1
Company X Balance Sheets, Flow-of-Funds Figures, and Adjusted Balance Sheet
($000)

	1979[a]	*Depreciation*	*Addition*	*1980 Recorded[b]*	*Relevant Price Level Index*	*1980 Adjusted[c]*	*1980 Difference*
Assets							
Monetary assets	$170		$30	$200		$200	0
Inventories	80		20	100	1.20	118	18
Equipment	350	$50	100	400	1.24	484	84
Buildings	450	50	100	500	1.20	590	90
Land	300			300	1.30	390	90
Total	1,350			1,500		1,782	282
Liabilities							
Debt	$610		$90	$700		$700	0
Equity	740		60[d]	800	1.20	1,082	282
Total	1,350			1,500		1,782	

Source: Tables 15–2 and 15–3.
[a]Opening adjusted balance sheet.
[b]Recorded conventionally on the basis of 1979 opening figures.
[c]Adjusted closing balance sheet.
[d]Of which $30 are retained earnings and $30 are issued capital.

1. Costs that stem from assets (historical depreciation expense and cost of materials from opening inventory), especially when the FIFO method is used. The adjusted costs can be calculated from the assets' adjusted values (based on detailed revaluation of each asset or group of assets) or by using the short-cut procedures in the first and fifth sections of chapter 10.

2. Interest expenses on debt. Although the costs that stem from assets are understated during inflation, the interest expenses are overstated because they include compensation for the decline in the debt purchasing power.

Rule 7: Yearly adjustment of costs of assets. When an adjusted opening balance sheet is available, and the balance sheet is adjusted every year (rule 5), two adjustments of costs are required as long as inflation persists:

1. The depreciation expenses derived from the revalued assets at the beginning of the year should be adjusted by the specific price level change during the year.

2. The cost of materials from opening inventory should be adjusted in a similar way when the FIFO method is used. However, when the LIFO method is used, usually no adjustment is required (see chapter 10). The adjustments are similar to those shown in rule 3.

Example. Consider the income statement of Company X for 1980 in table 15–3. Suppose it is a conventional income statement that is based on the 1979-adjusted opening-balance sheet. Because the LIFO method is used for materials, only the depreciation expense should be adjusted. Suppose the recorded depreciation (in \$000) is \$50 for equipment and \$50 for buildings.
Solution: To arrive at the price level for the last day of 1980, the depreciation expenses are adjusted (using the relevant price indexes from table 11–1) as follows (in \$000):

Equipment:	$50(I_{\text{specific}}) = 50 \times 1.24 =$	\$62
Buildings:	$50(I_{\text{specific}}) = 50 \times 1.20 =$	60
		122

The additional depreciation adjustment, to be deducted from the net earnings, is

$$122 - 100 = \$22$$

Rule 8: Estimating the real interest on debt. During inflation the actual interest expenses include compensation for the decline in the debt-purchasing power, in addition to the preinflation real-interest expense. The real-interest expense on debt is estimated by

$$\left(D + \frac{ND}{2}\right) i^*(1 + p)$$

where D is the debt, beginning of year; ND is the new debt acquired during the year; i^* is the preinflation interest rate on debt; and p is the general price level change during the year.

Example. Consider the financial data of Company X for 1980 in table 15–3. The actual interest expense (in \$000) is \$70. The preinflation interest rate on debt was 4 percent ($i^* = 0.04$), and the general price level change was 20 percent ($p = 0.20$).
Solution: The real interest expense (in \$000) is estimated to be

$$\left(610 + \frac{90}{2}\right) 0.04(1 + 0.20) = \$31.44$$

Because this figure is an estimate, it is rounded to \$32 for further calculations.

In practice the adjusted-interest expenses are higher than those calculated in the previous example. The real interest rate should be charged only on loans that finance assets whose value is inflation-adjusted, but not on liabilities that finance the accounts receivable. These liabilities should be charged by the current nominal interest rate because current receipts and payments are realized during the accounting year and are not adjusted.

Rule 9: Estimating the profit from operations. To estimate the profit that stems from the current operations, the adjusted costs that stem from assets (rule 7) and the adjusted-interest expenses (rule 8) should be deducted from the after-tax gross earnings (net earnings before interest). This profit measure can be used for performance evaluation.

Example. The net earnings for Company X before interest for 1980 (table 15–3, in \$000) were \$160, with net earnings of \$90 and interest of \$70. Solution: The adjusted profit that should be used for performance evaluation (in \$000), is

$$90 + 70 - (22 + 32) = \$106$$

Inflation Effects on Profit

The level of the adjusted total profit is affected by inflation through several variables, such as the composition of the items in the balance sheet (various types of assets or liabilities), the levels of the various price indexes, and the average interest rate. The effect of some of these variables on the profit can be estimated using the procedures in this section.

The total profit during inflation is calculated by adding balance sheet adjustments to the conventional profit figure (rule 14). The total balance sheet adjustment, as measured by the change in equity between the end and beginning of the period (rule 10) is partitioned into several components (rules 11–13).

Rule 10: Calculating total equity change. The adjustment of a company's assets changes the recorded equity. The equity in the adjusted balance sheet is derived by subtracting the debt from the adjusted assets. The change in equity is the period's increase in equity.

Example: Consider Company X balance sheets for 1980 in table 11–1. Solution: The change in equity for December 1980 (in \$000) is

Adjusted assets (example for rule 6)	\$1,782
Debt	(700)
Equity, adjusted	1,082
Recorded Equity	(800)
Change in equity	282

Rule 11: Calculating equity maintenance adjustment. The sum required to maintain the real value (purchasing power) of a company's equity in an inflationary year is measured as follows:

$$E_b(p_{\text{general}}) + NE(p_{\text{general},1/2})$$

where E_b is equity, beginning of year (opening balance sheet); NE is new equity, issued during the year; p_{general} is the general price level change during the year, which equals (Index at end of year/Index at beginning of year) − 1; and $p_{\text{general},1/2}$ equals one-half of p_{general}.

The inflation-compensated equity at the end of the year is

Recorded equity + equity maintenance adjustment

Example. The equity maintenance adjustment (in \$000) for Company X in 1980, assuming $p = 0.20$, is

$$740 \times 0.20 + 30\ (0.20 / 2) = \$151$$

The adjusted equity at the end of 1980 that would maintain its real value is

$$800 + 151 = \$951$$

This figure can also be derived as follows:

Opening equity, inflation-compensated	740 × 1.20 =	\$888
New equity, inflation-compensated	30 × 1.10 =	33
Retained earnings		30
Total		951

Rule 12: Calculating total assets gains. The balance-sheet gains on assets in the current year because of inflation is computed as follows:

Adjusted nonmonetary assets by specific price indexes (rule 6)
+ Monetary assets, end of year

− Adjusted equity, inflation-compensated (rule 11)
− Debt, end of year
= Gains on assets

Example. Consider the data of Company X for 1980 in table 11–1.
Solution: The total effect of inflation on assets (in \$000) is

Adjusted nonmonetary assets (example for rule 6)	\$1,582
Monetary assets (table 11–1)	200
Adjusted equity (example for rule 11)	(951)
Debt (table 11–1)	(700)
Gains on assets	131

This figure can also be derived as follows:

Equity from adjusted balance sheet (table 11–1)	\$1,082
Less inflation-compensated equity (example for rule 11)	(951)
Gains on assets	131

It can also be computed by deducting the equity-maintenance adjustment (\$151) from the total equity change (\$282).

Rule 13: Calculating asset holding gains. The holding gains of non-monetary assets are defined and measured by the difference between the estimated current cost or value of the assets (adjusted by means of specific price indexes) and the historical acquisition costs restated in terms of current price level (adjusted by means of the general price index). This sum is considered as a reserve for the renewal of assets.

Example. Consider Company X figures for 1980. The nonmonetary assets are adjusted by means of the specific price indexes in the example for rule 6, amounting to \$1,582 (in \$000).

Solution: The adjustment (in \$000) using the general price index (1.20) is

Inventories	$80 \times 1.20 + (20 \times 1.10) =$	\$118
Equipment	$(350 - 50)1.20 + (100 \times 1.10) =$	470
Buildings	$(450 - 50)1.20 + (100 \times 1.10) =$	590
Land	$300 \times 1.20 =$	360
		1,538

The asset-holding gains are

$$1{,}582 - 1{,}538 = \$44$$

Rule 14: Calculating total profit. The total profit to be allocated in the current year is calculated as follows:

Change in equity (rule 10)
− Equity maintenance adjustment (rule 11)
= Gains on assets (rule 12)
− Asset-holding gains (rule 13)
= Profit adjustment
+ Nominal profit
= Total profit

Example. Consider the data of Company X for 1980.
Solution: The total profit (in $000) is

Change in equity (example for rule 10)	$282
Equity maintenance adjustment (example for rule 11)	(151)
Gains on assets	131
Assets-holding gains (example for rule 13)	(44)
Profit adjustment	87
Nominal profit (net earnings from table 15–3)	90
Total profit	177

The total profit stems from operations and from inflation gains on debt (rule 15).

Rule 15: Estimating the inflation gains on debt. During inflation, the actual average interest rate paid on loans often does not provide full compensation for the decline in the purchasing power of the outstanding debt. In this case, the borrower reaps inflation gains.

The inflation gains on the company's net debt is estimated by deducting the profit from operations (rule 9) from the total profit (rule 14).

Example. The inflation gain on Company X debt in 1980 (in $000) is estimated to be

Total profit (example for rule 14)	$177
Profit from operations (example for rule 9)	106
Inflation gain	71

Table 11–2
Company X Timeseries Balance Sheets—1979 and 1980
($000)

	1979				1980	
	Recorded[a]		*Indexed to 1980*[b]		*Adjusted*[c]	
Monetary assets		$170		$204		$200
Inventories	$80		$96		$118	
Equipment	350		420		484	
Buildings	450		540		590	
Land	300		360		390	
Subtotal		1,180		1,416		1,582
Total		1,350		1,620		1,782
Liabilities	610		732		700	
Equity	740		888		1,082	
Total		1,350		1,620		1,782

[a]See table 11–1.
[b]Inflated by the general price level change—that is, by 1.20.
[c]Nonmonetary assets from the example for rule 6; monetary items from table 11–1.

Rule 16: Timeseries comparisons. To enable timeseries comparisons of the adjusted financial statements, and of the resulting financial ratios, the figures must be indexed as explained in rule 3. Indexation should be carried out by means of specific price indexes. However, for simplicity, the general price index can be used.

Example. Consider the data in table 11–1. To compare the figures in the adjusted balance sheets (the 1979 opening adjusted-balance sheet and the 1980 adjusted-balance sheet), 1979 data are indexed by the general price index (1.20), as illustrated in table 11–2. The indexation of 1979 data to the December 1980 price level enables comparisons of 1979 figures with 1980 figures. For example, the real value of assets (in $000) increased from $1,620 in December 1979 to $1,782 in December 1980, whereas liabilities decreased from $732 to $700.

Part IV
Costing and Pricing

12 Framework of Costing

The cost of a product is an important output of a cost-accounting system. When the company does not have a cost-accounting system, a product may also be costed by assembling the relevant data (actual or estimated costs and value of product) from various sources. Although both problems of costing are similar, in the second case there is no assurance that some costs are not omitted because the product cost statement is not an integral part of a cost-accounting system.

The total cost, the individual cost items, the value of product (in the case of a final product), and the profit should be used for decisions and control. Such decisions may determine resource allocation (such as a change in the scale of an activity or product, or a change of the input mix in producing a given product), or pricing, when prices are set by the producer. Control is exercised by setting predetermined benchmarks or standards to be attained and by comparing actual performance against those standards.

A company is usually organized into departments. A department may produce final products for sale, or produce intermediate goods or services for internal use. For costing purposes, the company is divided into cost (or profit) centers. A cost or profit center is an accounting unit for which a cost statement is prepared. Many cost items must be allocated to the cost centers by an accepted procedure; this process causes some arbitrariness in costing.

Costing procedures are discussed in chapter 13, whereas in this chapter we state the problems of costing a product. In addition, the relations among cost, profit, and volume of production are delineated.

Managerial Cost Statement

To arrive at a meaningful cost of production, detailed cost items should be stated in a cost statement. In the case of a product that is produced for sale, the cost statement may also include the value of the produce and the amount of the profit. In preparing a cost statement it is important to compute and state the cost items in such a way that when deducted from the value of the product, a true profit will be derived; this procedure is done by evaluating the inputs and products in terms of their replacement costs (rule 3, chapter 8).

Example. A managerial cost statement for a given product is illustrated in table 12–1. To simplify the illustration, only the main cost items are presented and grouped into variable and fixed costs. The difference between the value of the product and the variable costs is named "contribution." The variable costs and the contribution provide data for short-run decisions regarding changes in the input mix and the scale of operations.

Analyzing the Cost Statement

A cost statement is usually prepared for individual products and for individual segments of a company. The cost statement of a segment or of a product can be used for performance evaluation in a way similar to that used in financial statements analysis for evaluating the performance of a company (chapter 15). In other words, some of the procedures and tools that are applied to financial statements can also be applied to cost statements.

Rule 1: Comparison between cost statements. For comparing between cost statements (of different products or segments, or of different periods) the various categories and the main cost items should be presented as proportions (percentages) of the value of product.

Table 12–1
Cost Statement for Product A
($000)

Value of product		$1,550
Variable costs		
Materials	$400	
Labor	200	
Intermediate goods[a]	245	
Internal services[b]	72	
Interest on working capital	100	
Total		1,017
Contribution		533
Fixed costs		
Depreciation	70	
Interest on assets	80	
Intermediate goods	105	
Internal services	8	
Overhead	130	
Total		393
Profit		140

[a]Goods transferred from other departments.
[b]Maintenance, transportation, computer, and so on.

Example. Consider the cost statement in table 12–1. The proportions of the main categories to the value of product are

Variable costs	66%
Fixed costs	25
Contribution	34
Profit	9

The proportions of the main inputs to the value of product are

Materials	26%
Labor	13
Interest	12
Intermediate goods	23

Rule 2: Profitability analysis. A major indicator of profitability, besides the net profit, is the contribution ratio. The contribution is the difference between the value of product and the variable costs. The ratio of the contribution to the value of product indicates the change in the cash inflow (that is, receipts minus variable costs) that results from a one-unit change in the level of sales, given that the fixed costs do not change.

Example. Consider the cost statement in table 12–1. The contribution ratio is 34 percent. Thus, a $1 change in the level of production and sale will cause a corresponding change of $0.34 in the net cash receipts; that is, it indicates the contribution to the company's fixed expense and profit. This ratio holds as long as the change in the level of production does not affect the level of the fixed costs.

Rule 3: Performance evaluation through variance analysis. The relative performance of a segment can be evaluated by comparing the items in the cost statement to benchmarks or standards. Standards are based on performance in the past of other company segments or of other companies. Standards are planned as targets to be achieved, and the actual performance is compared with the standards. The differences or variances are reported to gauge performance. Only significant variances on controllable items (such as the level of production and variable costs) should be reported to enable "management by exception"; that is, examining only those variances that are judged by management to be worthy of control.

Example. Assume that the cost statement in table 12–1 is a planned statement; that is, the figures are predetermined standards per unit of product. Additional data and the corresponding calculations are presented in table 12–2. These figures show that the actual volume of production and the total contribution exceeded the plan. However, because the use of material exceeded the plan, there was a decline in per-unit contribution.

Analyzing the Cost Items

Each cost item in the cost statement is a result of either a simple or an elaborate computation. Understanding the problems involved in calculating each cost item is the key issue in correctly interpreting the cost statement and in constructing a new cost accounting system or in changing an existing system.

Rule 4: Cost of materials. Most of the direct materials are drawn from inventory. The choice of the inventory valuation method (such as FIFO and LIFO; see chapter 8) affects the level of the recorded cost. During inflation, these cost items may require adjustment, especially when the FIFO method is used.

Rule 5: Cost of labor. Labor cost includes several types of renumerations, which differ among different workers. Usually an average wage rate for a group of workers is used.

Rule 6: Cost of intermediate goods. A production department often utilizes intermediate goods that are produced by other departments. When the production process consists of several stages, intermediate goods are

Table 12–2
Performance Evaluation for Product A

			Variance		
	Planned	*Actual*	*Absolute*[a]	*Percentage Relative*[b]	*Evaluation*
Total production					
Units produced	100	120	20	20	Better
Total contribution	$53,300	$57,600	$4,300	8	Better
Per unit					
Contribution	$533	$480	$53	10	Worse
Materials	400	456	56	14	Worse
Labor	200	190	10	5	Better
Intermediate goods	350	360	10	3	Worse

[a]Actual minus planned.
[b]Absolute variance divided by planned level.

transferred from one stage to the next one. A given cost item may be miscalculated in each stage, thus augmenting the mistake up to the final product. The fact that intermediate goods (work in process) are inventoried in every stage of production introduces complications into the cost computations.

Because the total costs of intermediate goods include both variable and fixed costs, each type of cost should be channeled separately to the cost statement of the final product.

Rule 7: Cost of internal services. A production department usually utilizes services that are rendered by so-called service departments, such as maintenance, transportation, or computer services. The fact that service departments often render services to one another introduces a complication into the cost calculations. Again, the variable and fixed costs should be channeled separately to the cost statement of the final product. The unit cost provides a "transfer price" for the service, and its meaning should resemble that of the price of a service in the market.

Rule 8: Interest expenses. The use of capital involves costs (that is, interest expenses); each product utilizes the services of capital (working capital, assets) differently. Hence, to arrive at a genuine cost of production, imputed interest (cost of capital) should be charged to each product according to its use of capital services. Refraining from charging interest (as often is practiced in conventional cost-accounting systems) will result in under-costing of products that intensively use capital resources.

Rule 9: Depreciation expenses. Depreciation expense is the portion of an asset's acquisition cost that is allocated to a given year. The choice of the depreciation method (for example, straight-line or accelerated; see chapter 8) affects the level of the recorded cost. The allocation of the annual depreciation expenses to individual products is difficult when an asset serves several products. An appropriate allocation method must be used in this case as in the case of internal services.

Depreciation expense may be a fixed or a variable cost. It is a variable cost if the use of the asset causes a real depreciation in its value. During inflation, the historical depreciation expense should be consistently revalued.

Rule 10: Overhead expenses. The overhead costs incurred for managing the company should be allocated to the individual products to arrive at full costs. Because the services rendered by management to the individual cost centers and products are generally not measurable (in contrast to the case of internal services), these costs must be allocated by using an arbitrary procedure. The procedure of allocating these costs affects the final cost of each product. The allocation of overhead implies charges for covering management expenses; as a result, the process of allocation to some extent resembles tax levying.

Mechanism of Costing

Costing a product or a service is elaborate because of the interrelationships among internal services, intermediate products, work in process, and the final products. The end result is that all the costs incurred are channeled or allocated to the final products.

Costs Flow and Allocation

Costs of production can be viewed as flowing in both temporal (time) and spatial (location) senses. The cost statement is an attempt to summarize the costs incurred in different periods for producing a given good or service. Because the costs incurred by the company must be allocated to both periods and products, costing can become complex and arbitrary.

Rule 11: Cost allocation for total production. When a cost statement is prepared for the total production of a company, cost must be allocated only in the temporal sense—the acquisition costs of assets and inventories and costs of goods in process are allocated to a given period (usually a year). Thus, the larger the share of costs that originate from past acquisitions or activities, the larger the complexity and arbitrariness of the costing and the less objective the results.

Rule 12: Cost allocation for a given product. In the case of a cost statement for a given product (final or intermediate), costs must be allocated in the spatial sense (between departments, cost centers, and products), in addition to the allocation in the temporal sense (assets and inventories). Thus, the greater the number of cost centers (types of services, number of stages in production, or number of production departments) and of products in each center, the greater the complexity and arbitrariness of the costing and the less objective the results. The complexity of cost allocation in the spatial sense can be seen from the illustration in table 12–3.

Transfer Pricing

As shown in table 12–3, many inputs (cost items) in each cost center originate from another cost center; that is, the inputs are processed and transferred from one center to another within the company. For costing purposes, these transfers should be priced.

Table 12–3
Cost Flow among Cost Centers

Materials

Beginning inventory
\+ Purchases
− Ending inventory
= Cost of materials issued to all centers

Production stage 1

Beginning inventory
\+ Materials
\+ Other costs
\+ Services
\+ Overhead
− Ending inventories
= Cost of intermediate good to stage 2

Final product

Beginning inventory
\+ Materials
\+ Other costs
\+ Intermediate goods
\+ Services
\+ Overhead
− Ending inventory
= Cost of goods

Service 1

Materials
\+ Other costs
\+ Services
\+ Overhead
= Cost of service,
− Allocation to other service centers and to production centers
= Over- or underallocation to profit-and-loss account

Overhead

Materials
\+ Other costs
\+ Services
= Total cost
− Allocation to other centers
= Over- or underallocation to profit-and-loss account

Rule 13: Predetermined transfer prices. Under conventional cost accounting procedures, the unit cost of production provides the transfer price of the intermediate goods and internal services. Hence, the higher the cost of production, the higher the transfer price. To eliminate temporary fluctuation of the transfer price, a predetermined rate is used, that is

$$\frac{\text{Estimated costs}}{\text{Estimated volume}}$$

The use of a predetermined rate also enables preparation of the cost statements without waiting for completion of unit-cost calculations by the supplying cost centers.

Charging predetermined transfer prices causes over- or underallocation of costs because the actual unit costs differ from the predetermined rates. Over- or underallocations are charged to the profit-and-loss account.

Rule 14: Market price for internal transfers. When an intermediate good or internal service has a market price, this price should be used instead of the predetermined cost-based price for an internal transfer price. In this case, the price of the good or service has an economic meaning and the over- or underallocation has a meaning similar to that of profit. This procedure reduces the arbitrariness of cost allocation, and the corresponding cost centers become contribution or profit centers.

When the company's assets can be traded in an active market and there is a market price for these assets, this market price should serve as a transfer price for transferring the assets from one year to the other. In other words, the arbitrariness of the temporal cost allocation can be reduced if the depreciation is calculated on the asset's market value and inventories are valued at market prices.

Rule 15: Transfer pricing in centralized and decentralized companies. In a centralized company the transfer price of intermediate goods and services is usually set by central management. In a decentralized company, on the other hand, the managers of the various divisions are involved in setting these prices.

Rule 16: Negotiated transfer price. Just as the price in the market is often set by negotiation, the transfer price in a decentralized company should also be set by negotiation. The best conditions for the negotiation to result in an optimal pricing are as follows:

1. There is an opportunity for both sides to sell or buy in the outside market.
2. Central management prefers inside to outside trading, but it does not dictate it.
3. Central management may be called to settle a dispute on price negotiation, but such a call is viewed as a failure of both managers involved in the dispute.

Adhering to this procedure will ensure that the decisions at the division level will meet the objectives of the conglomerate company, the profit of the division can be measured correctly, and the autonomy of the division managers is observed.

Cost-Accounting Sheet

The final result of costing is presented in a cost-accounting sheet. This sheet consists of the cost statements of the individual departments. All the cost items allocated to the departments appear on this sheet.

Rule 17: Presenting a cost-accounting sheet. A cost-accounting sheet is composed of all the cost statements of a company. Each column represents a cost or profit center (such as department or product) and each line represents an input or service. The unique aspect of this sheet is the presentation of the internal transfers (including intermediate goods, internal services, and overhead). The procedures for allocating the various cost items among cost and profit centers are delineated in chapter 13.

Example. A cost-accounting sheet for Company X is presented in table 12–4. To simplify the illustration, only the main types of cost and profit centers are presented, without a breakdown by individual products and intermediate goods and products.

Each column represents a cost statement; for example, the column for product A has been presented as the cost statement in table 12–1. Each line

Table 12–4
Cost-Accounting Sheet, Company X
($000)

	Internal Services		*Overhead*	*Intermediate Goods*		*Final Products*		
	1	*2*		*Stage 1*	*Stage 2*	*Product A*	*Product B*	*Total*
Internal transfers								
Service 1		20	10			40	40	110
Service 2	15			40	60	40	45	200
Overhead	10	15		40	60	130	155	410
Stage 1					330			330
Stage 2						350	390	740
	25	35	10	80	450	560	630	1,790
Variable costs								
Materials	30	80	40	90	60	400	600	1,300
Labor	20	30	200	50	100	200	250	850
Depreciation	10	10	30	30	50		100	230
Interest	5	20	30	20	20	100	150	345
	65	140	300	190	230	700	1,100	2,725
Fixed costs								
Depreciation	5	15	60	30	30	70	100	310
Interest	5	10	40	30	30	80	120	315
	10	25	100	60	60	150	220	625
Profit calculations								
Total cost	100	200	410	330	740	1,410	1,950	3,350[a]
Total transfers	110	200	410	330	740			
Value of products						1,550	2,200	3,730
Profit	10	0	0	0	0	140	250	400

[a]Total includes variable and fixed costs and excludes internal transfers.

Table 12–5
Section of Company X Cost-Accounting Sheet
($ 000)

	Product A	
	Variable Costs	*Fixed Costs*
Internal transfers		
Service 1[a]	$40	
Service 2[b]	32	$8
Stage 2[c]	245	105
Overhead		130
Variable costs		
Materials	400	
Labor	200	
Interest	100	
Fixed costs		
Depreciation		70
Interest		80
Total	1,017	393
Profit calculations		
Value of product	1,550	
Contribution	533	
Variable costs		1,017
Total costs		1,410
Value of product		1,550
Profit		140

[a]All the costs are variable because market price is used for transfers.
[b]Variable costs are 80 percent of total costs.
[c]Variable costs are 70 percent of total costs.

in the upper section of table 12–4 represents the cost allocation of an internal transfer.

Consider the column "Internal Service 1." This department consumes the regular variable and fixed costs (recorded in the corresponding column in $000), and it uses $15 of Service 2; $10 overhead costs are allocated to this center. The allocation of overhead to a service department enables a correct comparison of total costs among all the departments. Because Service 1 has a market price, this price is used as an internal transfer price for the service it renders (recorded in the corresponding line in $000). This department renders $110 services ($20 to Service 2, $10 to overhead, $40 to product A, and $40 to product B), while total costs are $100; thus, the profit is $10.

If a predetermined rate or price had been used to allocate overhead, Service 2, and the intermediate goods, over- or underallocation would have appeared in the last line for these cost centers.

The last column on the cost-accounting sheet in table 12–4 lists the total cost of each input item. The total cost incurred by the company includes the variable costs ($2,725) and the fixed costs ($625). The total costs of $3,350 equals the total costs of the final products ($1,410 and $1,950) less the profits, if any, of the internal transfer centers ($10 for Service 1).

The contribution is not listed in table 12–4. Presentation of the contribution requires the partitioning of each column into two categories, one for variable costs and the second for fixed costs, as illustrated for product A in table 12–5.

Cost-Volume-Profit Relationships

The volume of production and sales affects the level of unit cost and the level of total profit because of the existence of fixed costs. The effect of the volume of production and sales on profits is analyzed through the contribution ratio, breakeven analysis, and the contribution-sales curve.

Contribution Ratio

The difference between the value of product and the variable costs, called contribution, provides the contribution toward covering the fixed costs and profits.

The positive contribution represents the net cash inflow to the company (that is, receipts minus variable costs). Contribution is an important parameter in measuring performance, such as the performance of production managers and salesstaff (for example, sales commissions can be based on the contribution). When the total contribution exceeds the total fixed costs in a given period, a profit is recorded in the income statement.

Rule 18: Calculating the contribution ratio. The contribution ratio is the contribution divided by the value of sales. That is

$$\frac{\text{Sales} - \text{variable costs}}{\text{Sales}}$$

Alternatively, it is the unit contribution divided by the price of the product. That is

$$\frac{p - vc}{p}$$

where $p - vc$ is the unit contribution, p is the price of product, and vc is the unit-variable cost.

The contribution ratio indicates the change in the cash inflow that results from a one-unit change in the volume of sales, given that the fixed costs are constant and the unit contribution does not change.

Example. Consider the cost statement in table 12–1. The value of product is \$1,550 and the variable costs \$1,017.
Solution: The contribution margin is \$533 and the contribution ratio is

$$\frac{533}{1{,}550} = 0.34 = 34\%$$

Breakeven Analysis

Breakeven analysis is usually presented in a graphic form, as shown in figure 12–1. The breakeven point is determined by the intersection of the sales curve with the total cost curve. When production exceeds the breakeven point, the income statement will show a profit, and vice versa.

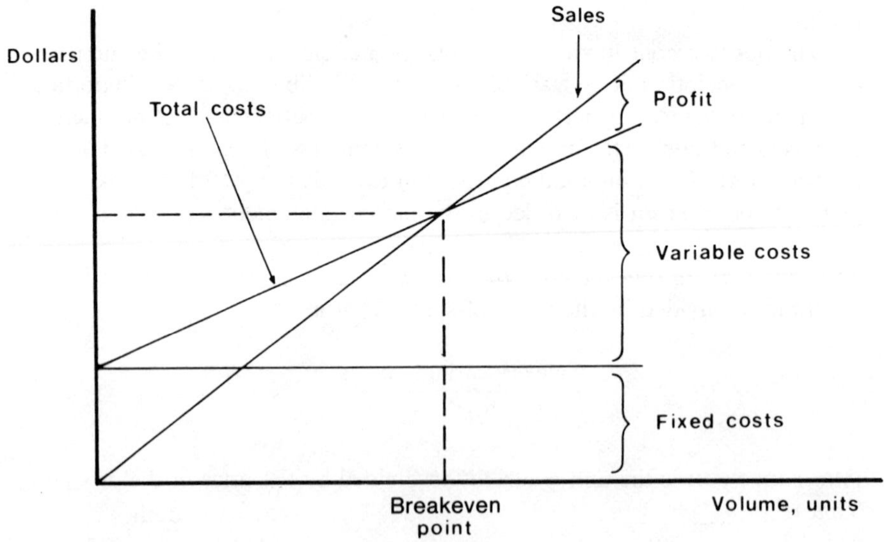

Figure 12–1. Breakeven Analysis

Rule 19: Breakeven analysis for planning. Breakeven analysis is used for determining the minimum volume of production and sales before the fixed costs are committed, as in the case of a new investment evaluation. Breakeven analysis is also used in planning the target volume needed to recover the fixed costs for the next period. In these cases, the target return on investment can be added to the fixed costs in determining the breakeven point for covering the full costs.

Rule 20: Calculating the breakeven point. The breakeven point is that volume of production where the contribution equals total fixed costs (or alternatively, where sales equal total costs). The breakeven point may be stated in units of product. That is

$$\frac{\text{Total fixed cost}}{\text{Unit contribution}} = \text{Breakeven point in units}$$

Alternatively, it may be computed in terms of dollars, using the contribution ratio (rule 18):

$$\frac{\text{Total fixed cost}}{\text{Contribution ratio}} = \text{Breakeven point in dollars}$$

Example. Consider the cost statement in table 12–1, and assume that this statement is for 100 units. The relevant figures are fixed costs, \$393; price, \$15.50 per unit; and unit variable cost, \$10.17.
Solution: The breakeven point is

$$\frac{393}{15.50 - 10.17} = 73.73 \text{ units}$$

The contribution ratio is

$$\frac{15.50 - 10.17}{15.50} = 0.34$$

Thus, the breakeven point in dollars of sales is

$$\frac{393}{0.34} = \$1{,}155.88$$

Contribution-Volume Curve

Breakeven analysis is based on several limiting assumptions, particularly the fact that the price of the product is determined by the market and both price and unit variable costs are constant.

To overcome these limitations, sensitivity analysis can provide a range of production levels for use in management decisions. This analysis can be accomplished by constructing a contribution-volume curve and using the contribution ratio as the decision variable.

Rule 21: Constructing the contribution-volume curve. The contribution-volume curve is constructed by using the formula for the breakeven point (that is, fixed cost / contribution ratio). Given the level of fixed costs, the breakeven point for various levels of contribution ratios can be computed and then graphed as a curve, as shown in the following example.

Example. Suppose the level of fixed cost is \$100; then the breakeven point for a contribution ratio of 0.1 is

$$\frac{100}{0.1} = \$1{,}000$$

These computations are repeated for various levels of the contribution ratio, providing the following values:

Contribution ratio	Breakeven point for \$100 fixed cost
0.1	\$1,000
0.2	500
0.3	333
0.4	250
0.5	200

These figures are graphed as the lower curve in figure 12–2. This curve shows the breakeven points for various levels of production and contribution ratios; it also indicates the minimum required volume, in dollars, to cover total costs, given the contribution ratio.

Rule 22: Breakeven volume. Given the contribution ratio and the level of fixed cost for a company or product, the breakeven volume is graphed in figure 12–2.

The breakeven point in terms of units of the product is computed by

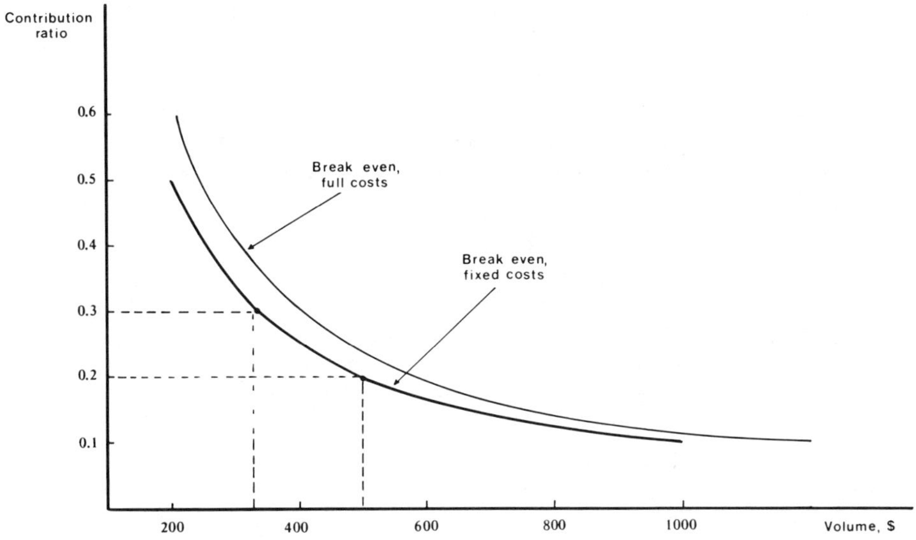

Figure 12–2. Contribution-Volume Curve

dividing the volume of sales in dollar terms by the anticipated product price. That is

$$\frac{\text{Breakeven point}}{\text{Price}} = \text{Breakeven point in units}$$

Example. The planned costs for a given product are: fixed costs, $100,000; price, $5 per unit; and unit variable costs, $4.
Solution: The contribution ratio is

$$\frac{5 - 4}{5} = 0.2$$

The lower curve indicates that for a contribution ratio of 0.2, the breakeven volume is $500 (move along the broken line from point 0.2 on the ordinate to the break-even curve and then move down). Because the breakeven curve is constructed for $100 fixed cost, the breakeven volume for $100,000 fixed costs is $500,000. The breakeven point is

$$\frac{500{,}000}{5} = 100{,}000 \text{ units}$$

Because the contribution of each unit is $1, the total contribution of 100,000 is $100,000, a sum that equals total fixed costs.

Rule 23: Constructing the full-cost curve. Full cost implies the inclusion of the target return on investment in the cost of product for pricing purposes (see chapter 14). To construct a corresponding contribution-volume curve, add the target return on investment to the fixed cost and proceed as explained in rule 22 for constructing and graphing another curve.

Example. Consider the data in the example for rule 21. Suppose the target return on capital is 20 percent of the fixed costs; that is, the fixed costs and the target return total $120. Using this figure, a second contribution-volume curve is constructed and graphed in figure 12–2 (the upper curve).

Rule 24: Sensitivity analysis of sales. Contribution-volume curves can be used for sensitivity analysis. The sensitivity is in respect to inclusion or exclusion of the target return on investment, changes in the level of the fixed costs, or the level of the planned contribution ratio. A planned or conceivable change in the price of the product and in the unit variable costs affects the contribution ratio directly.

Example. Consider the data in the example for rule 22, where the contribution ratio is 0.2 and the breakeven volume of sales is $500. Taking into account the target return on investment, the breakeven volume should be at least $600. This can be seen on the full-costs curve in figure 12–2 (move from point 0.2 on the ordinate to the full-costs curve and then move down).

Suppose management considers raising the unit price of the product from $5.00 to $5.70, resulting in a contribution ratio of

$$\frac{5.70 - 4.00}{5.70} = 0.3$$

rather than 0.2 as planned. Checking the two curves in figure 12–2, we find that for the contribution ratio of 0.3 the breakeven volume for covering the fixed costs is $333 and the breakeven volume for covering the full costs is about $400. Because the planned fixed costs are $100,000, the breakeven volumes are $333,000 and $400,000, respectively. The corresponding breakeven volume in units of the product are

$$\frac{333{,}000}{5.70} = 58{,}421 \text{ units} \qquad \frac{400{,}000}{5.70} = 70{,}175 \text{ units}$$

compared to 100,000 units and 110,000 units, respectively, for the unit price of $5.00.

Rule 25: Uncertainty considerations. Uncertainty implies a premium cost which, in turn, reduces the contribution margin. Therefore, the minimum volume of sales will generally be above the volume shown by the contribution-volume curves for any planned contribution ratio. That is, uncertainty shifts the curves upward.

Rule 26: A general contribution-volume curve. The contribution-volume curve that is constructed for $100 of fixed costs, as graphed in figure 12–2, can be used as a general curve. For any level of fixed costs and contribution ratio, a breakeven volume can be determined by multiplying the results by the ratio

$$\frac{\text{Actual fixed costs}}{100}$$

A second curve can be graphed (for example, for 1.20 of the fixed costs) to provide for sensitivity analysis in respect to target return on investment and uncertainty.

Because the curve is a rectangular hyperbola, drawing the second curve is simple. It should be 20 percent higher than the first curve. In general, if target returns are b percent of the fixed costs, the curve will be b percent higher than the fixed costs breakeven curve for every volume, or will be b percent to the right for every contribution ratio.

Relationship between Productivity and Size

The relationship between productivity or efficiency and the size of the operation is an important attribute of a series of data (timeseries or cross-section). A positive correlation between productivity and size means that the large segments are more productive.

Rule 27: Size-productivity indicator. The correlation between the numerator of a ratio (such as profit or production) and the denominator of the ratio (such as sales or workers) is approximated by the following steps:

1. List the data pertaining to the numerator Y (profit or production), and the denominator X (sales or workers) in two columns and compute for each observation (such as a given year or department) the ratio Y/X and record it in an additional column.

2. Compute the average (arithmetic mean) for each of the three columns (the two data columns and the ratios column) by summing each column and dividing it by the number of observations.

3. Divide the resultant average of the first column by that of the second to arrive at the weighted average (weighted by the denominator; see rule 36 in chapter 3). That is

$$\frac{\sum Y_i}{\sum X_i} = \bar{Y}_w$$

where $\bar{Y}_w$ is the weighted average.

4. Calculate the ratio between the weighted average (resulting from step 3) and the arithmetic average (resulting from step 2). If the resultant ratio is greater than one, then the correlation between Y/X and X is positive, and vice versa (see example in table 15–10)

Example. Consider the data in the first three columns:

Year or department	Profit Y	Sales X	Profit margin Y/X
1	$45	$500	9%
2	70	700	10
3	50	1,000	5
4	35	300	12
5	40	400	10
6	62	1,200	5
7	45	900	5
Total	347	5,000	56
Average (total ÷ 7)	49.57	714.29	8

Solution: the weighted average of the profit margin is

$$\frac{347}{5{,}000} = \frac{49.57}{714.29} = 0.069 = 6.9\%$$

The ratio of the weighted average to the arithmetic average is

$$\frac{6.9}{8} = 0.86$$

Because the weighted average is smaller than the arithmetic average (their ratio is smaller than one), there is a negative correlation between the profit margin and size. In other words, there are decreasing returns to size in the population analyzed—the larger segments (such as departments or years) are less efficient.

Types of Costs

The term "cost" is used in many ways. It has many implications, and there are many cost classifications. The main types of costs are summarized in this section.

Direct versus Indirect Costs

Direct cost is the cost of an input that can be traced to a cost center or to a product. Direct materials and labor are usually considered as the main direct costs. Indirect cost, on the other hand, is the cost of an input that requires the use of some cost-allocation procedure to charge it to a cost center or to a product. A given cost item may be a direct cost for one cost center and an indirect cost for another.

Controllable and Avoidable Costs

Controllable cost is the cost of an input that can be controlled by the manager. Avoidable cost is the cost of an input that can be avoided if the production process is terminated.

Controllability or avoidability of a cost item depends on the type of cost and on the point of reference. Many cost items are controllable or avoidable at a given time or at a given level of hierarchy in the company, and are noncontrollable or nonavoidable at a lower level of the organization or when the cost is already committed.

Variable versus Fixed Costs

The classification of costs as variable or fixed is related to the level of production. If the usage of an input varies with the level of production, it is a variable cost; if not, it is a fixed cost. The classification of costs into variable and fixed is of major importance for decisions. In the short run, only the variable costs should be considered, whereas for long-run decisions, all costs—variable and fixed—must be taken into consideration.

Marginal and Differential Costs

Marginal cost is an economic concept of the cost resulting from a one-unit change in the level of production. Differential cost (incremental or decremental), on the other hand, refers to the difference in costs at two examined level of production. The latter term is more applicable to real-life decisions regarding conceivable changes in output and input mixes.

Opportunity Cost

The cost of something is the amount of money that is sacrificed to obtain it. The opportunity cost of an input is measured by the net income that the input can yield in the best alternative use. An input will be allocated to the alternative that provides the highest opportunity cost. The alternative use of the input can be outside or inside the company.

External and Internal Opportunity Costs

External opportunity cost is the unit market price of an intermediate goods that is used in production rather than sold. External opportunity cost should be used as the transfer price of intermediate goods and services.

Internal opportunity cost is the per-unit contribution that a limited resource can generate in the best alternative production line. For example, equity capital has an external opportunity cost that is determined by the money market. This cost should be used for internal costing and as a benchmark in investment evaluation. Equity capital also has an internal opportunity cost—the rate of return of that alternative that will be sacrificed if the capital is invested in another project.

13 Costing Procedures

The cost of a product is a summary of the cost incurred in different periods and in different cost centers within the company. The final cost figure is the result of an elaborate mechanism of channeling and allocating costs in both temporal and spatial senses.

Because costing a product is an elaborate mechanism, accepted costing procedures are used to arrive at the final cost. Often, several alternative costing procedures can be used to solve a given costing problem. Furthermore, many costing procedures are arbitrary. Thus you must select that procedure which best suits the problem at hand that also minimizes the conceivable distortions which may result from applying it.

The main procedures for computing the various types of costs are summarized in this chapter. The major cost-accounting methods are first delineated to provide a background for the description of the costing procedures.

Cost-Accounting Methods

Cost-accounting methods are classified by three characteristics: the type of production process, such as job-order versus process; the types of data that are included, such as historical versus standards (or planned); and the items of costs that are included, such as total (that is, absorption or full costing) versus direct (or variable costing). Thus, any cost-accounting system is characterized by all three methods—for example, job-order, absorption, and historical cost accounting.

Job-Order and Process Costing

Job-order costing is used in those situations where many types of jobs and batches of production are produced simultaneously. Machine-tool manufacturing, construction, and CPA offices are typical business lines for which job costing is applicable. The job itself is considered as the cost center; the direct costs incurred for each job or batch (direct materials and labor) are recorded in a special job-order form. At the end of the period or when the job is finished, indirect costs are allocated to the job.

Process costing is used in those situations where a few homogeneous products are produced in large quantities. The product flows continuously through several stages of production. Cement production and canneries are typical processes for which process costing is applicable. The department is considered as the cost center; the costs (direct and indirect) in each department (stage of production) are accumulated for a period (such as a month) and then divided by the quantity produced to arrive at the unit cost of production.

Example. The managerial cost statement in table 12–1 suits both job-order and process cost-accounting methods. When a job or a batch of a given product is manufactured, the cost statement, as illustrated in table 12–1, summarizes its cost. This cost statement may also summarize the periodic cost of a department in which a product is manufactured under a continuous and repeated process.

Standard Cost Accounting

A standard is a goal to achieve or a predetermined benchmark for measuring performance. Standard cost accounting is a system that compares the actual cost and income figures against predetermined standards. The main aspect of this system is the so-called variance analysis. The difference between the actual figures and the standards, in respect to price and quantity, is used for control purposes.

Absorption and Direct Costing

When either job-order or process costing is applicable, the unit cost may present total cost, indicating absorption or full cost accounting. Alternatively, the unit cost may include only the direct (or variable or avoidable) costs; that is, direct costing is practiced. The cost statement in table 12–1 integrates the aspects of both absorption and direct costing for managerial purposes.

Rule 1: Profit level under adsorption and direct costing. Under absorption costing, the fixed costs are absorbed by all the units produced; hence, the profit is

$$S(P - C) - S\frac{F}{Q}$$

Q = units produced
S = units sold
P = selling price
C = variable cost per unit
F = total fixed cost

Under direct costing, on the other hand, the fixed costs are considered as the period's expense; hence, the profit is

$$S(P - C) - F$$

When there is a difference between the number of units produced, Q, and those sold, S, the profit level under each method differs, as follows. Subtracting the second formula from the first one provides

Profit under absorption costing
− Profit under direct costing
$= (Q - S)F / Q$

where $Q - S$ is the change in inventory. When production is higher than sales (that is, $Q - S > 0$), the level of inventory increases during the period, and the profit under absorption costing is higher than under direct costing, and vice versa.

Example. Consider the following data for a given department in units of product

	First quarter	Second quarter
Beginning inventory	0	10
Production	60	40
Sales	(50)	(50)
Ending inventory	10	0

Additional data and the income statements under both costing methods for the two quarters are presented in table 13–1. The gross margin under absorption costing is affected by the change in the level of inventory because a portion of the fixed costs is charged to the units in inventory. In other words, the production manager may affect the level of reported income by manipulating the volume of production.

Table 13–1
Income Statements, Department B

	January–March			April–June		
Absorption cost accounting						
Sales, 50 units @ $8			$400			$400
Cost of goods sold:						
Beginning inventory		$0		10 units @ $5	$50	
Cost of good produced	60 units @ $5[a]	300		40 units @ $6	240	
Less ending inventory	10 units @ $5	50	250		0	290
Gross margin			150			110
Direct cost accounting						
Sales, 50 units @ $8			$400			$400
Variable costs of goods sold:						
Beginning inventory		$0		10 units @ $3	$30	
Cost of goods produced	60 units @ $3[b]	180		40 units @ $3	120	
Less ending inventory	10 units @ $3	30	150		0	150
Contribution margin			250			250
Fixed costs			120			120
Gross margin			130			130

[a]Total costs per unit.
[b]Variable costs per unit.

Costing Intermediate Goods

An intermediate good is produced in one segment (such as a department) and transferred to another segment. To compute the unit cost, the segment's costs in a given period (such as a month) is divided by the number of units produced in the period. In the case of a continuous production process, in which a relatively large number of units are processed, the calculations take into account the existence of beginning and ending inventories of goods in process—the main issue in the so-called process cost-accounting method.

Example. The following data are used to illustrate other examples later in this chapter. Department C's figures for May in one year are as follows:

	Costs
Beginning inventory: 450 units, one-third processed	$ 315
Units started: 1,000	
Cost incurred	3,600
Ending inventory: 200 units, one-half processed	

Rule 2: Calculating the number of equivalent completed units. To compute

unit cost in a given period, the number of units completed (fully processed) should be calculated, as follows:

Beginning inventory
+ Units started
− Ending inventory
= Units completed

Example. The relevant figures for Department C are:

	Units
Beginning inventory	450
Units started	1,000
Ending inventory	(200)
Units completed	1,250

Of the 1,250 units completed, 800 (1,000 − 200) units were started and completed during the period.

Because the units in inventory are only partially processed, the level of process (that is, of completion) of the goods must be estimated and, accordingly, the number of equivalent completed units calculated. The procedure for computing the equivalent units depends on the method of costing used, as shown later in this section. Units are often lost during the production process and measurement units are transformed (for example, from gallons to pounds), which introduces further elaborations into the costing procedure.

Methods of Costing Work in Process

There are essentially two methods for computing the unit cost of work in process in each production stage. The number of equivalent units and the periodic costs are determined by the method used, as summarized in the following rules.

Rule 3: The moving average costing method. This method adds the beginning inventory (costs and units) to that produced during the period; the unit cost for all completed units (produced and from inventory) is

$$\frac{A + B}{T + I_1 b}$$

where A is the value of beginning inventory, B is the incurred cost, T is the units completed during the period, and I_1b is the units in ending inventory processed at level b (say $b = 1/2$ processed).

Example. The unit cost in Department C is

$$\frac{315 + 3{,}600}{1{,}250 + (200 \times 1/2)} = \frac{3{,}915}{1{,}350} = \$2.90 \text{ per unit}$$

The total costs are allocated as follows

Units completed, 1,250 @ $2.90	$3,625
Ending inventory, 200 units 1/2 processed	290
Total	3,915

Rule 4: The FIFO costing method. The FIFO method treats the beginning inventory separately from the current calculations; therefore, the calculations are more complicated. The unit cost of completed units during the period is

$$\frac{B}{T - I_0a + I_1b}$$

where I_0a is units in beginning inventory processed at level a (say, a = one-third processed).
The denominator represents the number of equivalent completed units.

Example. The unit cost in Department C is

$$\frac{3{,}600}{1{,}250 - 450 \times 1/3 + 200 \times 1/2} = \frac{3{,}600}{1{,}200} = \$3.00 \text{ per unit}$$

The total costs are allocated as follows

Beginning inventory: 450 units, one-third processed	$ 315
Completing 450 × two-thirds processed @ $3.00	900
Units started and completed: 800 @ $3.00	2,400
Ending inventory: 200 units one-half processed equivalent to 100 units @ $3.00	300
	3,915

The unit cost here ($3.00) is higher than that under the moving average ($2.90 in the previous example) because the unit cost of the beginning inventory was lower ($2.10 per unit, $315/150) than the current costs in May.

Rule 5: Moving average versus FIFO. The moving-average method is simpler to compute; thus it is preferable for its simplicity. However, during inflation, the FIFO method is preferable because it costs the period's production at current prices.

Costing Internal Services

The total costs incurred by a service department are, in general, divided by the amount of service rendered to provide the internal transfer price. The effectiveness of the service rendered (as measured by such factors as quality, timing, or availability in emergency cases) is usually more important than the cost aspect. Such intangible values should be taken into account when evaluating the performance of a service department. Furthermore, the demand for a service may be dictated by the consumer (for example, in products with seasonal or peak-load demand), thus affecting the unit cost.

Costing Interdepartmental Services

When services are rendered from one service department to another, the calculations of the unit cost should take into account the existence of the interdepartmental services. These services may be ignored or may be allocated accurately by using linear algebra or an iterative computation method. Two methods are summarized in this subsection.

Rule 6: Market price for allocating interdepartmental services. When a market price exists for an internal service and is used as a transfer price, the problem of costing interdepartmental services is solved simply. All the users of the service, including the service departments (and even the supplier itself) are charged the market price. This procedure is illustrated in table 12–4 for service 1. If a market price for a service does not exist, management should set a price.

Rule 7: The step method for allocating interdepartmental services. This method includes allocating the costs of the interdepartmental services to the service departments in a sequence. The sequence begins with the department that receives the lowest number of services from other service departments. After the costs of the first department have been allocated, a second department comes into the sequence.

Order the departments beginning with the one receiving the lowest number of services from other departments, as follows:

Department Rendering Service	Department Receiving 1	2	3	4
1		x	x	x
2			x	x
3		x		x
4			x	

Department 1 does not receive internal services, department 2 receives 2 services (from 1 and 3), and departments 3 and 4 receive from all other departments.

Example. Consider a company with two service departments and two production departments. The relevant data and computations are presented in table 13–2, which illustrates the step method of allocating the costs of the service departments starting with electricity. The allocation rate is computed by dividing the total costs by the amount of service rendered to other departments.

Costing for Seasonal and Peak-Load Demand

When the amount of service rendered is determined by seasonal or peak-load demand, as in the case of electricity, special machinery and hotels, the costing should be based on two charges (see also chapter 14). The use of two charges allocates the costs in a way that represents the special aspects of seasonal or peak load demand.

Rule 8: The two-part charging method. The costs of the service departments should be allocated by using two types of charges or rates:

1. A charge for the right to use the service, which is based on the cost of using the capacity or facilities (usually the fixed costs). This charge is allocated to the users of the service according to the planned capacity or the usage at the peak season (or load).
2. A charge for the actual use of the service, which is based on the direct

Table 13–2
Interdepartmental Service Cost Allocation

	Service		*Production*			
	Electricity	*Space*	*A*	*B*	*Total*	*Allocation Rate*
Data						
Electricity (K WH)	300	400	1,300	2,000	4,000	
Space (f^2)	100	—	300	600	1,000	
Cost before allocation	$296	$238	$2,000	$1,000	$3,534	
Allocation of services						
Electricity	$(296)	$ 32	$ 104	$ 160		$\frac{296}{4{,}000 - 300} = \$0.08 / \text{KWH}$[a]
Space	—	(270)	90	180		$\frac{270}{300 + 600} = \$0.03 / f^2$
Total	0	0	2,194	1,340	$3,534	

[a]Total cost of electricity divided by total usage of electricity minus the internal usage of the electricity department. This rate is applied to the amount of electricity used by each user. The allocation for space is made in the same manner.

costs incurred in rendering the service (usually the variable costs). This charge is allocated to the users of the service according to actual usage.

Example. Consider a company with two production departments that utilize internal transportation. The transportation capacity is 100 hours, according to the planned demand by the production departments. The relevant data and computations are presented in table 13–3, which illustrates the allocation of the transportation cost according to the two-part charging method and other methods. The two-part charging method allocates the cost in a way that motivates managers of production departments to prepare a better plan and to save in current usage of the service.

Overhead and Joint Cost Allocation

The allocation of both overhead and joint cost is arbitrary. It may distort the cost and profit figures and, in turn, may yield erroneous decisions based on those arbitrary figures. However, for various purposes (such as valuing inventories) and for arriving at full cost of production, these costs should be allocated.

Rule 9: Allocating overhead. When the amount of service rendered cannot be measured, as in the case of management, bookkeeping, and research and development, the costs are called overhead. Overhead is allocated to the various cost centers by using an accepted base that measures the volume of production, such as direct labor costs, total costs, or value of production. An alternative base is the contribution (that is, the value of the product minus variable costs). The choice of base affects the amount of cost allocated to a given cost center.

The use of direct labor costs as a base for allocating overhead has a serious drawback: a department manager views the overhead costs as added to the labor costs. Because direct labor is usually a variable cost, adding the overhead (which is generally a fixed cost) distorts the figures. The use of the value of the product or the contribution as a base for allocation eliminates such biases.

Example. Consider a company producing two products: the overhead expenses ($130) should be allocated directly to the two final products. The relevant data and computations are presented in table 13–4.

Rule 10: Allocating joint cost. In some cases, more than one product is produced from a given input, as in the case of crude-oil refining and meat-

Table 13–3
Internal Transportation Cost Allocation

	Department A	*Department B*	*Total*	*Allocation Rate*
Data				
Planned usage	60 hours	40 hours	100 hours	
Actual usage	40	40	80	
Capacity costs			$1,200	
Variable costs			800	
			2,000	
Cost Allocation				
By planned usage	$1,200	$800	$2,000	$\frac{2,000}{100}$ = $20 / hour[a]
By actual usage	1,000	1,000	2,000	$\frac{2,000}{80}$ = $25 / hour
Two-part charging method:				
For planned capacity	720	480	1,200	$\frac{1,200}{100}$ = $12 / hour
For actual usage	400	400	800	$\frac{800}{80}$ = $10 / hour
Total	1,120	880	2,000	

[a] Total cost divided by total hours. This rate is applied to the planned usage of each department. Other allocations are made in the same manner.

Table 13–4
Overhead Allocation

	Product A	*Product B*	*Total*	*Allocation Rate*
Data				
Value of product	\$1,550	\$2,200	\$3,750	
Labor costs	200	250	450	
Contribution	533	751	1,284	
Allocation of overhead				
Value of product	\$54	\$76	\$130	$\frac{130}{3,750} = 0.035$[a]
Labor cost	58	72	130	$\frac{130}{450} = 0.289$
Contribution	54	76	130	$\frac{130}{1,284} = 0.10125$

[a]Overhead divided by total value of products. This rate is applied to the value of product of each product. Other allocations are made in the same manner.

packing. The cost of the joint input is allocated to the joint products by using an accepted base that measures the volume of the joint products. Two bases are usually used: the value of product and the contribution, where the contribution is the difference between the value of product and the specific costs of the joint products.

The use of the value of product for cost allocation has a drawback: the allocated cost may be larger than the contribution of one of the joint costs (as illustrated in the following example), thus indicating loss, which may, in turn, distort decisions regarding processing the joint product in question. This situation may hold especially for by-products, which are, as a matter of fact, joint products.

Example. Consider the data for two joint products, as presented in the upper section of table 13–5. The application of the two methods of allocation is presented in the lower sections of the table. The use of the value of product as a base for allocation causes product B to show fictitious loss. This loss does not appear when the contribution is used as a base for allocation.

Rule 11: Profitability indicator of joint products. As long as the value of product of all joint products is higher than the total costs (that is, joint and specific), the processing of the joint input is profitable. Given this rule, as long as the value of product of each joint product is higher than the specific costs, the processing of the product is profitable. The use of the contribution as a base for allocation is preferable in view of this rule.

Costing Capital and Assets Services

The company's cost of capital in the form of interest should be imputed to the individual cost centers and products, just as all the other cost items are charged. The cost calculations of capital charges differ for the various types of assets.

During inflation, the inflation-free cost of capital (see chapter 1) should be applied to revalued assets. The application of the current rate to the revalued assets counts the inflation factor twice.

Rule 12: Costing nondepreciable assets. The annual cost of the capital that is invested in nondepreciable assets, like land, is

$$Ar$$

where A is the value of asset, in current prices, and r is the company's inflation-free cost of capital, before tax (chapter 1).

Table 13–5
Joint Cost Allocation

		Product A		*Product B*	*Total*	*Allocation Rate*
Data						
Value of product		$200		$50	$250	
Specific costs		60		40	100	
Contribution		140		10	150	
Joint cost					90	
Margin					60	
Allocation by value of product						
Value of products		$200		$50		
Specific costs	$60		$40			
Joint cost	72		18			$\frac{90}{250} = 0.36$[a]
Total cost		132		58		
Margin		68		(8)		
Allocation by contribution						
Value of product		$200		$50		
Specific costs	$60		$40			
Joint cost	84		6			$\frac{90}{150} = 0.60$
Total cost		144		46		
Margin		56		4		

[a] Joint cost divided by total value of products. This rate is applied to the value of product for each joint product. The other allocation is made in the same manner.

Example. A production process utilizes one acre of land that is valued at \$2,000. The inflation-free cost of capital is 5 percent.
Solution: The annual cost of the capital that is invested in the land is

$$2{,}000 \times 0.05 = \$100$$

Rule 13: Costing depreciable assets. The annual cost of the capital invested in depreciable assets, such as buildings and equipment, is composed of depreciation and interest on the average value of the asset. The interest is computed by

$$A(0.67r)$$

where A is this acquisition cost of asset, in current prices, and 0.67 is the interest add-on factor (rule 2, chapter 2).
Interest should not be computed on the basis of the depreciated value of an individual asset since the resultant charges are not equal over the asset's life.

Example. A production process utilizes a building acquired last year for \$10,000. Straight-line depreciation is used, assuming a life span of 20 years. The inflation-free cost of capital is 5 percent.
Solution: The annual cost of the capital that is invested in the building is

Depreciation:	$10{,}000 \times 1/20 = \$500$
Interest:	$10{,}000 \times 0.67 \times 0.05 = \$335$

Rule 14: Costing inventories. The cost of the capital that is invested in inventories is

$$A\frac{n}{12}r$$

where A is the value of inventory, in current prices, and n is the time of inventory turnover, in months (chapter 9).
This cost can be added to the standard cost of the materials, in addition to other holding costs.

Example. An inventory of a given material is valued at \$4,000. The holding time is 3 months and the cost of capital is 5 percent.

Solution: The cost of the capital that is invested in the inventory is

$$4{,}000 \times \frac{3}{12} \times 0.05 = \$50$$

During the year, the inventory is turned four times; thus, the total interest charges are

$$50 \times 4 = \$200$$

Rule 15: Costing operating capital. The cost of the capital that finances the acquisition of the variable cost items, until the revenue from the sale of the product is received, should be based on the actual schedule of payments and receipts. This cost item may be of significance in long production processes (such as construction and agriculture) when the interest rate is high.

The cost of operating capital can be approximated by the following steps:

1. Multiply each payment by the number of months until the revenue is received, to arrive at a "dollar × month" figure.
2. Accumulate these sums.
3. Apply the average monthly interest rate on current liabilities to the accumulated sum.

Example. Consider a production process for which the payments start (for example, in January) 5 months before revenue is received (for example, in May). The monthly interest rate is 1.5 percent. The payment schedule and the computations follow:

	Payments	Months of finance	Dollar × month
January	$500	4	2,000
February	200	3	600
March	200	2	400
Total	700		3,000

The cost of the capital that finances this production is approximately

$$3{,}000 \times 0.015 = \$45$$

This cost, divided by the total cost, is about 6.4 percent.

Suppose this production process is repeated five times in a year. Then, the total interest charges are

$$45 \times 5 = \$225$$

Rule 16: Accounting procedure of interest charges. The procedure of charging the individual products and cost centers by the imputed interest for the use of capital services resembles the procedure of using the market price to cost internal transfers (chapter 12). This resemblance implies that capital is considered as a contribution center in the cost-accounting system. This center is credited by the internal charges and debited by the actual interest payments on debt.

Example. Consider the data in the last four examples as representing a company. The total interest charges are:

Land	$ 100
Building	335
Inventory	200
Operating costs	225
	1,060

Against this total imputed interest, actual interest paid is debited (for example, $400). The difference ($660) is the imputed returns originating from the fact that equity is not costed in the accounting system.

Variance Analysis

The main objective of a standard cost-accounting system is to report the differences between the actual figures and the planned standard figures. This procedure is called variance analysis.

Rule 17: Decomposing the total variance. The difference between the actual and the standard figures for input (or output) items is usually decomposed into price and quantity variances. That is

$$\text{Total variance} = \text{Price variance} + \text{quantity variance}$$

$$P_aQ_a - P_sQ_s = Q_a(P_a - P_s) + P_s(Q_a - Q_s)$$

where P_a, P_s are prices, actual and standard, and Q_a, Q_s are quantities, actual and standard.

This variance analysis is depicted in figure 13–1. The price variance is calculated on actual quantity, and the quantity variance is measured in terms of standard prices.

Example. The standard for producing one unit of a product is 100 hours at \$4 per hour. The actual performance was 110 hours at \$4.20 per hour. The actual cost was \$462, compared to \$400 planned cost.
Solution: The price variance is

$$110(4.20 - 4.00) = \$22$$

The quantity variance is

$$4.00(110 - 100) = \$40$$

The total variance is

$$462 - 400 = \$62$$

Rule 18: Calculating price variance of materials. The control of the prices of materials should be carried out by computing the price variance immediately after the acquisition of the materials. This procedure implies that the price variance is separated and reported before the materials enter inventory. In turn, the inventory is valued at standard prices (chapter 8). The quantity variance, on the other hand, is separated and reported during the production process, either when the materials are issued or when production is finished.

This procedure implies that computing the price variance of materials is carried out without any connection to the quantity variance; the former is carried out on total purchases of all materials on acquisition, whereas the latter is carried out on materials actually issued for production.

Costing during Inflation

Costing during a period of inflation becomes more elaborate: various cost items, such as depreciation, cost of materials, and the interest rate should be adjusted; some cost items may become noncomparable, as in the case of costs incurred at the beginning and the end of a long production process; and variance analysis becomes almost impossible to apply.

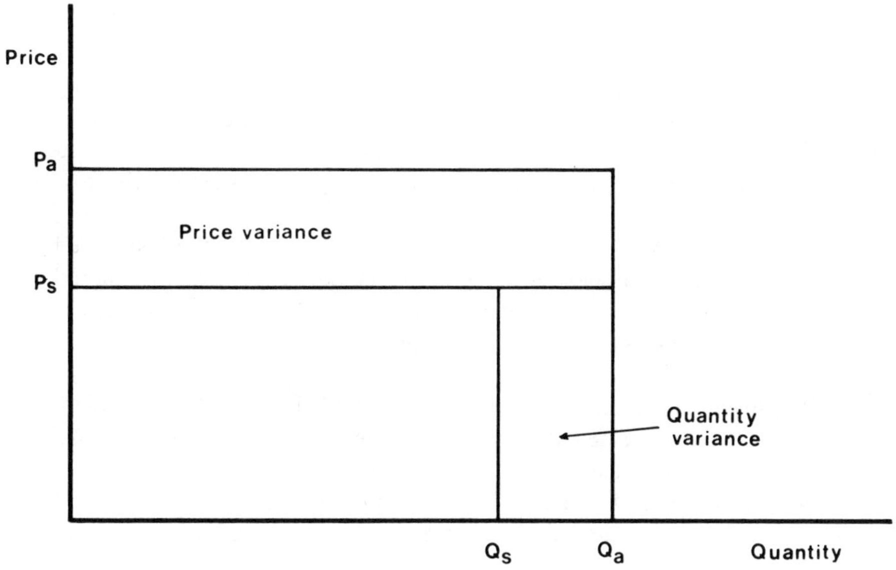

Figure 13–1. Variance Analysis

To arrive at a correct cost statement, the depreciation expenses and the materials drawn from inventory should be based on revalued figures. That is, these inputs should be based on current values. In contrast, the inflation-free interest rate (chapter 1) should be used rather than the current interest rate, which includes compensation for the decline in the real value of the capital. The inflation compensation of the capital is already carried out after revaluing the depreciation and the cost of materials drawn from inventory.

Assets Revaluation

For a company to survive in the long run, the revenue from the sales should cover the cost of replacing all inputs used in production, including materials that are drawn from inventory and depreciation derived from the replacement value of the fixed assets. Assets should be revalued also to provide a correct figure for insurance purposes and for computing the returns on investment.

Rule 19: Fixed asset revaluation methods. For costing purposes, the fixed assets should be revalued to represent their market value or their replacement cost. Several methods are in use.

1. Market value revaluation: In most cases, the market price of an

existing asset for which there is an active market (such as land, trucks, or livestock) is the best revalued figure.

2. Replacement cost revaluation: The replacement cost of an existing asset, for which there is no active market, is estimated by the current market price of this or a similar new asset, after deducting either the accumulated depreciation or the appraised reduced service ability of the asset relative to a new one.

3. Price-Level Adjustment revaluation: To arrive at the estimated current cost of a given asset or a group of assets, the acquisition cost should be adjusted by the specific price index (chapter 11). This adjusting procedure approximates the replacement cost of the group of assets at hand.

Rule 20: Inventories revaluation methods. Detailed revaluation of inventories is cumbersome, especially when there are many types of inventories. Several methods are in use.

1. When the FIFO method is used, both inventories and cost of materials used can be adjusted by using the short-cut procedures in chapter 10.

2. When the LIFO method is used, usually adjustment of the cost of materials is not required. However, adjustment of the inventories is not simple (chapter 10) and usually a detailed adjustment is required.

3. The next-in, first-out (NIFO) method is sometimes proposed for use in costing materials in time of high inflation. This method uses prices corresponding to the replacement costs that are anticipated to prevail at the time the final product is sold.

Indexing Operating Costs

When the inflation rate is high and there is a long time between the acquisition date of the inputs and the receipts of revenues, the operating costs should be indexed to arrive at a correct cost statement. The specific price index of each input should be used, or if it is not available, the general price index should be used.

Rule 21: Indexing lump costs. When the costs are incurred in a few lump sums, the indexation of each sum is

$$VC \times I$$

where VC is variable costs, and I is price index at end of production/price index at date cost incurred.

Rule 22: Indexing stream of costs. When the costs are incurred more or less at a constant rate over time, the indexation is approximated by

$$TVC\ (I_{\text{average}})$$

where TVC is total variable costs; $I_{\text{average}} = 1 + P/2$; and P is (price index at end of production/price index at beginning of production) − 1.
A more accurate formula, especially when the price level increase is not uniform over time, is

$$I_{\text{average}} = \frac{\text{Price index at end of production}}{\text{Sum of indexes over the period} / n}$$

where n is the number of price indexes between the beginning and end of production.

Example. Consider a construction project that started in May 1979 and ended in May 1980. In May 1979 the variable costs amounted to \$20,000, and since that time \$2,000 has been paid each month for acquiring inputs. You want to know the real cost of production in June 1980 price level. The construction inputs price index was 200 points in May 1979, 202 in June 1979, and 232 in June 1980.
Solution: The \$20,000 costs of May 1979, in terms of the June 1980 price level, are

$$\$20{,}000 \times \frac{232}{200} = \$23{,}200$$

Assume that the price level increased evenly over the period. The average price index is

$$1 + \left(\frac{232}{202} - 1\right)/2 = 1.0743$$

The total costs incurred during the period June 1979–May 1980 are \$24,000. In terms of the June 1980 price level, these costs are

$$\$24{,}000 \times 1.0743 = \$25{,}783$$

The total variable costs, in terms of the June 1980 price level, are

$$\$23{,}200 + 25{,}783 = \$48{,}983$$

compared to \$44,000 historical costs.

Suppose now that the price level did not increase evenly, but rather as follows:

June 1979	July 1979	August–December 1979	January 1980	February–May 1980	June 1980
202	220	220	225	225	232

The more accurate average index is

$$202 + 220 + 220 \times 5 + 225 + 225 \times 4 + 232 = 2{,}879$$

$$\frac{232}{2{,}879\ /\ 13} = \frac{232}{221.5} = 1.0474$$

The costs incurred during the period June 1979–May 1980, in terms of the June 1980 price level, are

$$\$24{,}000 \times 1.0474 = \$25{,}138$$

Specific Price Changes

During a period of constant price level, a change in the price level of a given input or output is noticed directly from the price figures. In time of inflation it is difficult to check the specific price changes. But it is important to know the effect of inflation on specific groups of items (inputs or outputs) used in your company, mainly for inventory and pricing policy and for decisions on product mix and on substituting inputs.

The change in the price level of a group of items in real terms can be determined if there is a specific price index for this group of items. The real price change is arrived at by neutralizing the effect of inflation.

Rule 23: Determining the real price change. The real price level change of a group of items is approximated by

$$p_{\text{specific}} - p_{\text{general}}$$

where p is the periodic price level change, which equals (price index at end of period/price index at beginning of period) − 1.
The accurate formula is

$$\frac{1 + p_{\text{specific}}}{1 + p_{\text{general}}} - 1$$

Example. Consider the following data

	Year 1	Year 2
Price index of chemicals	161	192
Consumer Price Index	225	248

Solution: The price level change during this year is

Chemicals $$\frac{192}{161} - 1 = 0.193 = 19.3\%$$

Consumer prices $$\frac{248}{225} - 1 = 0.102 = 10.2\%$$

The change in the real prices of chemicals during the year is approximately

$$0.193 - 0.102 = 0.091 = 9.1\%$$

The exact fiture is

$$\frac{1 + 0.193}{1 + 0.102} - 1 = 0.083 = 8.3\%$$

Variance Analysis during Inflation

During inflation it is very difficult to set standard prices. Therefore, in time of high inflation, a company usually does not conduct a detailed price variance analysis.

Rule 24: Determining the price variance. During a period of constant price level, price variance is measured by the difference between the actual and the standard prices. During inflation, it is possible to approximate the price variance for a group of inputs or outputs for which a specific price index is available. The price increase of the group of items is considered as the standard against which the actual price increase of a given item may be compared.

Example. A factory uses wood as a major input. The price index of wood rose during the last year by 20 percent; this figure may be used as a standard.

Suppose the price of the main type of wood purchased by your company rose by 25 percent. This implies that the variance is about 5 percent.

Suppose the quantity and mix of the wood acquired and used by the factory are more or less constant. Then the increase in the actual total payments during the year should be compared with the 20 percent standard increase in prices.

Rule 25: Determining the quantity variance. Quantity variance can be approximated by updating the standard value of the product, which neutralizes the effect of inflation on prices and leaves the effect of the quantity variance. This method is not accurate because the price index used for updating the standard value will usually differ from the price index of each input used in production.

Example. Consider the data in the example for rule 17, where the standard value of the product was $400. Suppose the price level increased by 20 percent; thus, the standard value is updated to $480. If the actual costs are $528, then the quantity variance is approximately $48.

14 Pricing Products and Services

There is no general rule for pricing products and services. Generally, pricing decisions depend on the customers, competitors and costs. Specifically, pricing decisions should take into account the kind of product, the company's market opportunities and competitive situation, and the company's objectives and financial position.

Products fall into three major categories:

1. Homogeneous products: The company's product has no special feature different from other similar products. In this case, the price is determined solely by the market mechanism and the company has no pricing problems. Farm products follow this type.

2. Nonhomogeneous products: The company's product has some special feature that differentiates it from the products of other companies. These features may be real—that is, they may have special qualities of their own—or they may be imaginary—that is, induced by advertisement and promotion. In either case, the pricing decision is in the hands of the company. The pricing in this case is carried out by either the so-called market method or the cost-plus method.

3. New products: The new product is new to the company as well as to the market. Such a product incorporates some major innovation. The pricing decision in this case is a major factor in product survival and success. After a period of time, a new product becomes a standard product, because of the introduction of similar products by competitors.

The company's pricing decision is also affected by its market opportunities, including such factors as the degree of market saturation, the number of competitive products, the market prospectives (whether inflation or recession is expected), the company's market share, and whether the company is a leader or a follower.

The company's objectives are also an important factor in pricing. A dynamic, growing company usually has a different pricing strategy from a stagnant one; the former considers the long-run horizon, the latter, a short horizon. The company's policy regarding profits—satisfying or maximizing—also enters its pricing decisions.

The financial position of the company is also important in pricing. Distress conditions resulting from a temporary fall in demand affect a weak company differently from a strong one. A weak financial position would induce the company to lower prices far beyond the point dictated by the market conditions.

Tools for Pricing

Cost markup, profit margin, and demand elasticity are used in pricing; these terms are related to one another.

Cost Markup and Profit Margin

Rule 1: Calculating the cost markup. Cost markup is the rate that is added to cost to determine the selling price. That is,

$$P = C(1 + MU)$$

where P is the price per unit, C is the cost per unit, and MU is the markup rate.

Example. If the cost is \$10 per unit and the markup is 40 percent, then the price will be

$$10(1 + 0.40) = \$14$$

Rule 2: Relations between markup, price, and cost. Given the price and cost, and markup is

$$MU = \frac{P - C}{C}$$

Given the price and the markup, the cost is

$$C = \frac{P}{1 + MU}$$

Rule 3: Calculating the profit margin. Profit margin is the ratio between profit and sales. The profit margin per unit of product is

$$PM = \frac{P - C}{P}$$

where PM is the profit margin.

Example. If sales amounted to \$140 and the profit to \$40, then the profit margin is

$$40 / 140 = 0.29 = 29\%$$

Rule 4: Markup versus profit margin. Given the profit margin, the markup is

$$MU = \frac{PM}{1 - PM}$$

Given the markup, the profit margin is

$$PM = \frac{MU}{1 + MU}$$

Example. In the first and second examples, the markup is

$$MU = \frac{0.29}{1 - 0.29} = 0.41 = 41\%$$

and the profit margin is

$$PM = \frac{0.41}{1 + 0.41} = 0.29 = 29\%$$

Rule 5: Costs to be considered. The costs to be considered in pricing depend on the market conditions. When the market is stagnant and there is idle capacity in the company, only the variable costs should be considered, excluding the fixed costs. On the other hand, when the market and the company are growing, the costs to be considered are the full costs, including fixed costs (overhead, assets services, and desired rate of return on capital, before income tax).

When a company is growing, it utilizes its facilities (which are sunk costs) and adds new facilities. Such growth implies that the return on capital is higher than the borrowing interest rate (otherwise the company would not grow), and that the sunk assets have an opportunity cost. Therefore, the fixed costs should be included in pricing.

Rule 6: Demand elasticity. Demand elasticity with respect to price is a coefficient that relates proportional changes between the quantity demanded for a given product and its price. The coefficient is usually negative but stated without the sign.

Example. The price elasticity of demand for a given product is 1.4. Elasticity means that when the price rises by 10 percent, for example, the demand for the product decreases by

$$10 \times 1.4 = 14\%$$

Rule 7: Price sensitivity. The higher the demand elasticity, the higher the price sensitivity. That is, a small change in price brings forth a large change in the quantity demanded.

Rule 8: Estimating elasticity. The demand elasticity of a product, for the market as a whole at a given point in time, can be approximated by the reciprocal of the industry's weighted average contribution ratio. That is,

$$E \cong \frac{\text{Sales}}{\text{Sales} - \text{variable costs}}$$

The elasticity of demand determines the price (and the marginal revenue), which in turn determines the contribution level for a given cost structure.

Example. You estimate that for a given product, the variable costs out of sale value are 60 percent on a national average.
Solution: The approximated market elasticity of this product is

$$\frac{1}{1 - 0.6} = 2.5$$

Rule 9: Relations between fixed costs and elasticity. The larger the share of fixed costs out of total costs in producing a given product (on the average for the industry), the smaller the market elasticity of this product.

Market Pricing Methods

Pricing under market methods takes into consideration the current market forces: competitors' reactions and demand conditions. These methods generally assume a static market condition regarding such factors as demand and number of competitors. In this respect, they are short-run factors because they do not take into consideration changes in demand over time.

Rule 10: Follow-the-leader pricing. Under this method the pricing strategy is simple: the price of the product is set equal or somewhat below (for example, 5 percent) the leader's price. If your company is a leader in the market, you may follow a maximizing policy, taking competitors into account (rule 12, later in this section).

Rule 11: Constant market-share pricing. The company's objective is to keep a constant share of the market. This policy is made known to other competitors. Essentially, the company has a quantity-setting policy and no direct price policy. The price is set by competitors, taking into consideration the expected action of your company.

The constant market share method has the long-run view as a policy and is suitable for a relatively large company and a growing demand. It discourages price retaliation and newcomers. However, if the operations of a company that sticks to this policy are relatively inefficient, the company may experience considerable loss.

Rule 12: Maximum profit pricing. This method suits a company that is a leader in the product market. Its share in the market is big enough so that its actions affect the market and cannot be ignored. The company strives to maximize its profits, taking into consideration the market conditions and the actions of its competitors.

The price is set so that marginal cost equals marginal revenue. A proxy for marginal cost is the company's current unit operating cost. The marginal revenue is calculated using an estimate of the price elasticity of demand.

The price that will provide maximum profit to the leader in the industry is approximated by

$$P = C\frac{e}{e - 1}$$

where C is cost per unit, as defined in rule 5, and $e =$ elasticity of the company's demand. The company's demand elasticity is derived from the market demand elasticity as follows:

$$e = \frac{E}{S + R(1 - S)}$$

where S is the company's market share, assumed to be constant; E is the market demand elasticity (rule 8), ignoring minus sign; and R is the proportion of the followers. The proportion of the followers is approximated by the percentage of competitors who are expected to follow your company's price actions. More accurately, if your company raises or reduces the price, R is the proportion of the volume of the residual market (the competitors) that will raise or reduce the price accordingly.

Example. You want to set the price of a given product for which your company is considered a leader. The market-demand elasticity of this product is 3. The company's market share is one-third and the cost per unit is \$10. You estimate that 40 percent of the competitors (in volume terms) react to your price changes.
Solution: The company's demand elasticity is approximately

$$e = \frac{3}{0.333 + 0.4(1 - 0.333)} = 5$$

The unit price that will maximize the profit of your company is approximately

$$\frac{10 \times 5}{5 - 1} = \$12.50$$

The unit profit margin is

$$12.50 - 10.00 = \$2.50$$

The cost markup is

$$\frac{12.50 - 10.00}{10.00} = 0.25 = 25\%$$

Rule 13: Effect of competitors' actions. The more competitors who follow the leader, the more the leader with the followers together become a monopoly in the economic sense; that is, the leader's price policy results in maximizing profits.

The higher the proportion of followers (that is, the higher R), the lower is the leader's demand elasticity and the higher is the actual markup and profit margin for the leader.

Example. Consider the previous example, but suppose that 60 percent of the competitors will follow your price actions rather than 40 percent.
Solution: The company's demand elasticity is

$$e = \frac{3}{0.333 + 0.6(1 - 0.333)} = 4.1$$

The recommended price is

$$\frac{10 \times 4.1}{4.1 - 1} = \$13.20$$

The unit profit margin is \$3.20 (compared to \$2.50). The cost markup is 32 percent (compared to 25 percent).

Cost-Plus Pricing Methods

The selling prices of a going concern must be sufficient in the long run to cover all costs of production, as well as to provide a reasonable return on the owners' investment. When the company is growing, the fixed costs have an opportunity cost (rule 5). Therefore, under cost-plus pricing, all costs, variable and fixed, are considered as costs that should be included in the price structure.

Underlying the cost-plus pricing (which businessmen consider as "fair") is a growing demand and a dynamic policy regarding such factors as investment, product design, and promotional strategy. As such, the method implicitly considers a long-run horizon.

Three methods are included in cost-plus pricing: absorption pricing, returns on capital pricing, and contribution pricing. The first two suit a growing demand; the third suits a temporary slackening in demand.

Absorption (Full-Cost) Pricing Method

The absorption approach to cost-plus pricing is to recover the full cost of the product. The unit cost is based on a periodic (usually annual) production and cost budget.

Rule 14: Absorption target price. The target price—that is, the full-cost price to be charged—is

$$P = C(1 + MU)$$

where P is the target price; C is the cost per unit, direct and indirect; and MU is the markup rate for desired profit before income tax. The total cost per unit is computed by

$$C = C_d(1 + OH)$$

where C_d is the direct manufacturing cost per unit, based on actual costs, and OH is the overhead rate, which equals indirect costs/direct costs. Indirect costs are based on the budgeted production volume and costs.

Example. Consider the following data that are drawn from table 12–4:

		Product A	Product B	Total
Units produced		10	100	
Direct costs:	Materials	$400	$600	$1,000
	Labor	200	250	450
	Intermediate goods	350	390	740
		950	1,240	2,190
Indirect costs				1,160
Total costs				3,350

Solution: The overhead rate is

$$\frac{1{,}160}{2{,}190} = 0.53$$

The total costs per unit are

Product A: $(950 / 10)(1 + 0.53) = \$145.35$
Product B: $(1{,}240 / 100)(1 + 0.53) = \$18.97$

To arrive at a target price, profit before tax should be included in the indirect costs or added as a markup on the total cost figures.

Rule 15: Classification of costs, absorption pricing. The most common classification of costs is as follows:

Direct costs = materials and labor
Indirect costs = maintenance, depreciation, manufacturing overhead, and financing, administrative, and selling expenses

There are, however, other classifications in which cost items are removed from the indirect group and added to the desired profit to provide the markup:

1. Financing expenses (interest on loans) may be included in the markup rather than in the overhead rate.

2. Financing, administrative, and selling expenses may be included in the markup rather than in the overhead rate.

3. The desired profit may be added to the indirect costs to provide only one aggregate markup.

The classification of costs into variable and fixed costs is superior to the classification into direct and indirect costs (see chapter 12). Furthermore, charging imputed interest (the company's cost of capital) as a cost item (see chapter 13) provides improved cost data for pricing.

Returns-on-Capital Pricing Method

The returns-on-capital approach to cost-plus pricing is to recover the full cost of the product over a period of several years. Large companies strive to minimize fluctuations of their product prices resulting from fluctuations in demand. Constant pricing offers market stability. Their policy is to receive a desired return on the invested capital over a budgeted horizon that will yield adequate returns to the owners and not invite entry of new competitors.

Under this method the costs of production are determined as standard costs, which are planned for a normal volume of production. The latter is usually determined as an average volume over the business cycle.

Rule 16: Returns-on-capital target price. The target price—that is, the full-cost price to be charged—is

$$P = C_s(1 + MU)$$

where P is the target price, C_s is the standard cost per unit, and MU is the markup.

Rule 17: Calculating the markup. The desired markup is computed by

$$MU = \frac{K}{SC}r$$

where K is the invested capital, depreciated; SC is the total standard cost to produce normal volume; and r is the desired rate of return on investment, before tax (chapter 7). The standard costs include all costs except interest expenses. In some cases, the depreciation expenses are excluded from the standard costs and are added as a rate to the desired rate of return.

Example. The standard costs to produce a normal volume are \$3,000, the depreciated assets are recorded at \$2,000, and the target rate of return is 15 percent.

Solution: The desired markup is

$$\frac{2{,}000}{3{,}000} \times 0.15 = 0.10 = 10\%$$

Suppose the standard cost is \$30 per unit; then the target price is

$$30(1 + 0.10) = \$33$$

Rule 18: Markup from industry average. The ratio of capital to standard cost in rule 17 can be substituted by or compared to a similar ratio that is available as an average for the industry. The capital-output ratio (or its reciprocal, the assets turnover; see chapter 15), which is published for many industries, can be used for this purpose.

The markup based on the industry's capital-output ratio is

$$MU = \frac{rK^*}{1 - rK^*}$$

where MU is the markup; K^* is the capital-output ratio, which equals invested capital / sales; and r is the desired rate of return on investment, before tax.

Example. The capital-output ratio for your company's industry is 1.2. The company's desired rate of return is 15 percent.

Solution: The target markup is

$$\frac{0.15 \times 1.2}{1 - (0.15 \times 1.2)} = 0.22 = 22\%$$

Suppose the standard cost is \$50 per unit; then the target price is

$$50(1 + 0.22) = \$61$$

Rule 19: Markup for a new investment. When a company considers a new investment for expansion purposes, the incremental capital-output ratio should be used instead of the average capital-output ratio. The corresponding markup is

$$MU = \frac{rK'}{1 - rK'}$$

where K' is the incremental capital output = incremental investment/ incremental production value.

Example. Consider the previous example and suppose the company plans to invest $1 million in a project that is anticipated to increase its annual output by $700,000.
Solution: The incremental capital output ratio is

$$\frac{1{,}000{,}000}{700{,}000} = 1.43$$

The target markup is

$$\frac{0.15 \times 1.43}{1 - (0.15 \times 1.43)} = 0.27 = 27\%$$

Contribution Pricing Method

The contribution approach to cost-plus pricing allows the company to differentiate between the minimum price to charge its customers when demand is slackening and the maximum price to charge when demand is high, in accordance with its policy for charging a given return on capital. The minimum price must be equal to the variable or avoidable costs; the maximum price will cover full cost and a desirable level of profit.

The contribution method is generally used for pricing special orders, taking into consideration the company's capacity condition (full or idle capacity). It may also be used to set different prices to different market segments, when this practice is allowed. (In the United States, the Robinson-Patman Act forbids charging different prices to different customers unless the price discrimination is justified by differences in costs.)

Contribution pricing yields a contribution—that is, a gross return on sales. This return should cover the fixed costs and returns on capital (chapter 12).

Rule 20: Pricing under low demand. During low demand the minimum price to charge is the variable cost per unit.

Example. Consider the following data that are drawn from tables 12–5 and 12–4.

	Variable		Fixed	
Product A		$1,017		$393
Product B:				
Direct cost	$1,100		$220	
Service 1	40		—	
Service 2	36		9	
Intermediate goods	273		117	
Overhead	—		155	
		1,449		501
Total		2,466		894

Units produced: Product A, 10 units; Product B, 100 units
Solution: The minimum price per unit is

Product A: 1,017 / 10 = $101.70
Product B: 1,499 / 100 = $14.49

Rule 21: Classification of costs, contribution pricing. Costs for contribution costing are classified according to variable and fixed costs. Variable costs usually include direct materials and labor; interest on working capital; and a portion of maintenance, overhead, and selling expenses. The fixed costs usually include depreciation; interest on loans; administration; and a portion of maintenance, overhead, and selling expenses.

Rule 22: Pricing under high demand. During high demand, full-cost (absorption) pricing should be used. The classification here is according to variable and fixed costs, whereas under conventional absorption pricing the classification is according to direct and indirect costs.

The markup for each department or product is

$$MU = \frac{\text{Fixed costs}}{\text{Variable costs}} = \text{operating leverage}$$

where MU is the markup.
The fixed costs include desired profit before income tax.

The target price—that is, the full-cost price to be charged—is

$$P = C_v(1 + MU)$$

where P is the target price and C_v = variable costs per unit.

Example. Consider the previous example.
Solution: The operating leverages to be used as markups are

Product A:	$393 / 1{,}017 = 0.386$
Product B:	$501 / 1{,}449 = 0.346$

The total costs per unit are

Product A, 10 units:	$(1{,}017 / 10)(1 + 0.386) = \$140.96$
Product B, 100 units:	$(1{,}449 / 100)(1 + 0.346) = \$19.50$

To arrive at a target price, profit before tax should be included in the fixed costs or added as a markup on the total cost figures.

Pricing for Seasonal and Peak-Load Demand

Services (and nonstorable products) for which the demand is seasonal or loaded in peaks, should be priced differently than regular services and products. Examples of such services are hotels, recreation, and farm machinery with seasonal demand; electricity, telephones, and transportation with peak-load demands. The demand in these cases is high in one period (peak season or load), and low in another period (off-peak). The pricing method that is designed for this situation is called peak-load pricing, or two-charge pricing (see also rule 8, chapter 13).[1]

Rule 23: Pricing storable products. When the commodity can be stored, the problem of pricing seasonal or peak-load demand is simplified. The peak price exceeds the off-peak price by the unit storage cost.

Rule 24: Classification of costs, seasonal pricing. The pricing in this case is based on two types of costs:

1. Capacity costs, which include all the cost incurred by the company to be able to provide the service or product at the peak. These costs, mainly the fixed costs, are charged only during the peak.

2. Operating costs, which include the costs needed to operate the capacity and to provide the service or the product. These costs, mainly the variable costs, are charged in both peak and off-peak seasons.

Rule 25: Full-cost seasonal pricing. Under full-cost pricing (rules 14 and 22) the company's policy is to recover all the costs of providing the service, with a markup for profit before income tax. This approach suits public utilities and a large number of unorganized competing companies.

The price to be charged during the peak is

$$P = C_o + \frac{\text{Capacity cost}}{\text{Units in peak}}$$

Alternatively,

$$P = C_o + \frac{C_c}{w}$$

where P is the target price, C_o is the operating cost per unit, C_c is the capacity cost per unit, and w is the fraction of peak period out of the whole period. The capacity cost should include desired returns on investment.

The price to be charged during the off-peak period is the operating (variable) costs per unit, plus a markup for profit.

Example. The capacity costs amount to \$500, and the operating costs amount to \$0.20 per unit. The units supplied total 800 during the peak and 400 during off-peak.

Solution: The price to be charged during the peak is

$$0.20 + \frac{500}{800} = \$0.825 \text{ per unit}$$

Alternative computation: The capacity cost per unit is

$$\frac{500}{1{,}200} = \$0.417 \text{ per unit}$$

The fraction of peak is

$$\frac{800}{1{,}200} = 0.667$$

The price to be charged is

$$0.20 + \frac{0.417}{0.667} = \$0.825 \text{ per unit}$$

The off-peak price is \$0.20 per unit. The total receipts are

Peak	$800 \times 0.825 =$	\$660
Off-peak	$400 \times 0.20 =$	80
		740

Rule 26: Profit maximizing, seasonal pricing. The profit-maximizing pricing method suits a large and leading company. The target price is arrived at in two steps. First, compute the prices for each period by rule 22. Then, multiply the results by

$$\frac{e_i}{e_i - 1} \quad \text{for the peak and for the off-peak}$$

where e_i is the elasticity of the company's demand; i equals 1 in the peak; and i equals 2 in the off-peak period, respectively.

Example. Consider the previous example and suppose the company's demand elasticity for the service is 4 and 5 for the peak and off-peak periods, respectively.
Solution: The target prices are

Peak
$$0.825 \times \frac{4}{4-1} = \$1.10$$

Off-peak
$$0.20 \times \frac{5}{5-1} = \$0.25$$

The total recepts are

Peak	$800 \times 1.10 =$	\$880
Off-peak	$400 \times 0.25 =$	100
		980

Pricing during Inflation

Inflation distorts some financial figures, especially those related to capital: assets values, depreciation expenses, cost of materials drawn from inventory, and cost of capital. Because pricing is based on these values and costs, inflation affects pricing.

Rule 27: Costs to be adjusted. Two sets of cost figures affect pricing: accounting figures (including assets, costs, and depreciation), and rates (such as interest and rate of return). The accounting figures are recorded at their historical cost and generally are not adjusted for price level. Rates, on the other hand, are generally adjusted through the market mechanism, which takes inflation into consideration. For example, the current rate of interest, say 15 percent, results from inflation.

The common procedure for overcoming the distortions caused by inflation is to use current prices for the costs related to capital; that is, to adjust or revalue the assets and depreciation expenses to the present price level and use the prevailing nominal cost of capital. This procedure is wrong because it counts the inflation factor twice in costing the capital services. This error occurs because the compensation for the decline in the real value (purchasing power) of the capital is covered by both revaluing the assets (which includes revaluation gain) and using the current cost of capital (which includes price-level compensation).

Correcting Inflation Distortions

For pricing purposes, the accounting figures (including assets, costs, and depreciation expenses) should be adjusted to the current price level. The rates (which include the interest rate, cost of capital, and rate of return) should be stated in real terms—that is, in inflation-free terms (chapter 1).

The application of this rule to pricing implies that the invested capital is financed solely by equity. When financial leverage exists, the actual interest expenses are already inflation-compensated, which should be taken into account in absorption pricing.

Rule 28: Absorption pricing under inflation. Three costs are considered for absorption pricing (rule 15) during inflation:

1. Historical costs, including depreciation and interest expense on loans financing the current assets.
2. Desired returns on revalued assets at the pretax inflation-free rate.
3. Adjustment for understated historical costs (depreciation and materials from opening inventory) computed as follows:

$$(\text{Revalued costs} - \text{Historical costs})\,(1 - f^*)$$

where f^* is the proportion of net debt to net debt plus equity (rule 3, chapter 19).

Example. The historical depreciation expenses are \$80 and the revalued depreciation is \$120. The LIFO method is used for valuing the materials.

Suppose the proportion of net debt to net debt plus equity (f^*; see example for rule 3 in chapter 19) is 0.38.
Solution: The adjusted costs of depreciation to be added to the historical costs are

$$(120 - 80)(1 - 0.38) = \$24.80$$

The total depreciation to be charged is

$$80 + 24.80 = \$104.80$$

Rule 29: Returns on capital pricing under inflation. For applying the returns on capital pricing (rule 16) during inflation, use revalued invested capital (depreciated) with the preinflation desired rate of return and revalued standard costs.

Rule 30: Updating the price during inflation. The rules in this section are designed to determine the correct values and costs to be used in pricing during inflation. After the price is set (for example, at the beginning of the year), it should be updated periodically by indexing. The period of adjustment depends on the rate of inflation and the company's objectives.

Strategies in Pricing a New Product

Pricing a new product or service is a puzzling marketing problem. The product is novel, the market is ill-defined, and the life-cycle potentials of the product are uncertain. Thus, no simple pricing rules can be followed throughout the product's life-cycle.

Yet, in the early stages of launching the new product, a company should choose between two pricing strategies: skimming pricing and penetration pricing. The following rules are of help in setting the product on the right track.[2]

Rule 31: Skimming pricing. This strategy implies high prices at the early stages of market development and lower prices at later stages. This strategy is followed in two cases. First, use skimming pricing when the product represents drastic improvements over other existing products. Such new products will usually enjoy high price, because of few competitors. A high price is an efficient device for breaking the market up into segments that differ in price elasticity of demand. The richer segment is price-insensitive (inelastic demand). Hence, at the early stages, catering to this segment will produce a greater dollar volume of sales than the other market segments. In later stages,when price will be reduced, poorer segments will also buy the product.

Second, skimming pricing should be used when the investment in development cost of the new product is low, and competition is expected to follow in a short time.

Rule 32: Penetration pricing. This strategy is basically a long-run strategy, compared to the skimming-pricing strategy; it uses low prices starting from the early stages to maximize profits over a long horizon. This strategy is followed in cases when the sales volume of the product is very sensitive to price for all market segments (elastic demand) and there is no elite market; when it is possible to achieve substantial economies in unit cost of manufacturing and distributing the product by operating at large volume. (The use of low prices is a way to get into large production volume early.); and when it is easy for competitors to produce close substitute products in a short time (a low profit margin discourages competitors).

Notes

1. Rules 25 and 26 are based on O.E. Williamson, "Peak-Load Pricing: Some Further Remarks," *Bell Journal of Economics and Management Science* (Spring 1974), pp. 223–228.
2. Based on J. Dean, "Techniques for Pricing New Products and Services," in *Handbook of Modern Marketing,* ed. V. P. Buell and C. Heyed (New York: McGraw Hill, 1970), pp. 51–61.

Part V
Financial Management

15 Financial Statement Analysis

The company's financial position is the final outcome of management's past actions and decisions, related to the industry's economic conditions. The financial position and other related activities—what has been achieved and what probably will be achieved—can to some extent be unveiled through financial statement analysis.

The financial statement analysis approach considers the company as an entity to be analyzed within the framework of its own industry. Its purpose is to put the company in the proper perspective with respect to other companies in the same industry regarding profitability, debt capacity, and risk of operation; investment policy and growth; and ultimately, the company's prospects for success or failure. As such, financial statement analysis is considered as a macro approach that not only can be applied for the purpose of evaluating the company's past performance, but also can be used by management to coordinate the company's objectives and to set the desired policy for an improved future performance.

Financial statements of companies and corporations are generally published and open to the public. Thus, the financial statement analysis serves outside people dealing with the company (such as investors, banks, credit analysts, or suppliers), as well as the company's shareholders and management.

The Financial Report

The financial report consists of financial statements and is prepared at least once every year. This annual report is required to show the company's activities and state of affairs for the year ended on a certain date. It is usually made up of the balance sheet, income (profit-and-loss) statement, and flow of funds (sources and uses) statement.

Balance Sheet

The balance sheet shows the outstanding balances of the assets and liabilities at a particular time—the end of the financial period (usually a year).

The balance sheet is made up of four basic building blocks as depicted in

Table 15–1
Framework of a Balance Sheet

Assets	*Liabilities*
Current assets	Current liabilities
	} Net working capital
Fixed assets	Long-term funds

table 15–1: current and fixed assets, current liabilities, and long-term funds. Working capital is the investment in current assets. The difference between the current assets and current liabilities is the net working capital, which, under normal business conditions, is financed from long-term sources.

1. *Fixed assets* consist of long-term assets, such as land, buildings, and equipment. Also included are long-term investments in other companies and good will. The buildings and equipment values are usually recorded in the balance sheet net of depreciation.

2. *Current assets* are assets that will be converted to cash during the next period. These assets include cash, short-term securities, accounts receivable, and inventories.

3. *Long-term funds,* as the name implies, are funds committed on a long-term basis, beyond one-year maturity. These funds include long-term loans, owners' equity, retained earnings, and reserves. Retirements of long-term loans due in the next period are usually transferred to current liabilities.

4. *Current liabilities* include accounts payable, short-term loans (less than one-year maturity), and other deferred payments due for payment in the next period. The working capital is financed from sources of current liabilities.

The book values are recorded in the balance sheet according to conventional accounting procedures as illustrated in table 15–2. One should not infer that these values necessarily are equal to market values. For analysis and valuation purposes, every item in the balance sheet should be scrutinized.

Income (Profit-and-Loss) Statement

The income (profit-and-loss) statement is a summary of the company's business activity during the reported period. It reports the total revenues and the expense items by categories, as illustrated in table 15–3.

Table 15–2
Company X Balance Sheets of December 31, 1979, and December 31, 1980
($000)

	1979		*1980*	
Assets				
Current assets:				
Cash	$ 15		$ 20	
Accounts receivable	155		180	
Inventories	80		100	
Total		$250		$300
Fixed assets:				
Equipment	350		400	
Buildings	450		500	
Land	300		300	
Total		1,100		1,200
Total assets		1,350		1,500
Liabilities				
Current liabilities:				
Accounts payable	$ 60		$80	
Loans	50		70	
Total		$110		$150
Long-term liabilities:				
Loans		500		550
Stockholders' equity:[a]				
Common stock	600		630	
Retained earnings	140		170	
Total		740		800
Total liabilities		1,350		1,500

[a]Market value of shares:

96,000 @ $0.0096	$922	
100,000 @ $0.0100		$1,000

Flow-of-Funds (Sources and Uses) Statement

The balance sheet presents the outstanding balance of the liabilities (sources of funds) and the assets (uses of funds). The flow-of-funds (sources and uses) statement is similarly constructed and can be considered as the incremental balance sheet for the reported period. It can be derived directly from the opening and closing values of a balance sheet. Like the balance sheet, this statement is composed of two parts (sources and uses) as illustrated in table 15–4. The totals of the two parts should agree, as in the case of the balance sheet.

Table 15–3
Company X Income Statements for December 31, 1979, and December 31, 1980
($000)

	1979		1980	
Sales		$800		$1,000
Operating costs:				
Wages and salaries	$200		$250	
Materials	300		400	
Depreciation	75		100	
Total		575		750
Selling, general and administrative expenses		45		50
Earnings before interest and taxes (EBIT)		180		200
Interest		60		70
Earnings before taxes		120		130
Income tax		35		40
Net earnings		85		90
Dividends		55		60
Retained earnings		30		30

Table 15–4
Company X Flow-of-Funds Statement for 1980
($000)

Sources		
Internal:		
Net earnings	$ 90	
Depreciation	100	
		$190
External:		
Issued capital[a]	30	
Long-term loans	100	
Short-term loans	40	
		170
Total		360
Uses		
Investments:		
Buildings	$ 100	
Equipment	100	
		$200
Current assets		50
Retirement of loans		50
Dividends		60
Total		360

[a]4,000 preferred shares @ $0.009, less cost of issue.

The flow-of-funds statement discloses the investment and financial policy of the company during the reported period. Relationships among the different items on each part, as well as between the two parts, are of paramount importance in understanding the company's actions and decisions.

The flow-of-funds statement, together with the balance-sheet data, are used to investigate the company's investment and financing policy over time. The flow-of-funds statement provides incremental ratios that should be compared with the corresponding ratios derived from the balance sheet and from the income statement.

Analyzing Financial Statements

Several methods can be used in analyzing financial statements; three are summarized below. In each method, cross-section (same period) and timeseries (several periods) data of financial statements are examined and often compared to the average of the related industry.

Common-Size Statements Analysis

For each period under analysis, the components of the financial statements can be presented as percentages of the totals, as illustrated in table 15–5. The

Table 15–5
Company X Common-Size Financial Statements for 1979 and 1980
(percentages)

	1979	*1980*
Balance sheet		
Current assets	18.52	20.00
Fixed assets	81.48	80.00
	100.00	100.00
Current liabilities	8.15	10.00
Long-term liabilities	37.04	36.67
Equity	54.81	53.33
	100.00	100.00
Income statement		
Operating costs	71.88	75.00
Selling, general, and administrative expenses	5.62	5.00
Interest	7.50	7.00
Income tax	4.37	4.00
Net earnings	10.63	9.00
	100.00	100.00

resultant figures are compared with the industry's percentages. Some agencies publish industry average common-size financial statements (for example, Robert Morris Associates' *Annual Statement Studies*).

Deviations of the company's data from the industry's average figures may shed light on the company's behavior, but do not always indicate conclusively whether the deviations are beneficial. This point is especially true when not all the deviations are in the same direction. For example, you may find that the inventory percentage is higher than the average (indicating poor management), while the cost of materials is lower than the average (indicating good management).

In timeseries analysis, the trends of the company's percentages are compared to those of the industry's. In this case, too, the conclusions reached are seldom definitive. Despite these limitations, the following percentage figures are useful for performance analysis and projection purposes.

Balance-sheet percentages. Current assets are an indicator of the working capital. Liabilities are an indicator of financial leverage.

Example. Consider the common-size financial statements in table 15–5. The current assets increased from 18.52 percent in 1979 to 20.00 percent in 1980. On the other hand, the liabilities are an indicator of financial leverage. In table 15–5, the liabilities increased from 45.19 percent (8.15 + 37.04) in 1979 to 46.67 percent (10.00 + 36.67) in 1980.

Income-statement percentages. The percentages of expenses to revenue, also called input-output coefficients, may be used for analyzing the causes of performance, as well as for projection purposes. This type of analysis may stimulate a further inquiry into the individual cost items and into the costing of the individual products.

Example. Consider the data in table 15–5. The operating costs increased from about 72 percent in 1979 to 75 percent in 1980, and the net earning decreased from 10.63 percent in 1979 to 9 percent in 1980.

Financial Ratio Analysis

The objective of the ratio analysis is to construct a framework of relationships that represents the economic and financial aspects of the company within its industry. Ratio analysis sheds light on past performance and enables forecasting and planning.

The financial ratios are constructed by using the data reported in the financial statements. Performance ratios are constructed from data reported in the income statement and the balance sheet. Investment and financing analysis should be based mainly on data reported in the flow-of-funds statement.

Some of the financial data, mainly the balance-sheet data, are usually recorded in historical values. To arrive at meaningful figures, the historical values that are recorded in the financial statements should be revalued—that is, restated in current prices (as shown in chapters 10 and 11). Alternatively, if revalued data is not available, the ratios should be constructed to minimize the effects of inflation (examples are provided in the next section of this chapter).

Each aspect of the business operation can be represented by several individual ratios. Generally, one or two ratios for each aspect will be sufficient.

Rule 1: Selecting ratios. Keep the following in mind when selecting ratios:

1. The ratios should represent different aspects of performance.

2. The ratio should be directly related to the level of success of the company; that is, under equal conditions, the higher the level of the ratio, the higher the level of success of the company.

3. Between two ratios having similar interpretation, choose the one which is easier to compute and the more familiar to the user.

4. The ratio should be able to explain the position of very successful and very weak companies. If the level of a ratio is relatively high for weak companies (or vice versa), don't use this ratio for evaluating performance.

Rating Method of Analysis

A complete analysis of financial statements requires comparison between the company's timeseries ratios and those of the industry's average. For example, a follow-up of six ratios over 5 years means a comparison among 30 company ratios on the one hand, and a comparison of those with 30 industry averages on the other. Fortunately, the analysis can be greatly simplified by using the rating method described later in this chapter.

Two kinds of ratings can be used:

1. Grades that are given by experts and published by various agencies—for example, in Best's Insurance Reports. The expert analyzes the financial statements of a company and provides a grade, say between A and D. The meaning of such a grade is straightforward but it cannot be used for time series analysis, especially when a company's grade does not change over time.

2. Grades that are derived from the financial ratio figures of both the company and the industry. The grade is stated as a number between 0 and 100, which expresses the ranking of the company's ratio relative to other companies in the same industry. For example, a company with a grade of 60 means that 60 percent of the companies in the industry have a lower level and, therefore, only 40 percent of the companies have a higher performance than the company in question.

Performance Ratios

The performance (level of success) of a company and its credit standing are evaluated by analyzing the company's financial ratios and comparing them with the average ratios of the related industry. The financial ratios are usually grouped into several categories; the main ones are summarized in this section.

The ratios to be analyzed should represent the aspects of performance that are specific to the industry. Several ratios for each category are provided below. These ratios, within each category, are meant to be applicable to a wide range of manufacturing activities. The results of applying these ratios to the 1980 data in tables 15–2 and 15–3 are presented below for each ratio (the figures are in $000).

Profitability Ratios

Profitability ratios measure the economic performance of the company in a specific reported accounting period. The ratios, which reflect relative profitability, relate different aspects of profit or earnings to total sales or to total assets or to equity.

$$\text{Profit margin} = \frac{\text{Net earnings}}{\text{Sales}} = \frac{90}{1{,}000} = 9\%$$

This ratio reflects the intensity and efficiency of input used in production. During inflation, net earnings are usually biased upward, mainly because of the downward biased historical depreciation expense.

$$\text{Capital margin} = \frac{\text{EBIT} + \text{depreciation}}{\text{Sales}} = \frac{200 + 100}{1{,}000} = 30\%$$

where EBIT is earnings before interest and taxes.

This ratio reflects the total returns on capital (net earnings, interest, and depreciation) as related to sales. It is not affected by the depreciation method that is used, by the level of interest expense (financial leverage), or by inflation.

$$\text{Return on assets} = \frac{\text{EBIT}}{\text{Assets}}$$

This ratio reflects the end result of assets utilization and is not affected by the financial leverage.

During inflation the revalued total assets, or the market value of equity plus total liabilities should be used in place of the book value of the assets. In this case

$$\text{Return on assets} = \frac{\text{EBIT}}{\text{Equity} + \text{liabilities}} = \frac{200}{1{,}000 + 700} = 11.8\%$$

$$\text{Return on equity} = \frac{\text{Net earnings}}{\text{Equity}} = \frac{90}{1{,}000} = 9\%$$

This ratio reflects the returns to the owners' equity. The market value of equity should be used for this ratio. Note that this ratio is the reciprocal of the price-to-earning ratio that is used extensively by stock market analysts.

Liquidity Ratios

Liquidity is the relative ability of the company to meet its short-term obligations without weakening its credit standing.

$$\text{Current ratio} = \frac{\text{Current assets}}{\text{Current liabilities}} = \frac{300}{150} = 2$$

$$\text{Quick ratio} = \frac{\text{Current assets} - \text{inventories}}{\text{Current liabilities}} = \frac{300 - 100}{150} = 1.33$$

$$\text{Net working capital} = \frac{\text{Current assets} - \text{current liabilities}}{\text{Sales}} = \frac{300 - 150}{1000} = 15\%$$

The first two ratios are affected by the method of inventory valuation (FIFO or LIFO; see chapter 8) and by inflation (chapter 8).

Leverage Ratios

The leverage ratio (also called capital structure ratios) reflect the level of outside funds and indicate the solvency of the company in the long run.

$$\text{Leverage ratio} = \frac{\text{Total debt}}{\text{Total capital}}$$

$$\text{Debt turnover} = \frac{\text{Total debt}}{\text{Sales}} = \frac{700}{1{,}000} = 70\%$$

$$\text{Long-term debt turnover} = \frac{\text{Long-term debt}}{\text{Sales}} = \frac{550}{1{,}000} = 55\%$$

$$\text{Average interest} = \frac{\text{Interest payment}}{\text{Total capital}}$$

The ratio of debt to sales (the debt turnover ratio) is more useful than the ratio of debt to capital because the credit standing of a company is usually measured by its total activity on the market. Moreover, both numerator and denominator are stated in current (nominal) values; hence, the ratio is not affected by inflation.

During inflation, revalued total assets, or the market value of equity plus total liabilities, should be used in place of total capital. In this case,

$$\text{Leverage ratio} = \frac{\text{Total debt}}{\text{Equity} + \text{liabilities}} = \frac{700}{1{,}000 + 700} = 41.2\%$$

$$\text{Average interest} = \frac{\text{Interest payment}}{\text{Equity} + \text{liabilities}} = \frac{70}{1{,}000 + 700} = 4.1\%$$

Rule 2: Transforming leverage ratio. The leverage ratio is often stated as

$$\frac{\text{Total debt}}{\text{Total equity}} = \frac{700}{1{,}000} = 70\%$$

One can be transformed from the other as follows. Let

$$\frac{\text{Debt}}{\text{Equity}} = d \qquad \frac{\text{Debt}}{\text{Equity} + \text{debt}} = f$$

then

$$d = \frac{f}{1 - f} \quad f = \frac{d}{1 + d}$$

Example. The ratios in rule 2 are $d = 0.70, f = 0.412$.
Solution:

$$d = \frac{0.412}{1 - 0.412} = 0.70 \quad f = \frac{0.70}{1 + 0.70} = 0.412$$

Activity Ratios

These ratios reflect the activity and, to some extent, the efficiency of the company in using its resources.

$$\text{Assets turnover} = \frac{\text{Sales}}{\text{Assets}}$$

$$\text{Inventory turnover} = \frac{\text{Sales}}{\text{Average inventories}} = \frac{1{,}000}{(80 + 100)/2} = 11.1$$

$$\text{Accounts-receivable turnover} = \frac{\text{Sales}}{\text{Average accounts receivable}} = \frac{1{,}000}{(155 + 180)/2} = 6.0$$

$$\text{Working capital turnover} = \frac{\text{Sales}}{\text{Current assets}} = \frac{1{,}000}{300} = 3.33$$

The assets turnover ratio usually indicates resource efficiency. The other three ratios are more related to production and marketing conditions than to resource efficiency.

During inflation, the revalued total assets, or the market value of equity plus total liabilities, should be used in the first ratio in place of the assets. In this case,

$$\text{Assets turnover} = \frac{\text{Sales}}{\text{Equity + liabilities}} = \frac{1{,}000}{1{,}000 + 700} = 0.59$$

Rating the Company's Financial Standing

Financial ratio analysis for performance evaluation requires the comparison of each ratio with the corresponding average industry ratio for several periods. This procedure provides a large volume of figures that are difficult to comprehend.

These figures are more easily dealt with if the ratios are transformed into ratings. The rating approach is based on the premise that interactions among different aspects of the company's activity are consistent enough to establish a regular pattern of financial behavior. A similar procedure (the "economic indicators" approach) is practiced by the U.S. National Bureau of Economic Research for explaining and forecasting economic events.

Rating Individual Ratios

The rating method interprets or transforms each ratio into a rating or grade that indicates the company's position relative to the industry. The average rating for the industry is usually between 50 and 60 because of positive skewness (chapter 3). (The average ratio for all the companies corresponds to a rating of 55, whereas the median is 50). If the rating of a given company is 80, it implies that approximately 80 percent of the companies in the industry perform below this company and approximately 20 percent above.

Rule 3: Computing a rating. A ratio is interpreted into a rating by the following steps:

1. Estimate the lowest possible value of the financial ratio in the industry. Subtract this value from both the company's ratio and from the industry's average ratio. The result is the transformed ratio.
2. Divide the company's transformed ratio by the industry's transformed ratio. This result is the relative ratio.
3. Find the corresponding rating in table 15–6 that pertains to the relative ratio derived in step 2. When the dispersion (for example, the standard deviation; see chapter 3) of the ratios is wide, take the right-hand value in table 15–6; when the dispersion is narrow, take the left-hand value.
4. Each ratio that is not stated in terms that are directly related to the level of performance (that is, the higher the ratio, the higher the level of performance) should be reversed. For example, the leverage ratios should be reversed by computing their reciprocals.

Example. The profit margin of Company X for 1980 is 9 percent (see the

Table 15–6
Rating Corresponding to Relative Ratios[a]

Relative Ratio	*Rating*
0.4	5–10
0.5	10–20
0.7	30–40
1.0	50–60
1.1	60–70
1.3	70–80
1.5	80–85
1.7	85–90
2.0	90–95
2.5	100

[a]Based on positively skewed distribution, where the ratio of median to mean is between 0.9 and 0.8, corresponding to a coefficient of variation between 0.5 and 0.7, respectively. Most business financial ratios fall in this range.

previous section), the average for the industry is 8 percent, and the smallest value for the industry is zero.
Solution: The transformed ratio for the company is $9 - 0 = 9$, and for the industry $8 - 0 = 8$. The relative ratio is $9 / 8 = 1.125$. The rating corresponding to 1.125 relative ratio is derived by interpolation, using table 15–6:

$$65 + \frac{75 - 65}{1.3 - 1.1}(1.125 - 1.100) = 66.25$$

where 65 is the average rating for the relative ratio of 1.1 in table 15–6 and 75 is the average rating for the relative ratio of 1.3 in table 15–6.
Because the average rating of the industry is expected to be 55, the resulting rating for Company X shows a relative high profit performance.

The ratings for additional ratios are presented in table 15–7. As can be seen in four ratios, the company's performance is above the average, whereas the performance is below the average in the leverage ratio.

Rule 4: Approximating the rating. The company's rating is approximately equal to one-half the relative ratio, multiplied by 100. The order of magnitude of the approximation is plus or minus 10 points.

Example. The average profit margin in a given industry is 10 percent. You

Table 15–7
Company X Ratios and Ratings for 1980

	Profit Margin	*Return on Assets*	*Current Ratio*	*Leverage Ratio*	*Assets Turnover*
Industry ratios					
Average	8	10	1.9	35	0.55
Smallest	0	0	0.7	10	0.15
Company ratios[a]	9	11.8	2	41.2	0.59
Transformed ratios[b]					
Industry	8	10	1.2	25	0.40
Company	9	11.8	1.3	31.2	0.44
Relative ratios[c]	1.13	1.18	1.08	0.80[e]	1.11
Ratings[d]	66	69	63	42	65

[a]From the section "Performance Ratios."
[b]Original ratio minus the smallest for the industry.
[c]Company's transformed ratio divided by the industry's transformed ratio.
[d]Interpreted from the relative ratio by means of table 15–6, and interpolating.
[e]Reciprocal of the relative ratio, which is 1.25.

inspect the financial statement of two companies and find profit margins of 18 percent and 5 percent, respectively.

Solution: Given that the lowest profit margin in the industry is close to zero, the respective relative ratios are

$$\frac{18}{10} = 1.8 \quad \frac{5}{10} = 0.5$$

The approximated ratings are

$$\frac{1.8}{2} \times 100 = 90 \quad \frac{0.5}{2} \times 100 = 25$$

The results of the approximations are usually biased in the following directions: for the cases above the average, the bias is downward; for the cases below the average, the bias is upward.

Composite Rating

The advantage of a rating over the conventional ratio is that it provides the level of the company's ratio relative to the industry's norm (the average ratio for the industry). Thus, the rating provides more information and reduces by one-half the volume of figures to be examined by the analyst (because the industry's figures are already incorporated into the rating). Still, the volume of figures is large. For example, a follow-up of six ratios over 5 years means a comparison among 30 ratings. The volume of figures can be further reduced by combining the ratings into a composite rating.[1]

Rule 5: Deriving the composite rating. A composite rating of a company for a given period is derived by calculating the average of the individual ratings of the company. A composite ratio should be derived from a minimum of four ratios (and maximum of eight ratios), with one or two ratios for each category of performance (profitability, liquidity, leverage, and activity).

Example. Consider the ratings in table 15–7.
Solution: The average of the ratings is

$$\frac{66 + 69 + 63 + 42 + 65}{5} = 61$$

This average is the composite rating. Approximately 60 percent of the companies in the industry perform below this company and approximately 40 percent above.

Rule 6: Confidence level of a rating. The composite rating is computed from several ratios that are, in the statistical sense, a sample of a population. Because sample estimates may differ from the true population value, a confidence level should be provided (chapter 3).

The 90 percent confidence level of a composite rating is about $\pm$ 10 points. For example, a composite rating of 60 may actually fall between 50 and 70, with an average value of 60.

Rule 7: Timeseries rating. Both individual and composite ratings can be used to follow up the company's performance level over several periods. This procedure relates the annual ratings of both the industry and the company to a base period to provide timeseries ratings.

A ratio is interpreted into a timeseries rating by the following steps:

1. Compute the individual company's ratings for each period in the same way as that used for computing the regular ratings (rule 3), using the industry's ratios of the base period.
2. Compute the individual ratings for each period for the industry's ratios as carried out in step 1.
3. Compute a composite rating for each period for the company and for the industry.

This procedure provides two series of composite ratings that are related to a base period, one for the company and one for the industry. These series are very informative and easy to grasp.

Example. Consider the example in table 15–7, and the data in the first two rows of table 15–8. The industry's ratios for the 1980 (table 15–7) are used as a base.
Solution: The industry and company ratings have been computed in the same way as illustrated in table 15–7. The results of the individual and composite ratings are presented in table 15–8.

The industry's composite rating did change slightly between 1975 and 1980 (54.5 and 55, respectively), but the individual ratings changed more significantly (42 to 73 in 1975; 55 in 1980). The company's composite rating, on the other hand, declined slightly (from 62.8 in 1975 to 61 in 1980).

Application and Implication of Ratio Analysis

Financial statement analysis is used extensively by both management and outside people. Thus, the procedure of applying the analysis and the implications of the analysis should be studied carefully.

Rule 8: Procedure of analysis. The procedure of analyzing financial statements should take the following directions.

1. *Results versus reasons:* First, the end result of the operations should be determined; next the reasons for the achieved result should be examined.

Table 15–8
Company X Ratios and Timeseries Ratings for 1975 and 1980

	Profit Margin	*Return on Assets*	*Current Ratio*	*Leverage Ratio*	*Assets Turnover*	*Average (Composite Rating)*
Ratios for 1975						
Industry	7	8	2	30	0.50	
Company	8	8	2.5	25	0.50	
Ratings, on 1980 base						
Industry:						
1975	47	42	63	73	47	54.4
1980	55	55	55	55	55	55.0
Company:						
1975[a]	55	42	83	87	47	62.8
1980	66	69	63	42	65	61.0

[a]Ratings are calculated relative to 1980 industry ratios.

2. *Macro versus micro:* First, the overall situation should be determined; next, the details should be examined. For example, analyze the statement in the following order: composite rating, individual ratings, financial statement items, and cost accounting items.

3. *Cross-section versus timeseries:* Level of performance is a relative measure; therefore, it should be compared to former performances and to other performances. The first comparison (timeseries) indicates the trend, but it is not sufficient to arrive at a conclusion. The second comparison (cross-section) indicates the achievable performance.

4. *Ex-post versus ex-ante:* Projection is based on information about the past. Hence, past performance (ex-post) should be analyzed first; next, projections and planning (ex-ante) should be carried out.

Rule 9: Industry averages as benchmarks. Performance and success are relative measures. To find the performance of a company relative to other similar companies, a standard or a benchmark is needed. The most suitable benchmark for a financial ratio is the industry's average ratio. Many agencies publish industry averages; for example, Dun & Bradstreet's *Key Business Ratios*; Robert Morris Associates' *Annual Statement Studies*; Leo Troy's *Almanac of Business and Industrial Financial Ratios,* and others. In some cases, data on quartiles of the industry's average ratio are also published. Some financial ratios averages for selected industries for 1975 are presented in table 15–9.

Effects of Scale of Operations

Financial ratios are meant to provide figures for which the effect of the scale of the operations have been eliminated. In economic jargon, the use of ratios assumes constant returns to scale. However, the scale of the company does affect the actual ratios because the distribution of the ratios is positively skewed. (This effect is the reason why the industry's average rating in table 15–8 is 55 rather than 50).

In the United States, the ratios of the large companies are lower than those of the smaller companies. This observation is implied from the data in table 15–10, where the simple average is, in most cases, higher than the weighted average. The weighted average is computed by summing the numerators for all companies, summing the denominators for all companies, and dividing the aggregate numerator by the aggregate denominator. A higher simple average indicates that the correlation between the ratio and the denominator of the ratio (which indicates the scale of the variable under analysis, as for example, sales) is negative (see rule 36 in chapter 3 and rule 27 in chapter 12).

Table 15–9
Financial Ratio Averages for Selected Industries

		Financial Ratios: 1975 Industry Averages								
SIC Code	*Industry*	*PM*	*ROA*	*ROE*	*CR*	*QR*	*LR*	*AT*	*IT*	*ART*
1311	Oil-crude producers	.19	.09	.17	1.55	1.21	.43	.48	17.6	4.9
2200	Textile products	.02	.03	−.03	2.98	1.56	.48	1.40	5.8	6.6
2300	Textile apparel mfg.	.02	.06	.09	3.49	1.73	.49	1.69	5.1	7.5
3311	Steel-minor	.04	.07	.10	3.25	1.57	.47	1.41	5.4	8.9
3679	Electronic components	.01	.04	.05	3.17	1.45	.52	1.37	4.0	6.2
3714	Auto parts and accessories	.03	.07	.14	2.78	1.23	.47	1.55	4.9	7.6
3999	MFG inds	.04	.07	.16	2.77	1.38	.58	1.52	4.9	7.0
4210	Trucking	.02	.05	.12	1.49	1.01	.56	1.70	64.7	12.2
4511	Air transport	.02	.04	.06	1.33	1.03	.68	1.15	38.2	10.3
4911	Electric utilities-flow thru	.13	.06	.12	1.15	N/A	.57	.39	N/A	N/A
4912	Electric utilities-normalized	.11	.06	.11	.79	N/A	.55	.36	N/A	N/A
4924	Natural gas companies	.07	.06	.13	1.02	N/A	.57	.68	N/A	N/A
5311	Retail department stores	.02	.05	.09	2.11	.88	.54	2.17	6.9	29.9
5411	Retail-food chains	.01	.05	.10	1.73	.56	.53	5.28	16.9	100.7

Source: George Foster, *Financial Statement Analysis*, © 1978, p. 59. Reprinted by permission of Prentice-Hall, Inc., Englewood Cliffs, New Jersey.

Note: PM = profit margin, ROA = return on assets, ROE = return on equity, CR = current ratio, QR = quick ratio, LR = leverage ratio, AT = assets turnover, IT = inventory turnover, ART = accounts receivable turnover, and N/A = data not available.

Table 15–10
Effect of Scale on Financial Ratios

	1965 Average		1970 Average		1975 Average	
	Simple	*Weighted*	*Simple*	*Weighted*	*Simple*	*Weighted*
P rofit margin	0.083	0.082	0.057	0.059	0.051	0.052
Return on assets	0.073	0.056	0.052	0.044	0.057	0.047
Return on equity	0.148	0.128	0.120	0.105	0.135	0.121
Current ratio	2.55	1.91	2.50	1.55	2.46	1.54
Quick ratio	1.64	1.29	1.60	0.95	1.51	0.98
Leverage ratio	0.52	0.40	0.56	0.48	0.56	0.49
Assets turnover	1.22	0.61	1.10	0.57	1.15	0.61
Inventory turnover	12.98	6.82	11.58	6.26	11.26	6.71
Accounts receivable turnover	10.82	6.05	8.92	5.34	9.39	5.78

Source: George Foster, *Financial Statement Analysis*, © 1978, pp. 157–160. Reprinted by permission of Prentice-H all, Inc. Englewood Cliffs, New Jersey. Computed from data of 1,200 to 1,600 companies.

Table 15–11
Effect of Inflation on Financial Ratios

	Bias of Variables	Direction of Bias
Profitability ratios		
1) Profit margin = $\frac{\text{Net income}}{\text{Sales}}$	Conv. > PLA Conv. = PLA	Upward
2) Capital margin = $\frac{\text{EBIT + depreciation}}{\text{Sales}}$	Conv. = PLA Conv. = PLA	None
3) Return on assets = $\frac{\text{EBIT}}{\text{Assets}}$	Conv. > PLA Conv. < PLA	Strongly upward
4) Return on equity = $\frac{\text{Net earnings}}{\text{Equity}}$	Conv. > PLA Conv. < PLA	Strongly upward
Liquidity ratios		
1) Current ratio = $\frac{\text{Current assets}}{\text{Current liabilities}}$	Conv. < PLA Conv. = PLA	Downward
2) Quick ratio = $\frac{\text{Current assets} - \text{inventory}}{\text{Current liabilities}}$	Conv. = PLA Conv. = PLA	None
3) Net working capital = $\frac{\text{Current assets} - \text{current liabilities}}{\text{Sales}}$	Conv. < PLA Conv. = PLA	Downward

Leverage ratios		
1) Leverage ratio = $\frac{\text{Total debt}}{\text{Total capital}}$	$\frac{\text{Conv.} = \text{PLA}}{\text{Conv.} < \text{PLA}}$	Upward
2) Debt turnover = $\frac{\text{Total debt}}{\text{Sales}}$	$\frac{\text{Conv.} = \text{PLA}}{\text{Conv.} = \text{PLA}}$	None
3) Long-term debt turnover = $\frac{\text{Long-term debt}}{\text{Sales}}$	$\frac{\text{Conv.} = \text{PLA}}{\text{Conv.} = \text{PLA}}$	None
4) Average interest = $\frac{\text{Interest payment}}{\text{Total capital}}$	$\frac{\text{Conv.} = \text{PLA}}{\text{Conv.} < \text{PLA}}$	Upward
Activity ratios		
1) Assets turnover = $\frac{\text{Sales}}{\text{Assets}}$	$\frac{\text{Conv.} = \text{PLA}}{\text{Conv.} < \text{PLA}}$	Upward
2) Inventory turnover = $\frac{\text{Sales}}{\text{Average inventories}}$	$\frac{\text{Conv.} = \text{PLA}}{\text{Conv.} < \text{PLA}}$	Upward
3) Accounts receivable turnover = $\frac{\text{Sales}}{\text{Average accounts receivable}}$	$\frac{\text{Conv.} = \text{PLA}}{\text{Conv.} = \text{PLA}}$	None
4) Working capital turnover = $\frac{\text{Sales}}{\text{Current assets}}$	$\frac{\text{Conv.} = \text{PLA}}{\text{Conv.} < \text{PLA}}$	Upward

Source: Based on Y. Goldschmidt and K. Admon, *Profit Measurement during Inflation: Accounting, Economic and Financial Aspects* (New York: Wiley, 1977).

Note: Conv. = conventional financial statements, PLA = price-level–adjusted financial statements, and EBIT = earnings before interest and taxes.

The data in table 15–10 indicate that the larger companies have lower returns on resources; lower liquidity ratios, presumably because they are less susceptible to financial stress; and lower financial leverage, presumably because they can more easily issue equity capital.

Distress signals

The financial ratios express the end result of the company's business activity. They should be used to identify problems not to solve them. Thus, a low relative financial ratio, or an adverse trend in the ratio (even when the relative company's ratio is high), expresses a signal of distress that should trigger a detailed investigation.

The reliability of a ratio is tested by the correlation of the ratio in one period to those in former periods. There is empirical evidence that the correlation of financial ratios between two adjacent years is over 0.8 and between ratios separated by 5 years is over 0.6. This indicates that the ratios can be used for projection purposes. The reliability of a composite rating is even higher because it is constructed from several ratios.

Rule 10: Distress for an individual ratio. An individual ratio with a relative value (in regard to the industry) of less than 0.8 (rating of 40) is a sign of distress or bad management. Because of the reliability of the ratios, one can predict that the distress would prevail in the future.

Rule 11: Distress for a company. A company with a composite rating lower than 30 has a low chance of survival. The chance of default of bankruptcy for such companies in a 5-year period is very high (above 80 percent, according to empirical evidence).

Inflation Distortions in Financial Ratios

The fact that a ratio is independent of the scale in which the original measurements are carried out may cause the impression that financial ratios are unaffected by the accounting distortion caused by inflation. This impression is false if the dollars in the numerator of the ratio differ from the dollars in the denominator.

Rule 12: Direction of effect of conventional accounting on the ratios. The effect of inflation on each of the ratios listed in the section on performance ratios is presented in table 15–11. At least one ratio has been included in each category that is not affected by inflation. Inflation causes the profitability ratios to be biased strongly upward, the liquidity ratios to be biased downward, and the leverage and activity ratios to be biased upward.

Rule 13: Correcting the accounting biases due to inflation. The biases in the ratios can be corrected by using revalued figures (chapter 10). This rule holds especially for the correction of income and assets values. The values of total assets, total capital and equity can be corrected by using the market value of equity plus total liabilities, as illustrated in the section on performance ratios—for example, for the returns on assets.

Revaluing the inventories is usually less reliable, especially when the LIFO method is used (chapter 8). However, the cost of materials already more or less represent the current values and usually it is not necessary to revalue these costs. When the FIFO method is used, the cost of materials should be revalued.

Note

1. This section is based on L. Shashua and Y. Goldschmidt, "An Index for Evaluating Financial Performance," *Journal of Finance* (June 1974), pp. 797–814.

16 Financing Management and Control

It is the responsibility of top management to coordinate the company's entire activities and to integrate the plans and objectives of its various parts. The company's plans and goals for the future are delineated through detailed budgets of sales, production, costs of materials, inventories, accounts receivable and payable, investments, loans, level of cash, and so on. This mass of details is ultimately translated into financial figures. The financial figures end up in cash, which is the ultimate resource of any business. The cash enables the business to acquire inputs and resources it needs to survive and flourish.

The approval of the final budget, which is stated in cash terms, rests with top management. The approval procedure is first to check the end result, as shown in the final budget, and next to examine the details and the reasons for the final results. Any change in the desired final outcome is then transmitted to lower management levels and worked through backward to the necessary details in the various budgets.

Once the budget is approved, the analysis of the actual events and the control of performance follow the same approach: first checking the end results, next examining the details, and checking the end results again. This feedback process is the core of financing management and control.

Tools of Financing Management and Control

Parallel to financial statements analysis, where the analyst is interested in the end results of the company's financial position, financing management and control also deals with the financial end results. Moreover, it seeks to find the main decision or control factors affecting these end results.

The tools needed by top management for financing management and control are similar both for approving the budget and for managing and controlling current company operations. These tools are:

1. *Income statement,* in terms of accounting and cash basis, for the whole period, usually 1 year.

2. *Flow of funds statement,* in terms of accounting and cash basis for the period.

3. *Consolidated cash budget* of sales and capital accounts, broken down by subperiods (quarters or months).

In addition to the conventional accounting-based budget, a cash-based budget should be prepared. A cash-based budget is a summary of all cash movements (receipts and payments) that are anticipated as a result of the projected operations. These two budgets are linked through the sums carried from the preceding period and to the following period.

Management should also receive, as an auxiliary to these reports, a more detailed cash budget (but still a summary), pertaining to production and to capital accounts. This summary is based on detailed production and investments budgets.

These tools for financing management are prepared in addition to the conventional accounting-based budget, which provides the projected income statement and balance sheet. The conventional budget by itself is prepared from several detailed budgets pertaining to the major aspects of the company's operations, such as sales, inventories, production, materials, labor, overhead, and selling and administration expense.

Approving the Cash Budget

The process of approving the budget starts after ensuring that the production and investment plans for the next period meet all the company's resource constraints and goals. The next step is to determine the effects of the budget on current earnings and on the current financial position of the company. The financial position is mainly determined by the level of sales and the costs incurred, as well as the level of gross investment, which is based on the company's long-run expansion goals.

Effects on Earnings

The effect of the budget on next year's earnings is analyzed through the projected income statements. The statement, according to an accounting basis, lists the anticipated value of production and costs by major categories. The cash-basis projected-income statement, on the other hand, lists the anticipated receipts from sales and anticipated payments for inputs by major categories, in accordance with the projected cash budget.

Projected dividend is excluded from the budget because the budget is seen by too many people in the company, whereas dividend policy is the responsibility of top management only. Thus, projected dividend should be seen as an addition to the final cash requirements as stated in the cash budgets.

Table 16–1
Projected Income Statement
($ million)

	Accounting Basis	*Cash Basis*
Value of production	310	260
Costs less depreciation	240	223
Depreciation	20	20
Net earnings before dividend	50	17

Example. Consider the projected income statement in table 16–1. To simplify the illustration, only the totals are presented. The accounting figures show that total earnings before dividend plus depreciation is $70 million. This figure, which constitutes 22.6 percent of sales, is satisfactory, based on past company performance and on the industry average. From this point of view, the production plan is found to be reasonable.

The cash-basis earnings, on the other hand, show a much lower figure than the accounting figure ($37 million). This low level presumably is the result of a low level of sales and the build-up of excessive inventories of finished goods or work in process (because of low demand or a drop in the company's share of the market), or to poor management of accounts receivable, or both. Hence, management has discovered a weak point with respect to this low level of cash earnings that must be explained by the managers in these areas.

Effects on Long-Run Liquidity

The effects of the budget on long-run liquidity are analyzed through the projected flow of funds statement. The common company policy is to finance all long-run capital uses through sources of long-run funds.

Example. Consider the projected flow of funds in table 16–2. The total uses, on an accounting basis, amounts to $140 million; this sum is perfectly matched with anticipated long-run sources as required. However, the cash-basis figures indicate that $23 million of short-term loans will be needed to finance the long-run capital uses, which contradicts the company's policy. However, because the flow of funds is properly balanced on an accounting basis, these short-term loans can be considered as a temporary source for capital uses, to be liquidated in the near future (next year).

Table 16–2
Projected Flow-of-Funds Statement
($ million)

	Accounting Basis	*Cash Basis*
Sources		
Net earnings	50	37
Depreciation	20	
Loans: Long-term	70	70
Short-term[a]	—	23
Total	140	130
Uses		
Investments:		
Equipment	40	40
Buildings	60	50
Retirements of loans	40	40
Total	140	130

[a]Increase in working capital requirement, financed by loans with less than one-year maturity.

Effects on Short-Run Liquidity

The effect of the budget on the company's liquidity in the next period is analyzed through the consolidated cash budget illustrated in table 16–3. This statement lists the projected total receipts and payments by subperiods (quarters). The first and last columns show the sums carried from the preceding year (that is, brought forward) and carried forward to the next year, respectively. In the case of receipts, the sums carried over represent the inventories of products and the accounts receivable, whereas in the case of payments the sums carried over represent the inventories of purchased materials and the accounts payable.

The difference between total cash receipts and total cash payments is the periodic cash requirement to be raised to finance the projected plan. The second line shows the cumulative cash requirements for each subperiod, starting from the first quarter. These requirements are the outstanding short-term loans (less than 1-year maturity) to be raised, in addition to the existing balance at the beginning of the first quarter, as shown in the last line.

The cash requirements, as shown in the last three lines of the consolidated cash budget, do not include projected dividends. If dividends are paid, the cash requirements would increase by the amount of the projected dividends.

Example. Consider the consolidated cash budget in table 16–3. First, consider the cumulative cash requirement. Total additional working capital

Table 16–3
Consolidated Cash Budget
($ million)

	Carried from Last Year[a]	Quarters[b] 1	2	3	4	Total Cash	Carried to Next Year[a]
Receipts							
Sales	50	50	60	90	60	260	100
Capital sources	10	10	10	30	20	70	10
Total	60	60	70	120	80	330	110
Payments							
Costs	15	59	60	58	46	223	32
Capital uses	—	40	45	25	20	130	10
Total	15	99	105	83	66	353	42
Cash requirements							
Receipts less payments	45	(39)	(35)	37	14	(23)	68
Cumulative cash requirement		(39)	(74)	(37)	(23)		
Outstanding short-term loans	50	(89)	(124)	(87)	(73)		(73)

[a]Sums recorded in the balance sheet.
[b]Amounts of cash.

needed (additional short-term loans) is quite high, starting with $39 million in the first quarter, and rising to a prohibitive level of $74 million by the end of the second quarter. These figures decline to $23 million by the end of the year, a sum which corresponds to the short-term loans listed on the flow of funds statement. This sum of $23 million corresponds to the difference between the sum carried to the next year ($68 million) and that carried from the last year ($45 million). This correspondence is exact only when the flow of capital funds is properly balanced on an accounting basis (that is, when capital uses are not financed by short-term loans).

The proposed cash budget in table 16–3 is, presumably, not acceptable to management because of the high cash requirements. Furthermore, these high cash requirements stem both from the sales forecast and from the capital uses. To pinpoint the reasons, management should inspect more detailed cash budgets for these two accounts.

Revision of the Cash Budget

The consolidated cash budget illustrated in table 16–3 is prepared from detailed cash budgets for each account. A revision of the consolidated cash budget requires the inspection of each detailed budget. The individual cash budgets have the same form as the consolidated cash budget, with the exception of the last column. The last column lists the total budget on an accounting basis. The accounting figures correspond to

Total cash
+ Carried to next period
− Carried from last period

Cash budgets of production and capital account are illustrated in tables 16–4 and 16–5, respectively. Each line is a summary of a major category for which a separate detailed sheet of cash forecast is prepared. For example, the detailed sheet for the first line (product 1) would list the sums carried from the last year (by inventories and accounts receivable) and sales of the budgeted year. In turn, these sums may be broken down by major sales outlets (such as customers or markets). The same goes for inputs, where the breakdown is by major inputs or by major suppliers or both.

Each of the cash budgets in tables 16–4 and 16–5—that is, production (sales and costs) and capital account (investments and loans)—should be revised. After the revisions have been decided on, a new set of budgets should be prepared and submitted.

Example. Table 16–4 indicates that the sales forecast of product 1 is reasonable in quarter 1, low in quarter 2 and quarter 4, and relatively high in quarter 3. Discussion with the sales manager reveals that sales receipts can be increased by $10 million in quarter 2 if cash discounts to customers are increased. On the other hand, the low sales receipts in the last quarter stem

Table 16–4
Cash Budget—Production
($ million)

	Carried from Last Year	*Quarters 1*	*2*	*3*	*4*	*Total Cash*	*Carried to Next Year*	*Accounting Basis*
Sales								
Product 1	20	20	20	40	20	100	40	120
Product 2	30	30	40	50	40	160	60	190
Total Production	50	50	60	90	60	260	100	310
Costs								
Materials	10	30	30	30	15	105	25	120
Labor	5	15	15	15	15	60	5	60
Interest expenses	—	7	7	7	9	30	—	30
Taxes	—	2	3	1	2	8	2	10
Overhead	—	5	5	5	5	20	—	20
Total Costs	15	59	60	58	46	223	32	240

Table 16–5
Cash Budget—Capital Account
($ million)

	Carried from Last Year	*Quarters 1*	*2*	*3*	*4*	*Total Cash*	*Carried to Next Year*	*Accounting Basis*
Uses								
Investments:								
Equipment	—	10	20	—	10	40	—	40
Buildings	—	20	10	10	10	50	10	60
Loan retirements		10	15	15	—	40	—	40
Total uses	—	40	45	25	20	130	10	140
Sources								
Long-term loans	10	10	10	30	20	70	10	70

from low seasonal demand, thus causing inventory build-up. The policy of increasing cash discounts is then approved by management and the sales receipts of product 1 in quarter 2 is anticipated to increase by $10 million, while the same amount is deducted from quarter 3. This revision reduces the cash requirement in quarter 2 by $10 million.

The cash forecasts of all the other categories in table 16–4 were inspected and found to be justifiable, according to the company's current policy. For example, the cost of delaying of accounts payable beyond the current policy of 1 month was considered and found to be too high.

The figures in table 16–5 indicate a high cash requirement of the capital account. A cursory inspection indicates that the source lies in investment timing in the first two quarters. Discussion with the responsible personnel indicate that no serious loss would be incurred if these investments start in the second quarter instead of the first. Consequently, the budget is revised by shifting the investment from the first to the second quarter, and that of the second to the third quarter of the year. This revision reduces the cash requirement by $30 million in the first two quarters.

Similar revisions should be introduced to all the detailed budgets. The total revised cash requirement of the consolidated cash budget is

Quarter	1	2	3	4
Cash requirement	(9)	(25)	(3)	14
Cumulative cash requirement	(9)	(34)	(37)	(23)

Discussion with the financial manager revealed that these cash requirements can be raised from proper sources at the prevailing terms. The revision did not adversely alter the original earning forecast; hence, the proposed budget is approved.

Table 16–6
Monthly Cash Budget and Report

	Budget (Revised)			*Actual*		
	Carried from Last Period	*Cash*	*Carried to Next Period*	*Carried from Last Period*	*Cash*	*Carried to Next Period*
Total receipts						
Total payments						
Cash requirements						

Current Financing Management and Control

Current financing management and control rely heavily on the budgeted statements as discussed and presented the previous section. But a budget is still a forecast that is based on prior information. As the year progresses, new information is added based on actual events and performance of your company. Thus, proper management implies periodic budget revisions. At the end of each quarter, management should receive a revised version of the budget for the remaining periods (by quarters or by months). This revised version should be studied by management and approved in the same manner as the annual budget.

The budget statements are usually broken down by quarters. For the purpose of control, actual results should be compared to the budgeted figures on a monthly basis. At the end of each month, management should receive cash statements by major categories as listed in the cash budget (tables 16–3, 16–4, and 16–5). A desirable format of the monthly cash statement corresponding to the annual budget in table 16–3 is presented in table 16–6.

The budget format in table 16–6 is for a given month (or quarter). All figures that will be listed in this format should correspond to the last revised period. Deviations between the budget and the actual figures should be discussed with the proper personnel to find the cause and decide what can be done to enhance performance.

Besides the monthly statements, corresponding statements should be submitted to management on a cumulative basis. The figures in these statements show the sum of the monthly statements from the beginning of the year up to the submitted date. Such a statement is very informative. It shows the total financing activity of the company during the period, and services as a *pro forma* financial statement on a cash basis. It also indicates the overall reliability of the budget as a tool for performance evaluation. The form of this statement is similar to the corresponding monthly statement illustrated in table 16–6.

17 Valuing Acquisitions

The acquisition value of a going concern is different for the buyer than for the seller. The price depends, among other things, on the seller's and buyer's motives and on their notions regarding the market conditions.

In the case of privately held companies, the maximum price a buyer should be willing to pay is the present value of the future net cash inflow of the acquired company, discounted at your after-tax cost of capital. In the case of public corporations, the maximum price the buyer corporation should pay is that which does not reduce the return on its equity. In both cases, the settled price is more a matter of bargaining than a clear-cut problem in capital budgeting.

Several methods of valuation are presented in this chapter. Because each method has some drawbacks, more than one method should be applied to arrive at an order of magnitude of the value of the candidate company.

In acquiring the stocks of publicly held companies, merger aspects should be considered in addition to the valuation itself. In all cases, the buyer is assumed to acquire both the assets and the liabilities of the seller.

Analysis of the Candidate

Before valuing the company which is a candidate for acquisition, a thorough analysis of that company should be carried out. This analysis should include the history records, the present situation, and a forecast of the candidate's future operations.

The first step is to analyze the candidate's financial statements:

1. Validate all the items in the financial statements for the last 5 years.
2. State the main items in terms of today's price level.
3. Rate the financial statements relative to the industry; apply financial ratio analysis and a composite rating (chapter 15).

The second step is to examine the various aspects of the candidate's activities:

1. Analyze risk in respect to environment, business, and finance (chapter 18).

2. Review physical and mechanical condition of the facilities, buildings, equipment, and inventories; estimate their market value.

3. Examine the market conditions for the products or services, particularly market share, sensitivity of demand with respect to changes in economic conditions, the candidate's plans for new products, the prospects for new markets, and substitute products.

4. Evaluate investments in research and development needed to maintain the present competitive condition.

5. Survey the labor and staff situation regarding such factors as wage and salary level, labor-management relations, the possibility of retiring and firing employees, the need for training and recruiting professional staff.

6. Perform a cost-benefit analysis of improving the candidate's present operation through management, labor, or technological means (for example, new equipment).

7. Assess the synergistic effects regarding the prospects of reducing operating and overhead costs of the buyer's and the seller's combined operations. For example, duplicate facilities can be eliminated, purchasing and marketing may be consolidated, finance costs may be reduced, or operating economies may be realized.

Accounting and Appraisal Methods of Valuation

Both the accounting and the appraisal methods of valuing acquisitions rely on data from the financial statements. The methods differ in the procedure used to determine the goodwill.

Rule 1: Valuing by the accounting method. The accounting method implies that the assets and liabilities of a going concern can be realized according to their market replacement values, item by item. The company's market value, above the value of its physical assets, can be assessed by the capitalized value of its expected future profits. This premium value is called goodwill.

$$\begin{aligned}\text{Sum to be paid} = {} & \text{Revalued assets} \\ & + \text{Goodwill} \\ & - \text{Liabilities}\end{aligned}$$

Goodwill is evaluated by summing the adjusted profits (or losses) in the past 4 to 6 years.

The adjusted profit used to calculate the goodwill is derived from the reported accounting profit less correction for understated historical costs (especially depreciation) and imputed cost of capital on equity. That is

$$\begin{aligned}\text{Adjusted profit} = {} & \text{After-tax earnings} \\ & - (\text{Revalued minus historical depreciation}) \\ & \quad (1 - f)(1 - t) \\ & - (\text{Equity})\, r\end{aligned}$$

where f is the proportion of debt out of total capital, t is the company's income tax rate, r is the buyer's cost of capital after-tax, and equity is the book value of equity, retained earnings, and reserves.

The reasoning for the correction for revalued depreciation is as follows: The buyer claims that he will have a higher depreciation expense than the prevailing expenses because the acquisition value will be higher than the present book value. This claim holds for only the equity portion of the finance of the assets (chapter 19). The seller claims that the increased depreciation will be tax-deductible; thus the tax saving should be deducted from the increased depreciation expenses. (The actual tax saving to the buyer will be the amount resulting from multiplying t by the total increase in depreciation expenses).

Example. Consider the financial statements of Company X in table 15–2 and 15–3 for 1980. The relevant data are book value of equity, \$800; market value of shares, \$1,000; liabilities, \$700; revalued assets, \$1,700; pretax earnings, \$140; after-tax earnings, \$100; historical depreciation, \$100; and revalued depreciation, \$110. The buyer's after-tax cost of capital is 6 percent. The goodwill is calculated on a 5-year basis.
Solution: The proportion of debt out of total capital, f, is

$$700 \,/\, 1{,}500 = 0.46$$

The company's income tax rate, t, is

$$40 \,/\, 140 = 0.29$$

The correction for the revalued depreciation is

$$(110 - 100)(1 - 0.46)(1 - 0.29) = 3.83 \cong \$4$$

The year's cost of equity is

$$800 \times 0.06 = \$48$$

The adjusted profit is

$$100 - 4 - 48 = \$48$$

The goodwill is

$$48 \times 5 = \$240$$

The sum to be paid for acquisition (revalued assets plus goodwill minus liabilities) is

$$1{,}700 + 240 - 700 = \$1{,}240$$

Rule 2: Valuing by the appraisal method. The appraisal method of valuing acquisitions differs from the accounting method in the manner of assessing the goodwill.

Sum to be paid = Revalued assets
+ Goodwill
− Liabilities

The goodwill is determined by applying the following goodwill factor to the revalued assets, that is,

$$\text{Revalued assets}\left(\frac{Y - E}{Y}\right)$$

where Y is the total returns on capital, which includes after-tax earnings plus interest and depreciation; and E is the imputed capital expenses, which include revalued depreciation plus interest (the buyer's preinflation after-tax cost of capital) on total revalued assets.

When the age of the stock of depreciable assets is not evenly distributed, the capital expense E on the assets in this stock should be computed by the corresponding capital recovery charges (chapter 5). The capital expenses for the other assets is computed by applying the interest rate to the revalued assets.

Example. Consider the first example. The total return on capital Y is \$270. The buyer's preinflation after-tax cost of capital is 6 percent.

Solution: The imputed capital expense (revalued depreciation and 6 percent on revalued assets) is

$$E = 110 + (0.06 \times 1{,}700) = \$212$$

The goodwill (on revalued assets) is

$$1{,}700 \times \frac{270 - 212}{270} = \$365$$

The sum to be paid for acquisition (revalued assets plus goodwill minus liabilities) is

$$1{,}700 + 365 - 700 = \$1{,}365$$

The goodwill here (\$365) is higher than that found by the accounting method (\$240). However, if a cost of capital of 8 percent is used (rather than 6 percent), the goodwill under both methods would be almost equal (\$151 for the appraisal method; \$160 for the accounting method).

The appraised goodwill has the following meaning. As Y represents the total returns on capital and E represents the total imputed capital expenses, the term $Y - E$ represents the net return on capital. The net return is related to the total returns Y to indicate the ratio of net return to total returns. The resultant ratio, which can be viewed as the rate of extra profit, determines the goodwill when applied to the revalued assets.

When the returns on capital Y are lower than the imputed capital expenses E (that is, in the case of losses), the goodwill factor is

$$\frac{Y - E}{E}$$

This formula would avoid underappraising the value (for example, when $Y = 0.5E$, then $(Y - E)/Y = -1$ and the appraised assets value will be zero).

Example. Consider the previous example, but suppose the total return on capital Y is \$200 rather than \$270.
Solution: The goodwill is

$$1{,}700 \times \frac{200 - 212}{212} = \$-96$$

The sum to be paid for acquisition is

$$1{,}700 - 96 - 700 = \$904$$

Economic Method of Valuation

The economic method of valuation determines the value of a going concern with repect to the future returns, whereas the accounting and appraisal methods determine the value with respect to the history of the company.

Rule 3: Valuing by the economic method. According to economic theory, the value of a company to the buyer depends solely on the cash flow the company generates.

Sum to be paid = Present value of future cash flow
− Liabilities at acquisition date

When the future cash flow is anticipated to be perpetual and constant and the depreciation expenses suffice for assets replacement (which maintains the present output capacity), the total value of the company is

$$\frac{Y}{r} + \text{Gains on } L$$

where Y is the after-tax earnings plus interest minus correct depreciation; r is the buyer's cost of capital, preinflation but after-tax; and L is long-term outstanding loans. The first term (Y / r) is the present value of the perpetual return (see chapter 5). The second term (gains on L) is the gain on the outstanding long-term loans in present-value terms (see chapter 4), approximated by

$$L\left(1 - \frac{CR_{n,i}}{CR_{n,h}}\right)$$

where $CR_{n,i}$, $CR_{n,h}$ are capital recovery factors for n and i or h (rule 1, chapter 2); i is the average interest rate on L, after-tax; h is the current cost of capital, after-tax; and n is the average life span of long-term outstanding loans, which equals L / retirement of L in current year (last section of chapter 9).

Example A. Consider the financial statements of Company X in tables 15–2 and 15–3. It is assumed that the average figures for 1979 and 1980 are representative and would prevail in the future. The buyer's preinflation after-tax cost of capital is 6 percent. The gain on the loan is ignored for simplicity. The after-tax earnings before interest are

1979:	85 + 60 = \$145
1980:	90 + 70 = 160

Solution: The average annual cash flow is

$$(145 + 160) / 2 = \$152.50$$

The present value of the average annual cash flow is

$$\frac{152.50}{0.06} = \$2,542$$

The sum to be paid is

$$2,542 - 700 = \$1,842$$

The rate of the cost of capital used for valuation affects considerably the final value; the higher the rate, the lower the resultant value.

Example B. Consider the previous example, but suppose the cost of capital is 8 percent rather than 6 percent.
Solution: The present value of the annual average cash flow is

$$\frac{152.50}{0.08} = \$1,906$$

The sum to be paid is

$$1,906 - 700 = \$1,206$$

When the after-tax future cash flow is anticipated to increase, the total present value as arrived at in the case of constant cash flow should be multiplied by a correcting factor:

1. When $r > g$, the correcting factor is

$$1 + g(PVA_{n,r-g})$$

where g is the rate of anticipated growth of after-tax cash flow; r is the buyer's cost of capital, after-tax; PVA is the present-value factor of annuity (rule 7, chapter 2) at rate $(r - g)$; and n is the number of years of anticipated growth.

2. When $g > r$, the correcting factor is

$$1 + g(FVA_{n,g-r})$$

where FVA is the future value factor of annuity (rule 5, chapter 2) at rate $(g - r)$.

3. When $g = r$, the correcting factor is

$$1 + gn$$

Example C. Consider example A for rule 3, but an annual growth of 5 percent is anticipated for 7 years. The after-tax cost of capital is 6 percent.
Solution: The correcting factor is

$$1 + 0.05(PVA_{7,0.01}) = 1 + 0.05 \times 6.728 = 1.336$$

The total present value is

$$2{,}542 \times 1.336 = \$3{,}396$$

The sum to be paid is

$$\$3{,}396 - 700 = \$2{,}696$$

The Hybrid Method of Valuation

The hybrid method is based on both accounting and economic methods of valuation. By combining them, some of the main limitations of the former two methods are overcome. This method is similar in principle to the economic method, but does not assume a perpetual cash flow. Because future cash flow cannot be predicted far in the future, the valuation is based on the anticipated outcome in the next 5 to 7 years. At the end of this period, the method assumes that the company will be disposed of at a value determined by the accounting method. The resultant value and the net cash inflow until the assumed disposal date are discounted to provide the present value.

Rule 4: Valuing by the hibrid method. According to the hybrid method, the value of a company depends on the future returns of a planned horizon.

$$\text{Sum to be paid} = \text{Present value of net cash inflow} + \text{Present value of disposal value}$$

The present value of the net cash inflow (chapter 5) is

$$\sum_{t=1}^{T} \frac{W_t}{(1+r)^t}$$

where W_t is the net cash inflow in year t, stated in nominal prices, which equals sales minus total costs except depreciation minus income tax minus investments for replacement (needed to maintain current activities); T is the last year in the analysis, or the assumed disposal date; and r is the buyer's cost of capital, nominal rate after-tax.

In the case of constant annual net cash inflow, the present value of the net cash inflow is

$$W(PVA_{T,r})$$

where $PVA_{T,r}$ is the present-value factor of annuity (rule 7, chapter 2). The present value of the assumed disposal value, in year T, is

$$\frac{S_T - L_T + \text{Goodwill}}{(1+r)^T}$$

where S_T is the revalued depreciated assets, at end of year T; L_T is the total outstanding value of loans, at end of year T; and goodwill is computed from the present financial statements (rule 1 or 2).

Example. Consider the financial statements of Company X in tables 15–2 and 15–3. It is assumed that the figures for 1980 are representative and will prevail in the next 5 years. The after-tax cost of capital is 6 percent. The replacement of assets is assumed equal to $110, and loan renewal is assumed equal to loan retirement. The anticipated annual net cash inflow is

Sales		$1,000
Direct costs	$650	
Selling, etc.	50	
Interest	70	
Income tax	40	
Investments for replacement	110	(920)
		80

The disposal value after 5 years is evaluated at $1,000 plus $240 for goodwill (based on the first example), totaling $1240.

Solution: The present value of the net cash inflow for 5 years is

$$80(PVA_{5,0.06}) = 80 \times 4.212 = \$336.96$$

The present value of the assumed disposal value is

$$\frac{1{,}240}{(1 + 0.06)^5} = \$926.60$$

The sum to be paid is

$$336.96 + 926.60 = \$1{,}263.56$$

Valuing Acquisitions for Merger

A publicly held large company may be interested in acquiring the stock of a smaller publicly held company to increase the long-run returns on its shares. The stockholders of the purchased company share the same goal.

Incentives for merger

These are several reasons for a merger:

1. Synergistic effects. The combined operating costs of both parties may decrease as a result of the merger or income may increase.
2. Reduction in financial risk. The seller is, usually, more levered than the buyer, to a point which adversely affects the maret value of its shares. The merger dilutes the leverage and reduces the risk of default.
3, Increase in debt capacity. The merger usually increases the debt capacity because of the increase in size.
4. Diversification. By acquiring a different line of business, the buyer reduces his business risk.
5. Market opportunity. In some cases, the seller is a moderate-sized company whose stock is not known and is not particularly marketable. Thus, its price-earning ratio is unduly low and therefore the merger is advantageous.
6. Tax consideration. Loss-carryovers of the seller may be utilized to recover part of the purchase price through future tax reductions. Because of the complexity of the tax laws, advance rulings on this subject are important.

The purchase price is paid in terms of the buyer's stock. The ratio of exchange between the seller's and the buyer's shares is then the main bargaining variable.

A necessary condition of the acquisition is that the appraised value of the seller, net of liabilities, is higher than the market value of his shares. Hence, prior to any negotation, the valuing procedure described earlier should be carried out by the buyer.

Rule 5: Determining the exchange ratio of shares for merger. The exchange ratio is the number of shares of the buyer to be offered for one share of the seller.

Example. Consider the data of the following two companies:

	Buyer	Seller
Total earnings	$ 50,000	$ 20,000
Number of shares	5,000	5,000
Earnings per share	$ 10	$ 4
Price per share	$ 200	$ 40
Price-earning ratio	20	10
Total stock value	$1,000,000	$200,000
Growth rate (%)	10	2

The high price-earning ratio of the buyer is the result of the high rate of growth in earnings.

Suppose that after due consideration, the buyer assesses the value of the seller as $300,000; he then offers the seller $60 per share, an enticing offer because the seller's shares are offered at a market price of $40.

The exchange ratio offered is

$$\frac{60}{200} = 0.3 \text{ shares of buyer to 1 share of seller}$$

The total new shares received by the seller is then

$$0.3 \times 5{,}000 = 1{,}500 \text{ buyer shares}$$

The Benefits to the Merging Parties

The combined operation, assuming the market value of the two stocks is not affected, is

	Buyer and Seller
Total earnings	$ 70,000.00
Number of shares	6,500
Earnings per share	$ 10.77
Market price per share	$ 184.62
Price-earning ratio	17.14
Total stock value	$1,200,000.00

The Buyer's Benefits

The immediate effect on the buyer is an increase in his earnings per share from \$10 to \$10.77. The reduction in his stock price (from 200.00 × 5,000 to 184.62 × 5,000) is not important because he is sure that, in the long run, the acquisition is worth \$300,000 as he assessed and not \$200,000.

The Seller's Benefits

From the seller's point of view, his stock is now worth a minimum of \$276,930 (184.62 × 1,500), an increase of about \$77,000. However, his total earnings are \$16,150 (10.77 × 1,500) instead of the \$20,000 received before the merger. The reduction in the seller's earnings is then \$3,850 per annum, against a total appreciation of \$77,000 in his stock. The trade-off between these two values can be assessed using the seller's after-tax cost of capital. Suppose the seller's after-tax cost of capital is 10 percent. Then his annual gain from the stock appreciation is \$7,700 annually, which is greater than his loss on earnings. Hence, the offered exchange ratio is acceptable.

Rule 6: Determining the range of the exchange ratio. The maximum exchange ratio the buyer can offer so that the seller's earnings do not decline is

$$\frac{\text{Earnings per share of seller}}{\text{Earnings per share of buyer}} = \frac{4}{10} = 0.4$$

This ratio corresponds to an offer price per share, for the seller, equal to

Buyer's price earnings ratio × seller's earnings per share

$$20 \times 4 = \$80$$

and the total new shares received by the seller is 2,000 buyer shares (0.4 × 5,000).

The minimum exchange ratio the buyer can offer so that the seller's stock value does not decline is

$$\frac{\text{Market price of seller's share}}{\text{Market price of buyer's share}} = \frac{40}{200} = 0.2$$

This ratio corresponds to using the seller's price-earnings ratio in evaluating the market price of his shares. This minimum is, of course, not acceptable to the seller, because the immediate effect is a considerable reduction in earnings. The minimum will be accepted only when the seller is on the verge of bankruptcy.

18 Uncertainty Analysis

Uncertainty analysis deals with the risk of accepting a forecast. It plays an important role in economic evaluation and decision analysis in business.

Forecasts are based on predicted data: estimates of future sales, prices, capital costs, inflation rate, and so on. Some of the data are under the control of the company; others are affected by outside influences. It is reasonable to expect, therefore, that each of the predicted data could have various outcomes and, consequently, the forecasts may not be accurate. The forecast value will fall within a range of values, and the distribution of these values is governed by the inaccuracy of the predicted data that make it up.

The decision-maker (such as an investor) faced with a range of possible forecasts of an event must make a decision. One way to arrive at a solution is to rely on the law of large numbers, which leads to decisions based on the most probable outcome or expected value (average, median, or mode). This approach implies that any positive or negative deviation of a given size between the realized and the expected forecast are valued equally. That is, the value of a $100 gain is equal to the negative value of a $100 loss. In practice this equality is not so. An investor will prefer a certain to an uncertain value; he will accept a risk only with extra returns.

Uncertainty is a state of ignorance, and ignorance can be reduced by collecting more information. This step, by itself, involves additional costs that should be weighed against the possible reduction in the forecast's range.

Uncertainty also involves a cost because business people are, in general, risk-averse; that is, they prefer a certain to an uncertain outcome. This cost of uncertainty, also called the risk premium, depends on the level of the risk and on the investor's degree of risk aversion.

The topic of uncertainty analysis deals mainly with the method of measuring the risk level and the risk premium and methods of incorporating them into the expected-value approach—that is, into the average of all possible outcomes. The conceptual aspects of uncertainty are summarized in the first three sections of this chapter; this concept is applied in the last two sections and in chapter 6.

Sources and Measures of Uncertainty

The sources of uncertainty of a forecast stem from the uncertain values of the predicted data. For example, a forecast (that is, the final outcome for decision) might be of the profitability of a proposed investment. The predicted data on which this forecast is based include sales level, prices, and costs. Each of these predicted data is uncertain.

Sources of Uncertainty

There are many sources of uncertainty. They can be classified under three major risk classes. Some sources of risk that cannot be reduced, or are not under a company's control, are called systematic risk in security analysis. For example, when a portfolio is diversified, the only risk remaining is systematic: the risk is due to and affected by the market's general conditions.

1. Environmental risk is the result of factors outside the company's control, such as climatic conditions, state of the economy, inflation rate, government policies, change in consumers' taste, future prices, or competitors' reactions. Prediction of the possible states of these factors can be improved by collection of information concerning the environment in which the company is operating and by proper market research.

2. Business risk is inherent in the physical operations of the firm, such as production, equipment breakdown, labor-management relationships, costs of production, bad debts, or operating leverage. To some extent, good management can reduce business risk. For example, adequate maintenance and replacement of equipment and proper inventory control reduce the risk of breakdowns and stock-outs. Another example is the use of operating leverage, which is the ratio of sunk to operating costs. When demand is unstable, a production process with a low operating leverage is preferable to a process with a high one.

3. Financial risk results from financial leverage. When the company finances its operation partly by debt, it takes upon itself a fixed commitment; it must meet repayment schedules on its loans or face bankruptcy. Furthermore, as the company's income is not certain, but the repayment on loans is certain, fluctuations in income increase the uncertainty on dividends and on the company's growth. Financial risk is under the company's control and depends entirely on the stockholders' risk aversion.

Measures of Uncertainty

An outcome, such as a cash return, is uncertain when it can take on one of a number of possible values. Once a probability is given to a value of an outcome, the value is termed risky. Uncertainty can be measured only when probabilities are attached to the uncertain values.

An event with many possible values with known probabilities is termed a random variable, or a risky event. A random variable is described by a distribution, usually characterized by a statistical measure of location (such as average or median) and a statistical measure of disperson (such as standard deviation or coefficient of variation).

The risk level of an uncertain event is the deviation between the realized value and its anticipated value. The anticipated value, lacking any further information, would usually be the expected value or the average, whereas the realized value is one of a number of possible values in the distribution. The average risk measure of the event is therefore given by a measure of dispersion, such as standard deviation or coefficient of variation (see chapter 3).

Screening of Risky Projects

Given the expected returns and the risk measure of a project, the value (or utility) to the investor depends on his risk-aversion level. Screening among projects, based on utility values, is then straightforward (see the section on certainty equivalent later in this chapter). In many cases, however, inferior alternatives can be successfully screened without knowing the investor's risk-aversion level. Two methods for screening are summarized in this section. (For a third method for screening investment proposals by the payback method, see chapter 5.)

Rule 1: The dominance criterion. Alternative *a* (such as a portfolio) is superior to *b*, when

$$E_a \geq E_b$$

and

$$S_a \leq S_b$$

where E is the expected value of uncertain return, which is the average value over all possible outcomes for alternative a or b; and S is the standard deviation for alternative a or b. Alternative a is said to dominate b, or alternative b is an inferior alternative. Thus, between these two alternatives, a is preferred.

Example. Consider the following data for two portfolios:

	A	*B*
Average return (%)	20	15
Standard deviation	5	5

Solution: Portfolio A is superior to B because

$$E_A > E_B$$

$$S_A = S_B$$

The average return of A is higher, whereas the risk of both is equal.

The dominance method is not always applicable, as a profitable project may also be risky (that is, high expected returns and high standard deviation). This deficiency is corrected by the following method.

Rule 2: Baumol's expected gain confidence limit criterion. Alternative a is superior to b, when

$$E_a > E_b$$

$$(E_a - zS_a) \geq (E_b - zS_b)$$

where z is the number of standard deviations below the mean, corresponding to p percent error in the lower tail of the distribution.[1] For 15.9 percent error, $z = 1$ below the mean, and for 2 percent error, $z = 2.3$ below the mean (see table 3–1). When alternative a is superior to b, using, say, $z = 2$, then it is true for any $z > 2$.[2]

The z value is given by

$$z = \frac{(E_a - E_b)}{(S_a - S_b)}$$

Example A. Consider the following data for two portfolios:

	A	*C*
Average return (%)	20	15
Standard deviation	5	2.5

Solution: The number of standard deviations below the mean, corresponding to a given percentage of error, is

$$z = \frac{20 - 15}{5 - 2.5} = 2$$

Using the normal table the resultant z corresponds to approximately 2 percent error.

Hence, we can state with 98 percent confidence that portfolio *A* is superior to *C*. There is, however, a 2 percent chance that portfolio *C* (in the previous example) may be the superior one.

AU: see note msp 423

Example B. Consider the following data for two portfolios.

	A	*D*
Average return (%)	20	15
Standard deviation	5	0

Solution: Portfolio *D* is less risky than *A*, but it is not necessarily superior. Using Baumol's criterion,

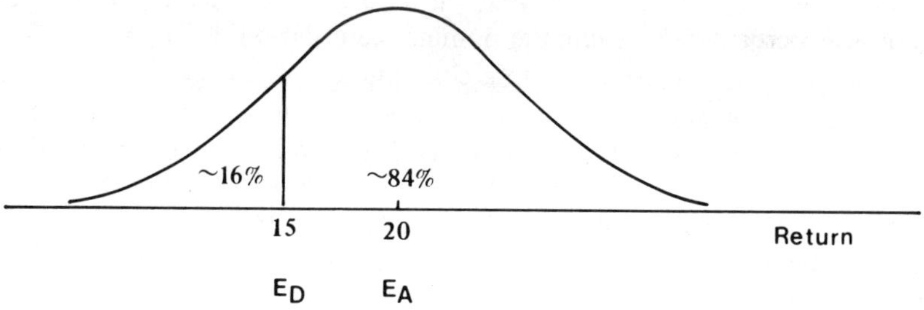

Figure 18–1. Distribution of Returns

$$z = \frac{20 - 15}{5 - 0} = 1$$

Using the normal table (table 3–1), the resultant z corresponds to approximately 16 percent error. Because $E_A > E_D$, we may conclude that portfolio A is superior to D with 84 percent confidence. This result implies that there is a 16 percent probability that the low outcome of A will be below the outcome of D, as depicted in figure 18–1.

Risk Aversion and Risk Premium

The degree of risk aversion can be determined from a risk-curve or from a utility function.

The Risk-Curve Approach

The degree of risk aversion depends on the investor's wealth and on the level of satisfaction he can derive from money. For any investor, one can derive a trade-off relation between his expected money earnings and the risk in obtaining this level of earnings, given his initial wealth position and a fixed level of satisfaction.

A risk curve can be constructed to represent a range of relationships between expected returns (average returns over all possible outcomes) and their risk levels (standard deviation) that provide the same level of satisfaction. Such a risk curve is depicted in figure 18–2. All the points on the curve have the same level of satisfaction or utility. The curve slopes upward, indicating that the investor requires higher and higher compensation for increasing risk. For example, a security with 9 percent return and 2 percent risk gives the same level of satisfaction as a security yielding 11 percent return at 5 percent risk. Using the dominance criterion described earlier in this chapter, every investment with a combination of returns and risk that is above the curve is superior to a combination of results below the curve.

The shape of the curve is different for different investors. For all investors, however, rational economic behavior indicates that the slope of the curve should be less than one (an angle smaller than 45°) at any point. Thus, beyond point B, the curve represents combinations of returns and risk that are not operative.[3]

The level of return with zero risk is given in the curve by the intercept A. This represents the level of certain return that gives the same level of satisfaction as any uncertain return along the curve. It is also called the certainty-equivalent value. For example, figure 18–2 reveals that the

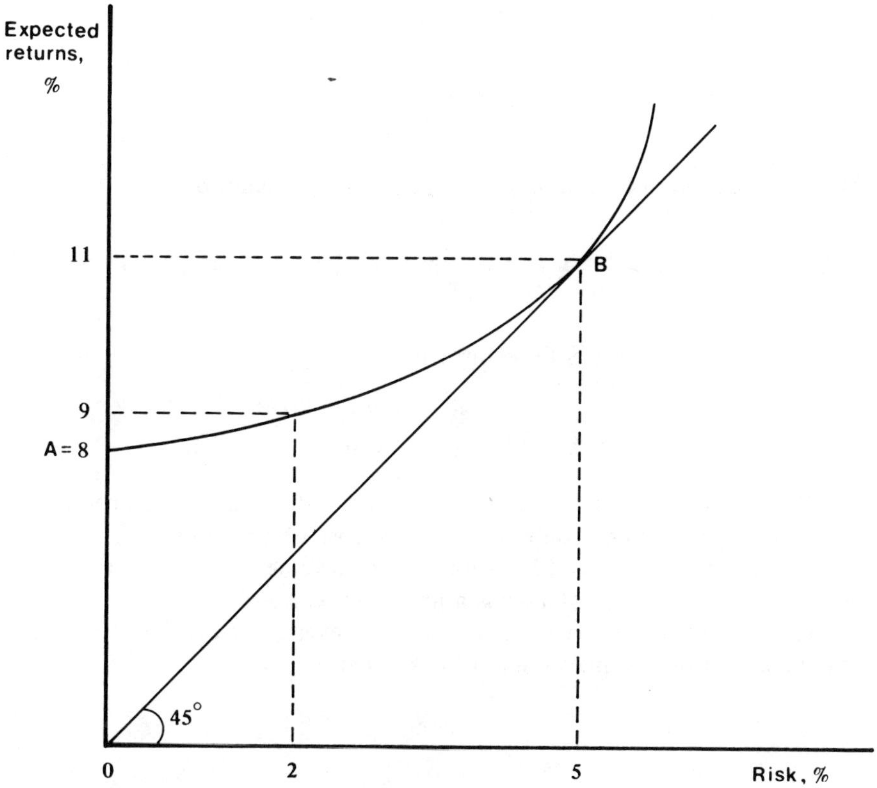

Figure 18–2. Risk Curve

certainty-equivalent value of the two securities (one with a 9 percent return at 2 percent risk, and the other with an 11 percent return at 5 percent risk) is 8 percent.

The relationships between an uncertain return and its certainty equivalent value can be approximated by drawing a straight line between point A and point B. Then

$$E = A + bS$$

$$A = E - bS$$

where E is the expected or average value of uncertain return; A is the certainty equivalent of E; b is the average slope, with value between zero and one; and S is the standard deviation.

Example. The average slope of the curve in figure 18–2 is

$$b = \frac{11 - 8}{5 - 0} = \frac{3}{5}$$

The expected return from a project corresponding to point B is

$$E = 8 + \frac{3}{5} \times 5 = 11$$

The certainty equivalent of the returns is

$$A = 11 - \frac{3}{5} \times 5 = 8$$

The risk premium is the difference between the value of an uncertain return and its certainty equivalent, or the cost of uncertainty. The risk premium is given by the term bS, with maximum value equal to the standard deviation (as the average slope has a maximum value of one).

At any point on the curve, the degree of risk aversion is equal to the slope of the curve at that point, per unit of risk. That is

$$r = \frac{\text{slope}}{S}$$

where r is the degree of risk aversion, corresponding to risk S.

Example. The slope at point B on the curve in figure 18–2 is one. Hence

$$r = \frac{1}{5}$$

The Utility Approach

A utility function shows the relationship between the amount of money and the level of satisfaction; that is, given a certain level of money, the function assesses the level of satisfaction (utility).

Given the utility function, the degree of risk aversion is

$$r = \frac{-U''}{U'}$$

where U', U'' are first and second derivatives of the utility function.[4]

A common utility function, called the power function, is

$$U(x) = Ax^e$$

where $U(x)$ is the utility of earning level x, x is the level of returns, A is a constant, and e is the coefficient of elasticity.

The coefficient of elasticity relates proportional changes in the level of satisfaction to proportional changes in the amount of money. For example, when $e = 0.9$, a 10 percent increase in the amount of money raises the level of satisfaction by 9 percent.

To determine the value of e, ask the investor the following single question: If the amount of your earnings doubles, by what percentage will your level of satisfaction increase? If the answer is, say 70 percent, then $e = 0.7$.

This form of utility assumes a constant degree of elasticity over all the person's level of earnings. Moreover, it is undefined or inapplicable for zero or negative wealth. Hence, this form of utility does not suit an individual person's utility function, but rather, it is applicable for a group of individuals.

The risk premium of an uncertain return, derived from the utility approach, is

$$\frac{-rS^2}{2}$$

where r is the degree of risk aversion and S is the standard deviation. For the power function, the risk premium is

$$\frac{(1 - e)S^2}{2\bar{x}}$$

where $\bar{x}$ is the expected or average level of returns and e is the coefficient of elasticity.

The certainty equivalent of an uncertain return with this form of utility (power function) is

$$\text{Certainty } (\bar{x}) = \bar{x} - \frac{(1 - e)S^2}{2\bar{x}}$$

where certainty ($\bar{x}$) is the certainty-equivalent value of $\bar{x}$

Example. The expected average return from a project is \$100 with a

standard deviation of \$80. The investor's coefficient of elasticity is 70 percent.
Solution: The certainty equivalent return is

$$100 - \frac{(1 - 0.70)80^2}{2 \times 100} = 100 - 9.60 = \$90.40$$

The risk premium is \$9.60.

Certainty Equivalent in Practice

In practice, both the risk curve and the utility approaches, as described in the previous section, are difficult to determine and apply. A practical approach is to approximate the utility function by linearizing its parts above and below the expected value. The satisfaction from a positive deviation is smaller than that from a negative deviation of the same amount. Such a function, as developed in the following subsection, is called the "kinked utility function."

Kinked Utility Function

To make the utility function meaningful to the investor it is desirable to express the level of satisfaction (utility) in units of money. In this way the utility function directly provides the certainty equivalent.

The utility of an investor for money returns above and below the average, according to the kinked function, is depicted in figure 18–3. The points on the kinked curve show the relationship between the level of return and the level of utility. The slope of the curve depends on the investor's wealth and on the level of satisfaction he can derive from money. At the point where the curve is kinked, the utility (\$500) is equal to the average returns (\$500). Above and below this point, the utility is lower than the return. The ratio between the utility and the returns is not equal along the curve. For example, when the returns are—for example—\$100 above the average (\$600), the utility is \$550 (\$50 above the average); when the returns are \$100 below the average (\$400), the utility is \$300 (\$200 below the average).

Rule 3: Interpreting the kinked utility function. The meaning of the kinked utility function is as follows: The utility for the average value is defined as being equal to the average earnings in dollars of the uncertain proposition, that is,

$$U(\bar{x}) = \bar{x}$$

For values above the average earnings—that is, for positive net returns—the utility is

$$U(x_1) = x_1 - a_1(x_1 - \bar{x})$$

For values below the average earnings—that is, for negative net returns—the utility is

$$U(x_2) = x_2 - a_2(\bar{x} - x_2)$$

where $U(x)$ is the utility for x; x_1, x_2 are values above or below the average, $\bar{x}$ is average returns, and a_1, a_2 are unit-risk premiums for positive or negative net returns (rule 5). The unit-risk premium (which represents the slope b of the risk curve in figure 18–2 for the whole distribution is

$$\frac{a_1 + a_2}{2}$$

Example. The expected value of the returns from a proposed investment is \$500, and the utility is also \$500, as shown in figure 18–3. What is the

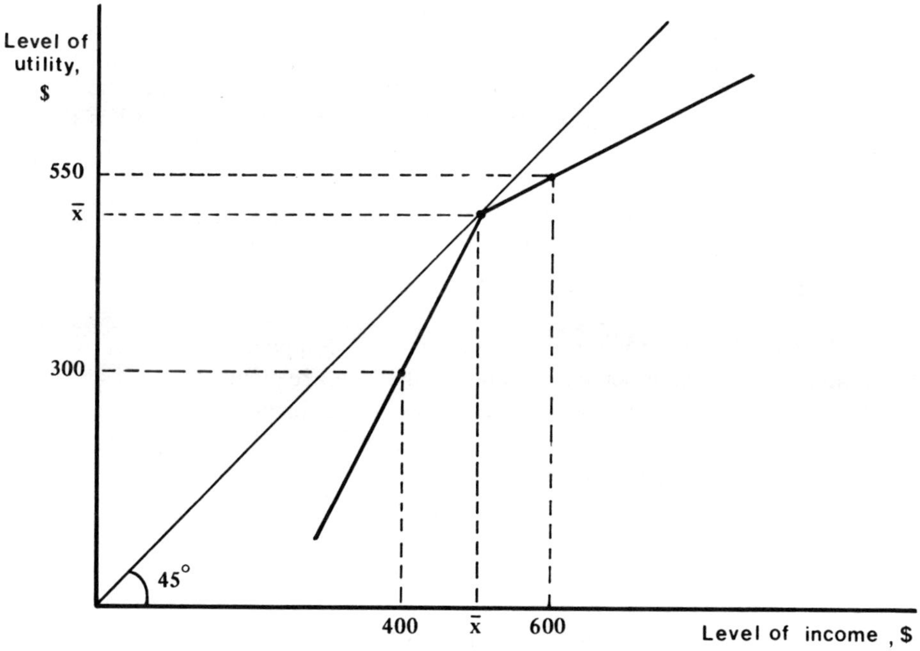

Figure 18–3. Kinked Utility Function

investor's utility from an outcome of \$600 and of \$400, given that his unit–risk premiums at these levels of return are 0.5 and 1.0, respectively? Solution: The utility for the positive outcome is

$$U(600) = 600 - 0.5\ (600 - 500) = \$550$$

The utility for the negative outcome is

$$U(400) = 400 - 1.0\ (500 - 400) = \$300$$

These results are shown by the curve in figure 18–3.

Rule 4: Determining the certainty equivalent from the kinked function. The certainty equivalent of the uncertain earning proposition is equal to the average uncertain returns less the risk premium. The risk of an outcome can be determined by the degree of risk aversion, using the kinked utility function as explained above. For the whole distibution of possible outcomes, the total risk is given by multiplying the standard deviation of the return by the relevant investor's unit risk coefficient.

For a risk-averse investor, the certainty equivalent value is

$$\text{Certainty}\ (\bar{x}) = \bar{x} - bS$$

where certainty ($\bar{x}$) is the certainty equivalent value of $\bar{x}$, $\bar{x}$ is the expected or average value of uncertain return, S is the standard deviation, and b is the unit-risk premium.

Rule 5: Determining the risk premium from the kinked function. The unit-risk premium coefficient b under the kinked utility function is determined as follows:

1. Ask the investor the following question: Suppose you receive with certainty the amount of cash equal to the average value of the earning proposition. This gives you a certain amount of satisfaction. Suppose now that the realized outcome turns out to be twice as much. By how much is your satisfaction increased? Suppose the answer is h percent.
2. Compute

$$a_1 = 1 - h$$

where a_1 is the unit-risk premium for positive gains (above the average) and h is the percentage on \$1.

3. Compute

$$a_2 = \frac{a_1}{1 - a_1}$$

where a_2 is the unit-risk premium for negative gains (below the average).

4. Compute the coefficient of unit-risk premium

$$b = \frac{a_1 + a_2}{2}$$

Example. Suppose the investor's answer to the question on his satisfaction from a doubled size outcome (first step in rule 5) is 70 percent.
Solution: The unit-risk premium for positive gains is

$$a_1 = 1 - 0.7 = 0.3$$

The unit-risk premium for negative gains is

$$a_2 = \frac{0.3}{1 - 0.3} = 0.429$$

The coefficient of unit-risk premium for this investor is approximately

$$b = \frac{0.3 + \dfrac{0.3}{1 - 0.3}}{2} = 0.364$$

(These figures appear in the third line in table 18–1.)

The relations between the average unit-risk premium per \$100 and those for the positive and negative net returns are presented as coefficients in table 18–1. These figures provide the level of risk per \$100 of earnings. For example, the 30 percent figure for positive gains means that the risk premium from \$100 above the average is 30 percent of \$100 (that is, \$30), whereas the utility of \$100 gain is \$70.

The first pair of coefficients in table 18–1 indicate that the satisfaction from a gain is not much larger than the dissatisfaction from an equivalent loss, that is, negative gain (10.0 percent against 11.1 percent, respectively). The pair of coefficients in the last line, on the other hand, implies that a \$1 loss is valued much higher than a \$1 net returm (a risk premium of 150 percent against 60 percent).

Table 18–1
Unit-Risk Premium Coefficients

Positive Gains (a_1)	*Negative Gains* (a_2)	*Whole Distribution* (b)
10.0%	11.1%	10.5%
20.0	25.0	22.5
30.0	42.9	36.4
40.0	66.6	53.3
50.0	100.0	75.0
60.0	150.0	105.0

Example: Evaluating investment. Consider the following data for two portfolios.

	A	*B*
Average return (%)	20	15
Standard deviation	10	2

The investor's coefficient of unit-risk premium is 0.364.
Solution: The certainty equivalent for portfolio A is

$$20 - 0.364 \times 10 = 16.36\%$$

The certainty equivalent for portfolio B is

$$15 - 0.364 \times 2 = 14.27\%$$

The result indicates that the investor will prefer portfolio A over B.

Suppose the investor does not like risk, so his unit-risk premium is relatively high—for example, $b = 0.75$, rather than 0.364. Then, the respective certainty equivalent values are

$$20 - 0.75 \times 10 = 12.50\%$$

$$15 - 0.75 \times 2 = 13.50\%$$

This investor will prefer portfolio B to A because his risk premium is high.

According to Baumol's criterion (rule 2), the level of the investor's risk aversion does not enter the analysis. Still, this criterion is applicable to provide additional information.

Example. Consider the previous example, using Baumol's criterion.

$$z = \frac{20 - 15}{10 - 2} = 0.625$$

Using the normal table (table 3–1), the resultant z corresponds to approximately 27 percent error. That is, if the first investor (whose unit-risk premium is 0.364) prefers portfolio A over B, the investor's risk of misjudgment is at most 27 percent. Despite this possible level of error, the investor perfers portfolio A.

The second investor (whose unit-risk premium is 0.75), however, prefers portfolio B. By being more averse to risk, he is not ready to take the risk of 27 percent that the returns of portfolio A will be below those of portfolio B. On the normal table, z corresponds to 27 percent error. That is, in preferring portfolio A over B when the risk premium is low and above A when the risk premium is high, the investor's risk of misjudgment is at most 27 percent, whatever his degree of risk aversion.

Diversification to Reduce Risk

Most business activities bear some risk. The general rule to reduce the overall risk is the principle: "don't put all your eggs in one basket." In business, this principle is known as diversification.

Diversification is another name for spreading the invested capital over several activities, so that lucky outcomes of some activities cancel out the adverse outcomes of some other activities. The effectiveness of canceling out depends on the number of activities and on the extent of the correlation of positive and negative returns. The larger the number of activities and the more negative the correlation, the smaller the overall risk of the investment. In the extreme case, if all the returns of the activities are perfectly negatively correlated, the risk reduces to zero. Usually, zero risk does not occur in the market. Hence, do not expect that an optimal portfolio has a zero risk. On the other hand, when the returns of the activities are perfectly positively correlated, diversification does not reduce risk.

In diversification, the investor is faced with two problems: the optimal number of activities, and the maximum allowed volume of each activity. This problem in capital budgeting is best solved by computer algorithms, such as by linear programming. The following heuristic approach usually gives satisfactory results when the only constraint the investor is facing is the budgeting of investment capital. The procedure assumes that the investor has already screened out inferior activities (see the earlier discussion in this chapter).

Rule 6: Determining the number of risky activities. Usually, increasing the number of securities reduces the risk of a portfolio to a certain extent. A further increase may not reduce it further, because of a possible increase in the average positive correlation among the portfolio's securities.

Rule 6A. Empirical evidence indicates that the optimal number of securities in a portfolio is between six and ten from different industries.[5]

Rule 6B. The risk of a portfolio is always smaller than that of the security with the highest risk. The relation is

$$S_r < \frac{S_m}{\sqrt{n}}$$

where S_r is the standard deviation of portfolio, S_m is the highest standard deviation of a single security in the portfolio, and n is the number of securities in the portfolio.

Rule 6C. Empirical evidence indicates that the risk of a portfolio properly diversified (equal proportions of different industries) is about one-half of the risk for a portfolio that is randomly diversified.

Rule 7: Determining the maximum allowed level of a risky activity. The maximum allowed level of a risky single activity depends on the number of activities of the company and on the maximum loss the company can bear before it is financially ruined.

Given that the number of activities is limited because of production and marketing constraints, the maximum level of any activity is approximated by[6]

$$\frac{L}{(2S - B)\sqrt{n}}$$

The more accurate formula is

$$\frac{L}{(t_{(a)}S - B)\sqrt{n}}$$

where L is the maximum allowed loss in dollars (named Shackle's Focal Loss), S is the standard deviation per unit of the activity, $t_{(a)}$ is the Student's t, for a level of risk error and n activities (table 3–3), B is the average expected net profit per unit of the activity, and n is the number of activities, limited by outside constraints.

Example. A farmer is contemplating 10 crops. His maximum allowed loss before ruin is \$50,000. Suppose the standard deviation of the ith crop is \$100 per acre, and zero expected net profit. What is the maximum acreage allocated to the ith crop?
Solution: The maximum level of activity is, approximately,

$$\frac{50{,}000}{2 \times 100 \times \sqrt{10}} = 79 \text{ acres}$$

The more accurate solution depends on the farmer's accepted risk error.
For the 10 percent maximum error, $t = 1.812$ (see table 3–3) and the maximum level of activity is

$$\frac{50{,}000}{1.812 \times 100 \times \sqrt{10}} = 87 \text{ acres}$$

For 5 percent maximum error, $t = 2{,}228$ (see table 3–3) and the maximum level of activity is

$$\frac{50{,}000}{2.228 \times 100 \times \sqrt{10}} = 71 \text{ acres}$$

Notes

1. W.J. Baumol, "An Expected Gain Confidence Limit Criterion for Portfolio Selection," *Management Science* (October 1963), pp. 335–346.
2. L.J. Robinson and P.J. Barry, "Risk Efficiency Using Stochastic Dominance and Expected Gain-Confidence Limits," *Journal of Finance* (September 1978), pp. 1244–1249.
3. S.C. Tsiang, "The Rationale of the Mean-Standard Deviation Analysis, Skewness Preference and the Demand for Money," *American Economic Review* (June 1972), pp. 354–371.
4. J.W. Pratt, "Risk Aversion in the Small and in the Large," *Econometrica* (January 1964), pp. 122–136.
5. Based on G. Foster, *Financial Statement Analysis* (Englewood Cliffs, N.J.: Prentice Hall, 1978), pp. 241–243.
6. Based on J.M. Boussard and M. Petit, "Representation of Farmers' Behavior under Uncertainty with A Focus-Loss Constraint," *Journal of Farm Economics* (November 1967), pp. 869–880.

19 Effects of Inflation on Financial Activities

Inflation is a general phenomenon in many countries, and every business has to live with it successfully. It affects almost all business decisions, which must be made quite differently from those under stable price level conditions.

The effect of inflation on business and economic variables is not uniform; that is, inflation affects various activities in different directions and to different degrees. Therefore, understanding the effects of inflation on specific aspects of business, economics, and finance is of paramount importance for successful management.

Inflation has a number of major effects on business activites:

1. The prices of inputs and outputs do not change at the same rate during inflation.
2. Overtaxation of inflationary returns on equity causes capital erosion.
3. The interest rate on loans usually lags behind inflation because of institutional intervention and market imperfections. Moreover, the interest rate on outstanding loans is usually not renegotiable and therefore is below the current rate.
4. The inflated value of the assets is only partly realized in the current period, whereas the inflation compensation on newly acquired loans is fully repaid during the current period in the form of high interest rates.
5. Financial leverage is increased because of demand for external funds induced by the preceding inflationary effects.

The various effects of inflation on business activities should be taken into consideration in costing and pricing, investment evaluation, planning and financing the company's activities, analyzing financial statements, and evaluating the performance of the company and its segments.

In addition, in times of inflation the value of money changes; as a result, the accounting system must be adapted to reflect the data in comparable units (chapter 11).

An amazing fact about inflation is that it increases reported profits at the same time it reduces corporate liquidity. This chapter highlights some important factors behind this phenomenon.

Overtaxation of Equity

During inflation, the returns on equity capital should provide for both preinflation return and compensation for the decline in the real value (purchasing power) of the invested capital. These returns on equity are recorded as regular profit and are subject to income tax. Thus, inflation induces overtaxation of equity and, in turn, capital erosion.

In addition to income tax authorities, other parties, such as management and labor, have claims to the reported profit (which includes the inflation-compensation of equity capital), thus augmenting the process of equity erosion.

Debt capital, on the other hand, receives its remuneration through the increased interest rate (which includes preinflation interest and compensation for the decline in the real value of the principal). Therefore, a hypothetical company financed totally by loans is not overtaxed, because the interest payments are tax-deductible.

Overtaxation Resulting from Inflation

During a period of inflation, the historical depreciation expenses and costs of materials that are drawn from inventory are understated. Because these expenses are tax-deductible, the result is overtaxation. Hence, overtaxation should be calculated on the difference between the adjusted figures and the historical figures.

Rule 1: Overtaxation under 100 percent equity. Overtaxation due to inflation-understated historical costs (depreciation and materials from inventory), under conditions of 100 percent equity finance, is

$$(t)\,(\text{Adjusted cost} - \text{historical cost})$$

where t is the income tax rate relevant to the analysis.

Example. The financial statements of a company that is financed solely by equity capital records $1,000 depreciation expenses and $2,000 cost of materials. The adjusted figures are $1,300 and $2,100, respectively. The relevant rate of income tax is 46 percent.
Solution: The company is overtaxed by

$$0.46(3{,}400 - 3{,}000) = \$184$$

Rule 2: Overtaxation under financial leverage. Overtaxation results from the fact that the amount needed for maintaining the real value of the equity during inflation is taxed. This rule does not hold for debt finance. Therefore, when the company is partially financed by debt, overtaxation should be computed only for the equity part. In general, the higher the proportion of debt to total capital (that is, the higher the financial leverage), the lower the overtaxation.

Under conditions of financial leverage, overtaxation resulting from understated historical costs (depreciation and materials from inventory) is

$$t(1-f)\,(\text{Adjusted cost} - \text{historical cost})$$

where t is the income tax rate and f is the proportion of debt to total capital.

Example. Consider the previous example, but with a share of debt in the balance sheet of 35 percent.
Solution: The company is overtaxed by

$$0.46(1-0.35)\,(3{,}400-3{,}000) = \$119.60$$

Rule 3: Determining the leverage for overtaxation. Consider a case where the company holds only fixed assets, the nominal value of which increases as a result of inflation. In this case the proportion of equity in total capital is

$$(1-f)$$

where f is the proportion of debt to total capital. This proportion should be used in computing the level of overtaxation.

However, companies usually also hold monetary assets, such as cash, accounts receivable, and bonds, the nominal value of which does not change as a result of inflation. To arrive at the proportion of equity for computing overtaxation, the monetary assets should be deducted from the debt to arrive at a net debt figure. Hence, we define the proportion of net debt (liabilities less monetary assets) to net debt plus equity (total assets less monetary assets) as follows

$$f^* = \frac{\text{Net debt}}{\text{Net debt} + \text{equity}}$$

Note that f^* is always smaller than f.

Example. Consider the balance sheet of Company X for 1980 in table 15–2. The following data are relevant (in $000)

Cash	$ 20	
Accounts receivable	180	
Monetary assets		$ 200
Inventories		100
Fixed assets		1,200
Total		1,500
Liabilities		$ 700
Equity		800
Total		1,500

Solution: The proportion of net debt in total assets (less monetary assets) is

$$f^* = \frac{700 - 200}{1,500 - 200} = 0.38$$

This proportion with the following data (in $000) is used for computing the overtaxation of Company X in 1980.

Assume that materials inventory is valued by the LIFO method. The adjusted depreciation expenses are $120, whereas the historical depreciation, as recorded in the conventional income statement (not on the adjusted 1979 opening balance sheet) is $80. The relevant income tax rate is 30 percent. Overtaxation is

$$(120 - 80)(0.30)(1 - 0.38) = \$7.44$$

Capital Erosion

Measuring the rate of equity erosion resulting from overtaxation is important in evaluating investments and making pricing decisions. Because the holding time of inventories is relatively short, the erosion from the overtaxation of equity invested in inventories is disregarded in this section.

The rate of equity erosion depends on the type of asset in which the capital is invested—whether it is a monetary or a 1-year asset or a depreciable asset or a perpetual asset.

Rule 4: Measuring erosion, monetary and 1-year assets. A monetary asset is an asset, the nominal value of which does not change as a result of inflation; a one-year asset is an asset with a life span of no more than 1 year.

The erosion at the end of the year on $1 of equity invested in monetary or 1-year assets is, in current prices.

$$tp$$

where t is the income tax rate and p is the inflation rate.

Example. A company invests $1,000 of equity in a battery that is disposed of after a year without a salvage value. After the battery was purchased, inflation started at the rate of 20 percent. The rate of income tax is 50 percent.

Solution: The equity erosion is

$$1{,}000 \times 0.50 \times 0.20 = \$100$$

Suppose the return on this investment before inflation started was 15 percent. The preinflation profit was

Gross return	$1,150
Cost of battery (depreciation)	(1,000)
Income tax (50%)	(75)
Profit after-tax	75

Suppose now that during the year the price level rose by 20 percent. To simplify the presentation, assume that the gross returns and the replacement cost of the battery rose also by 20 percent. Suppose the returns to the owners are kept in real terms—that is, they increased by 20 percent.

The corresponding profit at the end of the year is

Gross return ($1,150 × 1.2)	$1,380
Cost of battery (depreciation)	(1,000)
Income tax (50%)	(190)
Profit, after tax	190
Returns to owners ($75 × 1.2)	(90)
Extra cash	100

The cash for replacing the machine is $1,000 (depreciation) plus $100 extra cash—that is, $1,100; the replacement cost is $1,200. The difference of $100 is eroded.

Rule 5: Measuring erosion, depreciable assets. In the case of a depreciable asset, the erosion process is spread over the asset's life span.

Rule 5A. The erosion in a given year, on \$1 of original equity that is invested in depreciable assets in current prices is

$$E_m = td_m[(1 + p)^m - 1]$$

where E_m is the erosion in year m, d_m is the depreciation expense on \$1 historical acquisition in year m, $(1 + p)^m$ is the compounding p for m periods (rule 3, chapter 1), p is the inflation rate, and t is the income tax rate.

Example. A \$1,000 equity is invested in a project with anticipated uniform cash flow for 10 years and a life span of 10 years. The project will be straight-line–depreciated and the depreciation expenses will be reinvested in the project. After the equipment was purchased, inflation started at a constant annual rate of 20 percent. The rate of income tax is 50 percent. Solution: The erosion during year 1, in end of year 1 monetary terms, is

$$1{,}000 \times 0.50 \times 0.10[(1 + 0.20)^1 - 1] = \$10.00$$

The erosion during year 4, in end of year 4 money terms, is

$$1{,}000 \times 0.50 \times 0.10[(1 + 0.20)^4 - 1] = \$53.68$$

Suppose the gross return of this investment, before inflation started, was 15 percent. Then the annual return was

$$1{,}000CR_{10,0.15} = 1{,}000 \times 0.19925 = \$199.25$$

where CR is the capital recovery factor (rule 1, chapter 2)

The preinflation annual profit was

Gross return	\$199.25
Depreciation	(100.00)
Income tax (50%)	(49.63)
Profit after-tax	49.62

Suppose now that during the year all the prices rose by 20 percent as assumed in the example for rule 4. The corresponding profit at the end of year 1 is

Gross return ($199.25 × 1.2)	$239.10
Depreciation	(100.00)
Income tax (50%)	(69.55)
Profit after-tax	69.55
Returns to owners ($49.62 × 1.2)	(59.55)
Extra cash	10.00

The residue cash for replacement is $100 depreciation plus $10 extra cash—that is, $110; the replacement cost is $120. The difference of $10 is eroded.

Rule 5B. The total erosion on $1 of equity that is invested in depreciable assets, over the asset's life span, in present-value terms, is

$$t[(PVD)_r - (PVD)_h]$$

where t is the income tax rate; PVD is the present value of depreciation schedule (rule 7, chapter 2); r is the real (inflation-free) discounting rate after-tax; and h is the nominal (inflation-compensated) discounting rate after-tax.

Example. Consider the previous example and assume that the real inflation-free cost of capital is 5 percent.
Solution: Assuming that the inflation rate is 20 percent, the nominal, inflation-compensated cost of capital (rule 33, chapter 1) is

$$h = (1 + 0.05)(1 + 0.20) - 1 = 0.26 = 26\%$$

The present value of the 10-year straight-line depreciation schedule (rule 30, chapter 8) is approximately

$$\text{For } r = 0.05 \qquad 1{,}000 \times \frac{1}{1 + (0.67 \times 10 \times 0.05)} = \$749$$

$$\text{For } h = 0.26 \qquad 1{,}000 \times \frac{1}{1 + (0.67 \times 10 \times 0.26)} = \$365$$

The present value of total erosion is approximately

$$0.50(749 - 365) = \$192$$

Rule 6: Measuring erosion, perpetual assets. In the case of a perpetual asset, such as land, the principal is not returned except when sold. Hence, as long as the asset is not sold, there is no equity erosion due to overtaxation. Presumably, this advantage is one of the reasons that investing in land is considered as a hedge against inflation. However, when the asset is sold, the inflation-compensation of equity will be taxed.

Example. Equity of \$1,000 is invested in land with anticipated annual returns of 15 percent. The inflation rate is 20 percent.
Solution: The preinflation annual return was

Returns	\$150
Income tax (50%)	75
Profit after-tax	75

The profit at the end of the first inflationary year is

Returns (\$150 × 1.2)	\$180
Income tax (50%)	(90)
Profit after-tax	90
Returns to owners (\$75 × 1.2)	(90)
	0

The after-tax profit suffices for paying the preinflation returns to the owners.

Rule 7: Effect of assets' life span on erosion. The previous rules indicate that the longer the life span of the asset, the lower the overtaxation and, in turn, the erosion of equity because overtaxation is postponed.

Rule 8: Tax benefit from postponing returns. When money is invested in a savings account or a bond, the postponement of the payment of the returns reduces the total income tax payment and, in turn, the effective tax rate, provided the same marginal tax rate still holds.

Example. Consider a \$100 investment in a 5-year bond. The interest returns at 10 percent a year may be paid annually or may be deferred and paid on repaying the principal. Income tax is 50 percent in both cases.
Solution: In the case of annual payment, the after-tax return (rule 32, chapter 1) is

$$(100 \times 0.10)(1 - 0.50) = \$5$$

That is, 5 percent.
The after-tax total return after 5 years (rule 3, chapter 1) is

$$100 \times (1 + 0.05)^5 - 1 = \$27.63$$

In the case of deferred payment, the income tax will be levied at the end of the fifth year on the total returns. The after-tax total return is

$$[100 \times (1 + 0.10)^5 - 1](1 - 0.50) = \$30.53$$

The second alternative provides higher after-tax returns but the returns are available only at the end of the contracted period (in this case, after 5 years).

Effect of Inflation on Liquidity

The effect of inflation on the company's business is two-fold: an economic impact, expressed by gain or loss on debt, by capital erosion, and in turn by an increase in the level of the financial leverage on new investments; and a financial impact, expressed by a weakening of the liquidity position of the company, as shown in this section.

Liquidity is the relative ability of the firm to meet all its short-term obligations without weakening its credit standing (chapter 15). A necessary condition for a company to be liquid is that all long-term fixed assets are financed from long-term funds. Retirements of long-term loans and assets replacement should also be financed from long-term funds. During persistent inflation, the latter condition is impaired, both for privately held companies and for publicly held companies. Private companies will find it increasingly difficult to raise long-term loans; public companies will have difficulties in issuing new stocks and at the same time keeping the price of stocks from falling.

Inflation has an adverse effect on liquidity because of the divergence between the profitability of the investment (internal rate of return) and the cash returns, as explained in the following section, and overtaxation and equity erosion, as explained earlier. These effects reduce the internal funds (retained earnings and depreciation), which would not be sufficient to meet the requirement for asset replacement. The higher the inflation rate, the more serious is this phenomenon. The end result is an increase in demand for outside funds.

Rule 9: Illustrating the financial liquidity gap. The cash flow that is generated by an investment consists of returns and expenses. These flows (apart from the capital cost) increase in accordance with the rise in the general price level. The invested capital such as a loan, on the other hand, requires inflation-compensation in each period. (In contrast, when the loan is indexed, inflation-compensation is spread over the loan's term; see chapter 4). The mechanism of the inflation effect on liquidity is illustrated in the following examples.

Example A. Assume preinflation conditions and consider an investment of $1,000 with an anticipated constant net cash inflow for 10 years, yielding 5 percent annual returns, before tax. There is no salvage value.

The annual cash inflow (chapter 2) is

$$1{,}000(\mathrm{CR}_{10,0.05}) = 1{,}000 \times 0.1295 = \$129.50$$

Suppose the investment is financed by a 10-year installment loan at 4 percent interest per annum. The loan's annual payment on interest and principal (rule 7, chapter 4) is

$$1{,}000(CR_{10,0.04}) = 1{,}000 \times 0.1233 = \$123.32$$

The net annual pretax net cash inflow is

$$129.50 - 123.30 = \$6.20$$

The investment is thus economically sound, and its effect on liquidity is beneficial because there is an annual net cash inflow.

Example B. Suppose now that the same investment of $1,000 is considered under inflationary conditions, where prices are anticipated to increase by 20 percent annually for the next 10 years. The projected cash flow thus will increase at the rate of 20 percent per year. The internal rate of return at constant prices is not affected.

Profitability Considerations

The preinflation internal rate of return of the investment (5 percent), if stated in current prices (that is, fully inflation-compensated; see rule 33, chapter 1), is

$$(1 + 0.05)(1 + 0.20) - 1 = 0.26 = 26\%$$

Suppose again that the investment is financed by a 10-year installment loan. However, the interest on the loan has been raised to compensate for the decline in the real value of the principal because of inflation. To provide full inflation-compensation, the interest rate is

$$(1 + 0.04)(1 + 20) - 1 = 0.248 = 24.8\%$$

The investment is still economically sound because it yields a 26 percent rate of return in current terms compared to a cost of 24.8 percent. In other words, this investment (which is financed by the loan) should be undertaken on economic grounds.

Liquidity Considerations

The annual net cash inflow of the investment is anticipated to increase as a result of inflation by 20 percent per annum. The preinflation annual net cash inflow of $129.50 is anticipated to increase by 20 percent at the end of the first year; that is, to be

$$129.50 \times 1.2 = \$155.40$$

with a similar 20 percent increase each succeeding year.

The annual charge on the installment loan at 24.8 percent interest is

$$1{,}000(CR_{10,0.248}) = 1{,}000 \times 0.27835 = \$278.35$$

This charge is constant over the total period of the loan, whereas the revenues are increasing at the yearly rate of 20 percent because of inflation. The cash flows for the first 5 years are

Year	1	2	3	4	5
Net cash inflow from investment	155.40	186.48	223.78	268.53	322.24
Loan repayment	278.35	278.35	278.35	278.35	278.35
Anticipated cash flow	−122.95	−91.87	−54.57	−9.82	43.89

Effect on Liquidity

The previous example illustrates the harmful effect of inflation on the liquidity of a leveraged company. The negative net cash inflow has to be financed by new, probably short-term, loans, at a higher interest rate than the original loan. In an economic sense, nothing has changed because the investment's internal rate of return and the loan's cost did not change in real terms. However, part of the asset's appreciation in the early periods has to be refinanced from outside sources, which adversely affects the liquidity position of the company.

In actual life, only a portion of the investment would be financed by debt capital. This partial financing, of course, reduces the illustrated effect to the portion financed by debt out of the total financing. But too often the loan repayment term is shorter than the investment life span—a fact that enhances the liquidity problem. Furthermore, during inflation lenders often reduce the term of loans.

Rule 10: Determining the length of negative cash inflow. The length of the period of negative cash flow depends on the inflation rate and on the asset's life span. In general, this period of adverse liquidity is stretched over the first 30 to 40 percent of the assets' life span, assuming that the loan's term equals the asset's life span.

Risk from Increased Financial Leverage

The preceding discussion indicates that inflation induces an increase in financial leverage, which, in turn, causes an increase in risk.

The risk may be attributed to the equity that bears the risk or alternatively allocated to both equity and debt. This procedure enables you to arrive at the total cost of a loan—the interest and the risk premium.

The measure of risk level is defined as the standard deviation on total returns. The relative measure of risk is determined by the coefficient of variation, which is the standard deviation for $1 of invested capital (chapter 3). On the other hand, the risk measured in dollars (the risk premium) is the risk level multiplied by the investor's risk-averse factor (chapter 18).

Rule 11: Measuring the financial risk on equity. When an investment is financed partly by loans, the total dollar-risk premium would fall on equity alone, because the payments on the loan must be honored. This requirement increases the relative risk on equity—that is, the dollar risk premium on $1 equity.

The relative risk level on equity is

$$\frac{\text{Relative risk level}}{1-f}$$

where f is the financial leverage, which is the proportion of debt to total capital.

Example. The relative risk level on an investment, as measured by the coefficient of variation, is 0.50. The financial leverage is 40 percent.
Solution: The relative risk measure on equity (coefficient of variation) is

$$\frac{0.50}{1-0.40} = 0.833$$

Suppose now that because of inflation, the financial leverage on the new investment is 55 percent rather than 40 percent. Then, the relative risk measure on equity is

$$\frac{0.50}{1-0.55} = 1.11$$

which is higher than the former risk measure.

Rule 12: Allocating the risk premium between equity and debt. The dollar-risk premium is computed on total investment. It can be allocated proportionally between the sources of finance—that is, between equity and debt. The dollar-risk premium allocated to the debt should be considered as an addition to the cost of the loan in computing the profitability of debt financing (chapter 4).

Example. The total risk premium on a \$1 million investment is \$50,000 (chapter 6). Suppose this investment is financed partly by loans to the amount of \$400,000 (that is, the financial leverage f is 0.40).
Solution: The cost of the loan should be increased by

$$50{,}000 \times \frac{400{,}000}{1{,}000{,}000} = \$20{,}000$$

That is, in addition to the interest, the loan should be charged for the risk by

$$\frac{20{,}000}{400{,}000} = 0.05 = 5\%$$

If the dollar risk is attributed only to equity, the $50,000 risk premium increases the cost of equity by

$$\frac{50{,}000}{600{,}000} = 0.0833 = 8.33\%$$

Suppose now that because of inflation the investment is financed by a $550,000 loan, rather than by $400,000. Then, the cost of the loan in terms of risk does not change (it is still 5 percent), but if the $50,000 risk premium is attributed only to equity, the cost of equity will increase to

$$\frac{50{,}000}{450{,}000} = 0.1111 = 11.11\%$$

Rules for Producing, Investing, Borrowing, and Saving

The following rules of thumb fit a company with some initial stock of assets and working capital. The company can use its resources to produce, invest, and save. It can also borrow up to a certain proportion of its capital at a rate that may be greater than the rate of return on its savings.[1]

1. A company can produce, invest, and borrow if the price of the product covers both variable and fixed costs, where the fixed cost is calculated using the borrowing interest rate. Or equivalently, when the net rate of return on the invested capital, in current values (after allowing for variable costs and depreciation; see chapter 7), is greater than the borrowing rate.

2. A company can produce and invest, but not borrow if the rate of return on the invested capital in current values is greater than the lending rate but less than the borrowing rate. It is, therefore, profitable to invest the retained earnings only.

3. A company can produce and borrow for production only, if the price of the product covers variable costs; or the gross rate of return on the invested capital in current values (before allowing for depreciation) is greater than the borrowing rate.

4. A company can produce and save, but not invest if the price of the product covers variable but not fixed costs. Production using inherited capacity and working capital is profitable, but capacity addition is not. Hence, do not invest in your company. Retained earnings should be saved (invested outside the company).

5. A company should not produce or invest, but save only, if the price does not cover variable costs. In this case retained earnings, if any, cannot be invested profitably in the company and should, therefore, be saved (invested

outside the company). In short, the company should produce whenever expected price covers variable cost and invest whenever price is greater than variable cost plus total cost of capital. The company borrows if its cash constraint is binding and its expected revenue covers total costs evaluated at the borrowing rate of interest. When the uncertainty of the amount of future receipts is taken into account, the company should guard against possible future weak liquidity by not investing up to the limit of its borrowing capacity.

6. The rate of return on invested capital, as just discussed, in a period of stable prices is in real terms. In time of inflation, the rate of return is still in real terms because it is computed on current values. On the other hand, the rates on lending, borrowing, and saving are stated in nominal terms. Hence, first transform these rates into real terms as follows (using the rules in chapter 1):

$$\frac{i - p}{1 + p}$$

where i is the stated, nominal rate of interest; and p is the inflation rate.

Stating all the rates in real terms enables you to apply these rules in a period of inflation.

Rules for Combatting the Effects of Inflation

It is generally accepted that inflation benefits borrowers and harms lenders. Consequently, a company will have a great incentive to expedite and expand investments, mainly by debt financing. As expounded earlier in this chapter, debt financing may have a devastating effect upon the company's current liquidity when the inflation rate is high and persistent. Besides causing liquidity problems, inflation affects a host of business decisions so that they must be made quite differently from those made under stable price levels.

The following points concerning inflation effects should be considered by management in making decisions to combat the adverse effects of inflation. The higher the rate of inflation and the more persistent it is, the more devastating its effects. Furthermore, persistent inflation has additional cumulative effects.

1. Use updated financial data. Introduce procedures of current cost-accounting and reporting. Insist on receiving financial reports updated by the current price level. This step provides meaningful data and also reduces the tendency to blame inefficiency on increased prices.

2. Implement planning and control. Inflation increases uncertainty, especially in respect to cash flow. Use the cash budget (chapter 16) as the

main tool for controlling your company's activities. To reduce the uncertainty factor, you must revise all budgets, especially the cash budget, much more frequently than before, depending on the rate of inflation. During high inflation, you may have to revise budgets every month. These activities add costs that should be taken into consideration in costing and pricing. Bear in mind that control of the prices of inputs becomes very difficult (chapter 13).

3. Evaluate investments. The anticipated cash flow from a proposed investment should be estimated in nominal values, corresponding to the anticipated inflation, year by year. The discounting process should use the desired after-tax cost of capital, fully compensated by inflation (chapter 5). When an investment is partly financed by loans, the cash flow should be stated as net cash flow (that is, after deducting the loans' payments of principal and interest). This net cash flow may come out negative in early years. Additional loans, or equity, should be considered and the resulting net cash flow reestimated, to ensure that the net cash inflow in all years (except the original investment) is not negative. Only then apply the discounting procedure to calculate the present value of the investment.

4. Consider asset replacement. For a going concern to survive, it should at least maintain its productive capacity, if not expand it. This rule implies dynamic replacements of aging assets. In time of inflation, the replacements' requirements exceed the annual recorded depreciation. For example, when inflation is persistent at the rate of 15 percent and the average life span of the stock of assets is 10 years, the required replacement of the stock (that is, the revalued depreciation) is about twice the company's annual recorded depreciation (chapter 10). This fact should be remembered when decisions are made concerning income allocation among bonuses, dividends, and retained earnings.

5. Consider financial leverage. The rate of interest on loans often lags behind inflation. This, together with the fact that the interest expenses on debt are tax-deductible, encourages companies and individuals to take loans. You should increase financial leverage as long as the investment of the loan is profitable (that is, if the after-tax rate of return on the investment financed by the loan is higher than the after-tax interest rate; see chapter 5, plus the risk implied by taking out the loan; see chapter 6); and if the liquidity of your company is not impaired (that is, if the loan's term matches the investment life span and the periodic loan repayment is below the investment-periodic net cash inflow; see the earlier discussion in this chapter). When inflation is high and persistent, it increases the level of financial leverage even when no new investments are considered. This increase occurs because the inflated value of the assets is only partly realized through the inflated sales in the current period, whereas the inflation-compensation on loans (which is included in the higher interest rate) is due in the current period (except when

long-term loans are indexed; see chapter 4) and therefore is fully realized. To combat this effect, the only resort open to management in maintaining a constant level of financial leverage on the current value of assets is to increase the equity funds. A feasible method, preferred by shareholders, is to raise capital by issuing convertible shares instead of ordinary shares. This procedure has the advantage of preserving the shareholders' voting control and maintaining the debt capacity intact.

6. Review monetary assets. Balance-sheet items that are expressed in fixed-money terms are eroded in time of inflation. This group includes items of current assets, such as cash and debtors, and liabilities, such as creditors and loans. You should keep a careful eye on the balance between these two groups of items so that the company will gain from the decline in purchasing power of the net debt.

7. Assess effects on shares and land. Empirical evidence shows that during inflation the prices of shares of stock lag behind the inflation rate, whereas the prices of land run ahead. For example, in the last decade, the market value of the shares of U.S. nonfinancial corporations rose from $652 billion in 1967 to $858 billion in 1978, an average annual rate of about 2.5 percent in comparison to 6.3 percent average inflation rate in the same period. If the value of the shares had risen by the same rate as inflation, their value in 1978 would have been about 50 percent higher than their actual value. In contrast, the market value of U.S. farm land and real estate rose in the same period by an average annual rate of about 10.5 percent.

8. Control working capital. Inflation induces an increase in working capital requirements. On the one hand, suppliers tend to reduce the period of extended credit; on the other hand, debtors tend to stretch the period of payments. Banks become more cautious in extending credit in time of inflation, so that the working capital extended by banks often increases by a smaller proportion than the inflation rate. This limit on credit aggravates the liquidity problem. Furthermore, inflation increases the rate of interest on banking lines of credit and overdrifts. These effects increase the total interest expenses on working capital considerably (even doubling and tripling it, depending on the rate of inflation). For example, in Israel agriculture, the interest charges in 1970 on working capital constituted about 2 percent of the value of sales. In 1980, this figure climbed to about 10 percent of the value of sales. In this same period, the average annual inflation rate was about 40 percent. These charges are significant and should not be neglected in costing and pricing decisions.

9. Calculate total interest expenses. The effect of inflation on interest is much stronger than the effect on prices. As the result of increases in leverage, working capital and nominal rate of interest, the total share of interest payments out of total value of sales becomes more important in costing and pricing. For example, in U.S. agriculture, total interest expenses in relation

to sales rose by about 40 percent in the period 1967–1978 (from 5.1 percent in 1967 to 7.6 percent in 1978) and still are climbing. The average annual inflation rate in that period was about 6.3 percent.

10. Review costing and pricing. Increased interest payments, equity erosion resulting from overtaxation and over-requirements of various profit takers (such as management and labor), and the increased cost of planning and control should not be overlooked in costing, pricing, and investing evaluation. How frequently cost revisions and indexing should be applied depends on the rate of inflation.

11. Avoid contractual obligations. Contractual obligations, such as long-term contracts, should be avoided under conditions of high inflation or safeguarded through indexing. These obligations include both contracts to supply (such as supplying products, services, or building contracts) or to receive (from such sources as long-term loans or leases). For example, in time of inflation it may be preferable to lease or rent on a year-to-year contract than to buy.

Note

1. The first five rules are based on R.H. Day, S. Morley, and K.R. Smith, "Myopic Optimizing and Rules of Thumb in A Micro-Model of Industrial Growth," *American Economic Review* (March 1974), pp. 11–23.

Appendix A: Capital-Recovery Factors

Periods	*1%*	*2%*	*3%*	*4%*	*5%*	*6%*
1	1.010000	1.020000	1.030000	1.040000	1.050000	1.060000
2	0.507512	0.515050	0.522611	0.530196	0.537805	0.545437
3	0.340022	0.346755	0.353530	0.360349	0.367209	0.374110
4	0.256281	0.262624	0.269027	0.275490	0.282012	0.288591
5	0.206040	0.212158	0.218355	0.224627	0.230975	0.237396
6	0.172548	0.178526	0.184597	0.190762	0.197017	0.203363
7	0.148628	0.154512	0.160506	0.166610	0.172820	0.179135
8	0.130690	0.136510	0.142456	0.148528	0.154722	0.161036
9	0.116740	0.122515	0.128434	0.134493	0.140690	0.147022
10	0.105582	0.111327	0.117231	0.123291	0.129505	0.135868
11	0.096454	0.102178	0.108077	0.114149	0.120389	0.126793
12	0.088849	0.094560	0.100462	0.106552	0.112825	0.119277
13	0.082415	0.088118	0.094030	0.100144	0.106456	0.112960
14	0.076901	0.082602	0.088526	0.094669	0.101024	0.107585
15	0.072124	0.077825	0.083767	0.089941	0.096342	0.102963
16	0.067945	0.073650	0.079611	0.085820	0.092270	0.098952
17	0.064258	0.069970	0.075953	0.082199	0.088699	0.095445
18	0.060982	0.066702	0.072709	0.078993	0.085546	0.092357
19	0.058052	0.063782	0.069814	0.076139	0.082745	0.089621
20	0.055415	0.061157	0.067216	0.073582	0.080243	0.087185
21	0.053031	0.058785	0.064872	0.071280	0.077996	0.085005
22	0.050864	0.056631	0.062747	0.069199	0.075971	0.083046
23	0.048886	0.054668	0.060814	0.067309	0.074137	0.081278
24	0.047073	0.052871	0.059047	0.065587	0.072471	0.079679
25	0.045407	0.051220	0.057428	0.064012	0.070952	0.078227
26	0.043869	0.049699	0.055938	0.062567	0.069564	0.076904
27	0.042446	0.048293	0.054564	0.061239	0.068292	0.075697
28	0.041124	0.046990	0.053293	0.060013	0.067123	0.074593
29	0.039895	0.045778	0.052115	0.058880	0.066046	0.073580
30	0.038748	0.044650	0.051019	0.057830	0.065051	0.072649
31	0.037676	0.043596	0.049999	0.056855	0.064132	0.071792
32	0.036671	0.042611	0.049047	0.055949	0.063280	0.071002
33	0.035727	0.041687	0.048156	0.055104	0.062490	0.070273
34	0.034840	0.040819	0.047322	0.054315	0.061755	0.069598
35	0.034004	0.040002	0.046539	0.053577	0.061072	0.068974
36	0.033214	0.039233	0.045804	0.052887	0.060434	0.068395
37	0.032468	0.038507	0.045112	0.052240	0.059840	0.067857
38	0.031761	0.037821	0.044459	0.051632	0.059284	0.067358
39	0.031092	0.037171	0.043844	0.051061	0.058765	0.066894
40	0.030456	0.036556	0.043262	0.050523	0.058278	0.066462
41	0.029851	0.035972	0.042712	0.050017	0.057822	0.066059
42	0.029276	0.035417	0.042192	0.049540	0.057395	0.065683
43	0.028727	0.034890	0.041698	0.049090	0.056993	0.065333
44	0.028204	0.034388	0.041230	0.048665	0.056616	0.065006
45	0.027705	0.033910	0.040785	0.048262	0.056262	0.064700

Periods	*7%*	*8%*	*9%*	*10%*	*11%*	*12%*
1	1.070000	1.080000	1.090000	1.100000	1.110000	1.120000
2	0.553092	0.560769	0.568469	0.576190	0.583934	0.591698
3	0.381052	0.388034	0.395055	0.402115	0.409213	0.416349
4	0.295228	0.301921	0.308669	0.315471	0.322326	0.329234
5	0.243891	0.250456	0.257092	0.263797	0.270570	0.277410
6	0.209796	0.216315	0.222920	0.229607	0.236377	0.243226
7	0.185553	0.192072	0.198691	0.205405	0.212215	0.219118
8	0.167468	0.174015	0.180674	0.187444	0.194321	0.201303
9	0.153486	0.160080	0.166799	0.173641	0.180602	0.187679
10	0.142378	0.149029	0.155820	0.162745	0.169801	0.176984
11	0.133357	0.140076	0.146947	0.153963	0.161121	0.168415
12	0.125902	0.132695	0.139651	0.146763	0.154027	0.161437
13	0.119651	0.126522	0.133567	0.140779	0.148151	0.155677
14	0.114345	0.121297	0.128433	0.135746	0.143228	0.150871
15	0.109795	0.116830	0.124059	0.131474	0.139065	0.146824
16	0.105858	0.112977	0.120300	0.127817	0.135517	0.143390
17	0.102425	0.109629	0.117046	0.124664	0.132471	0.140457
18	0.099413	0.106702	0.114212	0.121930	0.129843	0.137937
19	0.096753	0.104128	0.111730	0.119547	0.127563	0.135763
20	0.094393	0.101852	0.109546	0.117460	0.125576	0.133879
21	0.092289	0.099832	0.107617	0.115624	0.123838	0.132240
22	0.090406	0.098032	0.105905	0.114005	0.122313	0.130811
23	0.088714	0.096422	0.104382	0.112572	0.120971	0.129560
24	0.087189	0.094978	0.103023	0.111300	0.119787	0.128463
25	0.085811	0.093679	0.101806	0.110168	0.118740	0.127500
26	0.084561	0.092507	0.100715	0.109159	0.117813	0.126652
27	0.083426	0.091448	0.099735	0.108258	0.116989	0.125904
28	0.082392	0.090489	0.098852	0.107451	0.116257	0.125244
29	0.081449	0.089619	0.098056	0.106728	0.115605	0.124660
30	0.080586	0.088827	0.097336	0.106079	0.115025	0.124144
31	0.079797	0.088107	0.096686	0.105496	0.114506	0.123686
32	0.079073	0.087451	0.096096	0.104972	0.114043	0.123280
33	0.078408	0.086852	0.095562	0.104499	0.113629	0.122920
34	0.077797	0.086304	0.095077	0.104074	0.113259	0.122601
35	0.077234	0.085803	0.094636	0.103690	0.112927	0.122317
36	0.076715	0.085345	0.094235	0.103343	0.112630	0.122064
37	0.076237	0.084924	0.093870	0.103030	0.112364	0.121840
38	0.075795	0.084539	0.093538	0.102747	0.112125	0.121640
39	0.075387	0.084185	0.093236	0.102491	0.111911	0.121462
40	0.075009	0.083860	0.092960	0.102259	0.111719	0.121304
41	0.074660	0.083561	0.092708	0.102050	0.111546	0.121163
42	0.074336	0.083287	0.092478	0.101860	0.111391	0.121037
43	0.074036	0.083034	0.092268	0.101688	0.111251	0.120925
44	0.073758	0.082802	0.092077	0.101532	0.111126	0.120825
45	0.073500	0.082587	0.091902	0.101391	0.111014	0.120736

Periods	*13%*	*14%*	*15%*	*16%*	*17%*	*18%*
1	1.130000	1.140000	1.150000	1.160000	1.170000	1.180000
2	0.599484	0.607290	0.615116	0.622963	0.630829	0.638716
3	0.423522	0.430731	0.437977	0.445258	0.452574	0.459924
4	0.336194	0.343205	0.350265	0.357375	0.364533	0.371739
5	0.284315	0.291284	0.298316	0.305409	0.312564	0.319778
6	0.250153	0.257157	0.264237	0.271390	0.278615	0.285910
7	0.226111	0.233192	0.240360	0.247613	0.254947	0.262362
8	0.208387	0.215570	0.222850	0.230224	0.237690	0.245244
9	0.194869	0.202168	0.209574	0.217082	0.224691	0.232395
10	0.184290	0.191714	0.199252	0.206901	0.214657	0.222515
11	0.175841	0.183394	0.191069	0.198861	0.206765	0.214776
12	0.168986	0.176669	0.184481	0.192415	0.200466	0.208628
13	0.163350	0.171164	0.179110	0.187184	0.195378	0.203686
14	0.158667	0.166609	0.174688	0.182898	0.191230	0.199678
15	0.154742	0.162809	0.171017	0.179358	0.187822	0.196403
16	0.151426	0.159615	0.167948	0.176414	0.185004	0.193710
17	0.148608	0.156915	0.165367	0.173952	0.182662	0.191485
18	0.146201	0.154621	0.163186	0.171885	0.180706	0.189639
19	0.144134	0.152663	0.181336	0.170142	0.179067	0.188103
20	0.142354	0.150986	0.159761	0.168667	0.177690	0.186820
21	0.140814	0.149545	0.158417	0.167416	0.176530	0.185746
22	0.139479	0.148303	0.157266	0.166353	0.175550	0.184846
23	0.138319	0.147231	0.156278	0.165447	0.174721	0.184090
24	0.137308	0.146303	0.155430	0.164673	0.174019	0.183454
25	0.136426	0.145498	0.154699	0.164013	0.173423	0.182919
26	0.135655	0.144800	0.154070	0.163447	0.172917	0.182467
27	0.134979	0.144193	0.153526	0.162963	0.172487	0.182087
28	0.134387	0.143664	0.153057	0.162548	0.172121	0.181765
29	0.133867	0.143204	0.152651	0.162192	0.171810	0.181494
30	0.133411	0.142803	0.152300	0.161886	0.171545	0.181264
31	0.133009	0.142453	0.151996	0.161623	0.171318	0.181070
32	0.132656	0.142147	0.151733	0.161397	0.171126	0.180906
33	0.132345	0.141880	0.151505	0.161203	0.170961	0.180767
34	0.132071	0.141646	0.151307	0.161036	0.170821	0.180650
35	0.131829	0.141442	0.151135	0.160892	0.170701	0.180550
36	0.131616	0.141263	0.150986	0.160769	0.170599	0.180466
37	0.131428	0.141107	0.150857	0.160662	0.170512	0.180395
38	0.131262	0.140970	0.150744	0.160571	0.170437	0.180335
39	0.131116	0.140850	0.150647	0.160492	0.170373	0.180283
40	0.130986	0.140745	0.150562	0.160424	0.170319	0.180240
41	0.130872	0.140653	0.150489	0.160365	0.170273	0.180204
42	0.130771	0.140573	0.150425	0.160315	0.170233	0.180172
43	0.130682	0.140502	0.150369	0.160271	0.170199	0.180146
44	0.130603	0.140440	0.150321	0.160234	0.170170	0.180124
45	0.130534	0.140386	0.150279	0.160201	0.170145	0.180105

Periods	*19%*	*20%*	*21%*	*22%*	*23%*	*24%*
1	1.190000	1.200000	1.210000	1.220000	1.230000	1.240000
2	0.646621	0.654545	0.662489	0.670450	0.678430	0.686429
3	0.467308	0.474725	0.482175	0.489658	0.497173	0.504718
4	0.378991	0.386289	0.393632	0.401020	0.408451	0.415926
5	0.327050	0.334380	0.341765	0.349206	0.356700	0.364248
6	0.293274	0.300706	0.308203	0.315764	0.323389	0.331074
7	0.269855	0.277424	0.285067	0.292782	0.300568	0.308422
8	0.262885	0.260609	0.268415	0.276299	0.284259	0.292293
9	0.240192	0.248079	0.256053	0.264111	0.272249	0.280465
10	0.230471	0.238523	0.246665	0.254895	0.263208	0.271602
11	0.222891	0.231104	0.239411	0.247807	0.256289	0.264852
12	0.216896	0.225265	0.233730	0.242285	0.250926	0.259648
13	0.212102	0.220620	0.229234	0.237939	0.246728	0.255598
14	0.208235	0.216893	0.225647	0.234491	0.243418	0.252423
15	0.205092	0.213882	0.222766	0.231738	0.240791	0.249919
16	0.202523	0.211436	0.220441	0.229530	0.238697	0.247936
17	0.200414	0.209440	0.218555	0.227751	0.237021	0.246359
18	0.198676	0.207805	0.217020	0.226313	0.235676	0.245102
19	0.197238	0.206462	0.215769	0.225148	0.234593	0.244098
20	0.196045	0.205357	0.214745	0.224202	0.233720	0.243294
21	0.195054	0.204444	0.213906	0.223432	0.233016	0.242649
22	0.194229	0.203690	0.213218	0.222805	0.232446	0.242132
23	0.193542	0.203065	0.212652	0.222294	0.231984	0.241716
24	0.192967	0.202548	0.212187	0.221877	0.231611	0.241382
25	0.192487	0.202119	0.211804	0.221536	0.231308	0.241113
26	0.192086	0.201762	0.211489	0.221258	0.231062	0.240897
27	0.191750	0.201467	0.211229	0.221030	0.230863	0.240723
28	0.191468	0.201221	0.211015	0.220843	0.230701	0.240583
29	0.191232	0.201016	0.210838	0.220691	0.230570	0.240470
30	0.191034	0.200846	0.210692	0.220566	0.230463	0.240379
31	0.190869	0.200705	0.210572	0.220464	0.230376	0.240305
32	0.190729	0.200587	0.210472	0.220380	0.230306	0.240246
33	0.190612	0.200489	0.210390	0.220311	0.230248	0.240198
34	0.190514	0.200407	0.210322	0.220255	0.230202	0.240160
35	0.190432	0.200339	0.210266	0.220209	0.230164	0.240129
36	0.190363	0.200283	0.210220	0.220171	0.230133	0.240104
37	0.190305	0.200235	0.210182	0.220140	0.230108	0.240084
38	0.190256	0.200196	0.210150	0.220115	0.230088	0.240068
39	0.190215	0.200163	0.210124	0.220094	0.230072	0.240055
40	0.190181	0.200136	0.210103	0.220077	0.230058	0.240044
41	0.190152	0.200113	0.210085	0.220063	0.230047	0.240035
42	0.190128	0.200095	0.210070	0.220052	0.230039	0.240029
43	0.190107	0.200079	0.210058	0.220043	0.230031	0.240023
44	0.190090	0.200066	0.210048	0.220035	0.230025	0.240019
45	0.190076	0.200055	0.210040	0.220029	0.230021	0.240015

Periods	*25%*	*26%*	*27%*	*28%*	*29%*	*30%*
1	1.250000	1.260000	1.270000	1.280000	1.290000	1.300000
2	0.694444	0.702478	0.710529	0.718596	0.726681	0.734783
3	0.512295	0.519902	0.527539	0.535206	0.542902	0.550627
4	0.423442	0.430999	0.438598	0.446236	0.453913	0.461629
5	0.371847	0.379496	0.387196	0.394944	0.402739	0.410582
6	0.338819	0.346623	0.354484	0.362400	0.370371	0.378394
7	0.316342	0.324326	0.332374	0.340482	0.348649	0.356874
8	0.300399	0.308573	0.316814	0.325119	0.333487	0.341915
9	0.288756	0.297119	0.305551	0.314049	0.322612	0.331235
10	0.280073	0.288616	0.297231	0.305912	0.314657	0.323463
11	0.273493	0.282207	0.290991	0.299842	0.308755	0.317729
12	0.268448	0.277319	0.286260	0.295265	0.304331	0.313454
13	0.264543	0.273559	0.282641	0.291785	0.300987	0.310243
14	0.261501	0.270647	0.279856	0.289123	0.298445	0.307818
15	0.259117	0.268379	0.277701	0.287077	0.296504	0.305978
16	0.257241	0.266606	0.276027	0.285498	0.295017	0.304577
17	0.255759	0.265216	0.274723	0.284277	0.293874	0.303509
18	0.254586	0.264122	0.273705	0.283331	0.292994	0.302692
19	0.253656	0.263261	0.272909	0.282595	0.292316	0.302066
20	0.252916	0.262581	0.272285	0.282023	0.291792	0.301587
21	0.252327	0.262045	0.271796	0.281578	0.291387	0.301219
22	0.251858	0.261620	0.271412	0.281232	0.291074	0.300937
23	0.251484	0.261284	0.271111	0.280961	0.290832	0.300720
24	0.251186	0.261018	0.270874	0.280750	0.290644	0.300554
25	0.250948	0.260807	0.270688	0.280586	0.290499	0.300426
26	0.250758	0.260640	0.270541	0.280458	0.290387	0.300327
27	0.250606	0.260508	0.270426	0.280357	0.290300	0.300252
28	0.250485	0.260403	0.270335	0.280279	0.290232	0.300194
29	0.250387	0.260320	0.270264	0.280218	0.290180	0.300149
30	0.250310	0.260254	0.270208	0.280170	0.290140	0.300115
31	0.250248	0.260201	0.270164	0.280133	0.290108	0.300088
32	0.250198	0.260160	0.270129	0.280104	0.290084	0.300068
33	0.250159	0.260127	0.270101	0.280081	0.290065	0.300052
34	0.250127	0.260101	0.270080	0.280063	0.290050	0.300040
35	0.250101	0.260080	0.270063	0.280050	0.290039	0.300031
36	0.250081	0.260063	0.270049	0.280039	0.290030	0.300024
37	0.250065	0.260050	0.270039	0.280030	0.290023	0.300018
38	0.250052	0.260040	0.270031	0.280024	0.290018	0.300014
39	0.250042	0.260032	0.270024	0.280018	0.290014	0.300011
40	0.250033	0.260025	0.270019	0.280014	0.290011	0.300008
41	0.250027	0.260020	0.270015	0.280011	0.290008	0.300006
42	0.250021	0.260016	0.270012	0.280009	0.290007	0.300005
43	0.250017	0.260013	0.270009	0.280007	0.290005	0.300004
44	0.250014	0.260010	0.270007	0.280005	0.290004	0.300003
45	0.250011	0.260008	0.270006	0.280004	0.290003	0.300002

Periods	31%	32%	33%	34%	35%	36%
1	1.310000	1.320000	1.330000	1.340000	1.350000	1.360000
2	0.742900	0.751034	0.759185	0.767350	0.775532	0.783729
3	0.558379	0.566160	0.573968	0.581803	0.589664	0.597552
4	0.469383	0.477174	0.485002	0.492865	0.500764	0.508698
5	0.418469	0.426402	0.434378	0.442397	0.450458	0.458560
6	0.386469	0.394595	0.402769	0.410991	0.419260	0.427574
7	0.365154	0.373488	0.381875	0.390313	0.398800	0.407335
8	0.350401	0.358943	0.367540	0.376188	0.384887	0.393634
9	0.339918	0.348657	0.357451	0.366296	0.375191	0.384134
10	0.332328	0.341249	0.350222	0.359246	0.368318	0.377436
11	0.326759	0.335842	0.344977	0.354159	0.363387	0.372659
12	0.322631	0.331860	0.341135	0.350456	0.359819	0.369222
13	0.319550	0.328904	0.338303	0.347743	0.357221	0.366735
14	0.317237	0.326701	0.336204	0.345745	0.355320	0.364928
15	0.315494	0.325051	0.334643	0.344269	0.353926	0.363610
16	0.314177	0.323812	0.333479	0.343176	0.352899	0.362648
17	0.313178	0.322879	0.332609	0.342364	0.352143	0.361943
18	0.312420	0.322177	0.331958	0.341761	0.351585	0.361427
19	0.311844	0.321646	0.331470	0.341313	0.351173	0.361048
20	0.311406	0.321246	0.331104	0.340979	0.350868	0.360770
21	0.311072	0.320943	0.330829	0.340730	0.350642	0.360566
22	0.310818	0.320714	0.330623	0.340544	0.350476	0.360416
23	0.310624	0.320540	0.330468	0.340406	0.350352	0.360306
24	0.310476	0.320409	0.330352	0.340303	0.350261	0.360225
25	0.310363	0.320310	0.330265	0.340226	0.350193	0.360165
26	0.310277	0.320235	0.330199	0.340169	0.350143	0.360121
27	0.310212	0.320178	0.330150	0.340126	0.350106	0.360089
28	0.310161	0.320135	0.330112	0.340094	0.350078	0.360066
29	0.310123	0.320102	0.330085	0.340070	0.350058	0.360048
30	0.310094	0.320077	0.330064	0.340052	0.350043	0.360035
31	0.310072	0.320059	0.330048	0.340039	0.350032	0.360026
32	0.310055	0.320044	0.330036	0.340029	0.350024	0.360019
33	0.310042	0.320034	0.330027	0.340022	0.350017	0.360014
34	0.310032	0.320025	0.330020	0.340016	0.350013	0.360010
35	0.310024	0.320019	0.330015	0.340012	0.350010	0.360008
36	0.310019	0.320015	0.330011	0.340009	0.350007	0.360006
37	0.310014	0.320011	0.330009	0.340007	0.350005	0.360004
38	0.310011	0.320008	0.330006	0.340005	0.350004	0.360003
39	0.310008	0.320006	0.330005	0.340004	0.350003	0.360002
40	0.310006	0.320005	0.330004	0.340003	0.350002	0.360002
41	0.310005	0.320004	0.330003	0.340002	0.350002	0.360001
42	0.310004	0.320003	0.330002	0.340002	0.350001	0.360001
43	0.310003	0.320002	0.330002	0.340001	0.350001	0.360001
44	0.310002	0.320002	0.330001	0.340001	0.350001	0.360000
45	0.310002	0.320001	0.330001	0.340001	0.350000	0.360000

Periods	*37%*	*38%*	*39%*	*40%*	*41%*	*42%*
1	1.370000	1.380000	1.390000	1.400000	1.410000	1.420000
2	0.791941	0.800168	0.808410	0.816667	0.824938	0.833223
3	0.605466	0.613405	0.621369	0.629358	0.637371	0.645408
4	0.516665	0.524666	0.532700	0.540766	0.648863	0.556992
5	0.466702	0.474884	0.483104	0.491361	0.499655	0.507985
6	0.435932	0.444333	0.452776	0.461260	0.469784	0.478346
7	0.415916	0.424542	0.433211	0.441923	0.450675	0.459467
8	0.402428	0.411267	0.420150	0.429074	0.438039	0.447042
9	0.393123	0.402156	0.411230	0.420345	0.429498	0.438688
10	0.386598	0.395801	0.405044	0.414324	0.423640	0.432990
11	0.381970	0.391320	0.400707	0.410128	0.419581	0.429065
12	0.378662	0.388136	0.397644	0.407182	0.416749	0.426343
13	0.376283	0.385861	0.395469	0.405104	0.414764	0.424447
14	0.374565	0.384229	0.393919	0.403632	0.413367	0.423122
15	0.373321	0.383055	0.392812	0.402588	0.412382	0.422194
16	0.372418	0.382209	0.392019	0.401845	0.411687	0.421543
17	0.371762	0.381598	0.391450	0.401316	0.411195	0.421085
18	0.371284	0.381157	0.391042	0.400939	0.410847	0.420764
19	0.370937	0.380838	0.390749	0.400670	0.410600	0.420537
20	0.370683	0.380607	0.390539	0.400479	0.410425	0.420378
21	0.370498	0.380439	0.390387	0.400342	0.410302	0.420266
22	0.370364	0.380318	0.390279	0.400244	0.410214	0.420188
23	0.370265	0.380231	0.390200	0.400174	0.410152	0.420132
24	0.370194	0.380167	0.390144	0.400124	0.410108	0.420093
25	0.370141	0.380121	0.390104	0.400089	0.410076	0.420065
26	0.370103	0.380088	0.390075	0.400063	0.410054	0.420046
27	0.370075	0.380064	0.390054	0.400045	0.410038	0.420032
28	0.370055	0.380046	0.390039	0.400032	0.410027	0.420023
29	0.370040	0.380033	0.390028	0.400023	0.410019	0.420016
30	0.370029	0.380024	0.390020	0.400017	0.410014	0.420011
31	0.370021	0.380018	0.390014	0.400012	0.410010	0.420008
32	0.370016	0.380013	0.390010	0.400008	0.410007	0.420006
33	0.370011	0.380009	0.300007	0.400006	0.410005	0.420004
34	0.370008	0.380007	0.390005	0.400004	0.410003	0.420003
35	0.370006	0.380005	0.390004	0.400003	0.410002	0.420002
36	0.370004	0.380003	0.390003	0.400002	0.410002	0.420001
37	0.370003	0.380003	0.390002	0.400002	0.410001	0.420001
38	0.370002	0.380002	0.390001	0.400001	0.410001	0.420001
39	0.370002	0.380001	0.390001	0.400001	0.410001	0.420000
40	0.370001	0.380001	0.390001	0.400001	0.410000	0.420000
41	0.370001	0.380001	0.390001	0.400000	0.410000	0.420000
42	0.370001	0.380000	0.390000	0.400000	0.410000	0.420000
43	0.370000	0.380000	0.390000	0.400000	0.410000	0.420000
44	0.370000	0.380000	0.390000	0.400000	0.410000	0.420000
45	0.370000	0.380000	0.390000	0.400000	0.410000	0.420000

Appendix B: Add-On Factors for Finding the Average Interest Rate

Interest Rate (%)	Periods 3	4	5	6	7	8	9	10
1	0.669	0.628	0.604	0.588	0.577	0.569	0.563	0.558
2	0.671	0.631	0.608	0.593	0.583	0.575	0.570	0.566
3	0.673	0.634	0.612	0.598	0.588	0.582	0.577	0.574
4	0.675	0.637	0.616	0.602	0.594	0.588	0.585	0.582
5	0.678	0.640	0.619	0.607	0.599	0.594	0.592	0.590
6	0.680	0.643	0.623	0.612	0.605	0.601	0.599	0.598
7	0.682	0.646	0.627	0.616	0.610	0.607	0.605	0.605
8	0.684	0.649	0.631	0.621	0.615	0.613	0.612	0.613
9	0.686	0.652	0.634	0.625	0.620	0.619	0.619	0.620
10	0.688	0.655	0.638	0.629	0.625	0.624	0.625	0.627
11	0.690	0.658	0.642	0.634	0.631	0.630	0.632	0.635
12	0.692	0.660	0.645	0.638	0.636	0.636	0.638	0.642
13	0.694	0.663	0.649	0.642	0.640	0.641	0.644	0.648
14	0.696	0.666	0.652	0.646	0.645	0.647	0.650	0.655
15	0.698	0.668	0.655	0.650	0.650	0.652	0.656	0.662
16	0.700	0.671	0.659	0.655	0.655	0.658	0.662	0.668
17	0.701	0.674	0.662	0.659	0.659	0.663	0.668	0.674
18	0.703	0.676	0.665	0.662	0.664	0.668	0.674	0.681
19	0.705	0.679	0.669	0.666	0.668	0.673	0.679	0.687
20	0.707	0.681	0.672	0.670	0.673	0.678	0.685	0.693
21	0.709	0.684	0.675	0.674	0.677	0.683	0.690	0.698
22	0.711	0.686	0.678	0.678	0.681	0.688	0.695	0.704
23	0.712	0.689	0.681	0.681	0.686	0.692	0.701	0.710
24	0.714	0.691	0.684	0.685	0.690	0.697	0.706	0.715
25	0.716	0.694	0.687	0.689	0.694	0.702	0.711	0.720
26	0.718	0.696	0.690	0.692	0.698	0.706	0.715	0.725
27	0.719	0.699	0.693	0.696	0.702	0.710	0.720	0.730
28	0.721	0.701	0.696	0.699	0.706	0.715	0.725	0.735
29	0.723	0.703	0.699	0.702	0.710	0.719	0.729	0.740
30	0.724	0.705	0.702	0.706	0.713	0.723	0.734	0.745
31	0.726	0.708	0.705	0.709	0.717	0.727	0.738	0.749
32	0.728	0.710	0.708	0.712	0.721	0.731	0.742	0.754
33	0.729	0.712	0.710	0.715	0.724	0.735	0.746	0.758
34	0.731	0.714	0.713	0.719	0.728	0.739	0.751	0.762
35	0.732	0.716	0.716	0.722	0.731	0.743	0.755	0.767
36	0.734	0.719	0.718	0.725	0.735	0.746	0.758	0.771
37	0.735	0.721	0.721	0.728	0.738	0.750	0.762	0.775
38	0.737	0.723	0.723	0.731	0.741	0.753	0.766	0.778
39	0.739	0.725	0.726	0.734	0.744	0.757	0.770	0.782
40	0.740	0.727	0.728	0.736	0.748	0.760	0.773	0.786
41	0.742	0.729	0.731	0.739	0.751	0.764	0.777	0.789
42	0.743	0.731	0.733	0.742	0.754	0.767	0.780	0.793
43	0.745	0.733	0.736	0.745	0.757	0.770	0.783	0.796
44	0746	0.735	0.738	0.748	0.760	0.773	0.787	0.800
45	0.747	0.737	0.740	0.750	0.763	0.776	0.790	0.803

Interest Rate (%)	*Periods* 11	12	13	14	15	16	17	18
1	0.554	0.552	0.549	0.547	0.546	0.544	0.543	0.543
2	0.563	0.561	0.560	0.559	0.558	0.558	0.557	0.557
3	0.572	0.571	0.570	0.570	0.570	0.570	0.571	0.572
4	0.581	0.580	0.581	0.581	0.582	0.583	0.584	0.586
5	0.590	0.590	0.591	0.592	0.594	0.595	0.598	0.600
6	0.598	0.599	0.601	0.603	0.605	0.608	0.610	0.613
7	0.606	0.608	0.610	0.613	0.616	0.619	0.623	0.627
8	0.615	0.617	0.620	0.623	0.627	0.631	0.635	0.639
9	0.623	0.626	0.629	0.633	0.638	0.642	0.647	0.652
10	0.631	0.634	0.639	0.643	0.648	0.653	0.658	0.664
11	0.638	0.643	0.648	0.653	0.658	0.664	0.670	0.675
12	0.646	0.651	0.656	0.662	0.668	0.674	0.680	0.687
13	0.653	0.659	0.665	0.671	0.678	0.684	0.691	0.697
14	0.661	0.667	0.673	0.680	0.687	0.694	0.701	0.708
15	0.668	0.674	0.681	0.688	0.696	0.703	0.710	0.718
16	0.675	0.682	0.689	0.697	0.704	0.712	0.720	0.727
17	0.682	0.689	0.697	0.705	0.713	0.721	0.728	0.736
18	0.688	0.696	0.704	0.712	0.721	0.729	0.737	0.745
19	0.695	0.703	0.711	0.720	0.729	0.737	0.745	0.753
20	0.701	0.710	0.718	0.727	0.736	0.745	0.753	0.761
21	0.707	0.716	0.725	0.734	0.743	0.752	0.761	0.769
22	0.713	0.723	0.732	0.741	0.750	0.759	0.768	0.776
23	0.719	0.729	0.738	0.748	0.757	0.766	0.775	0.783
24	0.725	0.735	0.744	0.754	0.764	0.773	0.781	0.790
25	0.730	0.740	0.750	0.760	0.770	0.779	0.788	0.796
26	0.736	0.746	0.756	0.766	0.776	0.785	0.794	0.802
27	0.741	0.752	0.762	0.772	0.782	0.791	0.800	0.808
28	0.746	0.757	0.767	0.777	0.787	0.796	0.805	0.813
29	0.751	0.762	0.773	0.783	0.793	0.802	0.811	0.819
30	0.756	0.767	0.778	0.788	0.798	0.807	0.816	0.824
31	0.761	0.772	0.783	0.793	0.803	0.812	0.820	0.829
32	0.765	0.777	0.787	0.798	0.807	0.817	0.825	0.833
33	0.770	0.781	0.792	0.802	0.812	0.821	0.830	0.838
34	0.774	0.786	0.797	0.807	0.816	0.826	0.834	0.842
35	0.779	0.790	0.801	0.811	0.821	0.830	0.838	0.846
36	0.783	0.794	0.805	0.815	0.825	0.834	0.842	0.850
37	0.787	0.798	0.809	0.819	0.829	0.838	0.846	0.853
38	0.791	0.802	0.813	0.823	0.833	0.841	0.849	0.857
39	0.794	0.806	0.817	0.827	0.836	0.845	0.853	0.860
40	0.798	0.810	0.820	0.831	0.840	0.848	0.856	0.863
41	0.802	0.813	0.824	0.834	0.843	0.852	0.859	0.867
42	0.805	0.817	0.827	0.837	0.846	0.855	0.863	0.870
43	0.809	0.820	0.831	0.841	0.850	0.858	0.865	0.872
44	0.812	0.823	0.834	0.844	0.853	0.861	0.868	0.875
45	0.815	0.827	0.837	0.847	0.856	0.864	0.871	0.878

Index

Absorption costing, 268
Absorption pricing, 297, 303, 306
Acceptance criterion, statistics, 73
Aquisitions, valuing, 343–355
Activity, ratios for, 321
Add-on factor for interest. *See* Interest add-on factor
Amortization of capital. *See* Capital recovery
Annuities: capital recovery, 25; compound amount, 29; decay, 36; future value of, 29; gradient, 37–40; growth, 35, 38; infinite, 32; during inflation 32–34; ordinary, 29–32, 34, 40; present value of 31, 33, 35, 36, 37, 39, 40; sinking fund, 30; varying, 34–40
Annuity due, 40–41; capital recovery, 41; future value of, 40; present value of, 40
Appraisal of company, 344
Assets: capital charges, 121; costing services of, 171, 181–182, 251, 279, 281; economic value, 32, 113–115, 169; holding gains, 241; life span of stock 200–202; nondepreciable 32, 113, 120; rate of return on, 153; replacement cost, 170, 234, 286. *See also* Book value
Assets replacement during inflation, 390
Assets revaluation: acquisition value of stock, 217–218; book value of stock, 218–220, 222, 225, 227; in costing, 233, 237, 285; in financial statements, 232–235; nondepreciable, 32, 113, 120, 217; replacement cost, 170, 234, 286; starting date for time series, 221; of stock, 213–232; timeseries, 220–228
Assets services, costing, 171, 181–182, 237, 251, 279, 281
Assets valuation: accounting method, 169, 344; for costing, 171, 181; economic method, 169, 347; implications from, 170; during inflation, 207; replacement cost, 170, 234, 286; single asset, 169–171; stock of assets, 204–109, 213. *See also* Assets revaluation
Average, 53, 67; weighted, 68, 264. *See also* Mean

Balance sheet: description of, 311; inflation adjustment, 235–236
Book value: and acquisition of stock, 204–209; and depreciation methods, 172, 173, 174, 176; revaluation of stock 218–220, 222, 225, 227; single asset, 172, 173, 174, 176; stock of assets, 204–209; stock during inflation, 207, 218–220, 222, 225, 227
Bonds: price and yield of, 103–107; regular, 104–105; serial, 106
Breakeven: analysis, 258–263; and planning, 259; and sensitivity, 262; and uncertainty, 263
Budgeting, cash, 335, 339

Capital budgeting. *See* Investment evaluation; Rate of return
Capital charges, 25, 28, 120–125, 181–182, 279–281
Capital erosion during inflation, 378–383; depreciable assets, 380; monetary assets, 378; nondepreciable assets, 382
Capital expense. *See* Capital charges
Capital recovery: advanced payments (due), 41; factor, 26, 393
Cash budget, 335, 339
Cash flow: discounting, 7, 113–117; expected, 136; future value of, 5; investment and, 111–129; present value of, 7, 113–116, 128–134; risk adjusted, 135–138
Certainty equivalent, 136, 362–371: from kinked function, 368; in practice, 366–371. *See also* Uncertainty
Coefficient of determination, 61
Coefficient of correlation; see correlation coefficient
Coefficient of variation, 48: standard error of, 70
Common-size statements, 249, 315
Composite index for rating companies, 324–326
Compound amount. *See* Future value
Compounding, 4; and inflation, 23
Confidence region, 70
Contribution pricing, 301
Contribution ratio, 249, 257
Contribution-volume: curve, 260–263; relationships, 260–263
Correction factor, statistics, 47
Correlation coefficient, 59–61; from scatter diagram, 60 standard error of, 70
Cost absorption, 268, 297
Cost accounting. *See* Costing
Cost accounting sheet, 254–256
Cost markup, 292
Cost of capital. *See* Discounting rate; Rate of return
Cost of failure, uncertainty, 145–150
Cost-plus pricing, 297, 303, 306
Cost statement, 247–250, 254

Cost-volume relationships, 257–263
Costing: absorption, 268; assets revaluation, 233, 237, 285; assets services, 171, 181–182, 237, 251, 279, 281; capital services, 279–283; direct, 268; Flow of cost, 252; and indexation, 286–288; during inflation, 192, 228, 284–290, 392; intermediate goods, 250, 270–273; inventory, 192, 228, 286; job order, 267; joint cost, 276–280; methods of, 267–270; operating capital, 282; of process, 267; seasonal demand, 274–276, 303–305; of internal services, 251, 273–277, 279; standard method, 268; by transfer price, 252–254; variance analysis, 249, 283–284, 289; work in progress, 271
Cost allocation, 252, 273, 276–279
Costs: avoidable, 265; classification of, 250–252, 265–266, 293, 298, 302, 303; controllable, 265; fixed, 265; items, 250–252; opportunity, 266; variable, 265
Current ratio, 319

Debt. *See* Loans
Decay, 9, 11; annuity, 36; during inflation, 12; in real terms, 13
Deflating. *See* Indexation; Price index
Depreciation: accumulated for stock, 209–210; choosing method of, 179, 180, 186; declining balance, 174, 184, 199, 200, 206, 209; double declining balance, 176, 185; for economic value, 178; effect on balance sheet, 179; implications of methods, 178–182, 185–186; and income tax, 186, 193–194; during inflation, 198, 213–217, 223, 226, 228; methods of, 172–178; present value of, 182–186; stock of assets, 197–200, 213; straight line, 172, 183, 198, 205, 207; sum-of-the-years' digits, 173, 183, 199, 206; switch-over, 175, 177. *See also* Costing asset services
Discounting, 6
Discounting Rate: risk adjusted, 138–141; sensitivity of, 145. *See also* Rate of return
Discounted cash flow, 7, 113–117
Dispersion: coefficient of variation, 48; effect on mean, 67; measures of, 43–49; range, 43; standard deviation, 45
Distribution, rare events, 62
Distribution curve, 49–54: constructing, 49; empirical, 49; graphing, 50; skewed, 52; normal, 51; standard normal, 52
Diversification: number of activities, 372; and risk, 371–373
Dominance criterion, uncertainty, 359

Economic value: of asset, 32, 113–115, 169; of company, 347; and depreciation, 178; of investment, 113–115; of land, 32; of loan, 88–93; of nondepreciable asset, 32
Elasticity in pricing, 293–295, 305
Equity maintenance adjustment, 240
Estimates: acceptance criterion, 73; rare events, 62; rejection criterion, 72; revision of, 73; significance of, 69; standard error of, 69
Exceedance, probability of, 63
Extreme data. *See* Statistics of extremes

Financial leverage. *See* Leverage
Financial liquidity. *See* Liquidity
Financial management during inflation, 375–392
Financial ratios: analysis, 316, 318–321; and scale, 327; during inflation, 319–321, 332; inflation distortions, 332; list of, 318–321; rating of, 317, 322; and signals of distress, 332
Financial standing, 322
Financial statements; common-size, 249, 315; description of, 311–314; inflation adjustment of, 233–243
Financial statements analysis, 311–325: for acquisition, 343; by rating, 317; by ratios, 318–321
Financing management, 335–342
Flow of funds statement, 313–315, 335–338
Future value of: annuity, 29; annuity due, 40; cash flow, 5; principal, 5

Geometric mean, 66
Gradient annuity, 37–40
Goodwill, valuation of, 344, 346, 347
Growth, 8: annuity, 35, 38; during inflation, 12; negative, 10; in real terms, 13

Holding gains, 241

Income statement: in costing, 254, 269; description of, 312–313; inflation adjusted, 236–239; projected, 337
Income tax: depreciation and, 186, 193–194; during inflation, 194, 376–378, 382; interest rate and, 20, 96; inventory and, 194; investment evaluation and, 125–130; loans and, 96, 127; postponing returns and, 382; rate of return and, 158–159
Indexation, 21–24: and compounding, 23; of costs, 286–288; of loans, 100–103. *See also* Price index
Indexed loan, 100–103
Inflation: annuities during, 32–34; assets valuation during, 207, 218–220, 222,

225, 227; capital erosion during, 378–383; cost of capital during, 161–166; costing during, 192, 228, 237, 284–290, 392; decay during, 12; depreciation during, 198, 213–217, 223, 226, 228; effects on business, 375; effects on financial activities, 375–392; effects on liquidity, 102, 383, 386; effects on profit, 239–242, 376–378; effects on taxation, 376–378, 382; financial leverage during, 377, 390; financial ratios during, 319–321, 332; financial statement adjustment, 233–243; growth during, 12; indexation, 21–24, 100–103, 286–288; interest rate during, 18–21, 98–99, 238, 389; interest expense during, 391; inventory during, 192, 194, 202–204, 228, 232, 237, 286; investment evaluation during, 131–134, 390; life span of stock during, 201; loans during, 98, 132–134, 242; overtaxation during, 376–378; pricing during, 305–307, 392; profit measurement during, 233–243, 376–378; rate of return during, 153, 161; rules for combating effects of, 389–392; variance analysis during, 289; working capital during, 391. *See also* Assets revaluation
Interest: after-tax, 20, 96; compound, 4; continuous rate, 15–17; daily rate, 15–17; discount, 6, 17; effective rate, 14; and financial leverage, 160, 164; financial ratio for, 320; in cost accounting, 283; during inflation, 18, 98–99, 238, 389, 391; inflation-compensated, 20; inflation-free, 18; monthly rate, 14, 16; negative inflation-free rate, 19; on loans, 79, 86, 87, 97, 238; periodic rates, 15; present value of, 95–96, 130, 132; regular, 17; rule of seventy, 9; simple, 3
Interest add-on factor, 27, 401: use of, 25, 28, 31, 38, 84, 86, 88, 92, 93, 105, 106, 111, 117, 118, 121, 138, 181, 182, 199, 201, 202, 216, 221, 281, 381
Interest charges. *See* Costing assets services
Installment contract, 79–82
Installment loan. *See* Loans
Intermediate goods, costing of, 250, 2
Internal rate of return, 117–120: by interpolation, 118; and payback, 110–112; sensitivity of, 119–120
Inventory: average method, 187, 231, 271; costing of, 272, 281; FIFO, 187, 189, 230, 272; FIFO for work in process, 272; and income tax, 194; during inflation, 192, 194, 202–204, 228–232, 237, 286; LIFO, 187, 190–191, 192, 194, 231; LIFO in costing, 286; revaluation of stock, 230–232; revaluation for costing, 228, 286; turnover of stock, 202–204; turnover of stock during inflation, turnover ratios, 321
Inventory accounting, 189–193: during inflation, 192, 194; periodic, 189; perpetual, 189
Inventory valuation, 187–192: during inflation, 192; methods, 187–189; replacement cost, 188; retail, 187; standard price, 188
Investment: decisions on, 109, 388; in loan, 88–93, 126–130, 132–134; return on, 152–154
Investment evaluation: certainty equivalent, 136; under financial leverage, 125–130, 134; and income tax, 125–130; during inflation, 131–134, 390; internal rate of return, 117–120; life span and, 114; methods ot, 109–125; payback period, 109–113; periodic capital expense, 120–125; present value, 113, 115, 129, 131; profitability indicator, 110, 116, 123; rating, 115, 116; risk-adjusted rate, 140; sensitivity analysis, 141–147; uncertainty, 112, 135–150, 359, 370

Job order costing, 267
Joint costs, 276–280
Joint products, 276–279: profitability of, 279

Kinked utility, 366–371

Lender's cost of capital, 99, 161–166
Leverage: cost of capital, 159–166; decisions on, 160, 377, 386, 388; during inflation, 377, 390; inflation and pricing, 306; inflation and taxation, 377; investment, 125–130, 134; rate of return, 156, 159–161, 163–166; risk from, 386–388. *See also* Loans
Life span: investment evaluation and, 114; of stock of assets, 200–202; remaining of stock, 202
Liquidity: cash budget and, 337–339; effects of inflation on, 102, 383–386; loans and, 102, 385; ratios for, 319
Loans: comparisons of, 88; cost and gains, 88–93; decision on, 388; economic value of, 88–93; equal-principal-payment, 85, 87, 92, 95, 101, 106; evaluation, 88–93, 126–130, 134; financial ratios, 320; indexation of, 100–103; and income tax, 96, 127; during inflation, 98, 132–134, 242; installment, 79, 84, 85, 89, 93; installment contracts; 79–82; and interest, 79, 86, 87, 97, 238; life span of

stock, 211; and liquidity, 102, 385; mix of two loans, 82; outstanding, 93–95, 210–211; partial payments of, 81; periodic payments on, 84, 87, 94; present value of, 89, 94; present value of interest, 95–96, 130; repayment methods, 84–88; sensitivity analysis, 91; standing, 85, 92, 102; stock of, 210–211, 238, 320

Markup for pricing, 292, 299, 300, 302
Mean: geometric, 66; relation between means, 53, 66–69; skewness, 53; standard error of, 69; weighted average, 68; weighted and simple, 68, 264
Measures of association, 54–61
Median, skewness, 53
Merger: benefits from, 353, 354; exchange ratio, 353; incentives for, 352; valuing acquisitions for, 352–355

Normal distribution, 51: standard, 52

Operating capital, costing of, 282
Opportunity cost, 266
Overhead expenses, 251, 276, 278
Outliers, statistics, 64–66

Payback: determining the period, 109; of investment, 109–113; and rate of return, 110–112; and risk, 112; for screening projects, 112
Peak-load costing and pricing, 274–276, 303–305
Performance evaluation, 249, 318: rate of return, 154
Periodic charges on investment, 120–125
Present value: annuity, 31, 33, 35, 36, 37, 39, 40; cash flow, 7, 113–116, 128–134; depreciation schedule, 130, 182–186, 193; factor, 7; interest on loans, 95–96, 130, 132; infinite series, 32; investment, 113–116, 128–134, 136; loan repayment, 89, 94, 130; principal, 6; valuing acquisitions, 348
Pricing, 291–308: absorption method, 297, 303, 306; categories of products for, 291; contribution, 301; cost classification for, 293, 298, 303; cost plus (full cost), 297, 303, 306; demand, 293, 301, 302; elasticity for, 293–295, 305; elasticity and fixed costs, 294; during inflation, 392; market methods, 294; markup, 292, 299, 300, 302; methods, 294–303; new product, 307–308; peak load (seasonal) demand, 303–305; return on capital, 299, 307; strategies of, 291, 307; tools for, 292–294
Price index: changing base period, 22; deflating and inflating, 23–24
Probability of exceedance, 63
Process cost accounting, 267
Productivity and scale, 263, 327
Profit, during inflation, 239–242, 376–378
Profit and loss statement, 254, 269, 312
Profit margin, 292, 318. *See also* Contribution ratio
Profit-volume relationships, 257, 260
Profitability analysis, 255, 257, 318, 384, 388
Profitability of investment, 110, 116, 123
Profitability of loans, 88, 90, 127, 132

Quartiles and standard deviation, 46
Quick ratio, 319

Range, 43–45: and standard deviation, 45; and regression coefficient, 58; relative, 44; spread of, 44
Rare events, statistics, 62–64
Rate of return, 151–166: accounting derived, 151–154; and financial leverage, 159–161, 163–166; financial ratios for, 319; and income tax, 158–159, 163; during inflation, 153, 161–166; internal, 110, 117–120; lender's, 161–166; on capital, 152; on investment, 152–154; and payback, 110–112; and performance evaluation, 154; required, 155–159; and risk, 138–141, 153; risk adjusted, 138; sensitivity, 119–120
Rating companies, 317, 322: composite index, 224–326
Ratio analysis. *See* Financial ratios
Regression, 55–61: small sample, 56
Regression coefficient, 57–59: from range, 58; from scatter diagram, 57; standard error of, 70
Regression line, 55–61: for small sample, 56
Rejection criterion, statistics, 72
Replacement-cost, 170, 188, 234, 286
Replacement of assets during inflation, 390
Return on capital, pricing for, 299, 307. *See also* Rate of return
Return on investment. *See* Rate of return
Return period, statistics, 61–63
Revaluation of assets. *See* Assets revaluation
Revaluation of inventory. *See* inventory
Revising sample estimate, 73–75
Risk: and payback of investment, 112; and rate of return, 138–141, 153; and kinked function, 368–370. *See also* Uncertainty
Risk-adjusted rate, 138–141
Risk aversion, 362–366
Risk curve, 362–364

Risk premium, 142, 362–368, 387
Risk. *See also* Uncertainty
Rule of seventy, interest, 9

Sample size, 44
Scale, relations to productivity, 263, 327
Scatter diagram, 55–58: and correlation coefficient, 60; preparation of, 55; and regression coefficient, 57
Sensitivity analysis: discounting rate, 145; investment under uncertainty, 141–147; loans, 91; internal rate of return, 119–120; sales, 262
Services, costing internal, 251, 273–277, 279
Sinking fund, 30
Skewness, 52–54: indication of, 53; coefficient of, 54
Sources and uses statement, 313, 335, 338
Standard cost accounting, 268
Standard deviation, 45–48: estimation of, 46–47, 136; and quartiles, 46; and range, 45, 51, 52; standard error of, 69; standard error, 69, 74
Standard normal distribution, 52
Significance, statistics, 69–75
Statistics of extremes, 61–66: outlying observations, 64; return period, 61
Student's T table, 71
Stock of assets. *See* Assets
Stock of inventory. *See* Inventory

Tax. *See* Income tax
Time series analysis, 220–228, 243, 325–327
Transfer price, 252–254
Turnover of inventory, 202
Two-part charging; see costing seasonal demand

Uncertainty: adjusted cash flow, 135, 138; analysis, 135–150, 357–373; and breakeven, 263; business risk, 360; cost of failure, 145–150; diversification and, 371–373; Dominance criterion, 359; environmental risk, 358; expected gain criterion, 360; financial leverage and, 386; financial risk, 358; investment evaluation under, 112, 135–150, 359, 370; kinked function, 366; level of, 142; measures of, 358–359; screening projects, 112, 359–362; sources of, 358; subjective estimate of, 46, 136, 368; utility approach, 364–366; volume of production and, 263. *See also* Certainty equivalent and risk
Utility Function, 264, 366

Valuation: by appraisal, 344; of acquisitions, 343–355; of goodwill, 344, 347. *See also* Assets valuation
Variance analysis, 249, 283–284, 289; during inflation, 289–296 Variation. *See* coefficient of variation

Work in process, costing of, 271
Working capital, 312, 319, 321: costing of, 282; during inflation, 391

About the Authors

Leon Shashua is head of the Department of Economics, Israel Bank of Agriculture, Tel-Aviv. He has authored many articles in prominent journals in the fields of finance,production economics, and statistical analysis. He is currently doing research on the effect of inflation on the financial behavior of firms. Dr. Shashua received the M.Sc. from Hebrew University and the Ph.D. from Cornell University.

Yaaqov Goldschmidt is professor at the Faculty of Management, Tel-Aviv University, and research director at Heshev—the Inter Kibbutz Unit for Management Services, Tel-Aviv. His books include *Production Economics, Information for Management Decisions, Managerial Cost Accounting,* and *Profit Measurement during Inflation.* Dr. Goldschmidt received the M.S. from the University of Arizona and the Ph.D. from Cornell University.